Mediation Ethics

Ellen Waldman, Editor

Mediation Ethics

Cases and Commentaries

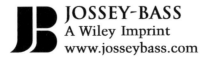

JOSSEY-BASS
A Wiley Imprint
www.josseybass.com

Published by Jossey-Bass
A Wiley Imprint
989 Market Street, San Francisco, CA 94103-1741—www.josseybass.com

Readers should be aware that Internet Web sites offered as citations and/or sources for further
information may have changed or disappeared between the time this was written and when it is read.

Limit of Liability/Disclaimer of Warranty: While the publisher and author have used their best efforts
in preparing this book, they make no representations or warranties with respect to the accuracy or
completeness of the contents of this book and specifically disclaim any implied warranties of
merchantability or fitness for a particular purpose. No warranty may be created or extended by sales
representatives or written sales materials. The advice and strategies contained herein may not be
suitable for your situation. You should consult with a professional where appropriate. Neither the
publisher nor author shall be liable for any loss of profit or any other commercial damages,
including but not limited to special, incidental, consequential, or other damages.

Jossey-Bass books and products are available through most bookstores. To contact Jossey-Bass
directly call our Customer Care Department within the U.S. at 800-956-7739, outside the U.S. at
317-572-3986, or fax 317-572-4002.

Jossey-Bass also publishes its books in a variety of electronic formats. Some content that appears in
print may not be available in electronic books.

Cover image: *Long Blue Form*, oil on canvas, copyright © 2010 by Annette Poitau.
http://annettepoitau.com

Library of Congress Cataloging-in-Publication Data

Mediation Ethics : Cases and Commentaries / Ellen Waldman, Editor. — First edition.
      p. cm
  Includes bibliographical references and index.
  ISBN 978-0-7879-9588-1 (hardback); ISBN 978-1-118-00132-5 (ebk);
  ISBN 978-1-118-00133-2 (ebk); ISBN 978-1-118-00134-9 (ebk)
  1. Dispute resolution (Law)—United States. 2. Dispute resolution (Law)—Moral and ethical
aspects—United States. 3. Mediation—United States. 4. Confidential communications—Lawyers.
I. Waldman, Ellen, date.
  KF9084.M435 2011
  347.73'9—dc22   2010048706

Printed in the United States of America
FIRST EDITION
HB Printing   10 9 8 7 6 5 4 3 2 1

To Seymour M. Waldman, a man of grace and virtue

~~~ **Contents**

Preface   ix

Acknowledgments   xiii

1 Values, Models, and Codes   1

2 Autonomy and Diminished Capacity   27
   Commentators: Carol B. Liebman and Mary Radford

3 Autonomy and the Emotions   55
   Commentators: Dorothy Della Noce and John Winslade

4 Disputant Autonomy and Power Imbalance   87
   Commentators: Forrest S. Mosten and Bill Eddy

5 Tensions Between Disputant Autonomy and
   Substantive Fairness: The Misinformed Disputant   113
   Commentators: Lela P. Love and Jacqueline Nolan-Haley

6 Information, Autonomy, and the Unrepresented Party   155
   Commentators: Michael Moffitt and Dan Dozier

7 Mediating on the Wrong Side of the Law   177
   *Commentators: John Bickerman, Jeremy Lack,
   and Julie Macfarlane*

8 Mediating with Lies in the Room   199
   Commentators: Dwight Golann and Melissa Brodrick

9 Confidentiality   227
   Commentators: Bruce Pardy and Charles Pou

10 Confidentiality Continued: Attorney Misconduct
   or Child Abuse   255
   Commentators: Art Hinshaw and Gregory Firestone

11 Conflicts of Interest   277
   Commentators: Bruce E. Meyerson, Wayne Thorpe,
   Roger Wolf, and Susan Nauss Exon

12 Mediating Multiculturally: Culture and the Ethical
   Mediator   305
   Commentators: Carrie Menkel-Meadow
   and Harold Abramson

13 Ethics for ADR Provider Organizations   339
   Commentators: Phyllis Bernard and Susan M. Yates

   Appendix: Model Standards of Conduct for Mediators   369

   Notes   381

   The Editor   419

   The Contributors   421

   Index   431

─◁◅◈▷▻─ Preface

I did not begin my legal career as a mediator or an academic. I started out as a litigator—filing complaints, writing motions, and pushing cases toward trial. However, early in my career, I had an interaction with opposing counsel that made me question if there wasn't a better alternative for resolving disputes. I was working on a personal injury case. My client, a seventeen-year-old girl, had suffered second-degree burns all over her body after the timer on a tanning bed malfunctioned. All parties agreed on the facts: the tanning bed had a timer; the timer had been set for fifteen minutes; the timer failed to go off; my client fell asleep and was exposed to the bed's ultraviolet lights for over an hour.

When the tanning bed manufacturer responded to our complaint and claimed they could not understand why they were being sued, I met with lawyers from the company to see if I could satisfy their concerns. My first meeting was with a lawyer who, like me, had been practicing for only a few years and had roughly my level of experience. The two of us had a reasonable conversation and were able to agree on some procedural points that would eliminate the need for a court hearing. On the second day of meetings, this younger attorney was accompanied by one of his senior, more grizzled colleagues. This more seasoned attorney drove the negotiation like a double-wide truck: he sideswiped the agreements his colleague and I had already reached and blocked any avenue for further negotiations. The result was an unnecessary court hearing, a waste of time and money for everyone involved.

The other young attorney and I were new to the law business. We adopted commonsense positions, took each other at our word, and made serious attempts to understand one another. We wanted to move things forward. We had impulses toward constructive collaboration. The more experienced lawyer, schooled in the art of escalation, took outrageous positions and seemed bent on sustaining discord.

My experience with this more senior lawyer made me wonder what becoming an experienced attorney would mean and what I would be like once my rookie reflexes were gone and I had begun to think and act like a pro. This episode taught me that garnering more experience as a litigator might blunt my native problem-solving skills—what I felt were my most valuable intuitions. This is not to say that all those in the legal profession practice scorched-earth litigation tactics incompatible with principled negotiation. Many attorneys practice in collaborative, problem-solving ways and mentor their younger colleagues in the usefulness of those methods. But it is true that some attorneys wander down side trails in order to push an aggressive agenda at all costs. The ethical imperative to be a counselor and help solve the client's problems can get lost.

The mediation field is similarly at risk. Intervening in other people's conflicts is an audacious act, its hubris justified only if the intervention is likely to make things better—or at least not make them worse. As a profession, the field seems to understand this. However, some mediators may find themselves practicing by rote, following well-worn wagon treads without reflection. My suspicion that some mediators operate on autopilot was confirmed when, a few years ago, I organized a dinner for local mediators to talk about ethics. I promised free food and wine. The only cost of admission was a description of the toughest ethical quandary each mediator had faced in practice. One veteran mediator accepted the invitation, but lamented that in his over-twenty-year career as a neutral, he had never seen anything resembling an ethical dilemma!

You'd think a field that self-consciously sees itself as "doing good" would have a well-developed literature on ethics, but ours does not. We are awash in texts that explain how to mediate effectively, profitably, spiritually, sensitively, and cross-culturally. But guidance in mediating ethically is in short supply.

I wrote this book to help conflict resolution professionals traverse the disorienting landscape of ethical decision making with greater clarity and deliberateness. In its case studies and commentaries, the book describes the often murky ethical terrain that mediators are likely to encounter and offers guidance on how to navigate it. This book is a trail guide; it will not always tell you where to go, but it will assess the allures and dangers of various off-road itineraries. After reading this book, it is unlikely you will suffer vertigo when facing a particularly precarious ridge or fork in the road ahead. You will become more adept at spotting potential roadblocks and reasoning through your options. Even on those occasions when all options seem bad, this book will help you become more conscious and confident of your own mediation orientation and forge a path that honors the important values at stake.

In the following chapters, you will hear from both me and other professionals in the field. In Chapter One, I discuss the underlying values of mediation, its regulatory codes, and emerging models of practice. The subsequent chapters introduce various ethical dilemmas, exemplified by both easy and hard cases. Each hard case is followed by commentaries from leading mediation scholars who explain what they would do in the case and why. Each commentator approaches conflict resolution with a different philosophy and articulates his or her approach to the case with deliberate attention to how an understanding of ethical obligations informs his or her thinking about the case. In the discussions that follow, you will learn what each commentator values most in the mediation process and how his or her values determine certain outcomes and discourage others.

The commentators in this book demonstrate the vast diversity that characterizes the field today. Evaluative, facilitative, narrative, and transformative mediators are all represented. In reading their work, you will be struck by the heterogeneity of their philosophical commitments. But note how all authors identify the values they hold most dear and how the priorities they set determine the action plans they adopt.

Acknowledgments

Some books yearn themselves into existence. They are written in a flurry of necessity, the words tumbling onto the page. This was not one of those books.

This meditation on mediation ethics took shape slowly, endured a protracted gestational period, and moved glacially toward birth. I'm sure my publisher thought forceps would be necessary. I'd like to thank all those who participated in the Lamaze classes and provided friendship and support throughout.

In terms of conception, I owe many thanks to Charlie Pou, Timothy Hedeen, and Judy Cohen for brainstorming with me about the need for a mediation ethics text that showcased the heterogeneity of thinking in the field. Charlie was particularly helpful in thinking through many of the basic structural questions and ended up contributing an insightful commentary on disclosure, secrecy, and the limits to mediation confidentiality.

Alan Rinzler, executive editor at Jossey-Bass, was another important early catalyst. Alan heard me give a talk at a conference in which I bemoaned the paucity of case-based ethics texts in the mediation field. He approached me after the panel, threw his card down on the podium, and said, "We want to do that book." Although writing a book was nowhere on my to-do list, coming from Alan, it felt like a challenge—one that I was surprised to find myself accepting. Although I would later marvel at the gap between identifying a need and actually attempting to fill it, talk about the need for an ethics text would have remained just that were it not for Alan's confidence and enthusiasm.

Along the way, colleagues and friends in a number of disciplines gave generously of their ideas and insights. Some read early drafts, others helped me talk through case studies, and still others offered materials that they thought would be helpful. Many, though not all, of these individuals wrote commentaries for the book. I thank

Hal Abramson, Gregg Bloche, Dwight Golann, Art Hinshaw, Lela Love, Julie Macfarlane, Steve Semeraro, Lois Waldman, and David Waldman for their special help along the way.

Seth Schwartz, Alan Venable, and Beverly Miller—talented writers and editors from the Jossey-Bass team—helped smooth the manuscript's rough edges. And I acknowledge my huge debt to Chris Sove of Sove Publishing, a former student with a gift for language who was there as a research assistant at the beginning and provided crucial support toward the conclusion of the project.

Writing is something we do alone. This solitude is bearable when leavened with good fellowship and camaraderie. I am so lucky in this regard. My friends Betsy Anderson, Patrick Burke, Julie Greenberg, Martha Hall, Barbara Hart, Kay Henley, Marybeth Herald, Scott Landers, Nina Markov, Joelle Moreno, Marina Greenstein, Bruce Pardy, Allison Taylor, Ben Templin, and Kenneth Vandevelde all remind me that ethics is not simply a matter of the head, but of what we give and receive in the way of love, care, and concern.

And, speaking of love, I owe both thanks and apologies to the two bookends of my family: my mother, Lois Waldman, and my daughter, Aviva. Thanks to my mother for her unfailing, unending nurture and for modeling each day, year after year, what it means to be a loving and encouraging parent. To my daughter, thanks for your vital, electric presence and for the fun and wonder you bring to me. I apologize for both my occasional distractedness and those moments spent tapping at computer keys rather than playing two-square, wrestling, or buying you a dog.

With a project of this duration, it is no surprise that life at its end would look different than it did at the beginning. My father, Seymour Waldman, died while this book was in process. He was, for me, the embodiment of grace and fair-mindedness. I have never met anyone else whose judgment was so untainted by bias or self-interest, so utterly committed to doing what was right and decent. He was, in every sense, Aristotle's man of virtue. I dedicate this book to him.

Mediation Ethics

CHAPTER ONE

Values, Models, and Codes

E thical decision making requires tough, sometimes tragic, choices. Difficult cases do not force us to choose between obviously right and obviously wrong paths. Rather, deciding which path to take is difficult precisely because there are compelling reasons to go in each direction. We want mediation to yield substantively good outcomes, and we want to honor disputants' rights to choose the best outcomes for themselves. In hard cases, it may not be possible to do both. We often can't pursue one value without forfeiting another.

Mediating ethically usually entails some loss. The difficult choices that professional mediators routinely make are often similar to the wrenching choices that faced the Greek hero Ulysses on his odyssey from Troy back home to Ithaca. At one point in the long journey, Ulysses was forced to steer his ship through a narrow strait of sea bordered on each side by ferocious monsters. On one side lurked Charybdis, whose yawning jaws sucked in and spewed out water three times a day, creating a whirlpool that destroyed any ship unlucky enough to drift too near. On the other side hovered Scylla, a six-headed beast with three rows of teeth in every mouth. No ship could pass within Scylla's reach without losing men to the monster's predations.

Ulysses' men were loyal soldiers and sailors, and he wanted to save them all, but he knew his whole ship would go down if he veered too close to Charybdis. However, sailing within Scylla's reach would mean the death of six oarsmen. With a heavy heart, Ulysses told his crew to row hard and give Charybdis's currents a wide berth. He stayed silent about Scylla for she was "a threat for which there was no remedy." Ulysses' men were easy targets for Scylla, who snatched the strongest and bravest among them. Ulysses' anguish is clear as he describes the sight: "When I turned to watch the swift ship and crew, already I could see their hands and feet, as Scylla carried them high overhead. They cried out and screamed, calling me by name one final time, their hearts in agony.... Of all things my eyes have witnessed in my journeying on pathways of the sea, the sight of them was the most piteous I've ever seen"[1]

Fortunately for us, mediation rarely poses such difficult matters of life and death. Still, the lesson from the *Odyssey* is clear: Ulysses could not save his ship without ethical compromise. Optimally the captain of a ship is truthful with his crew and safeguards the safety of every sailor. Ulysses deceived his men about the true dangers they faced and sacrificed six of his crew. But doing the right thing almost never involves following one mandate unflinchingly. When we consider the dire choices Ulysses faced, can we say this captain acted unethically? He saved the vast majority of those on board—all who could be saved. Where does truth rate when brute honesty threatens to fatally immobilize the entire ship? And how does one protect sailors' safety when the only choice is how many will die?

On a less stark scale, mediation ethics poses similar questions and teaches similar lessons. This chapter continues to weave the lesson of Ulysses into a discussion of the underlying values of the mediation field and their articulation in formal ethics codes. It highlights the inconsistencies that exist among and within various code sections and suggests that those inconsistencies reflect tensions among mediation's underlying values: disputant autonomy, substantive fairness, and procedural fairness.[2] Ideally mediators would maximally advance each of these principles in every intervention. Often this is not possible, and mediators have to decide for themselves how to prioritize and weigh these values when they push in competing directions. Mediator philosophy and the models that emerge from this philosophy play a significant role in how these balancing acts occur.

A BASE OF UNDERLYING VALUES

In the following chapters, you will hear from commentators with diverse approaches and philosophies. You may be surprised at the range of responses, but all of them pay deliberate attention to three underlying values that shape their understanding of what is at stake and what is ethically required in any given case:

- *Disputant autonomy:* A disputant's right to make choices based on personal beliefs and values, free of coercion and constraint
- *Procedural fairness:* The fairness of the process used to reach the mediated result
- *Substantive fairness or a good-enough outcome:* The acceptability of the mediated result

In cases that require difficult ethical decision making, these three values will likely be in tension. When mediators confront such cases, they need to reflect on whether any one of these values trumps the others or whether it is appropriate to compromise one or more of these values in the face of more compelling mandates. However, before a discussion of how the tension between these underlying values will influence a mediator's ethical decision making, I explore and define each of these values.

Disputant Autonomy

"You're not the boss of me." Any adult who has tried to issue an order to a child has probably heard that rebuff. The child is asserting her autonomy in the baldest way possible.

Most simply, autonomy, frequently referred to as self-determination in mediation codes and texts, means self-rule. Mediation strives to vest maximal control and choice with the disputant—not with the mediator, the state, or another third party. Unlike litigation, in which lawyers frame disputes and judges decide them, mediation assumes that disputants should retain control over how their conflicts are presented, discussed, and resolved. In litigation, fairness is discovered by looking to existing law. In mediation, disputants are urged to look to their own personal norms of fairness. Legal rules, social conventions, and other standards that might interfere with disputants' efforts to construct self-determining agreements are supposed to take a backseat.

Autonomous decisions express who we are—our preferences, desires, and priorities. They bear the imprint of our personality as it has developed over time. Determining whether decision making in mediation is truly autonomous requires a close look at internal and external conditions that threaten to influence or subvert our exercise of free will.

Internal threats inhere in the frailty of a disputant's mental or physical condition. If autonomous decision making reflects long-term values and an established pattern of belief and behavior, then illness, grief, or blinding rage may lead to decisions that subvert the values of a calmer, healthier self.

Situational threats arise from the dire, sometimes coercive, circumstances in which disputants find themselves. If you agree to hand me all your money because I put a gun to your head, can we say that you acted autonomously? If you haven't eaten in four days and agree to sign over the deed to your house in exchange for the rosemary-infused walnut baguette I'm waving under your nose, is that decision a true expression of free will? And if you agree to accept one thousand dollars from me for the broken elbow you suffered when I rear-ended you, ignorant that you could receive ten thousand dollars in court, how autonomous was your decision to settle?

Procedural Fairness

Procedural fairness examines the fairness of methods. When children are fighting in a nursery, a parent or caregiver may decide to handle all disputes about food by adopting a default procedural rule. That is, when, say, a cupcake is to be divided in half, one child gets to cut it and the other gets to choose the first piece. The adult has chosen not to dictate the size of the portions or who gets what. She is staying out of the substantive side of the dispute. Rather, she has decided to institute a procedure that encourages fair play in the division of limited sweets. The adult has made a decision, based on years of experience with children, that this rule, although imperfect, more likely than not creates fair results.

Long experience has taught mediation professionals that procedures such as preserving confidentiality and avoiding significant professional or personal relationships with clients facilitate settlements that are fairer and more satisfying to the disputants. In addition, research reveals that disputants are more likely to feel that they have been treated fairly in a dispute resolution process if they are given an opportunity to tell their story and feel listened to by a neutral and respectful third party. If disputants are treated with respect and dignity, they are likely to believe that the outcome reached in such a process is fair, even if actual terms of the agreement go against them.

Substantive Fairness

Substantive fairness treats the fairness of result. Consider a tug-of-war between two children over their favorite truck. The children are grasping opposite ends of the plastic vehicle, and one of them yells, "I had it first!" When you haven't seen what actually led up to this moment and both children are screaming like banshees, how do you arrive at a substantively fair result?

How you answer depends on your values. For some parents, given the uncertainty of what happened, a fair result would need to teach the value of peaceable coexistence. This might mean taking the truck away from both children. Other parents might surmise that the child who said she had it first did indeed have it first and decide that possession is nine-tenths of the law. Or maybe the parents would decide that because one child has had the truck for the past hour, it would be more important for her to learn a lesson about sharing. Are any of these conclusions right or wrong? In each case, the decision is based on your belief system.

What informs our substantive values? When working with children, we may be influenced by the way we were raised, institutional rules, or even the theories of our favorite child psychologist. When we mediate, we don't sit in a room with the parties isolated from the outside world; each of us comes into the room with our values in tow.

Most people would agree that people should receive their just deserts. But determining what people deserve will depend on the particular theory of justice one adopts. Should resources be divided equally, according to need, according to economic efficiency, or by some other criterion? If one hundred people need a new liver and only one liver becomes available in the next week, what does fairness require? Should the liver go to the sickest of the one hundred, the one most likely to benefit (who would definitely not be the sickest), or the individual who has the most dependents or contributes the most to society? And if contribution to society counts as a criterion, how should contribution be measured?

For some, formal law—judicial opinions, statutes, and constitutions—embodies important notions of justice. Legal rules that prohibit discrimination, protect consumers from dangerous manufacturing practices, and shift costs from injured victims to negligent actors are thought to capture important social judgments about the ways in which we should interact with one another. For this reason, many feel that legal rules have a role to play in mediation, functioning as placeholders for larger notions of equity and fair play. For others, formal law and justice diverge sharply. This view sees the law less as a reflection of our collective social conscience and more as a rigid set of rules that may do more harm than good. Think of the *Dred Scott* v. *Sandford* case of 1857, which ruled that African Americans who were imported to the United States and held as slaves were not citizens and therefore were not protected by the Constitution. For those who believe that formal law and justice do not always overlap, legal rules may have little compelling moral force and should play a minor role in private negotiation.

The mediation field is conflicted on the question of whether fairness of result matters. Some mediation scholars contend that mediators should be concerned with questions of fairness, however one might define that term. Others contend that courts and judges are uniquely situated to determine what is fair and that mediators have neither the institutional authority nor the expertise for such judgments.[3] But while not explicitly adopting substantive fairness as a formal value, many of the commentators in this book express concern about the possibilities for injustice and structure their interventions to guard against it. Many mediators aspire to be a force for good, without stating so explicitly. At the very least, they seek to avoid doing harm. Although most mediators are uncomfortable with the role of justice arbiter, they seek to facilitate a good-enough outcome—one that promotes party autonomy while satisfying minimal notions of fairness and equity.

BALANCING COMPETING VALUES

Adopting a practical approach to mediation ethics requires recognizing that value compromises and trade-offs are an integral part of doing ethics in this field. In the vast array of cases and contexts, it simply isn't possible to give voice and expression to every important value in every case.

Sometimes the goal of helping disputants meet their needs and interests must be tempered by other concerns, such as protecting vulnerable parties or advancing important societal interests. Taking actions that undercut or hinder disputant autonomy may sometimes be the most ethical choice. Value trade-offs are an inevitable end product of our efforts to attain the ethical golden mean.

Some Philosophical Precedent: W. D. Ross and Ethical Intuitionism

The notion that ethical behavior sometimes requires a balancing of important, divergent requirements is not new. In advocating this approach, I borrow from the theory of ethical intuitionism articulated in the 1930s by the Scottish philosopher W. D. Ross.

Ross was both a philosopher and a statesman, active in government task forces and in the administration of Oxford University where he taught moral philosophy. With one foot in the academy and the other in the bureaucratic trenches, he was interested both in questions of pure moral theory and in how moral theory could be made to work in the real world. In considering what makes actions morally correct, he opposed the absolute, unyielding quality of two dominant philosophical traditions: utilitarianism and deontology (a duty-based ethics).[4]

Utilitarians argued that in every situation, right action is that which brings about the greatest good, taking into account everyone affected. Because utilitarians defined *good* as happiness, the morality of an action was thought to derive entirely from the measure of resulting happiness. If an action yielded an overall increase in happiness, then that action was morally desirable. If an action decreased total happiness, it was morally undesirable. Under this theory, assessing morality becomes a mathematical process of calculating hedonic outcomes. Consequences supply the ultimate measure of right action.

Kantian deontology, a version of duty-based ethics famously elaborated by the German philosopher Immanuel Kant, denies these basic premises while adopting equally rigid criteria for moral action. According to Kant, morality is a matter of responding to "perfect duties"—duties that apply in every instance and admit of no exception. The prime directive for Kant requires that the maxims or principles on which individuals act are such that they can be universalized. For Kant, this meant that individuals must always treat others as ends in themselves and never simply as a means. These "categorical imperatives" can be further broken down into more specific obligations. For example, telling the truth and keeping promises are obligations that must be fulfilled, regardless of context.

Focusing on preexisting duties as opposed to consequences leads to dramatically different moral imperatives. For example, if it would maximize the happiness of a ten-person community to enslave one member and require him to attend to the every need of the other nine, then according to a utilitarian system, such enslavement would be morally acceptable. In a deontological system where respecting each individual's personhood is a "perfect duty," involuntary servitude, even servitude that would create maximal community happiness, would never be permissible. Utilitarians and Kantian deontologists similarly diverge when considering the "little (or big) white lie." If you were hiding a Jewish family in your house in Germany during Hitler's reign and the Nazis came knocking and asked if you were shielding fugitives, you would be compelled under Kant's theory to tell the truth and yield up your captives to certain death. The family's fate would not figure into the moral calculus. According to a utilitarian analysis, however, the benefits of truth telling would have to be measured against the harm that would be done to the family if discovered. One would have to consider which outcome—lying and saving the family or telling the truth and leaving the family to certain death—would maximize the overall quantum of happiness.

Although profoundly different, each of these theories offers its own unitary, monistic account of what morality requires. Each rule, applied uniformly in every circumstance, can be counted on to yield a singular measure of moral conduct.

Ross rejected the absolutist character of both utilitarianism and Kant's deontology. Although he was attracted to deontological thinking as a method, he did not subscribe to the notion of "absolute duties." Instead he postulated the existence of prima facie duties—duties that were presumptively binding but that on occasion, depending on context, must yield to other considerations.[5] Thus, for Ross, promise keeping and truth telling were not absolute duties to be kept in all circumstances, but rather prima facie duties that should ordinarily be kept, except when outweighed by other prima facie duties that, in the specific situation, carry a stronger imperative.

Thus, were Ross to consider the problem of the Nazi soldiers and the fugitive family, he would probably note that the Nazis' inquiry places the prima facie duty of truth telling in direct conflict with the prima facie duty of nonmaleficence—avoiding harm to others. Taking the situation as a whole, Ross would likely advise weighing these two prima facie duties and considering which, given these particular facts, is more compelling. After assessing the totality of the circumstances, Ross would conclude that the duty of truth telling—ordinarily a duty to be taken very seriously—must give way. Under these facts, shielding the desperate family is the primary moral imperative, and so one must come to terms with a breach of the truth-telling duty. Ethical intuitionism does not recognize absolute duties—only duties that become primary after considering the totality of the circumstances.

Ross didn't think there was any magic to the process of weighing and balancing the competing values at stake. No one rule could be laid down as to how to do it—other than to think hard and carefully about what is at stake and which duties seem most pressing under the circumstances. Rejecting methodological rigidity in favor of a fluid, intuitive approach, Ross wrote, "This sense of our particular duty in particular circumstances, preceded and informed by the fullest reflection we can bestow on the act in all its bearings, is highly fallible, but it is the only guide we have to our duty."[6]

Ethical Intuitionism and Mediation

Mediation has much to gain from Ross's ethical intuitionism. Mediators struggling to balance their duties to facilitate party self-determination with concerns about substantive outcome and procedural fairness may take comfort from the notion that duties that are undeniable in one case context may be subordinated to other priorities given a different set of facts.

The need for a context-driven balancing approach becomes even clearer when one looks at the regulatory landscape. In some professions, existing ethical guidelines are unified and consistent. This is not the situation in our field.

CURRENT ETHICAL CODES AND THEIR USES

For more than three hundred years in the United States, mediation occurred in an essentially rules-free, regulatory-ethics-free zone. With a few exceptions, no clear set of rules or guidelines steered informal dispute resolvers in an ethical direction.[7] Rather, early mediation pioneers were free to follow their own moral leanings and draw their own lines and boundaries.

Things are different today, at least for a large swath of the mediation workforce. Codes of ethical practice abound, formulated at national and state levels by trade groups and governmental entities seeking to establish basic principles of ethical practice. In subsequent chapters, we often note how a particular standard applies. In this chapter, I introduce the broadest national standards and the concept of specialized codes.

The Model Standards of Conduct for Mediators

Perhaps the most generalized and widely known set of guidelines is the Model Standards of Conduct for Mediators, a set of nine standards with commentary originally prepared and endorsed in 1994 by the American Arbitration Association, the American Bar Association Section of Dispute Resolution, and the Association for Conflict Resolution. In 2005, these standards were revised and reendorsed by these important trade associations.

The Model Standards are not very long and are reproduced in full in the appendix at the end of this book. Throughout this book, other commentators and I will be referring to portions of them. It would be worth your while to read them in full.

In the 2005 revisions, the drafters clarified that the Standards were to serve "three primary goals: to guide the conduct of mediators, ... inform the mediating parties, and ... promote public confidence in mediation as a process for resolving disputes."[8] As an aspirational guide, it is hard to overstate their significance. The Standards have assumed a Talmudic status in a field eager for direction. Like the Bible, Quran, or other holy texts, the Standards serve as the textual touchstone for virtually every argument regarding what mediation is or should be.

It is true that the Standards, except where explicitly adopted by state legislative bodies, do not enjoy the force of law. However, as the drafters point out, the fact that their text has been approved by the three largest trade associations in the field suggests that the Standards might be viewed as establishing a "standard of care" for mediators.[9] Moreover, a number of state courts and legislatures have either adopted the Standards wholesale or borrowed significantly from its language in creating their own regulatory codes.

For example, mediators who work on disputes involving federal agencies have been directed to follow the Model Standards, subject to a few caveats that apply specifically to federal employees and the constraints of working under government regulations.[10] Similarly, mediators working in court-connected programs in Arkansas, Louisiana, Maryland, Kansas, Michigan, Mississippi, New Jersey, North Carolina, South Carolina, and Virginia, as well as community mediators in New York State, are governed by codes that contain definitions of self-determination and impartiality nearly identical to those in the Standards.[11] Where state codes diverge from the Standards, they tend to allow mediators more latitude to provide evaluative information and charge the mediator more directly with a concern for the fairness of the mediated outcome.[12]

Specialized Codes

In addition to generalized codes that apply to mediation across a wide range of subject matter, there exist more specialized guidelines for particular types of cases. For example, mediators working in the area of divorce, criminal law, or disability rights all have particularized standards of practice that provide some ethical instruction.[13] Divorce mediators have the Model Standards of Practice for Family and Divorce Mediation (Divorce Mediation Standards), authored by representatives from the Association of Family and Conciliation Courts, the Family Law Section of the American Bar Association, the National Council of Dispute Resolution Organizations, and a host of other alternative dispute resolution (ADR) providers. Mediators working with those who are disabled have the Americans with Disabilities Act Mediation Guidelines, and victim-offender mediators have the Victim-Offender Mediation Association Recommended Guidelines.

Specialized standards like these alert mediators that if they wish to enter these subject matter arenas, they need to pursue additional training, become sensitive to the challenges raised by the subject matter, and pursue strategies different from those they might adopt in simpler, more generic cases.

INCONSISTENCIES AMONG CODES. With so many codes to consider, it would seem that ethical decision making would be a snap: just take a look at the Model Standards, review your particular state court rules, peruse the specialized codes for particular practice areas, and do what they say. But this linear approach will send you in circles because the codes governing professional conduct in mediation are inconsistent. Not only will applying two separate sets of codes to the same case often yield different directives, different provisions within individual codes themselves are in conflict as well. For instance, rules binding on mediators at the state level may not jibe with either the Model Standards or the specialized codes developed for particular types of cases. Let us review a fairly common scenario from the divorce arena.

Imagine you are a divorce mediator in Alabama working with a couple in which the husband is making aggressive financial demands and the wife is passively acceding to them. The husband wants a 75–25 split, saying he is entitled to the lion's share of assets because his wife wants the divorce and is eager to remarry. You know that no court would issue such an award. Given this couple's financial situation, a court would order a 50–50 split. You wonder, *Should I talk to the couple about a court's likely approach? How can I best promote each disputant's autonomy if each is operating with minimal information? How concerned should I be with the actual terms of the monetary split? Does substantive fairness matter? If I have doubts about their proposed agreement what should I do?*

If you looked at the generalized Model Standards, the Alabama Code of Ethics, and the Divorce Mediation Standards, you might come away confused. Each of the codes says mediation rests on the fundamental principle of self-determination. So maybe if the wife wants to give away something she is entitled by law to keep, it's consistent with promoting self-determination to let her. But the Alabama Code of Ethics also says that a mediator may withdraw if he or she believes any agreement reached would be the result of overreaching, and maybe the husband is overreaching here.[14] Furthermore, according to the Alabama Code, a mediator may discuss the possible outcomes of a case and offer an opinion regarding the likelihood of a specific outcome in court as long as the opinion is given in the presence of a party's attorney. In this respect, it could be argued that the Alabama Code would authorize—maybe even encourage—a discussion by the mediator of what an Alabama court would likely do if asked how to divide this couple's assets fairly.

Turning from the Alabama Code to the specialized Divorce Mediation Standards, one can discern a concern for the fairness of the ultimate agreement similar to that found in the Alabama Code. The Divorce Mediation Standards suggest you withdraw if the participants are about to enter into an unconscionable agreement or if one participant is using the mediation process to gain an unfair advantage.

Furthermore, to the extent provision of such information is consistent with standards of impartiality and preserving party self-determination, as determined under the Divorce Mediation Standards, mediators are authorized to "provide the participants with information that the mediator is qualified by training or experience to provide" so long as that information doesn't constitute legal advice.[15] This might lead our mediator to conclude that if he is a lawyer, it is permissible to give legal information about how community property is treated in that jurisdiction. But providing this kind of legal information threatens to transform the mediator from a neutral into a legal counselor, and the Model Standards explicitly say, "Mixing the role of a mediator and the role of another profession is problematic."

INCONSISTENCIES WITHIN CODES. With so many codes to consider, it is easy to understand how certain actions that are explicitly authorized by one set of standards may be considered problematic in another. But one needn't reach across two or more codes to find divergent instructions: most codes contain provisions that are in conflict with one another.

Take the Model Standards, for example. The Standards encourage mediators to recognize party self-determination as "a fundamental principle of mediation practice" and to work to ensure that parties are supported in making "free and informed choices as to process and outcome." This, of course, is to guarantee increased disputant autonomy. However, the Model Standards also contain provisions regarding procedural fairness and demand that mediators conduct their mediations in a strictly impartial fashion, avoiding any conduct that could lead the parties to think that the mediator favors one over the other.

The tension between promoting disputant autonomy while preserving procedural fairness emerges clearly when considering how the mediator should handle requests for legal information. If the wife asks you pointedly what sort of split a court would likely recommend, should you, if you are able, supply the information yourself? The Standards charge you with encouraging informed decision making. Optimally you would recommend that the wife elicit the information from her own attorney. But what if she doesn't have an attorney and refuses to get one? Providing the information yourself may seem harmless, but the Standards also eschew conduct that might lead one party to suspect partiality. If you were to provide such information, the husband may consider your disclosure to be partiality of the worst sort.[16]

Why the Codes Are Not Enough

When we apply the language from the Model Standards—either alone or in conjunction with other state or specialty subject matter codes—we reach three definite conclusions:

1. *The codes don't answer the question, "What is the ethical course of action in this case?"* There are simply too many contradictions and tensions between different codes and within individual codes. Ethical codes of conduct in mediation should be looked at as a place to start the ethical inquiry. Alone, they will not resolve the issue in any particular case.

2. *Most ethical dilemmas are not resolved by finding the one right answer.* Although certain discrete choices may fall beyond the ethical pale, usually there exists a range of ethically permissible responses and outcomes.

3. *It rarely makes sense to hold one value to be the one dominant principle that subordinates all others in every possible case.* Rather, the primacy of various principles should vary according to the particular facts of the case. For example, self-determination should figure more prominently in cases where the parties are evenly matched, fully competent, and informed and the outcomes contemplated don't threaten to harm third-party or societal interests. Similarly, quality of process and fairness concerns should garner more attention in cases where the ability of the parties to deliberate fully regarding their long-term best interests is in question and where the decisions may affect the well-being of those not at the bargaining table.

A BALANCING ACT: REJECTING RIGIDITY IN MEDIATION

Because the codes take us only so far, we must acknowledge the need to exercise discretion and balance competing ethical objectives. Adopting a practical approach to mediation ethics requires recognizing that value compromises and trade-offs are an integral part of doing ethics in this field. In the vast array of cases and contexts, it simply isn't possible to give voice and expression to every important value in every case.

Sometimes the goal of helping disputants meet their needs and interests must be tempered by other concerns, such as protecting vulnerable parties or advancing important societal interests. Taking actions that undercut or hinder disputant autonomy may sometimes be the most ethical choice. Value trade-offs are an inevitable end product of our efforts to attain the ethical golden mean.

In our divorce mediation example, we can profit from Ross's ethical intuitionism by first noting that it is unclear how best to satisfy the primary mandate of mediation to "respect party self-determination." Both the husband and wife profess to be comfortable with the 75–25 split. But what information are they working with? Although the exact components of autonomous decision making have never been fully defined, most in the mediation community have come to believe that decisions can never be fully self-determining unless they are reasonably informed; that is, the decision maker understands the risks and benefits that such a decision entails.

Does the wife have enough information to make a fully informed decision? Does she know that if the case were decided in a court of law, she would likely be entitled to half the assets? Must she know what a court would likely do before she can make an informed decision in mediation? If we facilitate the 75–25 split that both husband and wife are leaning toward, have we supported their self-determination, or have we simply helped them both make decisions that were only partly thought out? Exactly how much information does informed consent require?

If you asked these questions of half a dozen mediators, you might get at least six different answers. Most mediators would say they would do their best to make sure the wife knew what she was gaining, and giving up, by agreeing to an unequal split. But each mediator's personal "best" will differ depending on his or her understanding of what it means to promote disputant autonomy and procedural fairness, and the definitions adopted and weights assigned to achieving substantive fairness. Some mediators believe that settlement on almost any terms constitutes a good when compared to the alternative of continued discord or resolution through litigation. Other mediators believe that nonsettlement is preferable to an agreement that departs dramatically from societal norms. Thus, some mediators would be troubled by a split of marital assets that gave the wife much less than legislative and judge-made law would provide. Other mediators don't believe that legal norms should serve as any sort of benchmark of fairness, at least not in mediation, and so would not be disturbed by such a settlement disparity.

If you as mediator believe that self-determination means that the parties get to decide how much information they want or need, then you would favor letting the couple divide assets exactly how they want, regardless of what they know or don't know about prevailing legal norms. If you felt strongly that social norms are a relevant indicator of what is fair and just, then the couple's proposed split may trouble you even though you feel that the mandate of respecting party self-determination has been met.

Here, an ethical intuitionist such as Ross would likely counsel you to try to determine how much weight, in this case, the value of promoting self-determination should receive. At the same time, you would need to try to determine how important it is to strive toward an outcome that incorporates societal notions of equity in postdivorce property division.

The Range of Acceptable Action

Because mediators differ dramatically as to both their goals for mediation and the underlying values that shape those goals, there is a wide arena of conduct that most in the mediation community would condone as acceptable. For example, the following responses would all likely be seen as ethical by a vast majority of mediation experts in the field:

- Asking the wife if she has consulted with an attorney
- Suggesting the wife consult with an attorney
- Discussing in joint session the legal norms that suggest a judicial award of 50–50

Each of these options seeks to promote informed decision making while still protecting the parties' right to decide for themselves what they believe to be fair.

A tougher question arises if the wife says she has not consulted an attorney and does not care to. Options available to the mediator at this juncture range from the highly paternalistic to the more laissez-faire. If you were propelled by concern that all decisions made in mediation be informed, you could refuse to continue working on the case unless the wife agrees to obtain legal information from either you directly or outside counsel. Conversely, if you understood self-determination to require acquiescence to the wife's own judgment regarding the relevance of social norms to her negotiations with her ex-husband, then you would assist the parties in writing up their three quarters/one quarter split. Either of these options would fall well within the margin of acceptability given current thinking in the mediation world.

Beyond the Ethical Pale

Although mediators enjoy a large gray area in which they can safely work, there are some actions that many mediators would likely see as ethically out of bounds. For example, although a well-intentioned mediator, convinced that legislative and judge-made norms perfectly capture what should happen in all postdivorce splits, might be tempted to impose a settlement that fully incorporated her prediction of what a court might do, this would clearly cross the line.

While a mediator who imposes her preferred settlement is clearly too directive, mediators operating within the bounds of acceptable mediation practice vary in terms of how directive they are. Some mediators may closely question parties seeking to waive legal entitlements in order to make sure that they fully understand what they are giving up and how those waivers may affect their long-term self-interest. You may ethically ask:

> "Are you sure you are comfortable receiving only one-quarter of the property's equity when you would likely receive more if you went to court?"

> "How do you think you will feel about this decision in six months or a year?"

> "What is the benefit to you to come to this resolution now in this way? What are the possible costs?"

These questions are ethically acceptable: they serve to buttress mediator confidence that the party has thought carefully and deliberately about the waiver. But ethical dictates would require the mediator to abstain from requiring—or even pushing—the party to adopt any particular outcome. Mediator concern for substantive fairness can only trench so much on party self-determination. Arguably, mediators may impose on party autonomy by requiring the parties to acquire information. But what the parties do with that information is up to them. If a mediator is so troubled by the substantive outcome reached that she concludes it is unconscionable or the product of duress or overreaching, she can withdraw. But she cannot press the parties to adopt a particular outcome because it accords with her own sense of fairness, equity, or propriety.

The Role of Mediator Philosophy in Balancing Competing Value Commitments

Mediators everywhere say that promoting party autonomy, encouraging substantively good outcomes, and ensuring procedural fairness are important. But how they weigh and balance the three is in part a matter of mediation philosophy and model.

Mediators' models differ significantly in ways that are not simply stylistic variations on a common theme. Rather, they reflect divergent philosophies about conflict and human nature, as well as the primary goals and purposes of the mediation process. Because adherents to these different models are inspired by different ideological commitments, they deploy different ethical analyses and, unsurprisingly, sometimes reach different conclusions.

This does not mean that there is no overlap. And it does not mean that any action one would choose to take in mediation can be defended by some theory. Some actions would be considered unethical by mediators from every camp. It does mean, however, that there remains a considerable gray area where mediators working with different models would disagree regarding what should be done in any particular case. Given this impact of models, it is crucially important that mediators be clear about the models they are using and their own goals for the mediation process.

THE MULTIPLE MODELS OF MEDIATION

Numerous mediation schemata exist, and the nomenclature is vast and ever growing. For simplicity, we will focus on the distinctions between problem-solving and relationship-building approaches and explore briefly the subcategories that exist within each basic approach.

Problem-Solving Models: Evaluative Versus Facilitative

In 1996, Len Riskin developed a typology of mediation approaches that captured the mediation field's collective imagination and has gained increased traction ever since.[17] Indeed, when, nearly ten years later, Riskin himself attempted to rework his categories,[18] he found the original structure and vocabulary immovable. The second-generation terms and concepts that he described as allowing for a "new and improved" mediation grid simply have not caught on the way his first set of descriptors did. Given its widespread popularity and presence in training curricula, credentialing measures, and informal mediator chatter, it seems sensible to review the features of Riskin's typology that have had the greatest impact on the field to date.

Riskin's typology is oriented around problem solving. His models assume that the primary goal of the process is settlement. Within that basic framework, he identifies two different approaches—one facilitative, the other evaluative.[19]

FACILITATIVE MEDIATION. Facilitative mediators see their primary role as problem solving, but they adhere to clear limits in that role. Facilitative mediators "assume the parties are intelligent, able to work with their counterparts, and capable of understanding their situations better than either their lawyers or the mediator."[20] Because facilitative mediators vest ultimate confidence in the parties' own problem-solving capacities, they work mainly at developing those capacities through skillful questioning and listening. Facilitative mediators assist by helping parties better explore their underlying interests, develop proposals, and evaluate those proposals. They ask questions designed to help the parties probe in greater depth the likely consequences of settling or not settling. They encourage parties to assess the strengths and weaknesses of their various legal positions.

Notably the facilitative mediator does not evaluate the soundness or practicability of any party's stance. She does not judge the value or merit of any proposal on the table or offer up opinions about what would happen if the case settled or did not settle. She believes that such tactics impair mediator impartiality and stifle party autonomy. If a party appears to be sticking stubbornly to an unrealistic position, a facilitative mediator may ask questions in an effort to create movement. But she would stop short of giving her own view of the merits or offering an opinion of what a reasonable settlement option would be.

Because facilitative mediators seek to tap into the parties' own deep knowledge and understanding of the matters in dispute, they do not stress or claim to have subject matter expertise themselves. In fact, in Riskin's words, "too much subject-matter expertise" might be a hindrance for facilitative mediators because it would incline them "toward a more evaluative role, and could thereby interfere with developing creative solutions."[21] The facilitative mediator is like a symphony conductor: she brings the instruments together and works to help them play in harmony, but she does not add a bass or soprano voice herself. She is the maestro of process, but endeavors to have little influence on the actual melody that emerges.

EVALUATIVE MEDIATION. The evaluative mediator is also oriented toward problem solving, but she views her role in the dispute somewhat more expansively. The evaluative mediator "assumes that the participants want and need the mediator to provide some direction as to the appropriate grounds for settlement—based on law, industry practice or technology." She also assumes that "the mediator is qualified to give such direction by virtue of her experience, training and objectivity."[22]

Whereas facilitative mediators place the burden of developing and evaluating proposals firmly on the parties, evaluative mediators will, if need be, take on some of those tasks themselves. They feel free to offer their opinions regarding proposed settlement options and the legal merit of each party's positions. Because evaluative mediators introduce their own assessments into the mix, they view their own substantive expertise regarding relevant law, industry practice, or custom as a significant aspect of their skill.

DIFFERENCES IN DEFINING AND SUPPORTING AUTONOMY. Whereas both facilitative and evaluative mediators seek to support party autonomy, they differ on how to do so. Evaluative mediators believe autonomous decision making is better achieved when disputants are maximally informed about their best and worst alternatives to settlement. They view the provision of information regarding likely court outcomes as increasing, not diminishing, disputant autonomy. Facilitative mediators worry more about the possibly coercive effect of the mediator's opinion. If the mediator speaks, people, especially disputants, listen. According to the facilitative worldview, the mediator's provision of information risks overriding the disputants' own preferences and values; evaluations usurp, rather than support, party self-determination.

Thus, although both facilitative and evaluative mediators take party self-determination seriously, in their efforts to bring closure to disputes, they differ about what autonomous decision making entails and consequently adopt different attitudes toward offering opinions or evaluations.

DIFFERING VIEWS ON SUBSTANTIVE FAIRNESS. Writers who have set out to describe and advocate for either a facilitative or evaluative model have touched on the notion of substantive fairness only obliquely. Determining the relationship of these models to fairness concerns is thus, by necessity, somewhat speculative. Nevertheless, a few general observations can be made.

First, facilitative mediators are more likely to define fairness or justice as highly contextual and to take their cue from the parties' own perceptions. Thus, as two facilitative mediators have written, there is a difference between justice on high (what the law says) and justice from below (what the parties see as fair), and in their view, mediation is a place where justice from below should govern.[23]

Second, facilitative mediators would be loathe to vest formal rules or legal strictures with excessive moral authority and thus would be less likely to seek their recourse in considering whether outcomes reached are fair or equitable. Evaluative mediators are accustomed to referencing collective norms, be they legal, psychological, engineering, or grounded in some other customary practice. Because their expertise flows from knowledge of and facility with these norms, they are more inclined to endow them with some sort of moral authority. Many evaluative mediators look to legal or industry norms not simply as strategic tools that help settle cases but as authoritative benchmarks embodying societal judgments about what is fair and reasonable.

Relationship-Building and Personal Growth Models

Not all models view mediation as a tool for problem solving. Some adopt a broader vision, viewing mediation as a way to help people gain a deeper understanding of themselves and those they interact with. These models stress the potential of mediation to enhance relationships and encourage personal growth.

TRANSFORMATIVE MEDIATION. Unlike both facilitative and evaluative mediators, transformative mediators see problem solving as ancillary to the true goals of the process. Introduced by Robert A. Baruch Bush and Joseph P. Folger in their groundbreaking book, *The Promise of Mediation*, the transformative school views mediation's main task to be relational change and personal growth rather than dispute settlement.[24]

Conflict, according to Bush and Folger, offers disputants a unique opportunity to change the quality of their interaction and, in the process, develop into more morally and emotionally mature beings. While parties may enter into disputes feeling vulnerable and self-absorbed, mediation offers them the possibility of better understanding themselves and their underlying goals, as well as the perspectives and goals of their adversaries. Mediator strategies and techniques are thus entirely oriented toward promoting parties' recognition of their own needs and capacities and encouraging their ability to empathize with each other. Consequently, interventions that do not push toward party empowerment or recognition have no place on the transformative mediator's mental map.

For this reason, a transformative mediator would likely not see the use or merit of offering information or opinions to the parties. Empowerment, as defined by Folger and Bush, occurs when parties reach a clearer realization of their goals and interests and come to understand that "regardless of external constraints, . . . there are always some choices open and the control over those choices [is theirs] . . . alone."[25]

Like the facilitative model, the transformative model is wary of mediator interventions that might shift the focus or direction of the parties' discussion. The mediator's job, according to the transformative school, is to change the quality of the parties' interaction; to watch for and support shifts that reflect party self-confidence, agency, and empathy. Mediator interventions, according to this school, should help the parties better understand where *they* want to go with their dispute. Under no circumstances should the mediator intervene in ways that effect a shift in the substantive direction of the discussion. For that reason, in this model, offering an evaluation or assessment of the parties' position is never justified or warranted.

NARRATIVE MEDIATION. Like transformative mediators, narrative mediators also reject problem solving as the ultimate end goal of the process. According to Gerald Monk and John Winslade, the principal architects of this model, the goal of mediation "needs to be constructed in terms of a story. A story is not a one-time event but something that moves through time."[26] A successful conclusion to a mediation may be an agreement, but it need not be. Even if no agreement emerges, the process is successful if participants walk away with a new story about their interaction with one another. In the authors' words, the process has been successful if the parties have created a "sustainable, forward-moving narrative."[27]

Three interrelated assumptions shape narrative mediation practice:

- Foremost, language shapes reality. It does not merely transmit meaning; rather, it is a site where meaning is created.

- There is no such thing as an objectively fixed reality. Facts are always the product of a subjective perspective forged in particular social or cultural circumstance.

- Individual identity is a product of the multiple myths, traditions, and stories embraced by the surrounding culture. These stories shape and guide individual understandings and choices. These stories must be unpacked so that parties can gain a fuller sense of how they have imagined their conflicts and how they might reimagine them in a way that enables forward movement.

In narrative mediation, disputants come to the table with a "conflict-saturated story," and the job of the mediator is to deconstruct that story, expose those ideas "that masquerade as unquestioned truth,"[28] and help the parties work toward a more positive discourse. According to this view, shifting to an alternate narrative will effect shifts in the parties' relationship and situation.

Narrative mediation sees individuals trapped in conflict stories that emanate from and embody cultural myths and unexamined verities. The mediator expands party autonomy by "unpack[ing] the suitcase and tak[ing] out the pieces" and "hold[ing] them up for view."[29] The mediator helps parties look more closely at unexamined feelings of entitlement as well as scripts handed to them by virtue of their membership in family, religious communities, or society at large.

Substantive fairness is a concern in this model. Narrative mediation is sensitive to the role of power in mediation and seeks to destabilize existing and entrenched power relations. True to its postmodern roots, however, it does not see legal or social norms as necessarily delineating what is fair or right in any given situation. Rather, these norms are relevant to the discussion in that they are an important strand of the cultural script that parties work with.

The Effect of Mediation Model or Philosophy on Ethical Deliberation

This chapter has argued that weighing and balancing competing ethical mandates is an essential component of ethical deliberation. It suggests that thoughtful mediators, including the commentators in the following chapters in this book:

- Pinpoint the crucial values at stake
- Look for tension between those values
- Consider how the factual features of the case and their own mediation philosophy affect the balance of conflicting values and principles
- Select an action plan that honors the identified value trade-offs

Some ethical dilemmas point toward a common set of responses regardless of mediation philosophy. Conflict of interest and confidentiality problems would likely be diagnosed and understood similarly by evaluative, transformative, and narrative mediators alike. But other ethically challenging cases will look very different depending on the model employed. We will see, in the chapters ahead, that mediation philosophy plays a significant role in how various commentators balance commitments to disputant autonomy, substantive fairness, and procedural justice.

HOW THIS BOOK PROCEEDS: A ROAD MAP

The following chapters present hypotheticals designed to flush out some of the more difficult ethical dilemmas presented in practice. Each chapter begins with a brief discussion of the values implicated and guidance offered by existing codes and guidelines. This introduction features an editor's case—a relatively straightforward case that can be analyzed without great difficulty or controversy. Each chapter also features at least one, and sometimes two, commentators' cases: more difficult cases where the tensions between competing ethical values are posed more starkly. Prominent mediators and scholars have been recruited to discuss how they would proceed if faced with the dilemmas outlined in the commentator's case. They were recruited based on their experience and expertise and diversity of viewpoint. The book aims to showcase the heterogeneity of approach that characterizes the community of practicing mediators. At the same time, it seeks to reveal the common process of deliberation that undergirds each commentator's analysis.

A WORD ON MY BIASES

A crucial aspect of ethical practice involves being reflective about one's own biases. As editor, I have framed the issues, created the hypotheticals for discussion, and suggested that certain ways of proceeding are more advisable than others. In myriad ways, my biases shape the discourse that follows, and I wish to be transparent about the assumptions that suffuse my analysis:

- Only penetrating and sustained inquiry can determine the extent to which individuals are able to exercise and indeed are exercising their autonomy in mediation. Disputants can act autonomously only when certain conditions are in place, and mediators must attend carefully to constraints and pressures that may be impinging on and limiting a disputant's ability to act freely.

- Social norms, especially those embodied in the rule of law, constitute important guideposts to human behavior. They don't "do justice" in every individual instance, and thus the opportunity that mediation offers to reorient the negotiations around the disputants' idiosyncratic needs and interests is profound. Still, where extreme power imbalances exist, legal norms can be useful in delineating the minimal set of obligations owed the less powerful by the more powerful. Although mediators must be careful to preserve the unique capacities of mediation for innovative problem solving, they must also attend to the dangers of exploitation implicit in an unbalanced process.

- Intervening in others' conflicts is an act of temerity. It can be justified only if mediators embrace a duty of beneficence, aspiring to be a force for good. At the very least, mediators should embrace the less rigorous duty of nonmaleficence—the duty to avoid harm. Mediators should be concerned about fairness. They should ask the justice question while remaining humble about their ability to supply an answer and open to the possibility that multiple definitions abound.

Not everyone in the mediation community shares these views. Many would object to a searching inquiry of disputants' capacity to act autonomously, arguing that it imposes unnecessarily high barriers to the exercise of party self-determination. Mediation invites parties to expand and develop their sense of competence and agency. Why impose a burden of proof on disputants who accept the invitation? Similarly, many in mediation hold jaundiced views of the rule of law and the relationship of these rules to justice. They would assess mediation's efficacy according to its separation from, rather than incorporation of, legal norms in the parties' discussions. Moreover, the very idea that mediators should ask the justice question would be objectionable to many in the mediation community because it might encourage paternalism and place constraints on the sorts of unconventional outcomes that mediation makes possible. The notion that mediators should explicitly adopt a theory of beneficence, or at the least nonmaleficence, has not been widely articulated or embraced.

I have tried to provide some balance by recruiting commentators with diverse perspectives. It will be clear from their writings that they do not agree with me and would pursue different interventions than the ones I recommend. As the mediation field matures, it is likely that we will reach greater consensus regarding best practices in the field and what it means to practice ethically. For now, this book offers an opening to begin the conversation.

CHAPTER TWO

Autonomy and Diminished Capacity

Mediation seeks to help disputants make decisions that fit with their long-standing values. A disputant who values neighborly relations more than monetary comfort might choose to waive a significant legal entitlement in order to preserve peace. An aesthetically discerning business partner may choose to pay out a large slice of yearly profits in order to maintain authority over the visual details of the partnership logo. While perhaps not what everyone would do, these decisions are emphatically in line with these individuals' sense of what is fair and satisfying, and helping disputants arrive at internally coherent decisions is at the core of what mediation is all about.

But disputants may suffer from a number of conditions that put readiness or capacity to mediate at risk, including mental illness, physical illness, or substance abuse. What if disputants are so plagued by physical or mental difficulties that their current thinking or behavior appears to diverge from the values they have expressed consistently over the years? What if illness or disability interferes with their ability to weigh divergent options or participate meaningfully in mediation deliberations?

Ethical mediation requires judgment about a disputant's readiness to engage in mediation. How should such readiness be assessed? And how should a mediator balance a disputant's right to participate in mediation against the possibility that physical or mental impairment makes informed decision making impossible?

COMPLEXITIES OF DETERMINING CAPACITY

Determining disputant capacity is tricky, and the stakes, if error occurs, are high. Set the bar too high, and we risk excluding from mediation individuals who might benefit from presenting their views, forging creative solutions, and maintaining control over their own destiny. Set the bar too low, and we risk exposing vulnerable parties to an exploitative negotiation setting. Confused or cognitively impaired parties are unlikely to fare well when horse-trading with mentally agile bargaining opponents.

Cautions When Declaring a Disputant Unfit

Mediators should bear the following in mind before declaring a disputant unfit to take part in mediation.

First, medical capacity differs from legal competence. A determination of legal incompetence means that the state is acting in its protective capacity to curtail an individual's decisional rights in order to prevent harm. A determination of medical capacity looks at an individual's functionality in connection with particular tasks.[1] An individual may be declared legally incompetent to manage his or her financial affairs yet retain the capacity to engage in many other tasks, including mediation.

Second, capacity has meaning only in the context of a specific task or decision. We can't talk about people retaining or lacking capacity globally; rather, we have to ask, "Capacity for what?" It may be that an elderly person lacks the capacity to continue to live independently but retains the capacity to make simple health care decisions. Similarly, that same individual might lack the capacity to participate in discussions of complicated financial instruments, but be fully capable of engaging in straightforward talk about getting to the doctor and how food should be delivered and meals made.[2]

Capacity in Legal Settings

Capacity comes into play in a number of legal settings, be it standing trial for a criminal offense, signing a contract, or appointing a medical proxy. In each of these situations, the state will inquire into the psychological situation of the decision maker to determine whether he or she has the functional capacity to engage meaningfully with the choice to be made. The state does this for four main reasons:[3]

- It seeks to ensure that people don't make decisions that might thwart their longer-term best interests. For example, an individual in the grip of a paranoid delusion might wish to plead guilty to an offense he or she did not commit. Unburdened of that mental disability, our alleged criminal might deeply regret the guilty plea.

- It seeks to protect vulnerable third parties who might be disadvantaged by decision making tainted by incapacity. For example, our criminal defendant might have children who require care and nurturing that will be denied them if the guilty plea is uncritically accepted by the court. Or an impaired individual manipulated into changing her will might disenfranchise the very relatives she seeks to support.

- It seeks to enhance the efficiency and accuracy of the decision-making process. If a disordered individual cannot testify accurately or communicate reliably with advocate, judge, or jury, the possibility is strong that the final judgment will be in error.

- It seeks to preserve the dignity of the decision-making process. A criminal trial, probate hearing, or custody negotiation becomes a pantomime if the principal actors are unable to understand what the process means or what consequences hang in the balance.

Party capacity is similarly essential to ensure the integrity of the mediation process. Mediation's great promise is thought to lie in its ability to provide disputants greater autonomy in fashioning their own dispute endings. But autonomy is the exercise of self-rule, and if disease or other physical or emotional disturbance disorders the self beyond recognition, then the dispute ending may not be self-determining but rather self-defeating. Figuring out whether the disputant before you is capable of acting on and expressing her true self is crucial to determining whether the process can go forward.

Components of Capacity for Mediation

Assessments of capacity generally look to three areas of function: understanding, appreciation, and ability to communicate.

UNDERSTANDING. Parties must understand both the purpose and process of mediation as well as the issues the mediation was convened to address. Existing mediation codes and guidelines caution mediators to ensure that disputants are able to comprehend what is happening in the mediation and can participate without difficulty.[4] One set of guidelines crafted with disabled disputants specifically in mind states that all participants must be able to grasp "the nature of the mediation process, who the parties are, the role of the mediator, the parties' relationship to the mediator, and the issues at hand."[5]

APPRECIATION. Parties must also be able to appreciate the import of their decisions. This means they must be able to rationally consider the options on the table, weigh the costs and benefits associated with each option, and connect their choices with the consequences that logically follow.

COMMUNICATION. Parties must be able to relay their thoughts to other mediation participants. Some ability to express thought must be present, although it is important to remember that people can communicate in various ways, not simply through speech. Writing, sign language, and use of specially designed computers can all be means by which individuals with disabilities can make their wishes known.

The hard part of assessing capacity is maintaining focus on disputant functionality and not on the quality or sensibleness of the decision reached. If disputants can understand the relevant facts, appreciate how those facts relate to the available options, and engage in a balancing of benefits and harms, then they should be deemed capable of making decisions, regardless of whether they arrive at a solution that the mediator, or the rest of the world, would embrace. Disputants are entitled to assign their own unique meanings to the advantages and disadvantages that different options present. They are allowed to make decisions that the rest of us would consider irrational. They simply have to be capable of reaching those decisions through a deliberate and rational process.

Accommodations

It may be that an individual's impairments render capacity to mediate questionable, but accommodations could be made to bolster capacity. If this is so, provider organizations and individual mediators must endeavor to make those accommodations. For example, if a disputant is required to take medication that interferes with her ability to concentrate and focus, can the dosage be reduced temporarily, or are there periods between doses during which the mediation can be scheduled? Conversely, if a disputant has a mental illness that responds to pharmaceuticals, can the mediation be set during a period when the drugs are having their most salutary effect? Support personnel, representatives, attorneys, friends, or family may also be enlisted to help translate, explain, and otherwise assist in boosting an impaired individual's function.[6]

Capacity assessments can sound simple in the abstract, but let's look at the questions and concerns that might arise in a relatively simple case.

CASE 2.1: CAN MARY MEDIATE HER RESIDENCY?

Mary is an eighty-two-year-old retiree who has lived alone and independently since her husband died twenty-five years ago. She lives in the home they shared and has spent much of her retirement tending to the backyard flower and herb garden that, for many years, was the pride of the neighborhood. For years, Mary was the ambassador for her block, welcoming new families with freshly cut roses and homemade cookies. Always available if a friend needed help, Mary is famous for shunning help herself, priding herself on her ability to make do.

In the past few years, Mary's health has declined. She suffers from high blood pressure, congestive heart failure, and mild dementia. She has also become more withdrawn, visiting less often with neighbors and her friends at the senior center down the street. Mary was always forgetful, but now she is frequently late paying bills. Although she has plenty of money in her bank account, her water was shut off once because she sent off her payment without a stamp. Too frail to make it to the grocery store, Mary now allows a housekeeper, Ida, who comes once a week, to clean the apartment and bring in groceries. On Sunday mornings, her daughter, Elise, with whom she is not close, comes and takes her to church.

Two months ago, Mary forgot to take her heart medication. Ida came to bring groceries one morning and found Mary crumpled on the ground in the garden, pale, short of breath, and confused, wondering what plants she had come out to tend. Ida took her to the hospital where she was prescribed medication to stabilize her fluids and heart function.

Convinced that her mother is no longer capable of taking care of herself, Elise has hired a lawyer and filed a petition for guardianship. Mary opposes the petition and has hired a lawyer too. The judge assigned to the case has referred the case to you for mediation.

When you walk into the room, Elise and Mary are both there with their lawyers. You greet Mary and ask how she is. She answers you warmly and cogently. You ask if she has attended a mediation before, and she says no, but she says she knows that the idea is that she and Elise try to talk about where she should live and what sort of help she needs getting by. She looks alert and is talking logically with her lawyer.

Before you even begin your opening statement, Elise's lawyer asks to meet with you separately. He objects to the mediation, saying, "Look, Mary can't do this. If she were well and able to make good decisions for herself, we wouldn't be here. This case isn't appropriate for mediation. You need to cancel this, and we'll just make our arguments in court."

What do you do?

There are two main questions to address. The first is whether Mary is capable of participating in mediation. The second relates to mediation's end point: Does Mary possess the capacity to make an agreement? Should she be allowed to bind herself to a particular outcome?

Capacity to Participate

Essentially Elise's lawyer is suggesting that Mary isn't up to the task of mediating—that her health is so compromised that she lacks the cognitive ability to engage meaningfully with the process.

Although Mary has some health problems, she nevertheless appears to possess the capacity to participate actively in mediation. She has become withdrawn and forgetful, but nothing in the facts suggests that she is unable to understand the structure of the mediation process, why she has been asked to attend, and what the issues are. To the contrary, her answers to your questions suggest she possesses the minimal awareness required to engage in mediation.

Mary has already said she understands that the purpose of the process is to discuss with Elise whether she is able to continue to care for herself at home. To feel more confident that Mary is up to the task of negotiating, you might spend a bit more time providing her with information about the process and ensuring that she is able to absorb that information. You should methodically explain your role as facilitator and neutral intermediary, asking Mary questions to ascertain if she grasps the scope and limits of that role. Furthermore, you should try to determine what Mary understands regarding her attorney's function at the mediation and whether she regards her attorney as a source of information and support.

After explaining how you plan to proceed, either in joint session or caucus or some combination of both, you should again try to get a sense of whether Mary is following the description and understands the purpose and goals of these differently structured sessions.

If Mary can demonstrate that she understands why the mediation is taking place, what needs to be discussed, the ultimate goal of the process, and the respective functions of each participant, then she possesses capacity to proceed.

Capacity to Bind Oneself

Does Mary also possess the capacity to make an agreement? Should she be allowed to bind herself to a particular outcome? The case continues:

After the lawyers finish discussing the burden of proof for establishing need for a guardianship, Mary and Elise begin to talk. Mary asks Elise whether she is really worried about her or whether she has just been listening to the gossip of meddlesome neighbors who tell Mary and Elise alike that Elise is a bad daughter for allowing Mary to continue living alone. Elise confesses that she is tired of the neighbors' badgering, that they make her feel guilty, but that she also does worry about Mary living in her home alone.

Mary sighs and says, "Oh, Elise, you always cared too much about what others think. I know that my living alone is a burden for you, but that's just something you'll have to live with. Perhaps it's a bit risky for me to live like this. But you know me. I like managing on my own. I hate having others do for me. I probably need a bit more help with my medicine, but otherwise I get along fine. This house is everything to me. My garden reminds me of everything I've tended over the years. If I can still take care of my plants, then I still have a reason to move these sore legs of mine. If I move out, I lose my home, my garden, my memories, my life. Even if I went tomorrow, I'd go happy in the house where I lived so many joyful years with your father."

After two hours of frank exchanges and brainstorming, Mary and Elise agree that Mary will stay in her home. Mary agrees to tell her neighbors that Elise tried to get her to move in with her but Mary refused. Elise appears worn down by Mary's determination and resigned to follow her mother's instructions. Ida will come every morning to make sure Mary takes her medicine. Otherwise, because Mary insisted, no other interventions are planned. Ida will continue to bring the groceries once a week, and Elise will continue to take Mary to church.

- Can we be sure that Mary has the capacity to enter into a binding mediation agreement?
- Does she understand the raw facts of the situation?
- Can she appreciate the options on the table? Can she prioritize and assign weights to various values? Can she engage in a balancing process, finding that certain values are more dear to her than others? Can she draw logical connections between the options she chooses and the consequences that will likely follow?
- Can she communicate her preferences?

It appears that the answer to these questions is yes. Mary appears to understand that she runs some risk continuing to live alone.

She understands that she needs the medication for her health and understands that her forgetfulness sometimes gets in the way of her taking the medication.

She appears to appreciate the values at stake—safety, independence, privacy—and she can clearly assign weights to those values. She appears to be able to connect her embrace of a continued solitary existence with an elevated degree of risk. Similarly, she is able to link the guardianship option, and its concomitant move to Elise's home, with the loss of her familiar surroundings as well as her sense as an independent person.

The emphasis that Mary places on her garden and her attachment to the plants and physical structure of her house may seem eccentric, given the burdens of upkeep and her poor health. We may think that she is placing too much value on her role as gardener and not enough value on the importance of staying safe. The cost-benefit analysis she is engaging in may strike us as odd. But Mary is not out of touch with reality. She recognizes the dangers her choices pose. She seems to understand that remaining in the house is not the lowest-risk option in terms of her health. Still, Mary can articulate the joy that gardening and living independently give her and can weigh that joy versus the hardships that staying in her house entails. For that reason, her decision should be respected.

If you or I were Mary, we might opt for something different. If Mary were our mother, we might wish that the mediation had resulted in a more secure living situation for her. But we must be careful in engaging in capacity assessments not to import our own values—what we think is reasonable, rational, sensible, and secure—into the parties' discussions. Only if the disputants lack the functional abilities to understand, appreciate, and communicate should we intervene and consider terminating or otherwise altering the course of the mediation.

CASE 2.2: KEVIN'S DISABILITY—DREAMS AND DURESS

When Kevin was born, he suffered oxygen deprivation that led to moderate brain damage. He has been diagnosed as educable mentally retarded[7] and has been mainstreamed in the public school system. He attends some special education classes and receives private tutoring, but has been held back in his grade a number of times. Currently he has completed ninth grade, although if he had progressed through school at the average rate, he would be in his first year of college.

Kevin turned nineteen in August before beginning tenth grade. At that point, he was found ineligible to participate further in interscholastic sports according to a state regulation that prohibits students who turn nineteen before September 1 from participating on high school sports teams. Kevin is a talented football player, and his sports activities serve as an outlet for some of the frustration he experiences in the classroom. Kevin's coach has come to rely on him to score the winning touchdown in many games and is also convinced that Kevin's football prowess is central to his self-esteem and ability to connect with peers.

Kevin and his coach have brought an action under the Americans with Disabilities Act, claiming that Kevin is being discriminated against based on a disability. The complaint alleges that Kevin's mental retardation is the reason he is running afoul of the state's age limit at the beginning of his sophomore year. Were it not for his mental disability, Kevin would be proceeding through school at the expected rate and would be able to continue playing high school sports. Coach believes an accommodation should be made and that the age limit should be waived.

The state department of education counters that the state's limit for participating in interscholastic sports is based on a student's age, not mental abilities, and that the rule is applied uniformly among the student population. The case has been referred for mediation. Attending the mediation are Kevin, his coach, and a representative from the department of education.

At age nineteen, Kevin can do the academic work of a fourteen year old, but has the emotional maturity of a nine year old. He is concerned about fitting in and following rules and has become conscious that he is much bigger than the boys he plays with. Once last year, a tackle Kevin landed in an intramural game sent the opposing player to the emergency room with a fractured arm. Kevin was devastated and didn't come out of his room for the next two days.

Kevin is quietly ambivalent about continuing to play football. He does like the attention and the fact that he is good at football. But he is afraid of hurting others and wonders whether he might do better playing with those his age or with younger boys in sports with less body contact. But when he talks with coach, coach always says, "But the team needs you." And Kevin likes being needed. He doesn't feel that in many other areas of his life.

What should a mediator taking on Kevin's case do?

Comments on Case 2.2

Carol B. Liebman

In this mediation, as in so many others, the ethical issues can, for the most part, be resolved by good practice. While it is important for mediators to be aware of the ethical challenges Kevin's case triggers, including the principle of self-determination, mediator compe- tence, quality of the process, and party capacity, the answer to the question of whether to mediate will be found through attention to mediator skills.

If Kevin has the capacity to participate in the mediation process and the capacity to make a reasoned decision about what is best for him, then the process should go forward. Many individuals with disabilities can participate in mediation, so long as the mediator makes accommodations to help them engage in the communication and cognitive tasks at the heart of the negotiations.

In this case, it would appear that Kevin—with the intellectual capacity of a fourteen year old and the emotional capacity of a nine year old—is capable of taking part in the discussions. The challenge for the mediator is how, given Kevin's intellectual and emotional limitations, to best structure the mediation process to enable him to participate, as fully as his capacity will allow, in discussions about whether he will continue playing football on the school team.

Whether Kevin possesses sufficient capacity to bind himself to a final resolution depends on his ability to understand and appreciate the consequences of the decision reached, whether that is to continue to play on the team or not. Kevin's grasp of the situation will become clearer once the mediator has a chance to draw him out about what he wants and why. Given Kevin's limited emotional development, the mediator will need to pay attention to Kevin's ability to consider long-term consequences (a task difficult for young children) and will need to probe to ensure that Kevin is asserting his true preferences and not trying to please others (such as his coach).

While this discussion will focus on steps the mediator might take to help Kevin participate fully in the mediation, it is important to remember that the mediator is not Kevin's advocate and that process choices made to support his participation must not put the other participants at a disadvantage.

STRUCTURING THE MEDIATION. In order to support Kevin's full participation, the mediator needs to consider the following questions:

- What should the mediator do to develop this case before the mediation begins?
- Who should be at the table?
- What decisions is Kevin capable of understanding and participating in, and what decisions should be made by others in his best interest?
- Does the mediator need special knowledge or skills to handle this case?
- How should the mediation be structured to best support Kevin's participation?
- What about the interests of those not at the table?

What Should the Mediator Do in Advance? In many situations, mediators work with the participants before the formal mediation begins. They conduct an assessment of the case in order to determine who should be at the table or what issues should be on the agenda. They may hold a premediation conference call with the parties or their representatives. And some mediators, especially in complicated or emotional cases, have premediation caucuses with the parties and their representatives, just before the mediation or several days before, to learn about any process concerns and to provide a bit of coaching about how best to use the process. These premediation activities give mediators a better sense going into the formal mediation of how they can be most useful and also allow them the opportunity to begin to gain the trust of the parties.

In Kevin's case, a premediation meeting between the mediator and Kevin would have a number of benefits. The mediator could explain the mediation process in a setting where Kevin could ask questions and express concerns without worrying about the impact of those questions on others at the table. And the mediator could assess Kevin's ability to participate in the mediation discussion. The mediator could also talk to Kevin about whether there is anyone he would like to have at the mediation to help him make decisions. Obvious possibilities include his parents, an older sibling, a counselor or therapist, his tutor, or a teacher who is not involved with the athletic program. The mediator will need to be sensitive about the need to support Kevin's autonomy in any discussion about bringing a support person to the mediation.

A premediation meeting will also give the mediator a better sense of Kevin's ability to bargain for himself and may help Kevin gain a sense of ease with the mediator so that he will be more comfortable during the formal mediation. It might also be useful for the mediator, with Kevin's permission, to talk to his parents, a school counselor, and anyone else identified in a conversation with Kevin to get a better idea of how best to support Kevin during the mediation and to learn about the limits of his decision-making capacity. If Kevin does not want the mediator to talk to these people, the mediator must respect that choice. (I assume that Kevin does not have a legal guardian. If he did, the guardian would have to be involved in the discussions.) And, of course, if the mediator meets privately with Kevin prior to the formal mediation, she should have similar meetings with other participants.

Who Should Be at the Table? The issue that most concerns me in Kevin's case is the potential conflict between the coach's interest and Kevin's interest. The coach is obviously a very important figure in Kevin's life and seems to care deeply for Kevin. But he also cares about having a winning football team. While it sounds as if the coach views himself as Kevin's advocate, there is a serious possibility that the conflict will limit his effectiveness in that role. The coach wants Kevin to play both because he realizes how important playing is for Kevin and because Kevin helps the coach's team to win. Kevin wants to play because doing so gives him a sense of achievement and belonging, but he is also concerned about causing harm to other players. One can imagine a resolution that meets Kevin's interests but does not involve his continued participation on the team, for example, serving as the team manager or joining a team not affiliated with his school whose players are Kevin's age.

Having an additional advocate for Kevin participate in the mediation would help offset this potential conflict. But inviting another advocate to the mediation will have to be done in a way that does not damage the relationship between Kevin and the coach and respects the coach and his needs.

What Decisions Is Kevin Capable of Understanding and Participating In, and What Decisions Should Be Made by Others in His Best Interest? It is important in this case to define the issues that will be decided at the mediation and then to determine the appropriate level of participation for Kevin in resolving each. My instinct is that Kevin is capable of participating fully in all the decisions that will have to be made to resolve this conflict: that he is capable of understanding the role of the mediator and the others at the table, able to understand the alternatives that will be discussed during the mediation, and able to make choices that reflect an understanding of the advantages and disadvantages of each. But the mediator needs to consider whether there are some decisions about which Kevin should be encouraged to give input but are beyond Kevin's ability to understand, on either an emotional or an intellectual level, and where the final decision making needs to be done by others concerned about his life.

Does the Mediator Need Special Knowledge or Skills to Handle This Case? There are two types of expertise that might aid the mediator in this case: experience working with people with developmental disabilities and knowledge about disability law. In order to best serve Kevin and the other participants in this mediation, the mediator should have a good understanding of the capacities and limitations of someone with Kevin's profile and be comfortable working with people of differing capabilities. If Kevin functions at the intellectual level of a fourteen year old but only on the emotional level of a nine year old, the mediator should have sensitivity and expertise (gained through education or experience) in order to read signals—verbal and nonverbal—correctly. For example, it would be helpful for the mediator to know that nine year olds tend to be self-critical[8] and are concerned about fairness.[9]

While I generally value process skills in a mediator over legal expertise, in cases like this, where at least two of the three participants—Kevin and the coach—are not lawyers, and the representative of the state department of education may or may not be a lawyer, the mediator should have a basic familiarity with ADA law. She might also want to take a look at the state regulation limiting the age of athletes to see whether it has a waiver provision. I am not suggesting that the mediator become a case evaluator, but rather that she might need to provide the parties with legal information so that they can make informed choices.

How Should the Mediation Be Structured? The mediator can take many steps to structure the mediation to ensure the opportunity for all participants to speak, exchange information, develop options, and share in decision making. Measures likely to increase Kevin's ability to participate effectively include having the session in a place that is familiar to Kevin, taking frequent breaks, and having refreshments available. The physical setup is also important. Would sitting around a table be intimidating for Kevin? Is there a room available in the school with sofas and easy chairs? Once the mediation begins, will the use of caucuses make it easier to check on Kevin's understanding and answer questions, or will caucuses make him feel that he is being excluded and that people are talking about him?

Helping the parties generate options may be critical to successful resolution of this case. The scenario says Kevin is aware that he is bigger than other boys and that he was frightened when he harmed another player. Is there a way that Kevin could be on another team with older players? Is it possible to identify another team and a coach who would be sensitive to Kevin's special needs but also able to value what he brings in the way of physical ability without putting younger teammates at risk? Are there other sports that would draw on Kevin's physical ability without putting younger teammates in harm's way? Does Kevin have the ability to work with younger boys as a coach or a team manager? Are there other ways that he could belong without being in violation of the rules? The mediator will need to be sure not only that a number of options are explored but also that the discussion goes at a pace that is comfortable for Kevin and that Kevin's interests and values are honored by any decision that is agreed on.

How issues are framed may be important in terms of Kevin's ability to participate in a comfortable or meaningful way. For example, the impact of his physical size on other children, if framed as his being a threat to other children, might be quite distressing to him. Nine year olds have a fairly strong sense of fairness, so it might be easier for Kevin to discuss that issue in terms of fairness to the other players or in terms of his being a caring young man who does not want to hurt people.

What About the Interests of Those Not at the Table? Mediators differ in their views about whether they have a responsibility to those not at the mediation table but who will be affected by the mediation agreement.

We know that one child has been injured by Kevin during a football practice. It is likely that the age limit for participation on school teams was, at least in part, motivated by a concern for the physical risk to younger athletes by older and more physically developed players. If the representative of the state department of education fails to raise this issue, should the mediator do so?

In Kevin's case, there are two reasons the mediator might need to consider the interests of people who are not participants in the mediation, one ethical and one pragmatic. As a matter of ethics, the mediator might be unwilling to facilitate an agreement that satisfies the needs of Kevin, the coach, and the state representative but does so on terms that put others at risk of harm. For example, the mediator might conclude that an agreement granting Kevin a waiver so that he can continue to play on the football team puts the other children on Kevin's team and on opposing teams at an unreasonable risk of injury because of Kevin's size and strength. The mediator may be unwilling to continue in a process where her work will result in a threat to the well-being of nonparticipants.

Even if the mediator believes her responsibility is limited to those at the table, questions about the risk of harm to other players and, perhaps, of Kevin's team gaining an unfair advantage from his participation, should be raised by the mediator if the parties do not bring it up. Part of the mediator's job is to help the parties evaluate the viability and durability of the proposed agreement and consider how well it meets each of their short-term and long-term interests. The mediator should help Kevin think about how he would feel if there is another injury. She will also want to encourage both the coach and the state representative to consider the possible political, legal, and public relation consequences for both their careers and the welfare of their respective institutions, as well as for Kevin. The mediator might also want to discuss with the parties the possible fallout from players and coaches on other teams who feel that they are unfairly disadvantaged should Kevin be granted a waiver.

WHY I TILT TOWARD FINDING CAPACITY: MY "CRAZY" CLIENT AND HER PERFECT LETTER. In thinking that mediation is appropriate to resolve Kevin's conflict, I am influenced by a case I had many years ago when I was a legal services attorney in Boston. On the Friday after Thanksgiving in the mid-1980s, a woman came to our legal aid office saying that she had been locked out by her landlord on the Wednesday before Thanksgiving. She reported that she had spent a cold Thanksgiving living on a fire escape and, in addition, that animals were making noises and hurting her nose. I was the lawyer on duty that morning; a colleague was covering the office in the afternoon. I decided to deal with the immediate lockout problem first. I drafted the papers and turned the client and the motion for a temporary restraining order over to my colleague, who went to court that afternoon and succeeded in having the client returned to her apartment.

Early the next week, the client came into our office to prepare for the follow-up hearing. She announced that she had been raped by her boyfriend and was pregnant. I asked her to join me in a conference room and discovered that she was indeed pregnant, was not receiving prenatal care, and did not know where the "boyfriend" was. She reiterated that the animals were making noise and hurting her nose. She clearly was suffering from a major psychological illness with active hallucinations. I asked our office social worker to join us, and we talked to the client about getting medical care. She agreed, and over the next two or three months, the social worker drove her to the clinic for her appointments.

We had long discussions with the client about what she wanted to do once the baby was born and how she would care for the baby. She told us several times that she could not care for herself, and so she doubted that she would be able to take care of the baby. Ultimately she decided that she would like to talk to someone from the department of social services about giving her child up for adoption. Two or three weeks before the baby was born, the client wound up involuntarily committed to a mental hospital after she physically assaulted a family member. When the baby was born, our client called from the hospital to tell us and spoke of how beautiful the baby was. She also reiterated her intention to give the child up for adoption.

A few weeks later, on the day that she was going to sign the papers that would release her child for adoption, my social worker colleague and I met with the client in the mental hospital. First, we and our client met with the case workers from the mental hospital and the department of social services to talk about the process. I then met privately with my client to explain what was about to happen and to make sure that she understood that she was about to give up her child for adoption. The client accurately described the role of the psychiatrist and the adoption process and again said that she could care for Emily,[10] which is what she called her baby, when no one else could, but that it was now someone else's turn to take care of the child.

As she was leaving to meet with the psychiatrist for her competency examination, she paused and handed me a letter saying, "Carol, could you take a look at this, and see if it is okay. It is a letter I've written for Emily. I'd like to give it to her new mother so Emily can read it some day when she is old enough."

I took the letter, went back to the room with our legal aid office social worker, the department of social services social worker, herself a new mother, and the social worker from the hospital. I read the letter and passed it around to the other three. Each of us, as we read it, wound up in tears. If you had gathered all the best authorities on child development and the psychological needs of an adoptive child and had them draft the best letter they could to an adopted child, they could not have matched my client in the eloquence, love, care, and recognition of needs that this note communicated. It was the perfect letter from a birth mother to a child being given up for adoption.

That experience has always influenced my approach to working either as a lawyer or as a mediator with people with mental disabilities or mental illnesses. My client taught me that regardless of the labels society puts on people or our conventional views of their ability to make hard, important, meaningful decisions, there is often a core of competence that is too easily overlooked, ignored, or devalued by those in authority. I learned from this client to listen carefully, to give people a chance to demonstrate what they are able to do, and to respect their core of competence, their core ability to determine what is best for them and their loved ones.

Comments on Case 2.2

Mary Radford

Kevin's case presents a mediator with challenges on two levels. First, the mediator must determine whether Kevin, with or without accommodation, has the capacity to participate in the mediation. This ultimate decision rests with the mediator alone and requires a level of personal involvement with a party that is not a prelude to most mediations. Should the mediator determine that Kevin does not have the capacity to participate, the mediator should so inform the parties and either cancel the mediation or, if possible, proceed without Kevin.

If the mediator determines that Kevin does have the capacity to participate, the second challenge is how to conduct the mediation in a way that will maximize Kevin's ability to participate while not compromising the interests of the other parties to the process.

The question of whether and how this mediation should proceed cannot be answered in a vacuum. There is much at stake in the outcome, for the coach, the department of education, Kevin, and other tertiary stakeholders. The coach is interested in fielding winning teams, not just in this year but in the next two years that Kevin is in high school. The coach's future at the high school may depend on that, as may any opportunity he will have to pursue even better coaching jobs. The department is interested in upholding its rule for a variety of reasons, including promoting fairness among the state schools; discouraging children from delaying graduation in order to add value to their own sports records; protecting other school players from stronger, older players; and retaining the ability to make a bright-line and efficient assessment as to who should be allowed to play football without having to engage in a case-by-case analysis.

Kevin's well-being may be affected on a number of levels. Allowing him to play will increase his self-esteem, possibly encourage him to stay in school despite his academic frustrations, and maybe even help him to launch a career in professional sports. On the other hand, continuing to play beyond age eighteen may cause him to hurt himself physically or to injure another player, with the tragic side effect of psychological damage to him. Kevin's parents or guardians have both a financial and emotional stake in his well-being. Others whose fates may be affected are those players who may share in the glory of his victories, those players whom he may harm, and those players on other teams who may lose scholarship opportunities because their teams are outranked by Kevin's team.

FIRST CHALLENGE: KEVIN'S CAPACITY TO MEDIATE. In Kevin's case, the initial question that the mediator must answer for herself, before proceeding with the mediation, is whether Kevin will be able to participate in the mediation in a meaningful way, either on his own or with the aid of support persons or other forms of accommodation. The privilege of participating in dispute resolution processes that are crucial to one's future is a highly valued one, and the decision to exclude Kevin from that process should not be made without extensive thought, research, and dialogue. Persons with developmental disabilities have too often been presumptively denied the right to mediate under the theory that they did not possess the mental and emotional ability to engage in meaningful and informed decision making.

Capacity, Consent, and Preconceptions. Self-determination is a critical component of mediation. Intrinsic to the notion of self-determination is the concept of capacity to mediate. Despite the thoughtful analysis given this question by numerous scholars and mediators, the definition of *capacity to mediate* remains as amorphous as other definitions of *capacity* or *competence* (for example, capacity to contract, capacity to write a valid will, capacity to stand trial, among others). The ADA Mediation Guidelines provide a working definition of *capacity:* whether the party is able "to understand the process and the options under discussion and to give voluntary and informed consent to any agreement reached."

The facts of Kevin's situation should raise a red flag for anyone who is considering mediating his case. First, although Kevin's actual age is nineteen, he has been determined to have the intellectual abilities of a fourteen year old and the emotional maturity of a nine year old. Kevin's diagnosed intellectual and emotional "ages" should not in and of themselves bar his participation in the mediation. However, the mediator should not proceed without contemplating the potential downside of including him as a party whose consent will be necessary to any mediation agreement.

Every state has laws that make contracts entered into by minors void or voidable. The basic notion behind this is that minors do not have the intellectual capability to bargain equally in a contract situation. If the outcome of this mediation were to be a settlement agreement to which Kevin was a party, the mediator must be convinced that such a contract would be a valid one. The mediator can take some comfort in the fact that peer mediation in high schools has been quite successful. Observers of these procedures have reported that the participants understand the mediation process and participate actively in consensual decision making.

A second crucial fact of Kevin's situation is that he has been diagnosed as "educable mentally retarded" due to brain damage he suffered at birth. Most mediators have probably heard the term *educable mentally retarded,* but few have any training or expertise as to what the diagnosis entails. It would be useful for the mediator to do a bit of background work before even meeting with Kevin. This background work should include the mediator's taking some time to ask herself whether she has any preconceived notions about mental retardation, as stereotypes about this developmental disability abound in our society. For example, does the mediator have a subconscious vision of a mentally retarded man as having a temper that he can't control or as being sexually promiscuous or violent or as being "a child in a man's body"? This self-awareness on the part of the mediator will hopefully prevent her from reaching uninformed conclusions about Kevin's condition that might hamper her from assessing realistically his capacity to mediate.

A quick bit of research on educable mental retardation reveals that although the fourth edition of the American Psychiatric Association's *Diagnostic and Statistical Manual of Mental Disorders* (DSM-IV) defines this diagnosis only in terms of lower-than-average intellectual functioning (an IQ level of 50 to 70), the American Association on Intellectual and Developmental Disabilities (AAIDD, formerly the American Association on Mental Retardation) adds that the condition includes significant limitations on adaptive skills, such as conceptual, social, and practical skills.[11] Listed among the social skills are "self-esteem, gullibility, naiveté (i.e., wariness), social problem solving, and the ability to follow rules/obey laws."[12]

In addition, the functioning of persons with mental retardation has been found to be affected positively by personalized supports that assess each individual's needs and develop strategies for maximizing that individual's development over time. Support can be offered through a variety of people and means, including parents, teachers, tutors, friends, psychologists, or appropriate agencies. This information can help the mediator not only to comprehend the nature of Kevin's disability but also to begin analyzing what specialized techniques might facilitate his ability to mediate should the mediator decide to proceed.

A Dialogue with Kevin. In addition to performing background research, the mediator should not make any decision until she has engaged in a meaningful dialogue with Kevin about the upcoming mediation. To give structure to this dialogue, the mediator may consider asking the following questions:[13]

- Does Kevin understand the purpose of the mediation?
- Does he understand who the parties are?
- Does he understand what the role of the mediator will be (particularly that she will not be his advocate or his representative)?
- Can he listen to and comprehend the story of the other party (or parties)?
- Can he generate options for a solution?
- Can he assess these options?
- Is he expressing a consistent opinion?
- Does he understand and can he maintain the confidentiality of the mediation?

Adding detail to the last four questions, the mediator may ask Kevin why he thinks he should be able to play on the team and why he thinks he should not be able to play. She may ask him if there are other ways that he could be part of the team and still feel as good about what he does as when he plays in a game. The mediator should explore with Kevin how he felt when he accidentally injured a fellow player and how he would feel if that were to happen again.

Throughout the conversation, the mediator should assess whether Kevin's responses are cohesive and consistent or whether he is telling her only what he thinks she wants to hear. Finally, the mediator will need to decide whether Kevin can appreciate the concept and importance of "keeping a secret." The parties to a mediation often commit to confidentiality, particularly as to conversations that are had with the mediator in caucuses. In addition, if the setting of Kevin's case is a small town in which high school football makes news, the parties may wish to commit to keeping the substance of the mediation out of the hands of the press. Kevin could be particularly vulnerable to a shrewd reporter, and thus if the mediator foresees that a confidentiality agreement will be a part of this mediation, she will want to assure herself that Kevin understands and will be capable of living up to this agreement.

Should the mediator find Kevin's discussion about the above questions satisfactory, her next crucial step will be to determine if Kevin can participate meaningfully in a mediation in which his coach is a participant. The facts, which are consistent with the AAIDD description of people with Kevin's condition, indicate that adults in general and particularly the coach, as an authority figure as well as a respected mentor, may be able to exert tremendous influence over Kevin. It may be that Kevin cannot withstand this influence and that nothing the mediator can do will mitigate it. Should that be the case, short of conducting a mediation in which Kevin is isolated from the other parties, the mediator should probably conclude that the mediation should not proceed.

Possible Personal Support.   A final task for the mediator is to determine whether Kevin would be better served in the mediation with the aid of a support person and, if so, who that person should be. In their dialogue, the mediator could ask Kevin to suggest names of appropriate support persons. However, she should keep in mind that his most obvious choice—that is, his parents—may have a conflict of interest in this case. Their conflict may arise in two different ways. On the one hand, they may see Kevin's participation as a star football player as a stepping-stone to a future career for him, perhaps even in professional football. Although their desire to see their child succeed is laudable, the mediator should not forget that Kevin's success, particularly success as a pro, would be of substantial benefit to the parents also. For example, they may have been assuming that they were facing a lifetime of supporting him if he were unable to get a job due to his condition. This may cause them to be less mindful of the potential harms that may befall Kevin should he continue to play. On the other hand, the parents may be prone to keep Kevin off the team due to their fear that he would harm himself or others. Again, their overall aim is laudable, but the mediator must realize that their objectivity may be marred by their fear of financial liability should the worst-case scenario ensue.

The mediator may want to explore with Kevin whether he has a counselor or trusted adult friend who could stand by him during the mediation and help ensure that he understood the process as it was progressing and that he weighed fully all of the options presented and their various ramifications for him. The role of this support person will be a mixture of the roles typically played by a party's attorney and a party's guardian ad litem. The traditional role of the party's attorney is to advocate the desires of the party, while that of the guardian ad litem is to advocate the party's best interest. Kevin's support person will have the complicated task of helping him to digest the information he receives, weigh the advantages and disadvantages for his future as well as his present life, and reach decisions that maximize his own self-interest without dismissing the interests of others.

SECOND CHALLENGE: MAXIMIZING KEVIN'S ABILITY TO PARTICIPATE. Even if the mediator determines that the mediation should proceed and that Kevin can participate, the considerations discussed above cannot be put aside. As noted, the need for and identity of a representative or support person for Kevin must be nailed down prior to the mediation itself. The mediator should remain mindful that other accommodations may facilitate Kevin's ability to stay focused throughout the process. She should arrange for frequent breaks, a television or video games for downtimes, and snacks chosen for a teenage boy with the aim of keeping Kevin both alert and relaxed.

The question of who should participate in the mediation is one that must be given careful consideration. Kevin's parents or guardian clearly have a stake in the outcome. But just as with the coach, their presence adds the complication of Kevin's susceptibility to being swayed by authority figures. Other team members and players from other schools also have a stake in the outcome, but it is probably not advisable to add more teenage boys to the mix. The players for his home team could perhaps be represented by a teacher or parent. The players for the other teams will probably want a separate representative. Although they have the same interest in not being injured by an over-age player, their interest in whether Kevin's high school wins more games is the polar opposite of that of his own team's players.

Most important, should the mediation proceed, the mediator will be faced with a personal psychological challenge that will perhaps be even more daunting than that of determining Kevin's capacity. The process of determining Kevin's capacity has resulted in the mediator in Kevin's case spending extra time with him. She has given him special attention, talked with him about his hopes and fears, and helped him test the viability of the decisions he may make. Once the mediation begins, however, the mediator must assume the role of an impartial and neutral facilitator. As a neutral, she is obliged to ensure that the interests of all of the parties (not just Kevin's) are given equal respect.

This is not to say that she must remain passive if she discerns that one or more of the authority figures is taking advantage of his or her position to influence Kevin unduly. In fact, the mediator should also remain mindful that she too may have become an authority figure for Kevin and that his desire to please her and obey the rules could sway his actions. Maintenance of the power balance is an appropriate role for her and one that will require special diligence on her part in this case. On the other hand, the mediator should avoid the temptation to insert into the process, whether consciously or subconsciously, any of the conclusions that she herself has reached as to what is best for Kevin.

Once she has determined that Kevin has the capacity to engage in independent decision making, she must respect the decisions he makes. In particular, the mediator must safeguard Kevin's ability to change his mind. Even if he expressed to her in their premediation conversations that he was tending toward not playing, the mediator should be prepared for Kevin to reach an opposite conclusion in the mediation itself. Even if she personally thinks that is the wrong decision for him, once she has determined that Kevin has the capacity to mediate, she must remember that she has relinquished the right to "protect" him during the mediation itself. If she remains convinced that he and his support person are capable of weighing the options, the mediator must not intervene if the conclusions they reach do not seem appropriate to her. Even though neutrality and impartiality are ingrained in the minds of most mediators, the prelude to this mediation will test severely the mediator's ability to maintain that stance.

In summary, Kevin's case presents challenges that go to the very heart of two important values in any mediation: that of party self-determination and that of ensuring the quality and integrity of the process. It is crucial at the outset that the mediator determine that Kevin does have the capacity to participate in the mediation. As noted above, this assessment will require the mediator not only to examine Kevin's intellectual and functional abilities but also to measure the degree to which he can remain autonomous in the face of authority figures like his coach and his parents. If the mediator does determine that Kevin has capacity, she then, in a sense, must switch gears. Her goal prior to the mediation was to protect Kevin's right to self-determination. Once the mediation begins, the mediator's goal from that point on is to ensure a quality process for all of the parties, not just Kevin. The quality of this process and of any outcome that is reached is dependent on the mediator's ability, as an impartial facilitator, to provide the opportunity for each party to exercise the full range of his or her decision-making capacity.

Editor's Thoughts on Case 2.2 and the Comments

Both Liebman and Radford agree that Kevin's mediator must consider two separate questions. First, given Kevin's intellectual and emotional deficits, does he have the capacity to participate in an authentic and engaged way in a mediated negotiation? Second, given those same deficits, would it be fair and ethical to allow Kevin to bind himself to an agreement reached during those negotiations?

Liebman believes that the ethical challenges that Kevin's case poses can be addressed through careful practice; and both commentators devote significant attention to the preliminary spade-work that a mediator must do to help ensure that the basic parameters of ethical practice are met. Liebman suggests a premediation meeting with Kevin to answer questions, allay concerns, and begin thinking about possible support persons. She also recommends the mediator gain familiarity with the ADA and related state regulations governing high school athletics. In similar fashion, Radford recommends the mediator do background work on the stereotypes that might attend the label "educable mentally retarded" and learn what social and practical functions might prove difficult for Kevin throughout the process. In addition, Radford suggests the mediator investigate Kevin's capacity to mediate by posing a series of questions relating to his understanding of mediation's goals and direction and taking note of the consistency and cohesiveness of his answers.

Both commentators worry a bit about the presence of and possible pressure exerted by Kevin's coach. Both observe a conflict of interest in that the coach purports to be an advocate for Kevin's interests, but also harbors an independent interest in deploying Kevin's bulk and power in the service of a winning season. Radford notes that individuals with Kevin's diagnosis are impressionable and easily subject to social pressure from authority figures. And while Liebman suggests that an additional support person be brought to the table to counteract or neutralize the coach's influence, Radford wonders whether it is truly possible for Kevin to participate meaningfully in a mediation where the coach is present.

Liebman approaches Kevin's case with a fundamental confidence that individuals with a host of impairments nevertheless possess a "core of competence" that is "too easily overlooked, ignored, or devalued by those in authority." This confidence comes from her experience as a legal services attorney servicing mentally ill clients who nonetheless were capable at times of stunning acts of grace, insight, compassion, and care. From this work, Liebman came away with the sense that sometimes seemingly "crazy" people know better than the sane world what self-preservation requires.

Radford concedes that Kevin may indeed be capable of mediating and committing to an agreement, but she says his situation raises red flags. She notes that mediation with the coach appears problematic and that if there is no way to mitigate his influence, "short of conducting a mediation in which Kevin is isolated from the other parties," the mediator "should probably conclude that the mediation should not proceed."

Radford also notes that mediating with a disputant such as Kevin forces the mediator to assume two distinct stances that dovetail poorly with one another. In the first, the mediator must serve as helpmate, assessor, assistor, and confidante. Prior to the actual mediation, she must make an effort to determine whether and how Kevin might be empowered to serve as an autonomous and capable participant in the mediation. To do this, she must ally herself with him; she must spend sufficient time and attention to understand his strengths and deficits. She must then work to expand his cognitive and affective capabilities to the greatest degree possible.

Once the mediation formally begins, the mediator must put all this behind her and function as a neutral and impartial intermediary. She cannot serve as Kevin's advocate or amanuensis, tempting though it may become.

Kevin's case, then, poses a variety of ethical and functional challenges. As both commentators agree, moving through them requires reflection, deliberation, and constant attention to the fundamentals of skillful practice.

CHAPTER THREE

Autonomy and the Emotions

What are a mediator's ethical responsibilities when working with disputants in the thrall of intense emotion? Does the level of emotion implicate a mediator's responsibility to ensure disputants' autonomous capacity? If so, how?

The question of how autonomy links up with emotion is complex. When people act in emotion's vise, are they engaged in autonomous self-governance? Are their emotional selves their true selves, or should we view passion's flare as a type of invasion that leads people to act uncharacteristically in ways that thwart their longer-term self-interest?

Philosophers and psychologists have long debated the question. Some argue that emotions embody a distinct and specific form of intelligence and communicate important judgments that we make about our interactions with the world around us.[1] When we feel joy, disgust, anger, or despair, we are applying our values to changes occurring in our environment. We are assessing how these changes affect our goals as well as our ability to cope with and respond to our altered environment. This largely unconscious and automatic evaluative process produces our cognitive and affective experience.

It could be argued under this view that disputants acting under emotion's sway are expressing their most fundamental beliefs and that mediators should accept a disputant's emotionally driven decision as an accurate expression of her autonomous will.

Other scholars focus on the distorting effects of emotion.[2] They note that strong emotion can erect a screen that skews our vision and leads us to a partially obstructed view of past events and present motives.[3] Indeed, common experience tells us that extreme emotion can usurp the self, leading people to act in aberrant and destructive ways. Think of King Lear, Hamlet, and Othello—tragic heroes led to ignoble acts by the disordering effects of anger, grief, and jealousy. Clearly if Shakespeare had consulted us about writing a mediation scene for these noble figures transformed by passion, we would have advised him to postpone it for a calmer day.

Assessing an emotionally upset disputant's capacity to mediate will involve the same questions reviewed in the previous chapter:

1. Does the disputant have the ability to understand the information being presented?

2. Can she appreciate the significance of that information for her own life?

3. Can she consider her options in light of her long-standing needs and interests?

Most of the time, disputants are able to perform these tasks, even if they are feeling sad or agitated. But extreme emotion can be both paralyzing and deforming; it can distract and disorient. When a disputant is so disordered that she cannot focus on her long-standing interests, the mediator should think about terminating or at least postponing the mediation.

THE CHALLENGING EMOTIONS

In *Beyond Reason,* law professor Roger Fisher and psychologist Dan Shapiro define emotion as "felt experience."[4] This definition stresses the somatic quality of emotions. We feel them on our clammy brow and in the pit of our stomach. But emotions are also cognitive. As psychologist Richard Lazarus writes, "Emotion cannot be divorced from cognition, motivation, adaptation, and physiological activity.

When we react with an emotion, especially a strong one, every fiber of our being is likely to be engaged—our attention and thoughts, our needs and desires, and even our bodies. The reaction tells us that an important value or goal has been engaged and is being harmed, placed at risk, or advanced."[5]

Lazarus argues that every emotion reflects a perception of change in our relationship to our environment. Emotion assesses whether that change and the new situation are congruent with or harmful to our goals and well-being. This appraisal in turn prompts a series of physiological changes that prime us for action.[6] Positive emotions like happiness, pride, and compassion—Lazarus calls them "congruent emotions"—reflect our sense that our individual goals are in sync with our environment. Negative emotions—such as anger, anxiety, and grief—reflect a perception of dissonance or incongruity between our goals and our current situation. Theoretically it is possible for a person to be disordered by happiness, compassion, or love. But usually happy negotiators are easier to coax toward agreements, and the agreements are sensible and synergistic.[7]

In mediation, negative emotions threaten constructive decision making. These emotions precipitate physiological changes that may constrict a negotiator's vision and obstruct creative thinking. In addition, these emotions may lead to impulsive and destructive behavior. For this reason, they warrant further examination.

Anger

Anger is a response to perceived threats to personal or social identity. According to Lazarus, a person gets angry not simply when a goal is thwarted, but when the thwarting also involves a perceived personal slight or offense.[8] Typically anger requires a target who is seen as having control over her actions and is intentionally acting in a demeaning fashion. A driver who cuts in front of us because she is trying to avoid a newly fallen tree doesn't make us angry; a driver who cuts in front of us for no reason other than to gain a lead does.

As an evolutionarily honed response to perceived environmental threat, anger triggers physiological reactions. Neural and hormonal signals prime the body to either fight or flee. In preparation for these physical stresses, our heart pumps faster, blood pressure rises, and we sweat to maintain body temperature equilibrium. Our breathing quickens and becomes shallower, which leads to changes in blood chemistry that make the heart work harder. These responses combine to perpetuate a nervous sensitization that keeps our body in global alert.

These physiological changes are adaptive if we are mustering the strength to swing a heavy weapon or flee from a dangerous foe. They are less helpful if the task is to calmly approach a problem and deliberate on the possibilities for resolution.

While the body's sympathetic nervous system is busy maintaining a physiological code red, its cognitive system is similarly employed. People prone to anger are likely to cycle into a series of cognitive biases that feed their ire and propel them to rage These biases include

- *Suspicious and negative imputation of motive*—assuming others' behavior communicates hostility when other plausible explanations exist.

- *Catastrophizing*—assuming that things are much worse, or will become much worse, than they actually are.

- *All-or-nothing thinking*—assuming that only extreme options exist, usually in ways that diminish self-esteem or the perceived character of others.

- *Unrealistic demanding*—assuming unrealistic expectations for oneself and the rest of the world. One researcher called this form of rigid thinking a "hardening of the oughteries."[9]

- *Overgeneralization*—assuming one negative experience can be broadly generalized to predict all other situations.[10]

These cognitive biases fuel dysfunctional anger and impair the capacity to engage in productive mediation. A disputant who views every proposal from the other side as malevolently motivated is poised to reject all offers. Catastrophic thoughts make discussion of possible positive outcomes seem utopian and naive. All-or-nothing thinking—"either I get what I want or I'm a weak loser"—makes compromise impossible. Unrealistic demanding makes anything short of total victory seem like humiliating loss. And overgeneralization hinders disputants' ability to see that past disappointments aren't a necessary prelude to future betrayal.

Angry disputants are likely to miss the opportunities that mediation presents for settlement. However, it is unlikely that the process of mediating will be harmful to them or that they will agree to a settlement that does violence to their longer-term best interests. More likely, they will fail to reach a settlement that would satisfy their interests to a greater degree than their best alternative to a negotiated agreement (BATNA). But this is a practical failure, not an ethical concern.

Assessing from an ethical standpoint whether an angry person has the capacity to mediate, the mediator should consider two questions:

- Do the level and intensity of emotion doom the process to failure?
- Might the disputant's emotionality place the other disputant at risk for emotional or verbal abuse?

If the answer to either of these questions is yes, the mediator should forgo the mediation or suggest it be rescheduled.

Anxiety

Like anger, anxiety is a response to threat characterized by both physiological changes and cognitive responses. Anxiety is similar to fear, but whereas fear has a specific eliciting stimulus, anxiety often involves a vague and undirected sense of foreboding. And whereas anger may be the prelude to retaliation or aggression, extreme anxiety often prompts paralysis and inaction.

Like anger, moderate fear and anxiety are adaptive. At an earlier stage in our evolution, direct neural pathways formed between our sensory organs, our nervous system, and our amygdala (a site of emotion production). The effect of this connection was to help us react quickly to danger. With direct pathways established, if we stepped in the dark on the slippery back of a snake, we would immediately perceive the danger and reflexively leap away. All bodily functions would be directed toward the effort. Adrenaline secretion leads the liver to release glucose. Cardiovascular changes speed blood to the major muscle groups and away from the skin and viscera. Oxygen import increases, pupils widen to let in more light, digestive activity slows, and muscles tense. This automaticity has obvious benefits for survival. As one set of researchers notes, "When a tiger bounds toward you, what should your response be? Should you file your toenails? Do a cartwheel? Sing a song? Is this the moment to run an uncountable number of randomly generated response possibilities through the decision rule? . . . The alternative: Darwinian algorithms specialized for predator avoidance, that err on the side of false positives . . . and constrain your response to fight, flight or hiding."[11]

Useful as this reflex is, being overprimed toward anxiety has deleterious consequences. When calm deliberation, not sprint or attack, is called for, readying for disaster is maladaptive. As psychologist Harriet Lerner has written: "When anxiety gets really bad, prepare to shake; hyperventilate; feel nauseated; throw up; get dizzy, sweaty, antsy, jittery, tense, irritable, agitated and otherwise hyper-aroused. You may have difficulty swallowing and feel a constant lump in your throat.... You may feel numb, faint, physically immobilized, exhausted, detached from your body, and, at the same time, unbearably stuck in it."[12] In short, anxiety revs us up but gives us no place to go.

The effect on cognition is similarly disruptive. In moments of stress, neurotransmitters suppress frontal lobe activity essential to short-term memory, concentration, inhibition, and rational thought.[13] Anxiety "scrambles the brain in . . . ways that leave us feeling helpless and self-doubting."[14] The mind perceives threats where none exist. Moreover, once attention has focused on threat, it is difficult for anxious people to cognitively refocus elsewhere. One researcher notes, "The attention of people with high anxiety may get stuck on threatening events around them, which may interfere with flexible deployment of attention according to current performance demands."[15]

In mediation, anxious disputants focus selectively on facets of the dispute that appear threatening. They

- Fix on the possibility that their adversary is not operating in good faith.
- Perseverate on the uncertainty surrounding their settlement alternatives.
- See only the downsides of any offer from the other side.
- Worry about buyer's remorse.
- Obsess over being perceived as weak if they make an offer themselves.

In sum, although small doses of anxiety helpfully sharpen the negotiating mind, large doses fatally constrict the thinking brain into little more than a risk perceiver. Thus, when a mediator is considering whether a particularly anxious disputant has the capacity to mediate, the primary danger is that a disputant will be unable to take advantage of the opportunities mediation presents to bring the dispute to closure. That an intensely anxious disputant would reach a decision that poses more risk than her alternatives is unlikely. But if mediation offers a situation of possible gain, a mediator might want to think about counseling an anxiously overwrought disputant to work on lowering anxiety before squandering what may be limited opportunities for settlement.

Sadness, Grief, and Depression

Since disputes often arise in the wake of loss (injury or death of a loved one, professional or financial disappointment, reputational harm), it would be surprising if disputants in mediation didn't often come to the table feeling blue or down. In terms of assessing disputant readiness to mediate, however, it is important to distinguish between functional grief or sadness and dysfunctional depression.

SADNESS AND GRIEF. According to most researchers, sadness and grief are similar but distinct.[16] Sadness typically connotes a relatively brief response, whereas grief connotes a more enduring state that can persist from several weeks to several years. Sadness is typically a monochromatic emotion—a simple and straightforward "appraisal of permanent loss."[17] In contrast, grief is often complicated by a diverse crowd of negative (anger, contempt, fear, guilt) and sometimes positive (affection, pride) feelings. If a significant person has died, the bereaved may grieve not only the loss of the person, but also the loss of a stable set of meanings and identities that death has thrown into disarray. Sadness usually involves short-term coping strategies. Grieving requires more protracted coping efforts aimed at coming to terms with both concrete and ineffable dislocations, including changes in social roles, familial relations, and economic status.

As with other emotions, sadness serves an adaptive function: it promotes reflection. Our physiology slows, allowing for a time-out to revise cognitive structures and replot our course.[18] Abundant empirical research links sadness with greater detail-oriented information processing and less resort to heuristic or stereotype-driven decision making.[19] Our cues for arousal dim, creating more cognitive availability for complex problem solving. Sadness also curtails our confidence in first impressions, so we second-guess and reassess. As one researcher concluded, "With sadness comes accuracy."[20]

DEPRESSION. If sadness morphs into extreme grief or depression, cognitive function declines. Depressed individuals typically experience pronounced changes in sleep, appetite, and energy. They have difficulty thinking, concentrating, and remembering.[21] Problem-solving capacity decreases, as does the ability to sustain social relations. Depressed individuals are vulnerable to a negative ruminative response, which involves "repetitively and passively focusing on symptoms of distress and the possible causes and consequences of these symptoms."[22] This constant rumination feeds pessimistic thinking and saps motivation for positive change. Depression leaves its victims feeling worthless and empty.[23]

Mediation assumes that disputants can concentrate on the problem at hand and make decisions based on a careful evaluation of the benefits and risks of settlement. Depressed individuals have difficulty seeing the good in anything, much less making cost-benefit assessments about whether the good outweighs the bad. Whereas mild sadness may improve a disputant's ability to analyze the relevant facts, a global depression will defeat such an effort.

The challenge for the mediator is to identify when a disputant is not merely sad but disabled from depression. Mediators who are not psychologists by training lack the expertise to engage in sophisticated diagnostics. All mediators can, however, keep the possibility of disputant depression in mind and remain alert to its dangers. If a disputant's affect seems particularly flat and grim, it may be appropriate to ask a few questions and perhaps consult with colleagues with expertise in mental health. In a private caucus, the mediator could probe to determine if that individual is suffering from sleep disturbances, changes in appetite, difficulties maintaining relationships, lack of self-confidence, and a subjective sense of hopelessness.[24] Alternatively, mediators who feel uncomfortable with this line of inquiry could refer disputants to consultants who could explore these matters. If a determination is made that a participant in the mediation is acutely or chronically depressed, the mediation should be delayed. Otherwise two risks may ensue. First, a disputant's basic hopelessness about the future may blind her to the possibility of a positive outcome.[25] Second, her lethargy and lack of interest in her own life may lead her to conclude a disadvantageous agreement out of disregard for her own welfare.[26]

Fortunately, depression is not permanent. Multiple treatments exist, and the sensitive mediator may suggest that a disputant put off mediation until she is better able to harness her thoughts and feelings in the service of making good mediation decisions.

Shame and Guilt

Shame and guilt are often termed "the self-conscious emotions"[27] because they require two things that more basic emotions such as joy or fear do not require: the internalization of social standards, rules, or goals and a firm notion of the self.[28] Both shame and guilt involve a negative evaluation of the self in relation to external standards, but shame is more global than guilt is. The shamed individual feels that as a person, she has failed to measure up, whereas the guilty individual acknowledges the fault in a particular action. Shame asks, "How could I be this way?" whereas guilt asks, "How could I have done that?"

These self-conscious emotions are adaptive in that they promote the formation of complex social hierarchies through adherence to established social norms. Conformance with these norms allows communities to form in which individuals inhabit stable hierarchies and fulfill roles vital to communal survival.

And yet both shame and guilt are exceedingly painful emotions. The shamed individual feels unworthy and inadequate. She may engage in self-destructive or self-sabotaging action in an unconscious desire to punish herself for "being bad." Guilty feelings may also inspire irrational compensatory measures.

As is the case with depression, a guilt-stricken individual is not in a good place to negotiate. She may sell herself and her interests short out of a sense that she doesn't deserve a good outcome. If the mediator senses that a disputant is using the mediation process as a form of self-retribution, she should raise this issue with the disputant and consider whether going forward is in either of the disputants' best interests.

Case 3.1 includes anger but is more centrally concerned with guilt.[29]

CASE 3.1: HARRY'S WILL

Mike and his younger brother, Larry, have come to mediation to resolve a dispute over their father Harry's will. Harry divided his (not very large) estate equally between the sons, except that he left his deceased wife's piano, a fine Steinway, to Larry, who has taken lessons since he was a boy.

Harry was a foreman in a machine shop, a good worker with limited education and no management skills. He trained younger men who invariably received the promotions Harry yearned for. Over time Harry grew bitter at the younger men whose education allowed them to progress in ways he could not. He drank and would come home and rail against "those college boys with their books."

The elder son, Mike, was not a good student and eventually followed his father into the machine trade. Mike did not pay much attention to his work and always remained at a fairly low level. He also drank heavily like his father did.

Younger Larry excelled in school despite the taunting he received from his older brother and father. His mother, a passive woman, didn't interfere but quietly supported his efforts. She also bought him piano lessons and encouraged him to play the piano she had inherited from her mother. Larry left his small town, went to medical school, and specialized in neurology. When his father developed Parkinson's disease, Larry returned home and cared for his father during the last three months of his life.

Mike contends that Harry resented Larry, was angry when he left, and would never have bequeathed him their mother's piano. He is arguing that Larry exercised undue influence during the last few weeks of Harry's life and coerced him to change his will.

In mediation, Larry is quiet and passive. He is adamant that he had no discussions with his father about the will or the piano during the last three months of his life. He also admits in private discussion with the mediator to feeling guilty about surpassing his father and brother professionally and receiving special attention from his mother as a result of his academic and musical prowess.

Mike is angry throughout the mediation and accuses Larry of believing that because he is a doctor, he is entitled to the few fine things the family owned, like the piano. Larry is visibly hurt by these accusations. In caucus, he asks the mediator if indeed it is selfish to want the piano. Upset and visibly cowed, he tells the mediator that although he'd like the piano for sentimental reasons, he feels, given that he has lived most of his life away from the family, that maybe he doesn't deserve it. He says he is inclined to "just let the whole thing go."

What's Going On?

A psychotherapist would likely have many observations about Larry and Mike and their family dynamic. Although we don't have much information about Larry's daily life, we do know that in mediation, he expresses a sense of guilt about both literally and metaphorically leaving his family of origin behind. A therapist might identify Larry as suffering from a variety of survivor's guilt grounded in his perception that he has betrayed his family by outdoing them, abandoning them, and appropriating the love that he feels should have been bestowed on his brother.[30] Each of these imaginary crimes is commonly identified by therapists treating individuals whose happiness is marred by a sense of guilt and unentitlement. It may be that Larry's willingness to accede to Mike's accusation and just leave the piano behind are driven by a more global sense of familial guilt.

But mediators are not therapists, and mediation is not therapy. A mediator is not brought into a dispute to plumb the parties' deep past, as would be needed in order to diagnose whether Larry's thinking about the piano is clear or muddied by long-standing patterns of self-flagellation. Larry might be punishing himself for imaginary crimes. Or maybe he is simply making a rational cost-benefit decision that the piano is not worth worsening his relationship with his sole surviving brother.

Two Possible Tracks

There are essentially two tracks that the mediator in this case may follow, each calling for a different level of intervention on his or her part.

MINIMALLY INTRUSIVE. One track is minimally intrusive and assumes that disputants' emotional states reflect their basic values and orientations. This track is consistent with both the facilitative and transformative models of mediation, models whose orientation toward party control and responsibility would likely lead to adoption of less demanding or stringent criteria for decisional capacity. These models would likely find a party capable of participating and reaching agreement in mediation unless he or she was clearly mentally ill or disabled. According to this way of thinking, even if Larry is driven by self-punishing guilt, that guilt is part of who he is; when he acts according to its dictates, he is nonetheless expressing his autonomous self and the mediator should not question this form of motivation. Challenging Larry's decisions also entails a degree of paternalism that many mediators would disavow, asking, "According to what authority or training does the mediator assume the mantle of diagnostician—identifying Larry's pathologies and striving to limit their role in mediation?"

A mediator whose primary goal is to avoid paternalism in practice would likely take at face value Larry's desire to end the dispute by giving up the piano. She might ask some gentle and rather generic questions about how Larry will feel in six or twelve months if he walks away from the piano. She might ask Larry if he wants to discuss, either in private or with Mike in joint session, the legitimate reasons that his father might have left him the piano and assess whether those reasons might be seen as compelling. But the mediator would not be trying to assess or illuminate the role, if any, that survivor's guilt is playing in Larry's decision.

MORE INTERVENING. The second track is more interventionist, consistent with more evaluative or directive models. Pursuant to this approach, the mediator would engage in a more pointed series of questions focused more directly on Larry's stated sense of guilt and lack of entitlement. This approach is more concerned with the disordering or destabilizing effect of strong emotion and would seek to ensure that Larry's decision making really does reflect who he is and his longer-term best interests.

The mediator might ask Larry why he thinks it would be "selfish" to want the piano and whether his feelings about leaving home and "abandoning" his parents and brother are affecting his decision making in mediation. The mediator might spend some time with Larry trying to understand how Larry views the pros and cons of walking away from the piano without even making those views known to Mike. The mediator might ask Larry whether he has always felt he abandoned his family and how that has shaped his decision making over time.

Overall, it does not appear in this case that Larry's guilt feelings threaten his decision-making capacity. It does not appear that he is having trouble understanding relevant information or appreciating how that information affects him or will likely affect him in the future. It is also true that the stakes in this mediation are not high. He may want the piano for sentimental reasons, but he does not need the piano to eat, sleep, or stay healthy. His livelihood or basic well-being is not at issue.

CASE 3.2: LAURIE AND PAUL'S DIVORCE

In this case, the stakes are a bit higher, and although the facts are not explicit, we might assume that at least one of the protagonist's feelings of guilt are affecting her decision making. Like Larry, Laurie in the case below is contemplating walking away from assets that would likely be within her legal rights to claim. The question is whether a mediator should probe those decisions, especially when strong emotions may be at work.

Laurie and Paul have come to you hoping you will mediate their divorce. They are in their late twenties and have no children. Paul is a policeman with a modest salary; Laurie works as an assistant in a child care facility. They have little in the way of savings but have a house with over $125,000 in equity.

Laurie is romantically involved with the owner of the child care facility, an affair that ended the marriage. She feels guilty and uncomfortable talking with Paul and wants to end the marriage as soon as possible. Paul is very angry. He has an authoritarian personality and has turned harsh and unforgiving since he found out about the affair.

Laurie has been informed in mediation that their house is community property and that she is entitled to one-half of its value once it is sold. Paul has said that he wants the house appraised by a number of experts. Laurie, in response, says that she wants to relinquish her interest in the property so as to sign the papers sooner rather than later.

At the first session, you advised Laurie to talk to an attorney about her plan to relinquish her claim to the equity in the house. She returns at the second session saying she consulted briefly with an attorney and wants to go forward with the plan. When asked who she saw, she says she doesn't remember. You suspect she didn't see an attorney, but is simply in a rush to end negotiations that she finds difficult and painful.

What do you do?

Comments on Case 3.2

Dorothy Della Noce

This hypothetical case features a possible ethical tension between the mediator's sense of responsibility for the quality of the outcome and the participants' freedom to make their own decisions, by suggesting that (1) the quality of a mediated outcome can somehow be measured (or ensured) by the extent of its conformity with legal norms and (2) the mediator has a duty to ensure such conformity.[31]

To offer a meaningful contribution to the discussion of this hypothetical, I must begin by describing my theoretical framework regarding the nature and goals of the mediation process and the policy of the jurisdiction in which I practice. I will also describe the context I would foster in a mediation session.

THE TRANSFORMATIVE MEDIATION MODEL. A mediator's theoretical orientation to conflict shapes his or her assumptions about the nature and goals of the mediation process.[32] I identify as a transformative mediator. The transformative model posits that despite the potentially alienating and dehumanizing impacts of conflict interaction, people in the midst of conflict are capable of shifting their empowerment and recognition: they can, and desire to, change the quality of their interactions to reflect relative personal strength, self-confidence, or agency (the empowerment shift); they can, and desire to, change their relative openness or responsiveness to the other (the recognition shift).

The model assumes that the transformation of the quality of the interaction itself is what matters most to parties in conflict—even more than simply settling on favorable terms. Therefore, success in mediation is measured not by settlement per se but by party shifts toward personal strength, interpersonal responsiveness, and constructive interaction. The mediator's goal flows from this definition of success, namely, supporting the parties' efforts to change the quality of their interaction from destructive to constructive. Effective practice is focused on supporting empowerment and recognition shifts, by supporting party deliberation and decision making, and interparty perspective taking, in various ways.[33] In sum, this means that as mediator, I am committed to supporting, and not supplanting, each party's decision-making process and at the same time supporting, but not forcing, party efforts at building interpersonal communication and understanding. That is the essence of "good" (that is, ethical) practice in the transformative framework.

POLICY OF THE JURISDICTION. The setting in which a mediator practices is also relevant to a discussion of ethics. Some localities and institutions promulgate rules for mediation practice that encourage some forms of practice and constrain others, whether explicitly or implicitly. Fortunately, my use of the transformative model is supported by the legal and regulatory framework for Virginia mediators.[34] Virginia defines mediation broadly as "a process in which a neutral facilitates communication between the parties and, without deciding the issues or imposing a solution on the parties, enables them to understand and to reach a mutually agreeable resolution to their dispute."[35] This definition reflects a general policy that runs through most of Virginia's regulations regarding mediation practice: that the mediator should focus on supporting interparty communication and party self-determination and avoid making decisions for the parties or imposing solutions on them.[36] Therefore, my use of the transformative framework in Virginia would be considered ethical practice.

THE CONTEXT I WOULD FOSTER IN THE MEDIATION. My model for practice and Virginia's policy both affect how I engage and work with mediation clients. In order to discuss what I would and would not do in this case of divorce, they also force me to depart from the terms of the proposed hypothetical to an extent. The hypothetical itself assumes a different form of practice from what I have described and interventions I would be unlikely to have used. For example, in light of my transformative approach, it would be inappropriate for me, as a mediator, to diagnose a party's personality, judge his or her motivations, single a party out for advice, or determine the standards by which a party should make his or her decisions. So let me reset the case a bit as I explain what I would do.

Explaining the Model. When I initiated the mediation process, I would have discussed with the parties that I follow the transformative model and offered a detailed explanation of what exactly that means.[37] I would emphasize that I focus attention on the communication between the participants, with the goal of helping them to improve their understanding of each other's perspectives and the nature of the situation, and to make their own decisions about whether and how to proceed. The parties would have the choice of proceeding further or not. If they chose to proceed, my duty from that point forward would be to keep my word: to attend closely to the parties' conversation, highlighting opportunities in that conversation for parties to gain increased personal and interpersonal insight and make decisions about how to have the conversation and what outcomes to craft, if any. I would avoid any action that could suggest that I am deciding for the parties what a "good-quality" outcome may be because such a decision would undermine the fundamental principle of party self-determination contained in both the law and my contract with the parties.

Considering External Norms. Of course, there is always the possibility that there are external norms that may influence the parties' decision-making process, including but not limited to legal norms. The question then becomes one of assessing the weight these norms should have in the decision-making process of the parties and the extent of the mediator's duty, if any, to educate the parties about the norms and see that the agreement conforms to them.

Because both my model for practice and Virginia policy support the primacy of party determination, the decision of how much weight to accord legal norms for decision making must be left with the parties. The law is only one of a host of relevant factors on which parties can base their decisions. This is an important principle to bear in mind. Otherwise I fear that mediation would be reduced to a very conservative, narrow, norm-enforcing process, devoid of creativity and contextualized considerations. The risk is that it ultimately would not be an "alternative" dispute resolution mechanism at all, just a rather dangerous mechanism for the private imposition of private interpretations of legal norms without the protections of due process.

However, this does not mean that the parties proceed blindly, unaware that there are legal norms to consider. It does mean that there is an effort to balance the value of considering legal norms with the value of making a choice about the course of one's own life in the midst of conflict. In Virginia we strike this balance in several ways. First, Virginia obligates the mediator to disclose in a general way that the law may be an important consideration in the parties' decision-making process and that legal advice is not provided by the mediator. The Standards of Ethics require mediators to inform the participants of what is colloquially known as "the four legals":[38]

1. The mediator does not provide legal advice.

2. Any mediated agreement may affect the legal rights of the parties.

3. Each party to the mediation has the opportunity to consult with independent legal counsel at any time and is encouraged to do so.

4. Each party to the mediation should have any draft agreement reviewed by independent counsel prior to signing the agreement.

It is important to observe here that the mediator's duty to inform is framed in a general way, and the mediator is not expected to focus on particular legal consequences that the mediator believes he or she can foresee. Moreover, the responsibility for securing legal advice and review of any agreement reached is placed on the parties, not the mediator. In other words, it is their choice.

Second, Virginia also strikes a balance in favor of party self-determination with respect to the issue of whether mediators should provide legal information (although they cannot provide legal advice). The Standards of Ethics provide in section F, Professional Information:

1. The mediator shall encourage the participants to obtain independent expert information and/or advice when such information and/or advice is needed to reach an informed agreement or to protect the rights of a participant.

2. A mediator shall give information only in those areas where qualified by training or experience.

3. When providing information, the mediator shall do so in a manner that will affect neither the parties' perception of the mediator's impartiality, nor the parties' self-determination.

This provision suggests that the responsibility for obtaining professional information rests with the parties, and it is one of the many choices they are free to make in mediation. The mediator's duty is to tell them there is information and/or advice available from independent sources. However, the mediator is not obligated to provide specific information or advice. In fact, the wording of the provision suggests that a mediator actually treads on dangerous ground by providing specific professional information, by either exceeding his or her own qualifications or making choices that threaten party self-determination and mediator impartiality (such as choices about what information is relevant, what information to provide, who needs information, and how to frame that information).[39] Finally, the law explicitly acknowledges, as a policy matter for mediators, that agreements do not need to conform to legal norms.[40]

So in the context of my practice, I can assume that I have taken appropriate steps to inform the parties in advance that they might benefit from obtaining from independent sources relevant legal and other information about their situation and their choices, that there may be important legal ramifications to the decisions they make in mediation, and that they are encouraged to seek legal advice. After suggesting to both parties at the beginning of the mediation that obtaining independent expert information is advisable, I would not have singled Laurie out again or pushed her to act on this general advisory. The choice to gather information and consult with professionals is not mine; it remains with the parties.

Moreover, assuming for the moment that the parties go forward with the agreement on the terms proposed in the hypothetical, and I as the mediator record the terms of that agreement with them, they have also been advised to have the draft reviewed by counsel before signing it. Finally, referring again to common practice in Virginia, many mediators who draft documents with the parties in the course of mediation include the four legals in the text of the document as yet another reminder to the parties to consider the legal consequences of their choices.

SO WHAT DO YOU DO? I feel limited in what I can say about what exactly I would do. The difficulty is that a satisfactory answer requires knowing more about the communication that is going on than the hypothetical provides. Details of communication are essential: transformative mediators practice with what is known as a "microfocus"—attending to each move in the interaction as well as the patterns of moves that develop over time.[41] So if I had a tape or transcript of an actual interaction, I could tell you what I would be most likely to do or say at a particular critical moment and little more. And what I would do or say would depend on what opportunities for empowerment or recognition were offered by the parties in their communication and what shifts to empowerment and recognition were taking place. This is a much more dynamic and contextualized process than a hypothetical can capture.

Nonetheless, I can say with some confidence that depending on the interaction that is unfolding in the room, what I *might do* is reflect back to Laurie or Paul, individually, the essence of what each is saying if they speak with me directly; or summarize the similarities and differences between Laurie and Paul that emerge as they talk together; or summarize the decisions they have made so far in the session and the decisions they still face, followed by a question about what they want to do next or what they need to hear from each other or anyone else in order to make their decision. Each of these kinds of moves supports the parties' own process of communication, deliberation, and decision making.

I can also say with some confidence that what I would not do is establish rules for how clients are to behave in mediation, determine what information a client needs or on what standards a quality decision should be based, decide for a client that compliance with what the law might provide is the only or most important criterion for evaluating a decision, suggest to a client that I know better than he or she what is best for his or her life, or direct a client to demonstrate to me that he or she has followed (obeyed) any suggestion I might have (mistakenly) made in mediation. Such moves undermine party empowerment and self-determination. So, yes, the bottom line is that I do not enter the mediation with a predetermined standard for whether Laurie can make this decision or any other, or a toolbox of strategies for dissuading her or Paul from making certain decisions and encouraging them to make others. Laurie and Paul would be free to proceed together to their own decisions that emerge from a conversational process that fosters empowerment and recognition for and between both of them.

Comments on Case 3.2

John Winslade

First let me frame the task of responding to this scenario. I am committed to exploring the practice of mediation from a narrative perspective and shall approach this scenario from that angle. A narrative perspective encompasses what I believe to be a distinctive ethical position and therefore provides many places of entry to discuss this scenario. The ethics that I am referring to are more than, but include, the ethics of professional practice. They are about the application of an ethical stance to the practice of living as well as to the practice of professional participation in other people's lives. I do not believe those two orientations can be completely separated and that the glib assurances of neutrality in the dominant discourse of mediation act often as a smokescreen for the projection of particular ethical principles by mediators onto the lives of others.

ETHICS FROM A NARRATIVE MEDIATION PERSPECTIVE. Narrative mediation draws consciously from the challenges posed to the Enlightenment agenda of rationality by postmodern and poststructuralist thought. In particular, these challenges have focused on the means of warranting truth claims with reference to a particular set of assumptions of superiority:

- The superiority of the scientific method
- The superiority of particular versions of rationality over other ways of knowing
- The superiority of Western knowledge over other cultural traditions
- The superiority of individual self over collective selves
- The superiority of rights-based democratic government of lives over other possible conceptualizations of government

These are what Lyotard (1984) referred to as the grand narratives of the modern world. Each of these claims represents statements of value with regard to other possibilities, but they have become so commonplace and so unremarkable in our thinking that they are scarcely noticed as the basis for ethical stances. The postmodern challenge asks us to reconsider their automatic dominance. It asks us to poke behind the curtain of conventional rationality, which often treats empirical facts as rising above questions of ethics and, in the end, consigns ethics to a more limited place.

It is this kind of inquiry that I would like to bring to a consideration of this scenario. Therefore, I cannot start with what is expressed in codes of ethics. I have in fact written such codes myself and am familiar with the debates that go into their construction. From this experience, I am convinced that, while necessary, they will at best reflect the dominant consensus within a profession and constitute an attempt to regulate that consensus as a minimum basis for practice. Some who have felt awkward about the limits of the prescriptions for ethical practice that are embodied in ethical codes have argued for the development of aspirational ethics or virtue ethics rather than minimal ethical rules. I think these positions are valuable, and they have thrown up some useful challenges to what can be achieved by simple application of the rules.

EXPLORING PARTY NARRATIVES. I read this scenario as one in which the question posed—"What do you do?"—is based on a sense of discomfort with the application of the rules embodied in codes of ethics. For the mediator to have any question at all about Laurie's desire to make an "autonomous" decision in the way she proposes, there must be some ethical doubts in the mediator's mind. Where do these come from? Perhaps they come from the discourse of the marketplace. In this discourse, the market works most efficiently when we think of ourselves primarily as individual selves competing with other individuals for the satisfaction of our interests or assumed underlying human needs. Laurie should construct herself as a self-interested party in the marketplace of matrimonial property, and she makes us uncomfortable because she is somehow not playing that game. She appears not to be acting out of legitimate self-interest, and the mediator is disturbed. She is not, we might say, acting from within the dominant cultural understandings of what someone in her situation should do. She has been referred to a culturally sanctioned arbiter of the cultural norms (a lawyer) to moderate her culturally deviant response and has returned uninfluenced by this moderation, if it ever took place.

So from a narrative perspective, what might I do? Well, the first ethical principle I would seek to exercise would be the demonstration of curiosity. In narrative mediation, such curiosity is intended to be an expression of profound respect. It says that I am interested in the meaning of what you are saying and I am not going to assume that I know in advance what it means. So I shall set aside comparisons with dominant cultural stories and seek to understand your preferred decisions in your own terms. A narrative method is founded on the asking of questions, often deconstructive questions that seek to open up for examination not just the individual's thoughts, feelings, or intentions, but the context in which those expressions are being formed—the influences on them and the impact of cultural norms, or of the grand narratives of the modern world, on those expressions.

The first thing I would do, therefore, is ask lots of questions. The hypothetical scenario, as given, is very thin. What Clifford Geertz (1983) calls a much "thicker" story would be needed in order to participate in a useful professional conversation. I am not criticizing the scenario here either. In any mediation, the starting place must be a thin story. Those are the stories that are told first. When Fisher and Ury (1981) first argued for the broadening of the mediation conversation from a focus on initial positions to a focus on underlying interests, they were beginning the process of thickening the story. A narrative inquiry, however, does not assume that the only place that we can go to thicken the story is deeper into the individual's intentions, feelings, or thoughts. Deconstructive inquiry also goes into the cultural conditions out of which thoughts and feelings are constructed and on the basis of which they make sense. It necessitates an inquiry into meaning. But personal meaning is not assumed to originate within the individual as it is in modernist practice. Instead the role of discourse is stressed much more prominently.

From a narrative perspective, we form our internal stories out of the material given to us in the dominant discourses of the world around us. For example, the assumption that an affair has to end a marriage comes from the dominant discourse. This does not make it wrong or inappropriate. But there are many possible contexts in which people might decide differently. I would assume, therefore, that there are cultural discourses at work to produce the guilt that Laurie feels and the anger that Paul feels and that these responses do not just emerge out of their own heads.

So here are some initial lines of inquiry that I might pursue. I would ask Laurie questions like these:

- What have been the influences on your proposed decision?
- Some might read your idea as influenced by a desire to escape a situation. Is this accurate? If so, to escape from what exactly?
- On what basis have you been feeling guilty?
- What background influences are shaping your thinking about that basis for feeling guilty?
- Does this guilt apply only to the recent affair, or does it say something about your marriage?
- Is the decision to divorce based only on the affair, or is it based on other aspects of your marriage?
- What advice did your lawyer offer? Was that useful to you or not useful? Why?
- What have other people been saying to you about this issue?
- Is there an ethical principle you are standing for other than guilt in considering this option? What might that be based on?

- What has your experience been of Paul's stance during this time of trouble in your marriage?
- Has Paul influenced your decision about matrimonial property in any way?
- What do you imagine he might be thinking about what you are proposing?

The questions I would ask would be not only directed at Laurie. Why not? Because narrative mediation is about privileging relational decisions ahead of individual ones, and one of its starting ethical principles is that personal motivations are always relational rather than just expressions of the inner processing of one individual. So I would assume that Laurie's statement is not just about herself alone but about her positions in a relationship with Paul. So I would need to know more about that relationship from the perspective of both parties' positions within it. She might have comments about that, but ethically it would be important for him to have his own voice in this discussion. Therefore I might ask Paul some questions like these:

- What has been your experience of Laurie's affair? What impact has it had on you?
- What has been your participation in the decision to end the marriage?
- Some people in this situation might seek to repair the damage that has been done to their relationship. I am curious about why you have not chosen that route.
- Was what Laurie did a challenge to your position in your marriage? Can you help me understand how that was?
- How would you like to end your marriage? What sort of story would you like to have in the future about this stage in your life?
- What values are important to you at this time? For example, would it be important for you to get all that you can get from her and make her pay, or be fair to both of you, or reach some compromise position, or what?
- What life experiences are influencing your answer to the previous question?

- Why do you think Laurie is considering assigning all the matrimonial property to you alone? What is your opinion of what is influencing her to think of this outcome?
- I understand that Laurie consulted a lawyer about this decision. Have you also done that? What advice were you given, and how useful was that to you?
- What have other people been saying to you about this issue?

All of these questions are general inquiries intended to open up the personal issues and the shaping forces at work in the construction of those personal issues. There are, however, further inquiries that I would need to make in order to be satisfied that I was acting ethically. These inquiries would focus on the operation of power in the relationship. I understand ethics in the end to be about the moderation of power in ways that produce outcomes that are experienced as socially just.

EXPLORING THE OPERATION OF POWER (INCLUDING MY OWN). I want to be clear here that I am not talking about justice in terms of procedures. Ethical practice cannot be limited to the process of the mediation or to a promotion of what the law says. I am skeptical about the usual distinctions between process and content in this regard. It is not enough to say that mediators should attend to the process and leave the content of the decisions to the parties. Content influences process, and process decisions privilege certain content material. I assume that choosing what I ask questions about is an act of professional power. To act ethically, therefore, does not mean that I should remove all of my own assumptions from my utterances, an impossible task, so much as that I should be careful to be reflexive about how I use this power.

Reflexivity. To be reflexive, I need to ask myself some questions. What assumptions about divorce, extramarital affairs, the fairness of matrimonial current law, gender relations in general, will I bring to the table and find unconsciously infiltrating my process decisions? Whose story might I favor through the way that I interact? These are all ethical challenges that exist in any mediation conversation on a moment-by-moment basis. They are not easy to deal with. I would seek to handle them through making them as transparent as possible, through acknowledging where I might have biases and asking the parties to comment on those, and through regular checks on whether what I am doing is working for them or making them uncomfortable.

The ethical principles of reflexivity (not found in any ethical code) would suggest that I should seek to learn from Laurie and Paul, and be willing to some extent to be imposed on by their understandings, rather than only to impose my perspective on them. At the same time, I should be comfortable with the value of applying my own influence in the conversation (since this is inevitable anyway) on the basis of my experience and the deconstructive work I have done to think through the major discourses that produce divorce experiences for couples. I would hope that this background work brings some useful leverage to the conversation.

Inquiring into Relations of Power. One of the benefits I would hope a narrative perspective offers me in this context would be some training in the poststructuralist analytics of power relations (Foucault, 2000). Power, from this analysis, is about the ability of people to influence each other. It is also about how people's lives are governed systematically by larger social forces. Foucault teaches us to look beyond the individual's exercise of personal power on which most modern psychological and legal discourse is based. He focuses our attention on the work done by discourse to shape both the external actions and the inner experiences of people. He argues that in the modern world, processes of social control have developed sophisticated means of internalizing monitoring systems into people so that they do not so often have to be physically forced to comply with the rules of authorities. Hence, I would be interested in inquiring into the workings of power in the decisions this couple is making about the end of their marriage. Ethical practice would require this kind of inquiry from me.

There is not much information given in the scenario, but there are some hints at where relations of power might be found. Paul is described as having an "authoritarian personality." I would not accept this essentialist account of Paul's nature. An essentialist account is one that assumes that his actions are best explained with reference to an enduring essence inside him, to his "nature" or to how he just "is." It implies something fixed in him that cannot be changed or negotiated. I would want to respect him more than that, as someone who might have more identity stories available in his repertoire than this one thin story.

At the same time, the "authoritarian personality" story may suggest something of a discourse world that influences his thinking. Perhaps his attraction to the police force stems from a cultural background that emphasizes the rigid application of rules. Has he attempted to run his marriage in this way? Has he adopted a "head of the household" position and required Laurie to conform to his wishes? There are certainly cultural and religious discourses that would support him in this perspective. The law has certainly shifted and no longer regards the husband as entitled to govern his wife's behavior and to punish her when she does wrong. In this sense, the law has responded to some alternative discourses about equality at work in the modern world. But the more traditional patriarchal discourses are still available, are still well known, and are still in place in many daily interactions that take place between couples. Has Laurie's affair been in some way an expression of protest at how Paul has treated her? If so, what other methods of protest has she considered? Is the proposal to hand over matrimonial property another such protest? Does Paul want her to think of him in these terms from here on?

The no-fault divorce has been the norm in most countries in recent decades, but the older concept of adultery as the main grounds for divorce is still part of marriage discourse. It is sanctioned by many religious and cultural traditions, in some cases quite strictly. There is no mention of the couple's religious or cultural background in the scenario, a reflection in itself, perhaps, that the modern world has sought to govern people's lives more in terms of scientific truth and rational thought than in terms of religious truth or cultural tradition. But people do not always operate out of these dominant discourses. They draw on other discourses in making their decisions. So which of these might be at work on Laurie and Paul? And are there other alternative discourses that they might have considered but rejected? How does the legal discourse that featured in the advice that Laurie may have received square with the cultural and religious values that are important to her? How much does the adultery discourse position her as wrongdoer who deserves to be punished? Is there anything that could be said in her defense in relation to this discourse? Has her finding of herself as guilty been without any kind of trial to examine the mitigating circumstances?

Influence of the Listener. In any conversation, the listener exerts considerable force on the speaker's utterances. The speaker does not just speak in her or his own voice but anticipates what the other might say in response and shapes an utterance to take account of that. This idea would lead me to inquire more into Laurie's desire to give Paul all the matrimonial property. How much is this being influenced by what Laurie knows in advance that Paul will say? How does she know what he might say anyway? If she knows that he will be difficult to make any other agreement with, does she think that it is fair for him to exert that much control over her decision making? For that matter, does he think it would be fair for him to influence her decisions in such an overpowering way?

Paul may have grounds other than self-interest here for accepting or not accepting what Laurie offers. The logic of the marketplace, where all is fair and you get away with whatever you can, is not the only discourse that people can draw from in the formation of relationship stories. There are, for instance, many stories of altruism and dignity that are important to people in divorce contexts. Does Paul have a notion of fairness or of dignity here, despite his anger? I would ask, How much is anger in control of his responses, and how much is he in control of it? Does he think he has some responsibility to act in her interests as well as in his own? What will each of them say to themselves, when they look back at this situation in future, about how they ended their relationship and about the fairness of the decision reached? Will they, for instance, regard it as a decision reached on the basis of the emotions of the moment (guilt and anger) rather than on the basis of other considerations of their lives? If so, what other considerations could be included? What models of divorce have they known from others in their families and circle of friends, or from books or talk shows? Which of these models have they admired, and why? What would they have to do to divorce in that way? From within this model, how would they handle the matrimonial property issue?

An Agenda of Respect. All of these questions are not intended to push any particular outcome agenda. But they are an expression of the ethical agenda of respect for the effects of the operation of discourse power in people's lives and for the importance of choosing intentionally one's responses to that power. Respect for Laurie and Paul would be communicated by the effort to open up these lines of inquiry and not simply take the dominant discourse for granted. I would want to treat them as persons with agency and the ability to think creatively about forward trajectories if assisted a little to open up the field of possibilities. Because I am concerned about the operation of power in people's lives becoming expressed as dominance, I would feel an ethical responsibility to ask questions about whether there are unspoken power relations at work. In the end, it is up to Laurie and Paul how they make these decisions in mediation. My ethical task is to raise all sorts of questions to ensure that they make decisions based on a thorough deconstruction of the complex set of discourses running through their lives.

Editor's Thoughts on Case 3.2 and the Comments

Although the case of Laurie and Paul was crafted to highlight the challenges of mediating in the midst of what appears to be emotionally driven decision making, commentators Dorothy Della Noce and John Winslade found much else to discuss of ethical import. Della Noce focuses on the importance of respecting Laurie's choice to eschew legal advice and avoid considering legal norms in formulating her own divorce settlement. Deciding what information she needs to make an informed decision is, according to Della Noce, very much Laurie's prerogative. Winslade also expresses concerns that as a mediator, he should avoid imposing on Laurie and Paul his view of the dispute, but he appears to take as a given the likelihood that his interventions will play a role in substantively shaping the parties' conversations. While accepting the inevitable exertion of "professional power," he says that he strives to be open and transparent with regard to his own assumptions. The primary ethical task for Winslade is to open for examination the dominant discourses shaping the parties' belief and behaviors and uncover for exploration the operation of power in the parties' relationship.

It is noteworthy that both commentators begin by setting out the philosophical or theoretical commitments that shape their analysis. Della Noce identifies as a transformative mediator, while Winslade explores mediation from a narrative perspective. For Della Noce, this means that good or ethical practice would focus on the quality of the parties' interaction and on encouraging each disputant toward greater agency and self-confidence, as well as responsiveness toward the other. For Winslade, this means beginning with a questioning stance—challenging the assumptions of "conventional rationality," including the preeminence of individual over collective selves or rights-based governance over alternative forms of social organization. Both Della Noce and Winslade flat out reject the law or legal norms as a standard for measuring a quality outcome.

Both Winslade and Della Noce challenge portions of the hypothetical, indicating that there are behaviors or judgments reached in the scenario that don't conform with the way they practice. For example, Della Noce indicates that congruent with Virginia State codes and best practices, she would inform both Paul and Laurie generally of the "four legals"—advising disputants that mediated agreement may affect legal rights, that mediators don't function as attorneys and don't give advice, and that parties are encouraged to consult with and have draft agreements reviewed by counsel—and that following those general disclosures, she would not ask Laurie to see an attorney and would not question her decisions regarding how much legal information to obtain, if any. Winslade notes that he would not accept the simplistic and one-dimensional assessment of Paul as having an "authoritarian personality" and would oppose such a judgment as disrespectful. Della Noce echoes this when she says, "It would be inappropriate for me, as a mediator, to diagnose a party's personality, [or] judge his or her motivations."

Both Della Noce and Winslade note that the hypothetical is thin—that there are important stories, in terms of both the background cultural narratives that shape Laurie and Paul's choices and the actual minute-by-minute dialogue of the mediation, that are not included. Della Noce observes that it is hard for her, as a transformative mediator, to say what she would do without an actual transcript because transformative mediators practice with microfocus, that is, "attending to each move in the interaction as well as the patterns of moves that develop over time." Winslade also notes that the story, as provided, leaves open many questions about who Laurie and Paul are, what is really happening in their relationship, and what influences are shaping their mediation choices.

But whereas both Della Noce and Winslade make similar observations about the limits of the hypothetical, their solutions seem quite different. Della Noce speculates that depending on the unfolding interaction, what she might do is reflect back to Laurie and Paul the essence of their speech as they talk individually with her and each other. She might summarize the similarities and differences that emerge; ask the parties what they want to do next, if there is anything else they need to hear from one another to make future decisions; and summarize decisions that have already been made. The interventions seem to be largely those of reflection; questions are limited to asking the parties for their ideas of where they want to go and how they want to use the rest of their time in mediation.

By contrast, Winslade's interventions seem all about questions. Winslade would explore not only Laurie and Paul's thoughts and feelings but also "the cultural conditions out of which thoughts and feelings are constructed." He lists twelve representative questions that he would pose to Laurie and ten that he would pose to Paul. They probe the source of Laurie's guilt, the full reasons for the divorce, the advice she received from her lawyer, advice she may be receiving from other people, her experience of Paul in conflict, and other possible influences on her decision making. Questions to Paul also look to the reasons for the divorce, his role in that decision, his sense of his position in the marriage and whether Laurie has challenged it, whether Paul has consulted a lawyer and what the lawyer said, and what values are important to him as his marriage comes to an end. Winslade also observes that he would not leave himself out of the interrogation. He would ask himself tough questions about his own biases regarding marriage, infidelity, and divorce—and would try to be completely transparent with the parties about the scripts that influence his perceptions and judgments.

Winslade explicitly addresses the question of power. His training leads him to focus on the way language exerts a subtle and sometimes coercive force on the way people think and behave. Although he does not buy the simple story of Paul as an authoritarian personality, he would want to explore how the power dynamics of the marriage may be influencing the decisions Laurie and Paul are making in mediation. Winslade notes that the secular discourse of American divorce law envisions one set of power relations, but that alternative cultural and religious narratives may assume very different power allocations. Because he is "concerned about the operation of power in people's lives becoming expressed as dominance," Winslade feels a responsibility to learn the role these different narratives are playing in the couple's discussions.

Both Della Noce and Winslade seek to support party autonomy and provide an opportunity for untrammeled decision making. And yet their notions of how to do that appear different. In order to avoid having an undue impact on the parties' decision making, Della Noce appears to limit her interventions to those that summarize, highlight, or encourage party discussion. She does not ask challenging questions or push the parties to explain or examine their articulated positions. Winslade, however, would push the parties to consider the forces, both internal and external, that might be shaping their decisions. He asks them to consider the imprint of culturally dominant discourses as well as the impact of their own roiling emotions.

If Della Noce is intentionally following the parties' lead, Winslade appears to be "walking with the parties" and asking them to be more reflective and self-aware of their gait, pace, and direction. These different practices flow naturally from their respective starting points. For Della Noce, "good" (that is, ethical) practice entails "supporting, and not supplanting, each party's decision-making process and at the same time supporting, but not forcing, party efforts at building interpersonal communication and understanding." Winslade's conceptualizations of ethical practice include "the demonstration of curiosity . . . [as] an expression of profound respect" and "the moderation of power in ways that produce outcomes that are experienced as socially just." Inquiring into and unpacking party narratives while seeking to moderate power involve the mediator in a collaborative rewrite of the parties' conflict. If Della Noce adopts a meticulously supportive role, looking to reinforce particularly hopeful aspects of the parties' existing text, Winslade assumes a deconstructive stance that leaves the parties open to a new plot line—different and yet alike in their zeal and enthusiasm for the creative potential of the process. Together these commentators demonstrate the challenging, interpretive, dismantling, and synthetic roles that mediators of different orientations play in the service of good (ethical) practice.

References for Dorothy Della Noce's Comments

Antes, J. R., Folger, J. P., & Della Noce, D. J. (2001). Transforming conflict interactions in the workplace: Documented effects of the USPS REDRESS program. *Hofstra Labor and Employment Law Journal, 18,* 429–467.

Bush, R.A.B. (1992). *The dilemmas of mediation practice: A study of ethical dilemmas and policy implications.* Washington, DC: National Institute for Dispute Resolution.

Bush, R.A.B., & Folger, J. P. (1994). *The promise of mediation: Responding to conflict through empowerment and recognition.* San Francisco: Jossey-Bass.

Bush, R.A.B., & Folger, J. P. (2005). *The promise of mediation: The transformative approach to conflict* (2nd ed.). San Francisco: Jossey-Bass.

Bush, R.A.B., & Pope, S. G. (2002). Changing the quality of conflict interaction: The principles and practices of transformative mediation. *Pepperdine Dispute Resolution Law Journal, 3*(1), 67–96.

Della Noce, D. J., Antes, J. R., Bush, R.A.B., & Saul, J. A. (2008). Signposts and crossroads: A model for live action mediator assessment. *Ohio State Journal on Dispute Resolution, 23,* 197–231.

Della Noce, D. J., Antes, J. R., & Saul, J. A. (2004). Identifying practice competence in transformative mediators: An interactive rating scale assessment model. *Ohio State Journal on Dispute Resolution, 19,* 1005–1058.

Della Noce, D. J., Bush, R.A.B., & Folger, J. P. (2002). Clarifying the theoretical underpinnings of mediation: Implications for practice and policy. *Pepperdine Dispute Resolution Law Journal, 3*(1), 39–65.

Folger, J. P., & Bush, R.A.B. (1994). Ideology, orientations to conflict, and mediation discourse. In J. P. Folger & T. S. Jones (Eds.), *New directions in mediation: Communication research and perspectives* (pp. 3–25). Thousand Oaks, CA: Sage.

Folger, J. P., & Bush, R.A.B. (1996). Transformative mediation and third party intervention: Ten hallmarks of a transformative approach to practice. *Mediation Quarterly, 13*(4), 263–278.

Kolb, D. M., & Associates. (1994). *When talk works: Profiles of mediators.* San Francisco: Jossey-Bass.

References for John Winslade's Comments

Fisher, R., & Ury, W. (1981). *Getting to yes: Negotiating agreement without giving in.* Boston: Houghton Mifflin.

Foucault, M. (2000). *Power: Essential works of Foucault, 1954–1984* (Vol. 3; J. Faubion, Ed.; R. Hurley, Trans.). New York: New Press.

Geertz, C. (1983). *Local knowledge: Further essays in interpretive anthropology.* New York: Basic Books.

Lyotard, J. F. (1984). *The postmodern condition: A report on knowledge* (G. Bennington & B. Massumi, Trans.). Minneapolis: University of Minnesota Press. (Original work published in 1979)

CHAPTER FOUR

Disputant Autonomy and Power Imbalance

P revious chapters have examined internal threats to the exercise of disputant autonomy. Sickness, disability, and emotional extremity can all hinder disputants' ability to engage with the issues and press for the satisfaction of their long-standing goals and preferences. But threats to autonomy are not limited to impairments in an individual's physical, emotional, or psychological integrity. Some threats come from without, in the form of a power imbalance between the disputants in their overall relationship or in the mediation context.

It is universally acknowledged that mediation works imperfectly when parties come to the table possessing vastly different power reserves. At the extremes, when the power imbalance is too great, most commentators would say that mediation is inappropriate. Mediators confronting such an imbalance should simply refuse to proceed.

But how much is too much? Rarely do disputants enter mediation with exactly equal amounts of power. Some asymmetry is to be expected, and one cannot (and should not) decline every case where one party seems to hold a few extra cards. Two issues must be sorted out:

1. When is a power imbalance so great that the mediator should decline to proceed?
2. If existing imbalances are navigable, what strategies and safeguards should the mediator implement to ensure that the mediation proceeds in an ethical fashion?

CASE 4.1: DIVORCE, CUSTODY, AND DOMESTIC VIOLENCE

Case 4.1 presents a scenario in which the mediator must decide if the distribution of power between the parties is too unequal to allow quality mediation.

John and Karla have been married for ten years and have two children. John works as a security guard, and Karla has been a stay-at-home mom since she became pregnant with her first child soon after they married. Two months ago, Karla left John and moved with the children to a battered women's shelter. She has consulted with an attorney at Legal Aid and has been told that divorce filings in her jurisdiction must be accompanied by a session with a mediator if child custody or visitation is in dispute. Both John and Karla are asking for sole physical and legal custody. In addition, John is arguing that he should not have to pay spousal support because Karla obtained a physician's assistant certificate before they were married and can enter the marketplace and make a reasonable salary.

John denies that he has ever hurt Karla at any time in the marriage. When asked why Karla might leave and go to a battered women's shelter, John says he doesn't know. Karla, when questioned in caucus, is reluctant to talk about the possibility of abuse in the marriage. She does say that John has hurt her in the past, but never to the point of needing to go to the hospital or a doctor. She says, in an offhand way, that the real problem with her marriage to John is that he made her "feel small." When asked if she wants to proceed with the mediation, she shrugs and says, "I guess so. He is my kids' father, and he is going to want to see them, so we might as well do it this way." She mentions that she has begun attending support groups at the women's shelter and finds them helpful. When asked whether she feels that she was in an abusive marriage, she doesn't respond at first, but then begins to talk:

> He always found something wrong with what I did, even if I did what he asked. No matter what it was. It was never the way he wanted it. I was

either too fat, didn't cook the food right. . . . I think he wanted to hurt me in the sense . . . to make me feel like I was a nothing. . . . I don't know how to talk to people because my opinion doesn't ever count. I feel like I never had an opinion on politics or on life. I don't know how to interact because he would always be going like this to me [mimicking husband's gesture of drawing a line with his index finger]. . . . That was his big signal to make me shut up, or he'd be kicking me under the table to shut my mouth.[1]

Although Karla is ready to proceed, you wonder whether this case is appropriate for mediation.

This case poses the question of when the mediator should withdraw from a case on the grounds that the power asymmetry between the parties is too great. The question posed in Karla and John's case is whether John's domineering and demeaning treatment of Karla throughout the marriage has made it impossible for Karla to effectively negotiate with him regarding finances or the children.

Although disputants with a history of violence may sit on the extreme end of the power imbalance spectrum, the issues raised by their inclusion in the mediation-seeking population can be extrapolated to cases where the power differential is less extreme. In cases involving domestic abuse, as with cases presenting any troubling degree of power imbalance, it is important to ask the right questions. Mediators must focus specifically on the nature of the power imbalance and its effect on the disempowered party in terms of her being able to identify and advocate for her own interests and make free and uninhibited choices.

Types of Imbalance in Domestic Violence Cases

When domestic violence victims began to find their way into mediation, women's rights advocates sounded the alarm and urged a blanket prohibition. Couples with a history of domestic violence should, they argued, be categorically excluded from mediation caseloads. Feminists saw in mediation a dangerous venue where vulnerable women would agree to their impoverishment rather than face the wrath of their threatening partners. Women—and it was assumed that nearly all victims of domestic violence were women—would not be able to negotiate effectively with their abusers.

Second-wave thinking, however, has advanced a more nuanced approach. Experts in the area have moved away from bright-line rules in favor of more contextualized decision making. Research into domestic abuse has uncovered several different patterns of family violence that require individualized responses by the family mediation community.

Study of the nature of abuse between intimates has identified four distinct profiles.[2] Researchers are fairly consistent in labeling and describing the first two types but less consistent about the third and fourth:

1. *Imposing control.* This profile fits the popularly conceived image of domestic violence in which the abuse is part of a larger culture of battering. In this culture, the violence is not an outgrowth of conflict or disagreement within the couple, but exists to cement the abuser's efforts to impose absolute control and elicit absolute fealty. Men involved in the creation of this sort of culture are pathologically jealous and insecure. Their internal distress and pathology lead them to engage in repetitive and cyclical batter- ing. Violence within this culture of battering can easily escalate. Often it is fatal.

2. *Violence sparked by crisis.* Here, violence is not characteristic of the marriage. Rather, it is sparked by the crisis of separation and the shock of divorce. The propensity to violence in this profile is catalyzed by the dissolution of the marriage and fear of aban- donment. Usually the violence is perpetrated by the individual who is being left.

3. *Violence as conflict resolution.* This profile describes couples who mutually use violence as a mode of conflict resolution. The violence in this variant does not reflect fundamental personality pathologies, and it can emanate from either the woman or the man. Combatant couples who fall into this category fight physically, but the violence tends not to escalate to a truly dangerous level.

4. *Drugs or mental disorder.* Some researchers construct a separate category for violent behavior secondary to serious mental illness or substance abuse.

It is imperative that mediators figure out at the start which type of couple they are dealing with. If the husband is a compulsive and cyclical batterer and the wife is constantly on the alert for signs of the next explosion, then mediation is the wrong choice and the couple should be referred back to court. If, however, both members of the couple resort to violence and neither uses physical force as a means to dominate the other, then, with safeguards, the couple may be able to negotiate in mediation. The key, researchers say, is to determine whether a past victim of violence retains such fear, self-abnegation, or habits of submission that she will be unable to advocate forcefully in an informal negotiating session.

In Karla's case, the extent and severity of past violence is unclear. Nonetheless, what Karla has said is enough to raise red flags. Physical battering is only one aspect of the abuse prevalent between intimates, and mediators must be cognizant of the subjugating effects of these other forms of nonphysical subjugation.

Red Flags and Resilience

Emotional, sexual, or familial abuse or abuse of property can inflict grievous psychological scars and render effective negotiation difficult. Appropriate screening tools must not simply look at the presence, frequency, severity, and proximity of physical violence but also ask about other forms of intimidation and debasement. One domestic violence index asks about threats such as fist shaking, and another inventory asks victims if their partner "tried to make [them] feel like [they] were crazy."[3]

At their core, these inquiries seek to measure the reservoir of emotional strength available to the victim at the time of negotiation. They look at whether:

- The victim can face her partner in a confrontational way
- The victim can identify her own individual interests apart from his
- The abuser accepts responsibility for his behavior or whether, in his mind, everything remains his partner's fault
- The victim can act free of concerns about retaliation or retribution.[4]

If the answers to these questions are yes, then mediation may be a promising option. If not, the mediator should rethink.[5]

Should This Case Be Mediated?

Although Karla minimizes the degree of physical abuse in the marriage, she does admit that John has hurt her physically. It may be that the severity of the abuse was minor, or it may be that Karla, like many other battered women, is ashamed of having been beaten and is reluctant to acknowledge the pervasiveness or severity of violence in the marriage.

More important, Karla's comments about the emotional impact of her husband's behavior go directly to whether she is able to advocate on her own behalf. Karla says that her husband made her feel small, made her feel that her opinions don't count and that she was a "nothing." He continually motioned to her to shut up, and so she learned to keep her views to herself. If, going into the negotiation, Karla feels worthless and unentitled to her own opinions, cares, and concerns, then she will have difficulty asserting those concerns in the mediation. If she remains silent in the negotiation process, she is unlikely to end up with an agreement that meets her needs. Regardless of the level of physical battering in the relationship, the emotional abuse Karla suffered in the marriage renders mediation a risky proposition.

Mediation as a Future Option

Although Karla's current situation does not lend itself to a mediated solution, there is no reason to think that the power allocations in her relationship with John will remain static. Power riptides may shift dramatically, and it is possible that mediation could become a viable option for Karla in the future.

Imagine the following scenario:

Karla and John have been separated for one year, operating pursuant to a custody and visitation schedule negotiated by their attorneys. Karla has been living in a halfway house for the past year, attending individual therapy and support group meetings and working in a women's food cooperative. Her experiences in therapy have increased her self-esteem, and she has learned to identify, articulate, and push for her own interests. She has discovered that she has a talent for preparing fine foods and has begun to think about opening a small catering business specializing in baked goods. In addition, the children are older, and their school and after-school activities have changed. Karla would like to renegotiate the existing custody and visitation plan to better accommodate the children's schedule and her own career aspirations, and she would like to conduct the discussions with a mediator.

At this point, most mediators would likely be willing to assist Karla and John in renegotiating the child care arrangements. With counseling and support, Karla sees herself as worthy of attention and acknowledgment. She can have opinions, and she knows they count. She can identify her goals and interests and pursue them. It is likely that she would be sufficiently able to hold her own in a conversation with John that the informality of mediation's procedures and the avowed neutrality of the mediator would no longer be cause for concern.

Still, given the history of domination and abuse, a mediator would want to proceed with caution. Wary of the vestigial remainders of a deeply unbalanced relationship, a mediator may wish to put in place certain safeguards. After talking with Karla and ascertaining her wishes, the mediator could implement certain precautions to raise Karla's comfort level with the situation:

- If child care exchanges have always taken place in public and Karla still does not feel relaxed being alone with John, the mediator could arrange for escorts and staggered arrival and departure times, and make separate waiting rooms and common areas available.

- To increase the safety and comfort in the mediation room, the mediator could carefully monitor Karla and John's language and body language, prohibit drug and alcohol use, and be clear that no verbal or physical abuse will be tolerated during or outside the mediation sessions.

- The mediator could encourage the presence of support persons and attorneys.

POWER IMBALANCES IN MEDIATION GENERALLY

Disputes involving power imbalances come in all shapes and sizes. Regardless of subject matter—from contracts to consumer affairs, from will contests to juvenile dependency—any time that disputants appear before a mediator with vastly disparate power reserves, the mediator needs to ask: Is the power imbalance here too great? Answering this question requires an assessment of the risks and benefits of mediation as compared to the risks and benefits of alternative approaches. But before embarking on that analysis, it is important to understand where power comes from and how it manifests in the mediation process.

Power Sources in Mediation

Power in mediation represents the ability to shape both mediation process and outcome. A powerful disputant is better situated to exert control throughout the mediation discussions and obtain desired benefits. A less powerful disputant finds herself at a disadvantage in the effort to both secure gains and avoid undesirable consequences.

Power can derive from various sources:[6]

- *Resources: money, property, access to valuable contacts and expertise.* Disputants with ample time and a plush financial cushion can afford the transaction costs of disputing. They can afford to wait out the other side or ramp up the pressure by hiring advocates who will engage in exhaustive (and expensive) litigation maneuvering. Disputants with less money to spend face substantial pressures to settle simply to avoid the costs of keeping the dispute alive.

- *Knowledge, information, and accurate data.* In a dispute about the sale of an antique automobile, if one party is an expert in automobile markets and the laws of supply and demand for vehicles of a particular vintage, then that party will enjoy an advantage in the negotiations. She will know better what the street value is and what alternatives exist if a mediated outcome cannot be reached.

- *Merit in the eyes of the law.* A party whose position is strongly supported by existing legislation or case law enjoys a better bargaining position than one whose stance is legally tenuous. The disputant with the strong case can credibly claim that she will succeed even if the negotiations fail. The disputant with the weaker legal claim will be less inclined to risk judicial assessment and thus will be likely to make concessions in order to conclude the matter in mediation.

- *Moral conviction and certainty.* Parties with a strong belief that the forces of truth and justice are on their side are empowered by their own moral fervor. A fight over "the principle of the thing" pushes parties toward intransigence. When a party becomes the guardian of virtue, compromise takes on a moral taint. The conflict itself assumes the cast of a noble crusade, where being good means soldiering on, acknowledging no weakness, and brooking no compromise. Sometimes disputants with objectively weak positions with a meager power base can become powerful solely on the basis of their moral certainty.

- *Personal traits advantageous in mediation.* Eloquence, insight, logic, empathy, analytical prowess, and determination can compensate for other weaknesses in a disputant's stance. A disputant with a hopelessly grandiose wish list may still achieve many of her goals if she is a persuasive communicator and perceptive listener. Individuals with good personal and advocacy skills enjoy a significant advantage over those with less acumen in these areas.

- *The ability to inflict pain or irritation.* Individuals threatening to bring meritless lawsuits exert this form of power. Although the lawsuit may hold little likelihood of success, the prospect of being dragged into litigation, with all its attendant miseries, may be sufficient to induce cooperation. By threatening to impose pain, disputants can manipulate their adversaries into giving into demands that they would otherwise reject. And although other forms of power may be accessible to only a very few, nuisance power is democratic in that it is available to many disputants—even the puniest among us.

- *Perception.* Even if a disputant has no resources, legal authority, or nuisance capacity, she can exert power if she can convince her adversary that she does. Thus, a blustery disputant who has a big bark and puts on a show of overwhelming strength can benefit from her skillful projection of power, even if she lacks the capacity to make good on her threats.

Power Balance and Imbalance: Weighing Risks and Benefits

In mediation, power can be distributed in various ways. In some cases, disputants possess roughly equal supplies. This occurs when equally savvy professionals come to the table with experienced counsel, familiarity with the issues, and sufficient financial reserves to support settlement or continued litigation. Power may also be equally divided in a divorcing couple where one parent has greater experience with financial matters and possesses more marketable skills, while the other has more parenting skill and experience and can exercise greater leverage when it comes to the children. Since power may flow from different sources, one disputant's strength and authority in a particular realm may be undercut by his inexperience and comparative weakness in another. In this way, parties with very different sources of authority may find that they are equally matched in terms of their ability to press their interests and secure their aims.

In most cases, however, disputants are not evenly matched. There is always some power asymmetry. Executives with comparable corporate accounts may possess vastly different communication skills (and the same may be true of their lawyers). Divorcing women who command greater authority in the domestic realm may nonetheless find themselves outmatched if their husbands can draw on significantly more extensive negotiating experience, financial reserves, and marketability.

When facing these imperfectly matched negotiating partners, mediators must decide if the risks of going forward are outweighed by the possible benefits.

RISKS OF MEDIATING IN THE FACE OF EXTREME POWER IMBALANCES. The main risk when one party is much more powerful than the other is that the latter will make decisions that do not represent her autonomous will. If the rationale for mediation is that it enables parties to make choices that truly reflect their values, then we must be sure that the parties' choices embody their deeply felt preferences and are free of external distorting effects. Here are some power dynamics to watch for:

- *Fear.* We don't want women in violent marriages to make ruinous financial or custody decisions in order to avoid angering an abusive spouse. In that situation, the choice to relinquish monetary entitlements or give in to a disadvantageous custody plan does not reflect a conscious deliberative process that furthers the victim's long-term goals. Rather, the concessions constitute capitulations made in fear: the victim is being driven by terror over consequences that should not, in proper circumstances, be affecting her decision at all.

- *Argumentative skills.* We don't want a verbally unskilled disputant to be corralled into an agreement because the other disputant was a high school debating champion. Again, the concern is that one party's mastery of quick, slick, or sly rhetoric may lead the less skilled wordsmith to make concessions that do not reflect her true preferences.

- *Lack of time, money, or other necessities.* When one party decides to agree to his adversary's terms and conditions because he says "he has no choice," we should worry if the power differential has induced a sense of hopelessness and defeatism, making the mediation merely a stage for surrender rather than a forum for considered decision making.

- *Informational imbalance.* The exercise of choice furthers self-determination only if the choice is informed. In other words, we act in a way that furthers our autonomous will only if the action is based on an accurate assessment of our situation. If our decisions are based on a misunderstanding—of both what we are agreeing to and what the consequences of that agreement will be—then our decision is not self-determining but self-subverting.[7] Thus, informational asymmetries where one party understands the consequences of settling or choosing not to settle and the other party doesn't challenge mediation's core values.

- *Effects of informality.* The position of the less powerful disputant in mediation is thought to be rendered particularly tenuous by mediation's informal structure and commitment to neutral intervention.[8] It has been argued that informality potentiates the expression of prejudice, whereas formal policies and procedures serve to blunt it.[9] In mediation, disputants and mediator alike sit close together, speak to one another informally, and are encouraged to bring up whatever seems factually or emotionally important. No one wears a robe or a wig or sits on a lofty podium. The absence of this pomp and ceremony, it is thought, disinhibits the participants and allows buttoned-up bias and prejudice to slip into the discourse.

- *Unprotectedness.* As compared to the litigation process where advocates play a prominent role, the weaker party in mediation cannot necessarily rely on another participant for protection. Counsel may, but need not, be present. And the fewer resources a disputant has, the less likely she will be able to afford an attorney. In addition, the mediator is prohibited from advocating on the weaker party's behalf because such advocacy would violate the mediator's vow of impartiality. Although mediators can and do work to soften power disparities, those moves must be carefully calibrated to avoid creating the appearance that an allegiance has been formed with one side against the other.

Because mediation thrusts parties into a free-wheeling discursive process with only a neutral facilitator to guard against foul play, it is thought that the process might not adequately serve the interests of the disempowered. For this reason, mediators must mull over how to proceed, or even whether to proceed, when confronted with a case involving a clear have and a have-not.

But before adopting too broad an exclusionary rule, we should look at the other side of the equation.

BENEFITS OF MEDIATING VERSUS THE ALTERNATIVE. Although mediating in the face of gross power asymmetries poses risks, there may be benefits as well. Parties who possess less power than their counterparts may nonetheless feel that mediation offers the most supportive, autonomy-enhancing path available to them.

Although they may lack the money, verbal skill, or knowledge base of the other disputant, the real question is whether they possess enough of these attributes to assert their interests and deliberate thoughtfully about the options presented. Even in a one-down position, the less empowered disputant will have an opportunity to explain her side of the dispute, present her needs and interests, and explain why her view of fairness and equity should be taken seriously. It may be, even in the face of real dangers, that the opportunities presented in mediation surpass those available elsewhere.

Thus, any consideration of the benefits of mediation and the risks must also address the alternatives. Mediation instead of what? What will our less empowered disputant do? Where will she go if she does not proceed in mediation? Two choices exist: maintain the status quo or litigate.

If the weaker party is seeking recompense or redress, then abandoning the conflict means abandoning the possibility of receiving something of value from the other side. In addition, if both disputants are intertwined personally or professionally, maintaining the status quo may mean sustaining a state of war that imposes myriad emotional and financial costs.

The second option is to pursue resolution through other means, usually litigation. In most situations, litigation does not level the playing ground between unequally situated parties.[10] To the contrary, it tends to exacerbate existing power imbalances.

Litigation is famously expensive. In complex cases, parties must secure skilled counsel to help them achieve their aims and counsel can usually be obtained only through a retainer and the promise of additional funds. Even if counsel agrees to work on commission, litigants must still pay the costs for court filings, experts, deposition fees, and the like. A disputant with meager resources will find herself at a disadvantage once the discovery games begin.

It might originally appear that the formality of litigation protects against the sorts of exploitation that can occur when a fast-talking disputant runs verbal circles around a less assertive fellow negotiator. And it is true that evidentiary rules and procedural requirements can hamstring a sly disputant's efforts to use rhetorical sleights of hand to extract extravagant concessions. But if that disputant has enough money to hire a facile attorney, he may be able to achieve significant gains through similar forms of manipulation. Moving from an informal but relatively inexpensive process to a more formal but unrelentingly costly process may merely shift the gamesmanship and agency from the disputant to the attorney.

Another problem with litigation is that power differentials based on time increase. The pace of litigation is famously slow. A party who is squeezed for time will feel the obligation to participate in court proceedings and postpone resolution until the litigation has run its course, a source of continued strain and pressure.

Still another downside of litigation may be that the problem is punted to a judge, who may not be in a good situation to understand the problems of the more vulnerable party. After all, most judges come from relatively privileged backgrounds and lead relatively privileged lives. Their ability to understand the motivations and needs of disputants operating under radically different sets of pressures may be limited.

In sum, the informality of mediation and the mediator's neutral stance may potentiate poor outcomes for some of mediation's less powerful disputants, but litigation poses its own problems. Depending on the victim's particular situation, the expense, delay, and highly complex nature of the adversary process may render it less attractive than the mediation bargaining table.

Though mediation works suboptimally where power imbalances exist, we cannot blink at the alternative. The adversary system tends to reflect and instantiate existing power relations. Excluding from mediation all situations where a diminutive David squares off against a hulking Goliath merely leaves David adrift in an adversary system that might paradoxically accentuate his deficits and blunt his ability to tap his strengths.

Although a case may present troubling power disparities, after giving serious thought to the risks and benefits, a mediator may still see mediation as an ethically viable course. Then the question becomes how best to proceed in light of the disparities.

DECIDING TO PROCEED: MEASURES TO HELP COPE WITH THE POWER IMBALANCE. If the mediator decides to proceed, it is important to gear the process to account for the existing imbalances. Fortunately, mediators are trained to cope with some measure of power asymmetry. Helping disempowered parties find their voice and push their agenda is part of the mediator's task. Here are three classic power-balancing techniques:

- *Ensure equal time.* Where the imbalance is personality based, the mediator can be diligent in making sure that the discussions are balanced and that each party, regardless of verbal skill or agility, gets a turn to talk. Timid and tentative disputants can be encouraged to fully elaborate their viewpoints and take a commanding role in the process. The mediator can encourage this by emphasizing that the process can work only if all participants are assertive.

- *Police intimidating behavior.* If one party throws his weight around by being insulting or abusive, the mediator can make clear that such intimidation is not tolerated throughout the process. If the dynamics are such that the weaker party simply does not speak honestly or freely with the other party present, the mediator can move the bulk of the discussions into a caucus format.

- *Level the informational field.* If the imbalance stems from one party's informational deficits, the mediator can strive to equalize

the parties' understanding of their situation by becoming a
source of information or involving other expert parties.

Thus, in a divorce situation where one party is refusing to pay
child support because it was the other spouse's choice to divorce,
the mediator could bring the jurisdiction's child support guidelines
to the session and let both members of the couple see that taking
the initiative to divorce is not a legally relevant consideration when
calculating support. This would alert both parties that their best- and
worst-case option should the dispute go to court does not include a
judicial award penalizing the spouse who chose to end the marriage.

Although providing legal information in a neutral fashion is
ethically permissible (and common practice), some mediators are
reluctant to do so.[11] One of their several concerns is that providing
legal information, which is ethically well established, often inadvertently shades into giving legal advice, which is highly controversial
and indeed explicitly prohibited in certain state codes (though permitted in others). But distinguishing is difficult. Making all parties
aware of the existence of certain statutes, cases, or other regulations
could be characterized as providing legal information, but if the
educational intervention goes beyond handing over the documents
or their citations to explaining what they mean and how they apply
in the parties' dispute, the mediator is applying law to fact and giving
legal advice.

Many mediators are not comfortable attempting to straddle the
fine and confusing line separating out the provision of legal information from legal advice. For this reason, they adopt an upstream
prohibition against the permissible discussion of legal information
in order to avoid any downstream ethical muddle.

The second way of leveling the information field is bringing
third parties into the process to provide the missing information. In
this case, mediators urge disputants to confer with counsel or other
substantive experts, including accountants, engineers, or tax planners.
Of course, if a disputant refuses to follow the mediator's direction,
then an ethical, responsible mediator has to decide whether to allow
that disputant to bind herself to an agreement based on the limited
information at hand.

As should be clear by now, power imbalances pose some of the
most nettlesome ethical issues in mediation practice. They force
deeper consideration of the linkage between informed consent and

disputant autonomy as well as the mediator's role, if any, in ensuring some modicum of substantive fairness in the final agreement reached.

In the next case, our commentators take up the question of what to do when an aggressive personality pulls a power play in the middle of a mediation. Here, the question is not whether the case should be mediated. The power imbalance at the outset was not so extreme as to warrant exclusion from the process. But in the thick of it, how should the mediator respond to a rather obvious gambit on the part of one party to leverage his power to propel a particular outcome?

CASE 4.2: SUPER TOM

Mary, a social worker, and Tom, a highly positioned corporate executive, are divorcing. Mary has been largely quiet during the mediation, mainly deferring to her husband's views on the children and their best interests. Tom is charming and articulate, but is one of those individuals who seems to suck the oxygen out of the room. In the two sessions that have transpired thus far, the mediator has learned much about Tom's life, career, and views of the marriage; the children; and the relationship. He has learned little about Mary, but that may be simply because Tom has occupied so much of the verbal space in the mediation.

From the discussion thus far, the mediator has learned, from Tom, that the collapse of the marriage can be laid entirely on Mary's doorstep, and that Tom has always been the emotional, communicative, and financial rock of the relationship. Mary protested that Tom's narrative is a bit one-sided, but Tom seems unable to absorb any narrative in which he does not figure as the hero.

The third session has been designated to discuss property issues. The parties own their home and a rental home. Tom has indicated that he is stressed about managing current finances, including paying for the two homes, and he wants Mary to commit to taking over one of the homes, with full responsibility for its mortgage and upkeep. He has brought two quitclaim deeds (one for each party to receive a home) to the mediation session and announces that he has hired a notary to arrive in one hour at the mediator's office.

Tom has coupled his property proposals with a complicated financial deal that may actually be generous to the wife overall, but he says she has to accept it today and sign the deeds when the notary comes. Otherwise he will withdraw his generous proposal, terminate the mediation, and go to court. The wife asks the mediator to help her decide what to do; she doesn't want to go to court and wants to be free of her husband and the whole divorce process. The husband is agitated and wants to leave the room so the mediator can "show her how good a deal is on the table."

How should the mediator proceed?

Comments on Case 4.2

Forrest S. Mosten

POWER! Conflict resolution scholars have contributed a significant body of work on how it generates and sustains conflict and have provided many useful ideas and strategies to lessen power imbalances during negotiation.[12] Although it is important to understand power and its impact on mediation parties, such understanding is only the beginning of a mediator's work. The true work begins with the use of that understanding to design a mediation structure and employ theories, strategies, interventions, and reflection.[13] These are a mediator's means for helping parties move from their current positions (that often reflect power imbalances, among other variables) to exploring new perspectives and options that may lead to resolution of the conflict.

This hypothetical highlights the everyday power imbalance challenges facing all mediators. Power imbalances are everywhere in human interaction outside the mediation room, so it is no surprise that they surface at the negotiation table as well. The question for mediators is what to do when power is unbalanced, as it is in every conflict that I have mediated for the past four decades. Of course, in some situations, a power imbalance in favor of one party in one issue or area of a relationship can be offset by an imbalance in favor of the other party in other issues. Similarly, a party who uses a perceived power imbalance to apply leverage or take preemptive action may find that power is ephemeral and shifting if the other party retaliates or even abandons the conflict.

In the current situation, Tom may "suck the oxygen out of the room"—but does this mean that he has the real power? Does he even have an imbalance of perceived power? Two variables signal that Mary's power is not insubstantial.

First, just as mediators who try too hard and talk too much risk their power in the room, a charming and controlling party such as Tom often reveals his own perceived lack of power, real or illusory. Mary's coiled potential to walk from the room or let Tom keep negotiating against himself suggests that the real power resides with her. Second, Tom's almost desperate attempts to threaten and coerce may reveal his fears and lack of patience, which seem to demonstrate weakness rather than strength.

I do not generally find that a mediator's analysis of power is the key to resolution. As power is always present and constantly shifting, I find it much more useful to focus on the mediator toolbox of strategies and interventions to move the parties in baby steps toward agreement. Let us examine three tools that would be useful in this scenario.[14]

PRIVATE SESSIONS WITH PARTIES: CAUCUSES AND PRELIMINARY PRIVATE PLANNING MEETINGS. Tom's self-interested yet astute suggestion that I meet privately with Mary will benefit both parties. Traditionally family mediation was premised on exclusively joint sessions between the parties to maximize direct communication between the parties, enhance neutrality of the mediator, and ensure fairness and perceptions of fairness.[15] Today most family mediators incorporate caucuses into a predominant joint session protocol. Caucuses can help clients get their emotional bearings as well as permit the mediator to privately help parties evaluate proposals from the other side.[16] Such evaluation may be substantive (Tom's proposed package deal) or procedural (demand for a short fused time line and imminent arrival of the notary). Although Tom suggested an immediate caucus to have the mediator "sell the deal," whether or not Mary accepts, the private meeting between Mary and the mediator may empower her and help her sort out her own self-interest without the direct coercion and pressure exerted by Tom in the joint session.

Although a caucus is helpful, a less crisis-laden model for private sessions can be used in mediation. In my own work, prior to a joint working session, parties meet with me individually in a scheduled preliminary private planning meeting. These sessions generally last sixty to ninety minutes per party and offer an early opportunity for a party to bond with me, establish rapport and trust,[17] screen for domestic violence and other power imbalances, take a factual history, uncover party concerns, help the party learn about and prepare for the stages of mediation (for example, rehearse the opening statement or make an agenda), and consider what to ask for and how to ask for it (formulate and communicate negotiation proposals). In a preliminary private planning meeting, after learning about Tom's overbearing manner, I might have been able to encourage Mary to overcome her own reticence to speak up and even explore what resources she might need to balance power (a lawyer, more information, use of private meetings).

INVITING ALL THE FAIRIES TO THE TABLE. A key mediator strategy is to determine who should be present at the mediation session. I do so by asking the parties if they have read *Sleeping Beauty* to their children (every parent has). I ask why Sleeping Beauty slept a hundred years (she pricked her finger on a spindle lathered with sleeping potion). I next ask how the potion got on the spindle (the wicked fairy put it there), why the fairy put the potion on the spindle (she was mad), and why she was mad (she was not invited to the grand birthday party of Sleeping Beauty). And then I give the lesson: "Always invite all the fairies to the party!"[18]

In this scenario, Mary may need to decide whether she should consult an attorney outside the session to determine the "generosity" of Tom's proposal or ask an attorney to come into the session to speak for her or at least provide legal and emotional support.[19] Perhaps a comediator or consultant with a financial background could be invited to the mediation to help both parties analyze Tom's proposal and float different options.[20]

Even if another professional is not invited due to cost or time factors, Mary might benefit from a support or resource person such as a parent, member of the clergy, or close friend.[21]

TRUST IN THE PARTIES: CAN THEY LIVE WITH IT? Finally, although most of my mediations involve high conflict and/or substantial assets and complex legal issues, ultimately the parties have the wisdom to make the best decisions for themselves. Despite Tom's pressure, Mary wants finality and to be able to move on with her life. Although Tom has schemed, uses manipulative tactics, and is creating a situation of duress, perhaps he is also fair, and Mary's acceptance of Tom's offer as is (or with slight renegotiation) might be in Mary's best interest.

The test of an acceptable settlement should not be what the party can get in court or by other means, what either party deserves, or what the legal rights are. Such variables might marginally increase the ultimate settlement amount but will rarely give the party such real benefits as finality, reduced financial costs, privacy, and the possibility of a future relationship with the other party.

In the caucus with Mary (as well as in joint session), the mediator might offer the following test for acceptance of a proposal: "Can you live with it? If not, let's keep talking."

CONCLUSION. Just as Monet never tired of painting water lilies and could always view them from another perspective, mediators committed to their craft are continually trying on new perspectives of conflict and sharing them with the parties. The goal should not be to convince a party to change. Change comes slowly, laboriously, if at all. The mediator should gently ask the parties if they want settlement more than they want conflict. If so, the next step is to ask the parties to try to consider the needs and concerns of the other party (recognition) without abandoning their own needs and concerns (empowerment).[22] This ability to at least understand and look at both points of view may be the foundation from which the mediator can skillfully use a toolbox of strategies to help the parties achieve movement toward resolution, and perhaps, find resolution itself.[23]

Comments on Case 4.2

Bill Eddy

This situation presents several ethical questions:

1. How should the mediator fulfill his responsibilities to preside over a quality process? How can he exercise his obligation to ensure a fair and balanced process?
2. How should the mediator handle bullying by one party?
3. How should the mediator ensure both clients' self-determination under these facts?
4. What, if any, role should evaluation play in this mediation?
5. What, if any, role should the mediator play in encouraging attorney review?
6. What, if any, role does the mediator's concern for reputation play in ethical decision making?

I address each question below.

1. **PRESIDING OVER A QUALITY PROCESS.** Standard I of the Model Standards counsels that the mediation process emphasizes informed consent, voluntary decisions, and an absence of undue influence. All of these are at risk if one party comes to the mediation with a notary waiting in the wings. While it is common for one party or another in mediation to threaten to quit negotiating and go to court, there is usually no third party waiting offstage to add external pressure to one side.

The mediator should make clear from the start that he is in charge of the process but not of the outcome. The process must be balanced, and any appearance of imbalance that is tolerated by the mediator would harm the overall process—not just for the parties in this case, but for parties considering mediation. For these parties and for the integrity of the process, the mediator should not allow the notary to come to or stay at his office. The mediator should block the signing of any deeds on the spot.

2. HANDLING BULLY TACTICS IN MEDIATION. Tom appears to be bullying Mary, no matter how you look at it. How voluntary can it be for her if Tom says, "Sign now—really, right now—or I'm going to court"? He knows that she does not want to go to court, so bringing in a notary for a quick deal signing adds emotional pressure without the opportunity for reflection and consultation, which are important components of a voluntary mediation process.

Yet I would recommend against the mediator's taking a harsh approach to Tom, so as not to appear to be "against" Tom and "for" Mary. The mediator should simply inform the parties that the process does not allow for the signing of deeds without time for reflection and consultation. Blame it on the process, not on Tom.

There is also the unknown of prior domestic intimidation or violence. Perhaps it is common practice for Tom to coerce Mary into signing documents or making other decisions. The mediator may be wise to separate the parties and ask Mary in private if there is a pattern of intimidation or violence in the relationship. If so, the mediator will need to decide whether it is appropriate to proceed further with the mediation. Perhaps the mediator might require them to obtain separate attorneys before meeting in future mediation sessions.

3. CLIENT SELF-DETERMINATION. One of the key aspects of mediation is that the clients make the decisions, except for a few decisions about the integrity of the process as described above. If both parties were to say, "That's fine; let's sign the deeds today. We're ready," then the mediator should allow them to do so. But in this situation, it appears that Mary is very uncomfortable, and therefore it would not promote her self-determination to have deed-signing occur that day.

4. EVALUATIVE MEDIATION. If Mary and Tom both said the mediator could explain the pros and cons of Tom's settlement proposal to

Mary, that raises a different question about whether the parties have expressed a desire to participate in evaluative mediation. If the mediator provides evaluative mediation as an option, then it may be appropriate for the mediator to do so for these parties. Mediation can take many forms, and evaluative mediation is firmly within the mainstream of practice today, so if the mediator wishes, he should feel free to offer this form of service. Likewise, the clients should be allowed to decide whether they want the mediator's evaluation included in their mediation.

If the parties contract with the mediator to provide an evaluation of their proposals and the mediator has sufficient expertise to do so, this is an ethically acceptable course to take. Of course, the mediator should not offer opinions about the strengths of each party's proposals or positions without the advance approval of the parties for the mediator to do so.

The mediator may also caucus or meet separately with Tom and Mary if the parties have agreed in advance to include that format in the mediation. However, there is an air of imbalance to it if the mediator is basically meeting with Mary to go over Tom's proposal without Tom's presence. The mediator could require Tom to be present to explain his proposal more himself. However, when there is high tension between the parties, it is common mediation practice to use separate caucuses, if for no other purpose than to separate the parties and let one or both of them calm down. Therefore, I would recommend that the mediator meet with each party to discuss Tom's proposal and to help Mary consider alternate proposals she might want to make.

5. ENCOURAGING MEETINGS WITH SEPARATE ATTORNEYS. This case clearly has an air of intimidation and seems shaped by Tom's self-centeredness. One of the best ways to counterbalance this potential imbalance, while remaining a neutral mediator, is to encourage or require that the parties obtain separate attorneys. Even if this is just for separate consultations, it may address issues of undue influence and the possible need for court protective orders. The mediator should make this recommendation to the parties separately, in caucus, so that the question of using attorneys does not become a point of added conflict between them. Some bullies in mediation also try to bully the other party out of consulting with an attorney.

6. THE MEDIATOR'S REPUTATION. Just as the mediation process needs to maintain credibility in the eyes of the public, a mediator needs future business. If the mediator allows a party to bring a notary to his office for a pressured settlement, it may damage his reputation in the mediation community, as well as for the mediation community. The mediation community is still vulnerable to attorney perceptions that the process is less tightly structured and more ripe for manipulation than litigation or attorney-led negotiations.

Maintaining his own reputation is important to the mediator but should not interfere with the other ethical values described above. If the mediator did not like the appearance of the notary but the parties were untroubled by it, the mediator would have two options: go along with it as part of party self-determination, or explain to the parties that it is not a procedure that the mediator is willing to participate in or have associated with his office. In the latter case, the mediator should inform the parties of other alternatives.

While the mediator's reputation should not dictate his every decision in a case, it is a justifiable factor to consider. All professionals—doctors, lawyers, engineers, and the like—make calculated assessments regarding how a particular action plan will affect their business. Big corporations aren't the only entities that worry about market share. So while self-interest should not be the sole engine of decision making, it would be unrealistic to suggest it will not or should not play a role. Fortunately, a mediator's concern for reputation, at least in this case, will likely encourage a more cautious approach to the power imbalance in the case. That is all to the good. It is possible in other cases that self-interest will not have such a salutary effect.

SUMMARY. Overall I believe that the mediator should tell Tom (and the notary) that it is not his practice to allow notaries to show up on behalf of one party in the mediation process and that mediation requires time for reflection and consultation. The mediator can go further and tell the parties that it is possible that an agreement or deed signed under those conditions could be easily set aside.

With such an approach, the mediator can resolve the situation without specifically criticizing one or both parties or appearing to blame one party in a process that should be characterized by respect for parties and balance.

Editor's Thoughts on Case 4.2 and the Comments

Tom and Mary's case prompts mediators Forrest Mosten and Bill Eddy to reflect on the uses and abuses of power. Mosten begins by making a few general observations based on his forty years of experience. He notes that power is fragmented, ephemeral, and nomadic. It is rarely spread equally and difficult to calibrate. Allocations change rapidly and subtly. For the mediator, knowing who has the power is less important than knowing how to manage its shifting distributions.

To do so, Mosten suggests mediators dig deep into their tool kit. He suggests that private sessions, both before and during the mediation, can be helpful. He also counsels the use of third parties as a possible mitigating influence.

Mosten makes reference to the age-old tale of Sleeping Beauty to remind disputants (and us) of the importance of issuing the proper invitations. Sleeping Beauty was cursed with eternal sleep because her guardians neglected to invite a powerful fairy to the party celebrating her birth. Similarly, Mosten notes that mediation negotiations may be less successful than they might be if important third parties like attorneys, financial consultants, or support persons are not "invited to the party."

Bill Eddy agrees that third parties, particularly attorneys, might be helpful to ensure that Mary understands exactly what Tom's offer entails. And he seconds Mosten's suggestion that private sessions could be useful for both screening and educational purposes. The mediator could caucus with Mary both to ascertain whether she and Tom have any history of violence or intimidation and also to educate her as to the risks and benefits of Tom's proposal. Before providing any sort of evaluation, however, the mediator should elicit Tom and Mary's preferences and make sure that is what they want.

Unlike Mosten, who leaves open the question of whether Mary might sign when the notary shows up, Eddy unequivocally rejects the possibility that the notary be allowed to enter the mediation and record Mary's signature. Allowing Mary to sign on the dotted line under the kind of time pressure Tom has orchestrated would, in Eddy's view, be inherently coercive and inconsistent with the mediator's duty to preside over a quality process.

Eddy notes that the mediator's concern for his own reputation, as well as the reputation the process enjoys in the community, are legitimate factors to consider. Attorneys concerned about the level of protection that mediation provides to vulnerable parties might look askance at Tom's imminently exploding offer and find fault with a mediator who didn't deactivate the bomb. Allowing this sort of maneuver to become the basis of a settlement might hurt the profession in the minds of skeptics who are already inclined to believe the worst. Eddy says reputational concerns shouldn't drive a mediator's decisions but should be acknowledged as having a legitimate place in any pragmatic calculus.

It is notable that neither Mosten nor Eddy thinks that Tom's power play invalidates the mediation as a means of achieving closure. Both think that with careful attention to the couple's individual and collective dynamics, and with a careful eye to the dangers posed by excessive pressure and intimidation, continued negotiations could yield a fair and satisfying conclusion.

CHAPTER FIVE

Tensions Between Disputant Autonomy and Substantive Fairness

The Misinformed Disputant

---◊◊◊---

Supporting disputant autonomy seems to be the obviously ethical thing to do when disputants make good choices. It's natural to want to respect and affirm decisions that are thoughtful, well informed, and productive of positive outcomes.

But what happens when disputants are inclined toward agreements that appear not to serve their long-term best interests? More complicated still, what happens when disputants are making those decisions based on incomplete or inaccurate information? In these circumstances, the mandate to honor party self-determination intersects awkwardly with the mediator's interest in facilitating fully informed decision making. In addition, if a party's haphazardly conceived choices yield unjust or inequitable outcomes, this raises questions as to whether a mediator bears any responsibility for the substantive fairness of the mediated outcome.

These are difficult questions that continue to inspire spirited debate. No consensus has emerged regarding how to honor these fundamental—and competing—values. Mediators who think party autonomy commands absolute fealty will be reluctant to challenge disputant deals on account of injustice. Mediators who see their role as promoting party autonomy in concert with other values will feel more comfortable inserting questions into the mix about equity and third-party effects. Both practices are ethically acceptable, though it remains important for mediators to be clear themselves on where they stand on these issues and communicate that stance to the parties.

DO THE CODES HELP?

National and state codes speak to this conundrum, but only obliquely. Rather than supply clear responses to the question of how mediators should balance party sovereignty with the demands of justice, the codes merely gesture toward permissive or disapproving attitudes without actually authorizing or restricting. Like traffic signs in a foreign language, the fine print can be indecipherable, but the red or green background gives hints of whether to speed or slow.

Over the mediator's role as educator, the Model Standards cast a yellow "slow": there's no outright prohibition, but proceed with caution. Some state code lights appear greener, though the actual language may seem muted and unclear. At the end of the day, mediators should remain alert to road signs but chart their own course, keeping in mind that reasonable and ethical people can disagree.

Informed Consent in the Model Standards

Although the Model Standards are ambiguous when it comes to specifying how respecting party autonomy accords with the interest in securing informed consent, they do state that informed decision making is important. It is a component of party self-determination—the foundational principle of the mediation process. The Standards also make clear that mediators—unlike physicians and other professionals—are not duty-bound to ensure that disputants' choices are knowledgeable or informed. The Standards specify that "where appropriate," a mediator should enlighten parties about "the importance of consulting" with other professionals to get the information they need.[1] This leaves open the obvious question: If the parties choose not to consult other professionals, what should the mediator do? What if the only way to see that the parties have information necessary for informed consent is to supply it yourself? Should you?

The Standards urge mediators to exercise caution when tempted to expand an uninformed disputant's knowledge base. For example, disputants often lack a realistic understanding of their options if they reject settlement and decide to try their luck in court. They may be overly optimistic or (though considerably less frequently) overly pessimistic when assessing their chances in litigation. They may misunderstand the mechanics of staging a trial, misperceive the remedial power of a court, and mistake the money, time, and trauma involved. A mediator may seek to perfect disputants' understanding by offering her own sense of the legal rules involved and how they might be applied to the disputants' situation.

But supplying legal information and discussing how that information affects the merit or validity of a legal position falls within the standard job description of an attorney. The Standards are careful to point out that the mediator role differs "substantially from other professional roles" and that mixing roles is "problematic."

Other provisos and qualifications follow. Mediators are allowed to provide information—but only if the content falls within their "training or experience" and only if doing so is consistent with other provisions—including the expectation of impartiality set out in Standard II. In addition, if providing information overlaps with an attorney's educational function, then Standard VI serves as a reminder that "a mediator who undertakes such [a] role assumes different duties and responsibilities that may be governed by other standards."

The Standards do not flat out forbid mediators from talking with disputants about the strength or weakness of their legal arguments, but they do freight the role with significance. They point out that mediators who supply information regarding the legal merits may be viewed as assuming a counselor role and will then be held to the standard of a reasonable "legal counselor." Because moving into this role significantly changes the dynamics, the Standards advise mediators to explain the shift in function to the parties and obtain explicit consent.[2]

Substantive Fairness in the Model Standards

The Standards are silent on the matter of substantive fairness. This is astonishing when one reflects that mediators are, after all, in the business of helping bring disputes to closure and that one fairly uncontroversial goal a society might hold for its dispute resolvers is to work toward agreements that are fair and just.

A look at professional standards in other fields highlights this gap. The codes of most other professions typically contain some discussion of the type of outcome to which its members should aspire. Codes of medical ethics exhort physicians to practice beneficently—to function as a force for good—and to consider justice in the allocation of scarce medical resources.[3] Psychologists are also urged to "safeguard the welfare and rights of those with whom they interact ... and to practice with the principles of justice and fairness in mind."[4] The preamble to social workers' ethics standards states that "social justice" is one of the profession's "core values,"[5] and the first sentence in the attorneys' Model Rules of Professional Conduct states that a lawyer is "a public citizen having special responsibility for the quality of justice."[6]

The Model Standards keep their distance from concepts like fairness and justice. Indeed, the Standards avoid setting any goals relating to the content of the agreements reached in mediation. Rather, all aspirations relate to process, not substance. Thus, the title of Standard VI is "Quality of the Process"; there is no standard that discusses quality of mediation outcome.

The Standards' structure assumes that striving toward a quality process will yield a qualitatively good outcome. That is why the Standards carefully delineate the components of procedural justice, including full party participation and capacity, mediator impartiality, and timely, diligent treatment of issues. And that is why explicit reference to substantive fairness is viewed as both unnecessary and potentially deeply problematic.

Understanding why talking about justice in an ethics code might be problematic requires a bit more attention to first principles. If one takes the underlying premise of mediation seriously, then it makes no sense to talk about substantive fairness other than through a renewed emphasis on party autonomy. After all, mediation explicitly rejects the idea that one must go to a judge—or consult any other external authority—to obtain justice. Rather, it holds that the parties are better situated to define what justice requires in their particular circumstance than is any public official. Given this rejection of the idea that social and legal norms capture globally authoritative truths, it seems safer to give concepts like fairness and justice a wide berth rather than to try to define them in some way that explicitly excludes legal texts and pronouncements.

In absolving mediators from attending to substantive justice issues in their work, the Model Standards take one side of a debate that has brewed in the mediation community for years. In the early 1980s, a celebrated exploration of these issues took place in the *Vermont Law Review* in which scholars Lawrence Susskind and Josh Stulberg battled over the question of mediator accountability. Pursuing the question in the context of environmental mediation, Susskind argued that it is not enough for mediators to guarantee full party participation, capacity, and balanced exchange.[7] Susskind claimed that "the success of a mediation effort must also be judged in terms of the fairness and stability of agreements that are reached."[8] Environmental mediation treats resources—air, water, land—that affect communities at large, not simply the parties at the table. Susskind was concerned that private negotiations over these public goods might yield wasteful and damaging outcomes. What if a powerful development company were able to bulldoze its way over representatives from an agency charged with protecting endangered animals, fragile ecosystems, or precious river rights? Valuable public spaces might be lost or compromised.[9] To prevent this, Susskind asserted, environmental mediation needed to accept responsibility for ensuring "1) that the interests of parties not directly involved in negotiations, but with a stake in the outcome, are adequately represented and protected; 2) that agreements are as fair and stable as possible; and 3) that agreements reached are interpreted as intended by the community-at-large and set constructive precedents."[10]

Stulberg forcefully demurred, objecting that nothing in the mediator's "obligations of office" equips or entitles him to assume the role of "social conscience, environmental policeman or social critic."[11] Stulberg argued that parties will reveal deal-enabling information— "statement[s] of . . . priorities, acceptable trade-offs . . . desired timing for demonstrating movement and flexibility"[12]—only if they know that the mediator has no stake in the outcome. Mediators can choose to end their involvement in a negotiation that they feel is leading to an unfair outcome, but "that judgment is one for the mediator qua moral agent, not mediator [qua mediator] to make."[13] In other words, for Stulberg, assuming responsibility for the fairness of the agreement represents a tragic abandonment of the neutral stance and an unwarranted expansion of the mediator's proper role.

Following Stulberg and Susskind's debate, the rest of the 1980s witnessed a flowering of criticism centered on the dangers of mediation's legal and normative agnosticism. Commentators ranging from Yale Law School professor Owen Fiss to anthropologist and social critic Laura Nader pointed to the alternative dispute resolution movement as a threat to public values such as equality and due process.[14]

Critical-race theorists and feminists worried that mediation's neglect of social norms meant that women and minorities would be denied the benefits that newly enacted civil rights legislation sought to confer. How ironic, they noted, that progress toward more gender- and racially sensitive laws in the formal adversarial system would be accompanied by a move to push cases out of that venue and toward more informal, less protective settings.[15]

More than twenty years later, the ranks of mediation's critics have thinned. Commentators today are more likely to lament that mediation looks too much like a judicial hearing, not too little.[16] Warnings that mediation delivers "second-class justice" to those who can't afford the price of entry to court have been supplanted by those who complain that it's now hard to tell the difference.

Still, Susskind's worry that private negotiations over public goods threaten important societal values continues to resonate. The call for mediators to pay attention to the ripple effects of what they do can be seen in a number of state ethics codes that support the notion that mediators may need to intervene, or at the least withdraw, when private party negotiations threaten to yield patently unfair outcomes.

Concern for Substantive Fairness in the State Codes

Although most states follow the lead of the Model Standards and make no explicit reference to substantive fairness, some do glancingly address the issue when specifying appropriate situations for withdrawal. Alabama states that a mediator *may* withdraw if the disputants' agreement seems to rest on fraud, duress, overreaching, the absence of bargaining ability, or unconscionability.[17] Arkansas and Florida go further in specifying that a mediator who detects these problems *shall* withdraw.[18]

Other states also authorize withdrawal in the face of an agreement that doesn't seem to meet a minimal standard of equity. Georgia gives a green light to mediators to "refuse to draft or sign an agreement which seems fundamentally unfair to one party,"[19] while North Carolina permits withdrawal in cases of bargaining inequality, fraud, or "any other circumstance likely to lead to a grossly unjust result."[20]

Note that these code provisions allow, and in some instances require, the mediator to pass judgment on the quality of the disputants' agreement. To be sure, the ambit of discretion is severely constrained. In a court of law, unconscionability is difficult to establish. An unconscionable agreement is so unfair and unbalanced that it "shocks the conscience." It is an agreement that "no man in his senses, not under delusion, would make" and "which no fair and honest man would accept."[21] In borrowing this draconian legal vocabulary, the codes signal that a mediator shouldn't reject the parties' agreed-on resolution unless it is seriously skewed and corrupt. Still, in identifying conditions where the ethical mediator could withdraw her imprimatur from the parties' desired outcome, the codes reflect an abiding concern with fairness and position the mediator as a final check against abuse or exploitation.

Concern for Informed Consent in State Codes

Consistent with the concern for fairness of state codes is a concern with the quality of party decision making. Spurred by the prospect of better party decision making, some states grant mediators considerable latitude in educating disputants regarding the risks and benefits of settlement. But the encouragement is always tempered by worry that a mediator might go too far. Even the most permissive codes imply that any opinions expressed should be carefully worded to avoid appearing as a command or directive. At every point, the desire for informed decision making is counterbalanced by an equally strong focus on the primacy of party views and preferences. Mediators can educate and opine, but their views regarding the law and the strength or weakness of a party's case should be presented as information, not deployed as persuasion in support of a particular outcome.

Although the intent animating the codes seems clear, sometimes the distinctions drawn are not. For example, Florida's Rules for Certified and Court-Appointed Mediators allow mediators to "point out possible outcomes of the case and discuss the merits of a claim or defense" while drawing the line at predictions "as to how the court in which the case has been filed will resolve the dispute."[22] Court-appointed mediators in Tennessee may "point out possible outcomes of the case and may indicate a personal view of the persuasiveness of a particular claim or defense," but they are instructed to "refrain from giving legal advice."[23] Guidelines drafted by the Department of Dispute Resolution Services of the Supreme Court of Virginia prohibit the provision of legal advice, defined as applying the law to specific case facts in such a way as to predict the outcome of the case or an issue in the case, or recommend a course of action based on the mediator's analysis.[24] North Carolina's guidelines also proscribe "taking the facts of a particular case, applying the governing law, and then giving advice based on these considerations."[25]

These codes limn the familiar fuzzy borders between legal information and legal advice in ways that amplify the space for speculation about the legal strength or weakness of the parties' positions. In their desire to create room for mediator opinion, these codes blur traditional definitions of legal information and legal advice, broadening out what we traditionally consider legal information and narrowing the sorts of behavior that would be characterized as prohibited advice giving.[26]

According to existing case law, giving legal information means talking about legal rules and standards in the abstract. Thus, a mediator who gave a couple a copy of the local jurisdiction's child support guidelines and said, "Here, read these," would be giving legal information. But once the mediator begins explaining how those guidelines would likely be read in the context of their own marriage, she would be seen as giving legal advice, and thus trespassing dangerously on forbidden ground.[27] Not only does the provision of legal advice transform a lawyer mediator from a neutral to an advocate, but it subjects a nonlawyer mediator to the threat of an unauthorized practice of law prosecution.[28] From many angles, giving legal advice as a mediator is a bad thing.

Yet some state codes, perhaps responding to market data that reveal many parties do want the mediator to help them expand their knowledge base, allow mediators to apply law to fact in the parties' concrete situation as long as they refrain from dictating how the parties should respond to the information. The Advisory Committee Comments to California's Code of Conduct for Court-Connected Mediators, for example, explains that a qualified mediator may "discuss a party's options, including a range of possible outcomes in an adjudicative process[,] offer a personal evaluation of or opinion on a set of facts as presented, . . . or . . . communicate the mediator's opinion or view of what the law is or how it applies to the subject of the mediation." A mediator can apply the law to the parties' set of facts as long as the mediator stops short of telling disputants what to do with the proffered analysis.[29] Thus, under the California Code, a mediator could say, "In my opinion, your claims on causation are weak. Despite damages of $500,000, I would estimate that your chances of succeeding at trial are less than 25 percent. Consequently, the maximum value I would assign your case is in a range between $75,000 to $125,000." What is forbidden is to follow the statement with, "So I'd take his offer of $135,000."

Although it is easy to see what the authors of the code were getting at, the actual line drawn between permitted and nonpermitted activity seems nonsensical. Wouldn't any disputant holding a $135,000 offer from the other side be heavily influenced to accept the offer if the mediator told her that her likely court recovery wouldn't exceed $125,000? Does allowing mediator opinions on the law while prohibiting prescriptive statements about the particular decision at hand successfully meet the twin goals of encouraging informed decision making while avoiding undue mediator influence?

If it seems that the California Code's parsing of the legal-information-versus-advice line leads to odd conceptual gerrymandering, it is important to remember that the trade-offs being managed are difficult and no clear balance can be struck that will work in all cases. Mediator discretion must be enlisted to determine when concrete applications of law to fact are called for, when they threaten to usurp disputant judgment, and how to tell the difference.

FACTORS INFLUENCING ATTITUDES TOWARD INFORMED CONSENT AND SUBSTANTIVE FAIRNESS

Ambiguity in the codes feeds confusion regarding how much and what sort of information mediators can or should ethically provide for disputants. The issue remains knotty. Although we are probably a long way from reaching broad consensus on how much information is enough, insufficient, or too much, we are now at the stage where we can identify the factors that shape our deliberations.

Factual Context of Case

Certainly the factual context of the case plays a role in most practitioners' thinking:

- Is each disputant represented?
- Does he or she have access to another expert who can provide the relevant data? Is the disputant able to use and amenable to using that expert?
- What information is missing? Is it material to understanding the nature and consequences of the contemplated agreement?
- What will the consequences be if the disputant enters into the agreement—or chooses to shun settlement—based on incomplete information or understanding? Who will be harmed? Will the harm be great?

Most mediators would think hard about such issues before deciding what to do with a disputant poised to make decisions without full command of the relevant facts.

The Mediator's Model

A second important feature relates not to fact but to mediation philosophy. As discussed in Chapter One, mediators hold different attitudes regarding the goals and purposes of mediation, and so they weigh competing values differently and reach divergent conclusions when presented with difficult ethical choices. The question of whether or how a mediator should influence the disputants' knowledge base requires both determining what informed decision making means and balancing that value with concerns about mediator impartiality and party self-determination. It is unsurprising that adherents to different models would reach varied states of equilibrium. Consider how facilitative, evaluative, transformative, and narrative mediators would view questions of informed consent and substantive fairness.

Facilitative mediators are uncomfortable giving disputants information about their alternative to settlement. They might sharply question the parties about their assumptions as to what will happen if they end up in court, but they will not provide their own assessments for fear of departing from a neutral role and having too great an impact on the substance of the parties' negotiations. Additionally, facilitative mediators do not set themselves up as arbiters of the fairness of what the parties decide. Rather, working with the conviction that parties know best what works for them, facilitative mediators equate justice with the parties' own choices.

Evaluative mediators are more comfortable talking to the parties about how they read the relevant law and what they think a judge or jury might do if the case ends up in court. Typically they are more concerned with the information base that parties are working with and more comfortable passing judgment on the equity of the parties' proposed outcome.

Tranformative mediators, focused as they are on encouraging shifts toward greater empowerment and recognition, steer clear of giving information about legal rights. Indeed, Bush and Folger explicitly caution against overenthusiastically pursuing informed consent. They call this problem the danger of "overprotection" and write:

> Because transformative mediation emphasizes party choice based on full consideration of options, mediators may think they have a special obligation to ensure that parties have adequate information before making decisions. After all, if a party lacks information—factual, legal or otherwise—how can that party make an informed choice about what to do? ... However, this view overlooks the point that party choice includes the choice of how much information to consider an adequate basis for decision making. While mediators can and should call parties' attention to the question of whether they think their information is adequate, it is possible to go too far on this point, as on others. When mediators do so, they can wind up discouraging decisions the parties themselves feel prepared to make. In effect, the mediator falls into the pitfall of "protecting parties from themselves," shifting from pursuing empowerment into protection—and disempowerment.[30]

Narrative mediators take a skeptical but inclusive view of the role of legal information in mediation. The principal architects of this model, Gerald Monk and John Winslade, are deeply concerned with fairness and equity, but they don't believe that judges have any special monopoly on divining what those concepts require. Indeed, they opine, "The concept of the courtroom as a place where truth is shared and a fair and just outcome attained is not borne out in most courts."[31] They describe legal discourse as potentially oppressive, as the means by which "the public power of the state can be exercised to shape the private world of the family."[32] Still, law talk is part of the background script from which the parties draw their roles, so they concede the relevance of this talk to the mediation discussion. Importantly, though, narrative mediators would not see it as their role to provide legal information themselves; rather, they would likely see their role as helping the parties parse the role that "law talk" plays in their narrative and helping them examine the degree of authority such discourse should enjoy.

INFORMED CONSENT THROUGH A DIFFERENT LENS: A CLASSIFICATION BASED ON NORMS

Although classification systems that distinguish between problem solving and understanding are helpful in describing mediators' diverse goals, another typology also helps to explicate mediators' different ideas surrounding the provision of information and the duty to secure informed consent. More than ten years ago, I proposed three categories based on the mediator's approach to legal and social norms: norm-generating, norm-educating, and norm-advocating mediation.[33] The models differ primarily in the mediator's stance toward social norms and their inclusion, or exclusion, from the process. I believe this system is particularly useful in clarifying the different approaches to informed consent and substantive fairness that pervade the mediation field.

Norm-Generating Model

The norm-generating model assumes that the only norms relevant to the process are those the parties identify and adopt. Thus, legal precedent, legislative pronouncement, administrative regulation, and majority custom are not thought essential or important to the parties' negotiation. Societal norms on the topic may exist, but they do not hold sway. This model of mediation follows Lon Fuller's expectation that the process be "commonly directed, not toward achieving conformity to norms, but toward the creation of the relevant norms themselves."[34]

The mediator, then, sees her role as encouraging the parties to decide for themselves what is fair, equitable, sensible, and just.

Although there may be case or statutory law relevant to the parties' dispute, the mediator would not view that information as crucial to the parties' deliberations. Norm-generating mediators emphasize the potential of mediation for realigning power between disputants and the state. In traditional legal settings, parties give over their disputes to outsiders who look at it with an outsider's eye and bring external rules and standards to bear on the most intimate of issues. In mediation, party interpretation, value, and judgment remain paramount. Norm-generating mediators don't wish to bring external social norms into the conversation for fear of chipping away at the parties' unfettered elaboration of their own beliefs and priorities. Talking about what judges or arbitrators might say distracts parties from the creative and empowering task of forging their own norms according to their own values. Bringing legal information into the conversation is not something a norm-generating mediator would be tempted to do.

Norm-Educating Model

Like the norm-generating model, norm-educating mediation is also committed to party autonomy, but it holds a different understanding of how such autonomy is best achieved. For these mediators, parties cannot be fully self-determining unless they are positioned to make informed judgments. Making an informed judgment means knowing the risks and benefits of settling, as well as the risks and benefits of not settling and perhaps going to court. What judges and legislators have said on the topic, then, becomes important, not only so disputants can have a better understanding as to how well their views mesh with larger social judgments, but also so they can better assess the likely outcome if their case ends up in court.

Social norms can include legal, psychological, and other forms of information. An injured plaintiff struggling with a fractured knee might benefit from knowing how judges and juries value and seek to compensate such injuries. Quarreling ex-spouses may benefit from psychological data analyzing the impact of various custody arrangements on child development and well-being. Such information gives parties a broader perspective on their stated demands and helps them better assess the value of continued disputing versus settling on other terms.

Importantly, mediators in this model do not urge parties to adopt the social or legal norms presented. Rather, they present the information to enrich the parties' deliberations. If the parties decide to disregard what judges and legislators would advise and formulate an altogether different plan, the mediator is willing to facilitate this outcome. The norms are simply information that the parties can choose to incorporate into their agreement or ignore. What matters is that the parties know what the norms are and their decision to disregard them is made in knowledge, not ignorance.

Norm-Advocating Model

Like norm-educating mediators, the norm-advocating mediator works to apprise the parties of the relevant social norms. In this case, however, her purpose is not only to encourage informed decision making, but to ensure that the norms achieve some measure of expression in the parties' agreement. The norm-advocating mediator uses legal, political, or ethical norms as the starting place for discussion. Thus, Equal Employment Opportunity Commission (EEOC) mediators ground parties' discussions in norms that prohibit bias and disparate treatment. Employers can talk about how they would like to run their business, and employees can express their expectations about their place in the corporate hierarchy, but the parties' preferences and expectations cannot run counter to federal antidiscrimination statutes. Similarly, environmental mediators begin with clean air and water legislation and work to structure deals that comply with the mandates contained in those acts. Mediators in the norm-advocating model assume that social or legal norms contain important judgments about how we should treat each other and the environment and seek to incorporate those judgments into the particularized agreements the parties choose to adopt.

It may seem at first blush that norm-advocating mediation is scarcely mediation. If the mediator exists only to tell the parties about the relevant norms and ensure their compliance, then how are the parties getting to exercise their self-determination in crafting the agreement? What role can party autonomy conceivably play?

Party autonomy and the mediator's facilitation skills are nonetheless important in this model because most social or legal norms are articulated at a high level of abstraction. For example, the Equal Pay Act of 1963 provides that "a man and a woman working for the same employer under similar conditions in jobs requiring substantially equivalent skills, effort, and responsibility must be paid equally, even when job titles and assignments are not identical."[35] But what if a woman working as a clown in a circus claims she is being discriminated against by her employer because she is being paid less than the male clown in the show? The clown acts are different—different costumes, different props, and different forms of juggling—but the primary aim of entertaining the audience is the same. Moreover, the sight gags overlap in theme. Is the female clown being discriminated against? The EEOC mediator would likely want the discussion to begin with the concept of nondiscrimination—equal pay for equal work. But the parties' notions of what constitutes equal work and how the female clown's work can be adequately recognized and compensated are matters that could fruitfully be ironed out by circus management and the clown over the mediation table.

Mediators working in the norm-advocating model would feel strongly that parties should be provided information about the law or other relevant norms surrounding the dispute. Because of the mediator's attitude that legal norms provide a foundation from which to launch discussion, it is likely that she would be well educated regarding the content of those norms. And it is likely that if the parties were reluctant to enlist other professionals, the mediator would feel comfortable engaging in that discussion herself. In this model, concerns regarding neutrality and impartiality take second seat to worries that party agreements should not stray too far from social norms thought essential to the vitality and strength of our social fabric.

Choosing the Norm-Generating Versus Norm-Educating Versus Norm-Advocating Model

Sometimes mediator philosophy dictates the choice. That is, some mediators adopt and use one model exclusively, regardless of case context. A transformative mediator may decide that she will use that style—and remain faithful to its underlying assumptions—in all cases. Other mediators move between models depending on the type of case they are handling. Indeed an emerging theme among experienced mediators is eclecticism—that they will pinch and borrow from different models depending on the case they are handling. Some mediators may be primarily facilitative but adopt more evaluative approaches to information in cases where they feel strongly that the parties can benefit from their substantive expertise in that arena.

The choice of whether to use a norm-generating, norm-educating, or norm-advocating model appears strongly dependent on the nature of the case. Although different mediators may deploy these models differently, here I set out the types of cases where the advantages of each model might be most profitably exploited.

NORM-GENERATING MODEL. The norm-generating model is most usefully deployed when the substance of the mediation outcome matters less than the goals of enhancing disputant autonomy and preserving relationships. In these cases, the mediator is not burdened with sober concerns about the fairness or justice of the parties' agreement. Legal or social norms in these cases have little to say about how closure for the parties might best be reached. This may be true for a number of reasons.

First, there may simply be no consensus norm on point. Society may be sufficiently conflicted about the matter that although numerous viewpoints have been expressed and litigated, no authoritative judicial or regulatory statement has emerged. If no consensus norm exists, we cannot say that society has adopted any particular view about what is just in the situation at hand. Hence, the parties' views of fairness fill the void, with no worry that some important guidepost to human behavior is being neglected.

A second reason is that the parties may be disputing in an area so private or of so little public concern that it has not been the subject of regulation. Again, in this instance, no legal or social norm maps out preferable versus less desirable approaches, so the parties' own notions of propriety supply the text for action.

In other instances, public norms exist, but they are so inconsequential when compared to competing objectives that they may be overridden without fear of substantial harm to either the parties or the public interest. In these cases the benefits to the parties in ceasing discord, maintaining control, and achieving a self-determined outcome and closure overshadow whatever may be lost by deviating from a societally endorsed course of action.

NORM-EDUCATING MODEL. The norm-educating model is appropriate to disputes that implicate social norms that are on point and relatively compelling. These norms are protective in the sense of protecting one or both parties from exploitation or abuse. Spousal property division rules designed to shield women from poverty after divorce are protective norms. So are norms designed to protect racial minorities, homosexuals, or those who are disabled from discrimination in the workplace. Because these norms are protective in design and effect, it is crucial that parties be informed of their existence before making decisions that waive the entitlements these laws confer.

That the parties must be informed of these norms, however, does not mean that they must adopt them. In disputes where the norm-educating model is appropriate, the parties' interests in reaching settlement outweigh whatever societal interest exists in the application of these norms. This is so for several reasons.

First, the parties approach the mediation with sufficient resources that their waiver of the legal entitlement does not appear coerced by circumstance. The disabled worker or the divorced housewife is waiving the entitlement that the law confers not out of desperation or hopelessness, but after consciously weighing the risks and benefits of pursuing the legal option and deciding that settlement better meets his or her needs.

Second, the resolution of these disputes primarily affects only the parties at the table. Although the dispute involves important protective norms, their nonenforcement will not harm third parties or significantly weaken the norms or their power in American life. We would not want plaintiffs in school desegregation cases after *Brown* v. *Board of Education* to accept individual money awards in return for an agreement to remain in separate but grossly unequal school systems. Such a private agreement would weaken the equality message that *Brown* sought to instantiate as an important aspiration for American institutions and public life. However, a disabled faculty member in a school district may choose to trade off a legal right to be accommodated regarding office equipment for a benefit in the workplace that she finds more desirable. In these disputes, because the disputant comes to the mediation with some degree of power and strength, and because enforcement of the norms is not essential to maintenance of the social fabric, the disputant may waive them, and such waiver is unproblematic from both the disputant's and society's vantage point.

NORM-ADVOCATING MODEL. The norm-advocating model is appropriate in cases where the calculus of private benefit and public harm is different. These disputes implicate important societal concerns, *and* those concerns are so great that they outweigh the individual disputant's interests in forging her own idiosyncratic approach to the problem. So in cases involving important social values like school desegregation or prison reform, society has a stake in asserting the norms of equality or humane treatment, and that interest takes precedence over the autonomy rights of the individuals involved.

Mediators might also advert to the norm-advocating model when dealing with a party who comes to the table so structurally disenfranchised that allowing her to negotiate away legal rights and entitlements would contribute to her continued oppression. We may be comfortable allowing a well-informed, well-resourced wife to waive her entitlements to spousal support at the end of a long marriage; we may feel differently if the wife is unsophisticated, unrepresented, and underresourced. If she is terminating the marriage in poverty with no resources or market power, we might not simply wish to reference the social norms that provide a bridge to a better future; we might insist on some level of their recognition in the resulting agreement.

I next explore two cases in which the ethical question about decision making in the absence of information seems easily answered. The first involves a sexual harassment complaint on an assembly line, the second is a neighborhood dispute over the use of adjoining property. Two harder cases then follow.

CASE 5.1: VULNERABLE WORKERS AND AN OPPRESSIVE EMPLOYER

Jill and Rose have worked on the Miso Car Company assembly line for three years. You have been hired by Miso to serve as an independent neutral as part of their internal grievance procedures. The women have requested a mediation with their supervisor because they have been taken off their usual 9:00 to 5:00 shifts and been told to work the midnight to 8:00 A.M. graveyard shifts, which disrupt their family lives. When Jill and Rose raised the issue with their supervisor, Bill, he said that the schedule change reflected "changes in work requirements at the plant." Both Jill and Rose claim that they are being retaliated against for complaining about the behavior of male coworkers on the assembly line.

Jill and Rose tell the following story. Four months ago, they decided that a group of new employees were making work conditions for the twenty women unpleasant and that management needed to get involved. They went to Bill and told him that women felt uncomfortable at work and wanted the supervisors to do something. Jill and Rose complained that a group of the younger employees spent all day telling off-color jokes that portrayed women in a demeaning way. In addition, they had begun drawing obscene stick figures in the dust on the car windows as they made their way down the assembly line.[36] Jill and Rose say Bill responded by laughing and saying they should "lighten up." When they complained that nothing about their working conditions was funny, he growled, "I promise you, it could get worse." The next day they found themselves assigned to the graveyard shift.

Bill has been around the Miso plant for ages. He is unsympathetic to Jill and Rose's unhappiness—and that of the other women—saying only that "the boys can get a little playful." Bill's attitude is consistent with that of other supervisors. Although supervisors don't engage in "horseplay" themselves, they don't discourage it, and they tag women who complain as "troublemakers" and punish them.

Jill and Rose are unsophisticated regarding Title VII and the whole concept of protection from a hostile work environment. Essentially they have given up asking for the dirty jokes and the pictures to stop. All they want now is to get their daytime shifts back. They are both single mothers who make do with babysitting in the afternoon, but they need to be home at night to care for their children.

From what you've heard, you've concluded that Miso is acting badly—and perhaps in violation of federal antidiscrimination law. Bill, Jill, and Rose are coming close to an agreement by which Jill and Rose move to a noon to 8:00 P.M. shift, which is better than the midnight to 8:00 A.M. shift but not exactly what they want. In addition, in exchange for this more workable schedule, Jill and Rose must agree to promise in the future "not to be troublemakers" or complain to outsiders about plant conditions.

What do you do?

Facilitating Informed Decision Making and Paying Attention to Justice

Most mediators, regardless of their philosophy, would feel uncomfortable facilitating an agreement given the facts of this case. It's not entirely clear, but Bill may be running afoul of Title VII, and Jill and Rose don't even know that federal law supports their right to be free of workplace behavior that creates a hostile environment. They don't know that Miso's behavior might be roundly punished in court and are willing to drop their legitimate demands in order to be partially—though not entirely—free of retaliatory measures that Miso should never have imposed in the first place. If Jill and Rose settle with Bill under the terms contemplated, they will be relieved of their night shift, but they will still have to endure a suboptimal work schedule; additionally, the discomfort that they and scores of other women suffer will continue. Miso will remain free to flout legal decrees designed to facilitate gender equity in the United States.

Even mediators generally opposed to bringing social and legal norms into the discussion would likely work to change Bill's and Rose and Jill's attitudes toward the dispute. Transformative mediators believe it is important to help parties better understand their own and their adversary's needs. Thus, a transformative mediator might work with Rose and Jill to remind them about the reasons they approached Bill in the first place. And a transformative mediator might talk to Bill about whether he thinks the female plant workers' unhappiness, complaints, and low-level agitation are going to stop if conditions for women remain unchanged. Whether a transformative mediator would make reference to the existence of laws prohibiting such conduct would likely depend on the individual. At least some mediators of a transformative bent would encourage Rose and Jill, and Bill, to speak with attorneys and return to mediation after having obtained some information about the relevant law.

Facilitative mediators would likely ask Bill a series of probing questions regarding how he thinks a judge might view Miso's 100 percent tolerance policy toward sexual harassment and how his own reaction to Jill and Rose might be assessed. A facilitative mediator might ask Bill what he understands about federal and state law governing working conditions for women and question him about his understandings.

An evaluative mediator would probably give Bill information about Title VII and what it requires. Whereas a facilitative mediator might ask Jill and Rose to talk about what they think their rights to be free of harassment at work are, an evaluative mediator would almost certainly provide them some information about what sort of male "horseplay" is and is not permitted in the workplace. At the very least, both facilitative and evaluative mediators would likely require Jill and Rose to see an attorney before agreeing not to bring any more complaints to the attention of the company or outsiders.

Because of the importance of sexual harassment law in setting standards for how men and women should treat each other in the workplace, most mediators would likely reject the norm-generating model in favor of a model that brings these norms into the discussion. Whether the mediator, after notifying Rose and Jill of their rights or advising them to consult attorneys before proceeding further, would allow them to waive those rights for a modest improvement in their schedule is again a question of individual philosophy. Most mediators would certainly be concerned with the significant power differential between Bill and the women and might urge the women to take advantage of some of the entitlements that the law provides.

CASE 5.2: HEY, NEIGHBOR—DON'T TOUCH MY CLOTHESLINE OR COMPOST!

Irma has lived at 125 Natch Lane for twenty years, across the street from Frank, who moved to the neighborhood with his wife nearly twenty-five years ago. Irma has been an avid environmentalist who went "green" long before it was fashionable. She has a large organic garden in her backyard and has never used a washer or dryer. Instead, she washes her clothes and linens in her bathtub and dries them on a clothesline spanning the border between her property and Frank's. She also keeps a compost right next to Frank's house and on one side of the clothesline.

Irma was never close friends with Frank and his wife, but they were cordial and cooperative neighbors. About four times a year, Irma would invite everyone on Natch Lane over for a large vegetarian feast, and Frank, a wine connoisseur, would bring the wine.

Frank always admired Irma for "living her dream," but did find the clothesline an eyesore and the smells that wafted over from the compost on a hot day a bit "rich." Technically Frank knew from looking at the maps and deeds that Irma's compost and parts of the clothesline edged over onto his property, and there were times when he thought about raising the matter with her. But it never seemed worth the fuss. As his wife always reminded him, Irma was a nice, quiet neighbor, and the dinners she held did a lot to foster a happy communal spirit along the block.

Since Frank's wife died last year, he has been suffering from low-grade depression and insomnia. Suddenly things that didn't bother him before do. Now when he looks out his window, all he sees is that annoying clothesline, and the smells have recently become intolerable to him. When he went to see Irma about the clothesline and compost, he spoke gruffly, and she seemed offended. "Don't you want to help save mother earth?" she asked. When Frank said no and suggested she move the clothesline, she replied that the other side of her property is too shady and the clothes would never dry. With regard to the compost, she simply said, "Frank, it's my property, and you've eaten my lovely vegetables for years. What is the matter with you?"

Frank is sad and angry. There is nothing the matter with him that getting rid of that compost and clothesline won't fix. He consults a friend, a local attorney, who tells him that technically, Irma's clothesline and compost are on his property, but that she might claim something called adverse possession that might give her rights to keep them right where they are. This information riles Frank even more.

At his attorney's urgings, Frank and Irma have come to you, a mediator at the local neighborhood center, for help resolving the matter. You are knowledgeable about the law. You know that landowners can gain property rights through "squatting"—but that the squatting must be (1) under claim of ownership; (2) adverse or hostile; (3) open, notorious, and visible; (4) continuous and uninterrupted for a period of ten years; (5) exclusive; and (6) peaceful.

Irma has been told by her attorney niece (who hasn't seen the property) that she has a good legal case because the clothesline and compost have been in the same place for over ten years. Frank has been told by his brother-in-law that he has a good case, at least with regard to the compost, because it is underground and hard to see and thus not "notorious or visible." You agree there is plenty to argue about, and you could give them more information about the elements of proof required in an adverse possession claim.

Should you?

Encouraging Parties to Formulate Their Own Norms: When Justice Doesn't Require a Discussion of Law

Most mediators would feel comfortable proceeding without giving undue attention to the legal norms at issue. This is true for several reasons. First, it seems clear that what really matters is Frank and Irma's feelings and relationship. They have lived together in peace for twenty years, and that relationship is integral to their ability to enjoy their homes. Moreover, Frank is suffering some mental distress as a result of his wife's death. Helping him resolve this dispute in a satisfying and therapeutic manner would seem particularly crucial given his current fragile psychological state.

In addition, this property dispute has limited scope. It affects no one other than Frank and Irma. It does not raise essential questions about justice or implicate protective norms that confer entitlements on the disadvantaged. Ignoring or downplaying the law will not undermine the expression of values essential to our common community. Rather, mediator attention to technical questions surrounding judicial definitions of *notorious* or *exclusive* will simply distract from the more important questions of how the parties can satisfy their respective interests in enjoying their homes and how they can reestablish goodwill.

This would seem to be an ideal case for a norm-generating facilitative or transformative approach that pays little attention to social or legal norms and attends instead to the parties' idiosyncratic feelings and needs. Ensuring that these parties know the local rules governing adverse possession before they reach an agreement is less important than making sure they come away from the discussion with a clearer sense of what they need from each other as neighbors and helpmates.

A mediator with an evaluative or norm-educating bent might raise the ambiguities in the law to suggest that pursuing the matter in court would be a risky strategy for both Frank and Irma. But it is likely that even the most evaluative sort would minimize discussion of technical legalities in favor of strategies that focused on relationship repair and mutual expectations for harmonious coexistence.

Who can say what is fair with regard to Irma's clothesline and compost? Has she "earned" the right to keep these fixtures on Frank's land? Do the fixtures' longevity and Frank's past forbearance mean that Frank is forever consigned to a view of Irma's gray socks and the fragrance of rotting coffee grounds? It's not clear that the local law, or any other law, can answer that question. Does society, in the form of legislative enactments and judicial opinions, have anything more sensible to say than Frank and Irma do? Justice here does not seem to reside in a close parsing of adverse possession law; rather it seems to inhere in the opportunity Frank and Irma have to consider for themselves the relevance of past practice and to think about what they wish to change and what they wish to remain the same.

CASES 5.3 AND 5.4: ILL-INFORMED CLAIMANTS

The harder disputes that follow raise questions surrounding the interplay of informed consent, substantive justice, and disputant autonomy. Counsel are involved in these cases, but they are misinformed. What should the mediator do when she believes that the parties are operating under serious misconceptions of their legal entitlements? Two commentators take on this difficult question.

Case 5.3: Tongan Slip and Fall

You are mediating a slip-and-fall personal injury case. The plaintiff, a newly arrived immigrant from Tonga, was injured when he stopped into the defendant's convenience store to use the facilities on the way to a job interview. The defendant's cleaning crew had mopped the restroom area in the back of the store, but neglected to post a sign alerting shoppers that the floor was wet. The plaintiff suffered serious injuries, including permanent nerve damage, in the fall and has incurred significant medical debt because he has no health insurance. Defendant is arguing that plaintiff was not a customer, and thus they owed no duty to him to maintain the restroom floor in a dry, safe condition. The plaintiff speaks little English and cannot follow the proceedings. His attorney, a fellow Tongan who has been practicing law in the United States for only four months, appears to misunderstand the relevant legal doctrines on landowner liability that supply his client with compelling arguments for recovery. Because the plaintiff has no job and is concerned about paying some portion of his debt to the health care providers who serviced him, he is preparing to settle with the defendant store owner for 10 percent of what you believe to be a $200,000 claim.

Case 5.4: Wrongful Death

As a result of defendant insured's negligence, the plaintiff's brother was killed in a car crash. From your years as a trial attorney, you know that a brother has no standing to sue for wrongful death. Stunningly, none of the parties or their attorneys seem aware of the standing rules in the local superior court, because plaintiff has demanded $650,000, and defendant has offered $200,000. The disputants seem to be moving toward a settlement in the $300,000 to $400,000 range.

What do you as mediator do?

Comments on Cases 5.3 and 5.4

Lela P. Love

I begin with two topics: substantive fairness and informed consent.

SUBSTANTIVE FAIRNESS IN MEDIATION. What is a fair outcome? The question is philosophically daunting. As a modest start, one facet of fairness entails an outcome arrived at through a coherent process operating with integrity.

In court, a fair outcome is the impartial application of public law by the judge or jury to the facts that they find. In arbitration, empowered by the parties' consent, the arbiter—like the judge or jury—determines the facts and applies whatever law, industry custom, religious tradition, or contractual obligations that the parties choose to determine what's fair. Sometimes the law allows an unsavory person to win. Sometimes courts convict an innocent person. Sometimes arbiters simply get it wrong ("it" being either the facts or the law or both). Assuming the decision maker had no conflicts of interest, procedures were followed, and appeals were allowed, such outcomes are substantively "fair" as long as the rules or norms were impartially applied to arrive at the outcome and the parties had a chance to present all relevant evidence.

In mediation, substantive fairness is quite different. The parties are the arbiters of the relevant facts. A fair outcome is one that parties believe is acceptable and fair—not an outcome, necessarily, that would mirror what a court would do. It is certainly not the outcome that is in keeping with what the particular mediator would find legally or morally acceptable. Rather, the mediated outcome must rest easy with parties' values, principles, and interests, addressing their needs—psychological, moral, and practical—as they judge those needs to be. Even in hard cases, this principle seems relatively straightforward and easy to apply where the party knows about rights that society would grant, and the party chooses to ignore those rights or entitlements to pursue her own ends.[37]

For example, a woman in the process of a mediated divorce decides she cannot stand to fight with her spouse any longer. She wants a fresh start in life. She is willing to abandon what a court might give her. In fact, she sees any money coming from her spouse as tainted, as interfering with her intention to be wholly independent. If she knows what she might obtain in court, a mediator would say she is entitled to choose to accept something less than what she is due. Would a mediator press her to consider whether she would regret this decision at a later time? Yes. But if the woman persisted, her sense of fairness would be honored.

Or imagine someone has suffered from medical negligence: the doctor operated on the wrong knee. The doctor apologizes, and the patient chooses not to pursue the remedy a court would most likely give. The patient believes that mistakes happen, and in his calculus, the doctor has done the morally correct thing in apologizing. The patient is represented by competent counsel who urges the patient to demand a large settlement. The patient agrees to accept something less than what he is due. Would a mediator press him to consider the advice of his counsel? Perhaps. But if the patient persisted, his sense of fairness would be honored.

Even these are not easy cases for many people. Society approves of its own measures of a substantively fair outcome. Nonetheless, the mediator appropriately bows to the spouse who wants an entirely fresh start. The mediator accepts the patient's decision when he accepts an apology instead of a large sum of money. Fairness is achieved by the application of the parties' values to their situation and by the exercise of their self-determination to arrive at a freely chosen outcome.

INFORMED CONSENT. In the cases above, the parties know they might win in court what they choose to give away. The divorcing spouse knows that wives are entitled to a portion of their spouse's assets; the patient knows that he could get some compensation for the damage to his good knee. Part of the value each derives from the decision is a moral congruence, perhaps an affirmation that they are a strong or good person or that they have done the right thing. Nelson Mandela, Martin Luther King Jr., Mother Teresa—and many more not-so-famous people—would make decisions about what to take and what to give that might not be economically "rational." The decisions, though, are meaningful in part because they are informed; the parties know what is being chosen and why. In a situation where a party's choice is made without knowledge of the law or norm that is applicable, the question of what is ethically required of the mediator becomes more complex.

THE SLIP-AND-FALL CASE. What should the mediator do when confronted with the Tongan plaintiff who seems to be making a decision in ignorance of his legal entitlements? Should the mediator allow the plaintiff to settle for $20,000 when the mediator believes the claim is worth $200,000 and the plaintiff and his lawyer appear ignorant of the value of the case? The concern is whether the mediator should ensure that the plaintiff's consent to the settlement is informed by the knowledge of what the law would likely provide.

In the following, I analyze the case in terms of five important considerations:

1. A preference for informed consent
2. The imperative that the party must make the decision
3. The requirement that the mediator remain impartial
4. Power imbalance
5. The reality that nobody "knows" what a judge or jury would do

A Preference for Informed Consent. Of course, fully informed decision making is best. Any mediator would prefer that parties play with a "full deck."[38] Informed decisions enhance the durability of settlements and prevent the remorse that would accompany learning of possible foregone benefits too late. The Model Standards of Conduct for Mediators articulate a preference for informed party choice, defining *self-determination* as "the act of coming to a voluntary, uncoerced decision in which each party makes free and *informed* choices as to ... outcome [emphasis added]."

A premise of good practice for mediators is to ensure decisions are as thoughtful as they can be. A mediator—as a component of good practice—develops and expands the information base on which decisions are premised. She calls for the parties to uncover assumptions and refine evaluations—both practical and legal—in light of what the other side is saying and by further reflection and sometimes research. She may urge unrepresented parties to get legal counsel. She may ask lawyers to rethink their analysis.

In the Tongan case, she may ask the Tongan lawyer whether he may have overlooked arguments for recovery. She may also ask the lawyer for the convenience store whether there may be other legal theories under which the store would be liable to a potential customer, like the Tongan, who used the restroom or whether the lawyer would be comfortable making his legal argument to the judge. The mediator would properly explore with the Tongan client what costs the client foresees—in both the past and the future—given an injury of this nature. She may ask the Tongan lawyer (perhaps in a caucus so as not to embarrass him) whether he has checked with lawyers specializing in the area about the case's value and whether he has reviewed relevant guides regarding the value of the particular injuries. This urging of the mediator for the parties to inform themselves about the likely court outcome is a prompting toward informed consent. If a party, after being urged to inform himself, chooses not to do that, then regardless of the outcome agreed to by the party, the choice itself is informed by the decision not to seek further information. If, for a variety of possible reasons, the Tongan client prefers $20,000 now rather than making any further effort to research more thoroughly or rather than the possibility of $200,000 later, that is a choice that many might make.

To summarize, the preference for informed consent would mean that the mediator would properly

- Urge an unrepresented party to get professional advice (but then accept the party's choice not to do that).

- Ask whether the Tongan client would seek more if he thought the case were worth more. If the answer is yes, then urge more research. If the answer is no, then proceed with the settlement.

- Challenge the legal analysis of both attorneys if the mediator sees or suspects flaws in the analysis.

Even if the average person would want to make a decision in light of adequate information about his or her legal rights, a particular person might choose not to make the effort, take the time, or spend more money to do that. Some would prefer consulting an astrologer or a priest rather than getting more (or any) legal advice. Such preferences should be honored as long as the mediator has urged that the party consider getting informed. Note, though, that the mediator is not the source of the legal advice itself, but rather a catalyst for the party (and his or her attorney) to get more or better information—if the party wants to do that.

The Party Must Decide. The temptation the hypothetical dangles is that the mediator "knows" what the case is worth and consequently should tell the plaintiff. Even if it were possible to know the objective worth of a case (an assumption challenged below), the mediator does not know what the case is worth to the particular plaintiff:

- Maybe both Tongans don't want to appear in court for reasons of their own.

- Maybe the Tongan client really needs $20,000 today (to pay his debts, to secure a job, to make an investment, for his sick child), and the money in pocket is far more valuable than any future payment.

- Maybe the Tongans feel that $20,000 is a remarkable "gift"—given that no such settlement would ever occur in Tonga and the plaintiff feels bad about using the convenience store with no intention to be a customer.

In all cases, the Tongan, like the divorcing woman or the patient whose good knee was operated on, should be free to make a decision that serves ends that others might question. That is the meaning of freedom and self-determination. Even if the average person would always take more (money, land, goods), a given party might have unique priorities and preferences that should be honored.

The Mediator Must Remain Impartial. The preference for informed consent does not authorize the mediator to serve as the source of legal (or other) counsel that could direct a decision. Mediator impartiality is central to the mediation process. The Model Standards of Conduct for Mediators in Standard II, Impartiality, mandates not only that the mediator be impartial but also that the mediator appear impartial.

Any advice the mediator would give about the value of the case would favor one party over the other. If the mediator tells the Tongan that the case is worth $200,000, then the $20,000 offer is degraded in the eyes of the Tongans. Conversely, the mediator has handed the Tongans a bargaining chip worth (arguably) $180,000. Assuming that the defendants value the case far differently, the mediator may have succeeded in shutting bargaining down altogether. That shift from neutral to partisan is a shift that jeopardizes not only the mediator's actual neutrality, but also her perception of being neutral in the eyes of the parties. The mediator has done what a neutral expert would do and, in the shift in role, has lost her impartiality as a mediator.

So the mediator should not provide the evaluation, though she should urge the parties to seek it themselves—if they want to do that.

Of course, the mediator who urges parties to consider further legal counsel cannot escape the fact that such a suggestion in itself may be perceived as an evaluation that the proposed settlement figure is or may be out of line with the likely court outcome. The mediator response, however, is that she, in an evenhanded way, urges all parties to consider making more informed decisions. Asking questions is central to the mediator's job. Answering questions is not.

A Concern About Power Imbalance. The Tongan hypothetical is poignant because the plaintiff does not understand English (much less the nuances of a foreign country's law) and the plaintiff's lawyer appears inept. One imagines, with these facts, a weak plaintiff with a weak lawyer up against a corporate giant (the convenience store parent) with top-notch (and perhaps unscrupulous, given the legal theory advanced) counsel—a strong defendant with strong counsel. Does fairness demand that the mediator correct this power imbalance?

First, it is worth noting that a judge, jury, or arbitrator in an adversarial system cannot correct the power imbalance. Neither can—or should—the mediator equalize the power balance by becoming an advocate for the plaintiff or by supplying the legal counsel that the Tongan attorney seemingly fails to supply.[39]

Second, the mediator does empower the plaintiff by urging the plaintiff to become more fully informed. This begins, as a matter of good process, by the mediator's insisting on the presence of an interpreter for the non-English-speaking party so he can fully understand and participate in the process. By exploring with the Tongan team whether there may be more information worth obtaining before a deal is struck, the mediator does, again, address the imbalance. Knowledge is power, and informed decision making is at the heart of mediation. The plaintiff is not pushed into a deal but rather put on notice that he is responsible for obtaining information sufficient to ensure his own satisfaction with the fairness of the deal. The pause or check to the negotiation is some corrective to the power imbalance—at least as compared to negotiation without a mediator.

To change the hypothetical, if the plaintiff were unrepresented and defendant's lawyers were characterizing the law as giving plaintiff no cause of action, the mediator could quite properly note that plaintiff has heard the argument that defendant's lawyer will make and might want to hear what plaintiff's own lawyers would say in response! The presence of a poor lawyer in many ways makes the challenge more delicate and difficult for the mediator concerned about informed consent.

Nobody "Knows" What a Judge or Jury Would Do. The hypothetical is structured as if the mediator "knows" that the plaintiff's claim is worth $200,000. While one can make an educated guess about what a claim is worth, experts will differ on the same facts. There is no certain predictability with respect to any third-party evaluation. Consequently a mediator should not become a neutral expert or provide legal analysis. Judges, arbitrators, and neutral experts give decisions or provide advice because that is their job. Everyone knows that the answers provided by such decision makers are fallible conclusions. Supreme Court judges, after all—the most sophisticated jurists in the country—regularly come out differently on the same facts.

The mediator—by virtue of her job—knows that she does not know. She will never know all the relevant facts. She will never research the relevant law the way an attorney or neutral expert would. She is not charged with deciding like a judge or arbitrator. She is free not to know and retains much of her power and usefulness by knowing that she does not know the answer to the question the dispute poses. The answer is left to the parties.

If all parties requested that the mediator provide legal analysis, then the mediator might consider switching roles. However, her analysis is only as good as the process producing it. Did the mediator look at all the evidence the way an arbitrator would? Did the mediator go (metaphorically) to the library or seek advice from expert colleagues as a lawyer or expert would? Can the mediator screen out information learned in caucus that another neutral would never hear? The challenge with switching roles is being sure that the job is done—whatever the role requires—at the highest level.

THE WRONGFUL DEATH CASE. In the Tongan hypothetical, there is considerable latitude about what the plaintiff should know because of speculation about what a particular decision maker would do and because of the inevitable difference in opinion about the value of a particular case. How about a situation, like the wrongful death case, where clear standing rules appear to dictate—in a more cut-and-dried manner—the litigation outcome?

The analysis again starts with noting the preference for informed decision making. Here, both parties have attorneys who could and should supply information about the standing requirements. Consequently, a mediator should be able to relax as other professionals bear the responsibility of providing legal information as a base for informed decisions. The mediator might ask both attorneys whether they see any potential weaknesses or land mines in their case. If neither points out the potential standing problem and if the bargaining proceeds to a settlement, the mediator has done her job.

These facts do not present a problem of a power imbalance, as both attorneys seem (equally) inept without either having any noted handicap (like the Tongan lawyer). While the mediator would prefer that both sides fully understood the law (here, on standing), the mediator should not become a legal counselor, as such a move exceeds the limits of her job and, in this case, would grossly favor the defendant. It should be some solace to the mediator that perhaps case law has carved out some exceptions to the standing rule, and consequently the mediator may be wrong about the law. The principle of unknowability also suggests that there may be reasons, unknown to the mediator, explaining why the defendant is so ready to pay for the wrongful death. So the mediator should allow the bargaining to continue to its natural conclusion.

However, what if the plaintiff is unduly demanding and uncompromising? Ordinarily, the mediator would explore potential risks and weaknesses where a party is jeopardizing a settlement. In such a case, the mediator might—in a caucus with the plaintiff's attorney—inquire about the standing issue. Plaintiff's lawyer, after all, may have a good answer (the principle of unknowability and the mandate for mediator humility suggest this possibility). The most likely result of the inquiry would be to encourage plaintiff to take a more moderate position that might lead to a deal.

The same inquiry about standing, however, should not be made of defendant's lawyer because it would too radically interfere with mediator impartiality and might completely change the bargaining endowments of the parties. Asking defendant about the standing issue would give him a potent weapon, making his BATNA (best alternative to a negotiated agreement) radically better. The most likely result of the inquiry would be that defendant would feel so powerful as a result of his newly perceived BATNA that he would walk away from the mediation. Whatever sense of responsibility for the death of plaintiff's brother that defendant felt might be swallowed by his perception that he is untouchable in litigation. That information (if indeed it is accurate) should come from his lawyer.

The asymmetry of asking plaintiff about the standing question without giving defendant the same prompt is undeniably troubling, but less troubling than the consequences of raising the standing question with both parties. The asymmetry is in keeping with the mediator role of challenging parties with respect to potential vulnerabilities—"reality testing" positions and proposals. It is also in keeping with adopting an impartial position that does not radically favor one side or the other.

Assuming a settlement is reached with plaintiff knowing he would not have standing in litigation (thanks to the mediator's question) and with a defendant ignorant of that fact, fairness is satisfied by the fact that, whatever action the defendant took that resulted in the wrongful death, he was willing to pay for (at least when he thought a court might require a payment to the plaintiff), and he chose his legal adviser and must live with the quality of the advice.

DIFFERENT MODELS: DISCLAIMER. Different practice models might provide different answers to these hypotheticals. Evaluative mediators might be quite comfortable giving the Tongan case parties an acceptable settlement range or being more forthcoming on the standing issue in the wrongful death case.[40] Norm-educating mediators would freely share with the parties what the public norms were, and norm-advocating mediators would require that parties settle in keeping with public norms.[41] Mediators in these schools might be willing to tell the Tongans that the case is worth approximately $200,000, and they might be willing to raise the standing question with both plaintiff and defendant. Some mediators would be highly uncomfortable "allowing" a settlement that was too far out of the range they felt was appropriate or that differed significantly from the likely court outcome. If the parties affirmatively chose a model of mediation where the neutral was expected to provide such evaluative input, then its provision could arguably further self-determination.

I practice a facilitative approach to mediation, one that values the parties' sense of fairness in the mediation context over fairness embodied in public legal norms. So while informed consent is important, I must view it in the context that parties are informed by many things beyond legal norms, and that they are free to choose how much information they need to make a decision. By the principle of unknowability, I must be very humble about what I "know," preferring instead to charge the parties with learning more—if they choose to do that—and making their own decisions about what's fair, as well as about the sources of information that they choose to pursue.

CONCLUSION. Albert Einstein once said, "Whoever undertakes to set himself up as a judge in the field of truth or knowledge is shipwrecked by the laughter of the gods." Mediators do not share the power of judges and arbiters, who, in the context of resolving disputes, are charged with being godlike. Mediators do not have a final say, as an expert adviser would. In their more humble role of asking questions and letting the parties determine both the facts and the principles that will govern their decisions, mediators urge parties to be wiser and more careful. An advertisement for Ditech (which provides home financing) says: "You've Got a Brain. So We'll Treat You That Way." Like Ditech, mediators assume "People Are Smart" (the Ditech logo).

In the hypotheticals, neither the Tongan client nor the parties in the wrongful death action get what a client hiring an attorney bargains for: competent legal advice. However, they are not hiring the mediator to provide that service. They will hear the mediator asking questions.

They will see their attorneys in action. They can make ongoing judgments about the competence of their attorneys. For the mediator to provide legal information or advice when it radically benefits one side means that the mediator is stepping dangerously out of role and, at the same time, benefiting one party over another. The mediator will urge parties to get more information and gently push them—in appropriate circumstances where the mediator's neutrality is not compromised—toward certain sources of information.

Litigation and arbitration and expert opinions are all based on a paternalistic instinct that seeks a powerful third party who will sort things out for the disputants. Mediation is not paternalistic: the parties not only retain the power to decide the outcome; they also retain the power to decide what information they need to move toward a resolution. Where parties elect to have legal counsel but choose inept lawyers, the mediator cannot make up for the deficiency except insofar as the client or party is kept actively engaged in the mediation and can be an ongoing judge of the competence of the attorney he has chosen.

Comments on Cases 5.3 and 5.4

Jacqueline Nolan-Haley

The slip-and-fall case with the recent Tongan immigrant presents an uncomfortable scenario that sadly may be all too familiar to mediators in court-connected mediation programs, where settlement agreements are often made in ignorance of a party's legal entitlements. The Tongan plaintiff is arguably less sympathetic than the typical pro se[42] party in court mediation programs because at least he has a representative who has been designated to protect his legal rights. At the same time, however, he may be more sympathetic because of his misplaced trust in an incompetent attorney. The problem of attorney incompetence also arises in the wrongful death case.

Focusing on substantive fairness, both cases raise questions about the extent of a mediator's obligation to intervene when she thinks that a litigant is getting a raw deal due to counsel's mistakes. Assuming (as I do) that mediators should be concerned with the substantive fairness of agreements reached in mediation, the nature of an attorney's incompetence may make a difference in what a mediator does in the name of fairness or "fairness interventions." In these two cases, there should be greater fairness interventions with the Tongan plaintiff's attorney, who is unfamiliar with U.S. legal doctrine and local settlement culture, than with the attorneys in the wrongful death car crash case, who simply failed to read the relevant court rules.

THE PROBLEM OF INFORMED CONSENT. These cases trigger difficult issues related to informed consent, a fundamental principle of authentic mediation that requires parties to understand what they are doing when they agree to participate, while they participate, and when they reach a settlement in mediation. The principle of informed consent is not an end in itself but a means of achieving fairness, a basic goal in any dispute resolution system, and one that requires substantive as well as procedural justice.[43]

Contemporary mediation discourse reinforces the centrality of consent in mediation. The Model Standards require that the mediator conduct the process based on the principle of self-determination, "the act of coming to a voluntary, uncoerced decision in which each party makes free and informed choices as to process and outcome."[44] Similarly, the European Code of Conduct for Mediators requires that the mediator take "all appropriate measures to ensure that any understanding is reached by all parties through knowing and informed consent."[45]

There are two aspects of consent in mediation, one relating to participation and the other to outcome. Participation consent requires that parties make a conscious, knowledgeable decision to enter into the mediation process and to continue participating in good faith.[46] Outcome consent requires that an agreement be reached with an understanding of its content, its consequences, and what entitlements may be waived by giving consent.[47] The critical concern in these cases is the quality, and perhaps even the potential validity, of outcome consent. No doubt the Tongan plaintiff, suffering permanent nerve damage, incurring substantial debt, without a job and medical insurance, is "consenting" to the proposed outcome of $20,000 based on his obvious financial needs. But if the mediator is correct in her assessment that the case is worth about $200,000, how likely is it that this plaintiff is making an informed settlement choice? Likewise, in the car crash case, if the mediator knows for certain that the plaintiff has no standing to sue for wrongful death, then the defendant is probably bargaining in the dark, and any agreement reached will be suspect.

THE MEDIATORS' OPTIONS. Several unknowns in these narratives could affect the ethical course of action for these mediators. We do not know the context in which these mediations occurred. Were they in court? Were they mandated by the court? Context matters a great deal in mediation, and the ethical mediator's behavior may differ depending on the answers to these questions. We should expect higher levels of fairness interventions if mediation occurs in, or is ordered by, the court, particularly if there are power imbalances between the parties or if the court selects the mediator. Courts and society have a vested interest in the substantive fairness delivered by judicially sponsored mediation. Court mediation is linked to the public justice system and calls for more diligence in fairness interventions than does private mediation. Most parties who are required by courts to participate in mediation originally came to court with expectations of public justice reviewable through the appellate process. They did not intend a regime of secret justice without accountability.

Where should the ethical mediator look for guidance? Multiple ethics codes, many of which are internally inconsistent, adorn the mediation regulatory landscape.[48] Consider the Model Standards. Standard I, Self-Determination, requires that parties make free and informed choices as to both process and outcome. Comment 2 to that Standard then relieves the mediator of personal responsibility for decisions based on informed consent. Standard II, Impartiality, requires that the mediator conduct the process in an impartial manner and avoid conduct that gives the appearance of partiality. On the other hand, Standard VI, Quality of the Process, may affect mediator neutrality by requiring that the mediator promote honesty and candor and not knowingly misrepresent any material fact or circumstance in the course of the mediation.[49]

A mediator who is tethered to an absolutist interpretation of the Model Standards will become confused. Honoring the self-determination principle of Standard I but knowing that she is not responsible for ensuring informed consent, she could follow Comment 2 and "make the parties aware of the importance of consulting other professionals to help them make informed choices." But the parties in both these cases have already relied on legal professionals, albeit incompetent ones. Where does this leave the mediator?

Focusing on the impartiality requirement of Standard II, the mediator could take a "tough luck" approach and rely on the lawyers to do their job. If the parties have postmediation buyer's remorse, they may have legal recourse against their attorneys. Although this course of action sounds logical, reasonable, and legally defensible, it is not clear whether it would achieve justice. Would it be fair to a party and attorney who are unfamiliar with our legal system? Suppose the defendant in the slip-and-fall case is a repeat player who has settled similar cases with other unknowing immigrants? What happens to public confidence in the justice system and the Model Standards' goal to promote public confidence in mediation as a process for resolving disputes?[50]

Alternatively, the mediators could rely on the Standard VI requirement to promote honesty and candor and the caveat against misrepresentation of material facts. From this perspective, the mediator's silence in both cases might amount to misrepresentation of a material fact or circumstance, and she would be required "to take appropriate steps including, if necessary, postponing, withdrawing from or terminating the mediation."[51]

WHAT SHOULD THE MEDIATORS DO? These mediators need to work within the framework of the Model Standards, principles of substantive and procedural justice, and common sense. The Model Standards must be understood in context, not as absolutes.[52] Fairness principles of procedural and substantive justice should resolve any internal tensions between party self-determination and mediator neutrality. The mediator is more than a self-determination cheerleader for the parties' deal making or an impartial potted plant. She is involved in a trust relationship with the parties.[53] This relationship assumes that the mediator will be sensitive to substantive fairness issues and be concerned that parties do not unwittingly get a raw deal. While the principle of informed consent does not require that mediators offer parties and their attorneys specific legal evaluations (a risky proposition if done without party consent), it does require some mediator nudging in the interests of substantive fairness.[54] In both of these cases, mediator nudging is directed toward moving parties away from their proposed settlements.

The Slip-and-Fall Case. Fairness requires an explicit acknowledgment of the Tongan plaintiff's predicament, namely, that both he and his attorney are unfamiliar with the U.S. legal system and the local settlement culture in slip-and-fall cases. Presumably the defendant's attorney is familiar with both. This obvious power imbalance should motivate the mediator to engage in specific fairness interventions that include

1. Speaking privately with the Tongan attorney and asking him to review the relevant legal doctrine and then to rethink the settlement agreement.

2. Suggesting privately to the Tongan attorney that he consult with local personal injury lawyers before advising his client to settle for $20,000.[55]

3. Speaking with both the plaintiff and his attorney to suggest that they reconsider the amount of the settlement.

4. Reminding the plaintiff and his lawyer that by agreeing to resolve this claim through the mediation process, the plaintiff may be waiving greater rights and benefits that might otherwise be available.[56]

5. Suspending or terminating the mediation to give the parties time to decide what to do. If, despite the mediator's multiple efforts to get the parties to rethink the amount of the settlement, the Tongan plaintiff and his attorney still want to accept the offer of $20,000, that is their decision.

The Wrongful Death (Car Crash) Case. This case requires minimal fairness interventions by the mediator. In contrast to the Tongan plaintiff's attorney, these attorneys are familiar with U.S. law and the local settlement culture. They failed to read the local court rules, and there seems to be no excuse for their negligence. Nevertheless, because it appears that this mediation occurred in court, there is a higher threshold for fairness than would be required if this were a purely private negotiation. The mediator should meet privately with both attorneys before the mediation session begins, urge them to read the local court rules, and then discuss them with their clients. After all, the doctrine of informed consent also applies to the attorney-client relationship. If, after having read the rules, the attorneys and their clients still wish to mediate, the mediator could continue to facilitate their negotiations. Presuming good faith, the mediator could believe that the lawyers actually read the rules. There could be many reasons, including reputation and goodwill, that might prompt the defendant to offer a settlement despite the plaintiff's lack of standing to sue.

GOING FORWARD. Given the pervasiveness of judicially sponsored mediation programs, problems of substantive fairness are not going away. Going forward, we are challenged to develop new frameworks for safeguarding the integrity of mediation when it takes place in the civil justice system.

While mediated negotiations are not in any way akin to plea bargaining, it may be worth looking at what happens in the criminal justice system before parties give up their legal rights. In criminal cases involving plea negotiations, the judge is required to satisfy himself that the defendant's plea is voluntary and that the defendant understands the nature of the charges. To accomplish this, the judge engages in a colloquy with the defendant and asks a series of questions designed to inform the defendant of his rights and probe his state of mind. A sentence cannot be imposed until the judge is satisfied that the plea is voluntary and made with an understanding of its consequences.

In the civil justice system, in situations where the mediator knows for sure that one of the parties is unwittingly getting a raw deal, perhaps we should begin to imagine and construct a colloquy with the mediator and that party, and think about the kinds of questions that mediators should ask before a party agrees to a settlement. The end product could turn out to be a standardized process for safeguarding the substantive fairness of agreements reached in mediation.

Editor's Thoughts on Cases 5.3 and 5.4 and the Comments

Philosophically our two commentators begin at different points and emphasize different values. But when it comes to practical interventions in the cases provided, they do not end up so very far apart. Their preferred responses highlight what some say is the difference between evaluative and facilitative approaches: questions versus statements. Love would nudge the disputants toward information sources with a series of questions, Nolan-Haley with declarative statements.

But note that Love would defer to disputants who determine their information base is sufficient for decision, even if the mediator believes more information is warranted. Deciding how much information one needs to decide is, she states, part of self-determination. Nolan-Haley is not so sure, suggesting, in her coda, that perhaps in court-connected mediation, some colloquy between mediator and disputant is necessary to ensure that parties don't agree to bad deals due to an inaccurate or incomplete knowledge base.

Love's focus throughout her discussion is on ensuring that parties get to make all the important decisions in mediation, including how much information they want or need before reaching agreement. Justice in mediation, she reminds us, is what the parties decide, not what the mediator or anyone else would determine was a fitting conclusion to the dispute.

Those who would adopt alternative notions of justice in mediation must, she counsels, be both humble and pragmatic. Humility is called for because one can't really know what a judge or jury will do in a particular factual and legal context. A mediator who fixes on a predicted judicial outcome as the justice benchmark has to concede some level of fictive imagining. The true content of that benchmark is unknowable.

Pragmatism is called for because the power imbalance that is skewing decision making in mediation is sure to loom large in alternative forums as well. Litigation, Love notes, does not filter out power disparities. Often it accentuates them. And the mediator is not called in to the dispute to eliminate such disparities. She is there to help facilitate a resolution. The humble and pragmatic mediator will keep her limited capacity and authority in mind.

Nolan-Haley begins with the assumption that mediators need to be concerned with substantive fairness, even more so if the parties were sent or encouraged to try mediation by the court. In court-connected mediation, she observes, parties bring their dispute to the courts with an expectation that they will be receiving public justice. It is not right, in this context, to simply redefine the terms so that public definitions of equity no longer apply. In court-connected mediation, keeping an eye out for "public justice" and making sure parties don't get a "raw deal" is, she asserts, part of the mediator's duties of trust and fealty.

Nolan-Haley assumes that legal rules and decisions have something valuable to say about fairness and equity, and she doesn't seem overly bothered by the unknowability problem. But regardless of their different philosophical points of origin, both Love and Nolan-Haley come to occupy similar terrain when it comes to practical recommendations.

Both would press the plaintiff, his attorney, or both, to rethink their approach to the case. Love would ask questions—"If you thought the case were worth more, would you ask for more?" Nolan-Haley would speak to the Tongan attorney alone and "suggest" he consult with local personal injury lawyers or review relevant legal doctrine. Both would challenge the plaintiff attorney's legal analysis and push toward a reevalaution—with varying degrees of assertiveness and persistence.

Paradoxically, in the wrongful death case, Love's proposed intervention appears more forceful. She would speak specifically to plaintiff's counsel on the standing question, especially if plaintiff were in an obstreperous cast of mind. Nolan-Haley, feeling that interventions in this case are less called for, would simply remind counsel on both sides to read the local rules. If the parties continued to move toward a six-figure resolution, she would continue to assist on the grounds that defendant may have other good reasons, apart from the threat of litigation, to offer a sizable settlement amount.

It is easy to focus on the differences, but the commentators' shared common ground is more notable. In the Tongan slip and fall, both would work to expand the plaintiff's understanding of his situation but would avoid coaching him to ask for a specific sum of money. Both are sensitive to the dangers implicit in remaining passive in the face of the plaintiff's confusion, but they are also wary of assuming an advisory or overly paternalistic role. Both deliberate deeply about the meaning of justice in mediation and strive to mold their practice to that vision. Both acknowledge that there are no magic solutions to the tensions implicit in pursuing informed consent and disputant autonomy, but nevertheless forge reasonable and thoughtful compromises that accord with their individual value preferences.

CHAPTER SIX

Information, Autonomy, and the Unrepresented Party

C ase 5.3 in the previous chapter featured a disputant with an ill-informed attorney. This posed problems for the mediator because that disputant was settling without a clear or accurate picture of his legal rights. Unrepresented parties who enter into mediation with a fuzzy view of the legal landscape pose similar challenges.

COMPLEXITIES WITH UNREPRESENTED PARTIES

Mediating with an unrepresented party (as occurred in case 4.2) poses unique challenges. The presence of competent counsel helps the mediator rest easy on a number of fronts. First, the mediator can assume that the parties have been provided accurate and relevant information about their legal entitlements. Presumably counsel has discussed the downsides of pursuing litigation as well as the possibilities of a stunning victory. It may be that counsel has painted an overly optimistic picture or has glossed over aspects of the case that deserve attention, but it is unlikely that an ably represented party will enter into mediation with no notion of what lies ahead. Second, counsel will protect an unrepresented party from false bluster or intimidating maneuvers from the other side. The presence of counsel does not eradicate all power imbalances; parties still enter mediation with different resources and external constraints. Still, an advocate can blunt the rhetorical excesses of a swaggering opponent and provide a counterpunch when the other side hits below the belt.

It could be argued that we need not worry about litigants who proceed pro se because these disputants are exercising their autonomy in moving forward without counsel. If we are serious about autonomy, we shouldn't blink at this choice and resulting limited nature of their understanding of the legal consequences. Yet the choice to forgo counsel is not always entirely free; it can be a product of need and necessity. Given the high cost of legal representation, many disputants can't afford the retainer fee. If we assume that all litigants proceeding pro se are willfully eschewing the protection a lawyer can confer, we may be mistaking privation for autonomy. As Anatole France observed, "The law in its majestic equality, forbids the rich as well as the poor from sleeping under bridges,"[1] but only the homeless poor need the shelter that a stone archway can provide. In like fashion, both rich and poor disputants may decide to handle their conflicts without counsel, but our confidence that the choice to proceed pro se is a matter of preference and not exigency should be greater with the rich as opposed to the poor.

In addition to creating problems with securing informed consent, unrepresented disputants may confuse the mediator's role with that of an advocate. Disputants want help with the choices they face. With no other professional in the room, they often ask the mediator for information, advice, and guidance. It is easy to forget that the mediator is a neutral and not a knight errant ready to lend horse, shield, and lance to protect against the other side.

Keeping Roles Clear

Concern over this potential for confusion is evident in Rule 2.4 of the ABA Model Rules of Professional Conduct for attorneys. This rule governs lawyers serving as third-party neutral and addresses the danger posed when unrepresented parties appear before a lawyer mediator looking for guidance. The rule makes clear that lawyer mediators must "inform unrepresented parties that the lawyer is not representing them. When the lawyer knows or reasonably should know that a party does not understand the lawyer's role in the matter, the lawyer shall explain the difference between the lawyer's role as a third-party neutral and the lawyer's role as one who represents a client."[2]

Although the rule does not specify exactly what a lawyer mediator should say to make this distinction clear, a Resolution on the Unauthorized Practice of Law authored by the ABA Section of Dispute Resolution provides some guidance on what such a conversation might entail. Mediators should explain that while attorneys owe their clients duties of exclusive loyalty, these sorts of duties do not exist between mediators and disputants.[3] Mediators can't work to the protection of one party and the detriment of another. Thus, even if information is provided about what may happen in court, that information is being given to help everyone make realistic choices, not to give one side a bargaining chip over the other.

A lawyer mediator's explanation to an unrepresented party might go something like this:

> Mr. Jones, Mr. Smith—thanks for coming today. It's pretty obvious from my letterhead and the diplomas in the office where we first met that I'm a lawyer. But it is really important that you both understand that I'm not serving in that capacity here. I don't represent either of you. If I did represent one of you, it would be my job to fight as hard as I could to get one of you the best possible deal. I would be in one of your corners—and distinctly not in the corner of the other. As a mediator, though, I'm not in anyone's corner. I'm here to root for and support a good outcome. So even if I provide some information about what I think might happen if you don't settle here, I'm not giving you this information because I'm rooting for you and trying to help you "win." It also means I'm not against you and trying to help the other side win. What I'm really hoping is that there are no winners or losers here but people who are making informed and thoughtful choices about how they want to move forward.
>
> Sometimes when people get in the room with lawyers, they start to feel like that lawyer just automatically turns into a fighter. But you must understand that I'm not able to protect or advance either of your individual interests. I strongly recommend you do consult with an attorney about what we talk about and decide here—and get that person's independent advice. That person—if you choose to consult an attorney—will be the person looking out exclusively for your interests, not me. Do you both understand my role here today?

Guidance from the Codes in Pro Se Court-Connected Mediation

Where the parties have initiated litigation and been referred to a court-connected mediator, the court has an obligation to encourage informed decision making. As the National Standards for Court-Connected Mediation Programs state, unrepresented parties should be informed that mediation is an option for them, and they are protected against undue pressure to settle. The standards say that courts should avoid taking an overly enthusiastic or overly cautious approach to unrepresented parties. Some courts preclude the participation of unrepresented parties for fear that they will be manipulated and misled in mediation. This is a mistake because it prevents some parties who could ably represent themselves from benefiting from mediation's informal structure. Other courts, seeking to lessen their backload, refer all cases of a certain class or relating to a particular topic, regardless of the parties' amenability to mediation. As the Standards maintain, "Neither option provides unrepresented parties with the degree of information or choice that is desirable."[4]

Most state codes governing court-connected mediation programs don't provide specific guidance relating to unrepresented parties. One may surmise, however, that codes that authorize mediators to withdraw or discontinue mediations marred by gross power imbalance or unconscionability may have been drafted with the seriously outgunned pro se in mind.[5] Codes that do explicitly discuss obligations to unrepresented parties focus on flagging the risks in going through the process without the aid of counsel.

Arguably the strongest, most restrictive language can be found in the guidelines for mediators practicing in the Kentucky courts. These standards say that a mediator who has reason to believe that a pro se party does not understand the mediator's neutral as opposed to representational role should not convene the process.[6]

Massachusetts also requires its mediators to assess whether unrepresented parties are adequately protected in the process, but not in the context of aborting the mediation. Massachusetts rules state that where parties proceed pro se and the neutral believes that independent legal counsel or expert information is needed to reach an informed agreement or protect individual rights, the neutral must share that judgment with the parties.[7]

North Carolina's standards for professionals "participating in mediated settlement conferences" require that pro se parties receive an explanation that "there may be risks in proceeding without independent counsel or other professional advisors." However, if a party, after having been given this explanation, declines to consult with a lawyer, the mediator "shall permit the mediation to go forward according to the parties' wishes."[8]

Texas standards also specify that mediators should alert pro se parties to the possibility of risk, but they offer no guidance in the event the party decides to go it alone anyway.[9]

The codes are generally permissive. Mediators must take great pains to explain that they do not and cannot provide the sorts of protections that attorneys do provide, and they must alert unrepresented parties to the possibility that they may be at a disadvantage without the assistance of an attorney; but if a party wants to go ahead, generally the codes pose no obstacle. Only if the impending agreement is unconscionable, manifestly unjust, or marred by gross power imbalances would some codes urge caution in continuing.[10]

"Helping" the Unrepresented Party

Talking to unrepresented parties about the difference between the neutral and representational role is one thing; successfully conveying that distinction is another. Some parties, despite your best efforts, will still look to you to tell them what to do. They may ask, "What would you do in my position?" and you know whatever reply you give will be perceived as the magic answer. The codes are clear that mediators should be careful not to supplant disputant decision making. This is particularly difficult when dealing with a party who feels unequal to the task of deciding and may in fact be so given her lack of information. What to do in that situation? Case 6.1 takes up that conundrum.

CASE 6.1: A COSTLY SNAP

Joleen pays her rent by working during the day as a hygienist in a dental practice. At night and on the weekends, she works on portrait photography, a career she is desperate to transition into. Joleen knows the local environs well and decorates her office with photos of rugged mountain and desert scenes from nearby locales.

When Carla, a well-known fashion model, came into the office to have veneers made, she noticed a stunning photo Joleen had on her desk and asked who the photographer was. When Joleen said it was her work, Carla asked if Joleen would like to help her update and improve her modeling portfolio. Joleen jumped at the chance. She had to buy some higher-quality photography equipment for the job, but she figured that the hefty fee that Carla quoted would more than make up for the investment.

Joleen took several days off from work and shot photos of Carla in a swimsuit against a background of desert rocks. Carla told Joleen that she would include the shots in her portfolio and that they would be helpful in getting callbacks at some of the fancier modeling houses. The sunset shots, including a number of interesting cloud formations that seemed to mirror Carla's silhouette, were particularly striking.

The excursion ended badly for Joleen. Carla never paid her for her efforts, and Joleen went into debt on the expensive photo equipment she purchased. Joleen's efforts at speaking with Carla about the unpaid invoices were unsuccessful. The insult became immeasurably more painful when Joleen discovered the cloud silhouette photo in an upscale fashion magazine. No one had ever contacted Joleen for permission to use the photos. Indeed, the way the article was written, it appeared as if the photos were taken by the magazine's head fashion photographer.

Hurt and upset at not being given credit for the artistic photo, Joleen sued Carla for the five thousand dollar payment she was promised when Carla asked her to help with her portfolio. She does not know what, if anything, can be done legally about the unauthorized use of the photo.

The case is referred to Frank, a court-connected mediator. Carla does not show up, but an attorney for Carla's modeling agency appears in her stead. He has in his possession a draft answer to Carla's complaint. The answer includes a generic counterclaim for defamation, intentional and negligent infliction of emotional distress, and invasion of privacy. It demands $200,000 in economic and noneconomic damages.

Joleen is shocked and terrified. She is deeply fearful that she could be at risk for "losing a lot of money" if she goes forward with her suit. Frank explains to Joleen that he is not an attorney, that he must function in a neutral fashion, and that she might benefit from receiving the help of independent counsel. Joleen begins to cry and says she is already in debt and can't afford one.

Carla's agency lawyer offers five hundred dollars to "get rid of this nonsense." This does not even begin to cover Joleen's equipment debt of several thousand dollars and does nothing to remedy the unauthorized use of the picture, but Joleen is nervous and tempted to do anything to get rid of those scary counterclaims. She continually asks Frank whether she should "just take the money," whether he thinks their offer is "fair," and what he would advise if she were his client.

What should Frank do?

Frank has two predicaments. First, he needs to decide whether Joleen understands his earlier explanation about the limits of his role. He has told her that he cannot serve as her attorney, but her appeals to his judgment and legal expertise suggest she may be unable to conform her behavior to those constraints. The second predicament arises when she asks what he thinks she should do and what he would suggest if she were his client; clearly she is trying to push Frank out of the mediator role and into that of an adviser.

Frank could repeat his explanation, perhaps with some concrete examples of what it is an attorney typically does as opposed to what a mediator is authorized to do. He could tell her that as a mediator, he is not in a position to opine on what is "fair" and advise her as if she were a client. Moreover, he could explain that the other side might justifiably question his impartiality if he were to pretend she were a client and direct her as to the proper response to their offer.

Joleen may or may not be able to absorb this information. It may be that she is led by her anxiety to continue to look to Frank for advice. If that is the case, the prudent course for Frank is to halt the mediation and talk to Joleen about her options.

If Joleen is able to comprehend the limits to Frank's role and stops asking him to tell her what to do, Frank still has some decisions to make. Is this the sort of case where the outcome is so unconscionable, the balance of power so off-kilter, the result so inequitable that Frank should withdraw on the grounds that continuing would violate the mandate to preside over a quality process?

The first thing to say is that there is no ethical constraint on Frank's squeamishness. If Frank had received payment from the parties and felt compelled to withdraw at a very early point in the process, it may be appropriate for Frank to refund the fee. However, it is not coercive or undermining for Frank to decide that he wants to disassociate himself from a process that he is confident fails to serve Joleen's long-term interests.

Although the facts provided are cursory, certainly a case could be made that Carla has treated Joleen badly and is now using threats and intimidation to avoid having to make things right. It would appear that Joleen is due not only the promised five thousand dollars, but also compensation and perhaps equitable relief for the unauthorized use of her photo. We don't know much about Carla and Joleen's communications about the photos, but we know that Joleen expected she would be credited as the photographer and was surprised to see her work in a commercial venue without her knowledge, permission, or attribution.

It also appears as if the agency's counsel has appended counterclaims to their answer purely to frighten Joleen. Filing suit for nonpayment of a contractual obligation typically doesn't give rise to an intentional infliction of emotional distress claim or any of the other legal violations being asserted. Defendant's counsel seems to be using the legal process as a battering ram—arguably a tortious act in and of itself.

In addition to fairness concerns, Frank might justifiably wonder if Joleen truly understands her options. The Model Standards and state corollaries make clear that if the concept of a quality process is to mean anything, it must mean at a minimum that parties comprehend "the process, issues, [and] settlement options" under discussion.[11] If Joleen doesn't understand that she has ownership rights in the pictures she took and doesn't understand the meaning (and vulnerabilities) of the counterclaims asserted against her, arguably her lack of understanding impairs the quality and integrity of the process as it unfolds.

Frank, then, has a number of options:

- He can withdraw.

- If he wants to continue with the mediation, he can insist that Joleen gain more information about her rights to her artistic production and brainstorm with her several low-cost ways of accomplishing that. It may be that small claims advisers or other affordable services are available.

- If Frank adheres to an evaluative approach to problem-solving mediation, he might consider giving some information himself about the property rights that artists enjoy and the proof burdens involved in the tort claims being alleged. The difficulty here is that it is unlikely that Joleen would be content with general information. Given her anxiety, it is likely that she would press Frank to tell her what to do with the information he is providing—and that is a line Frank must be careful not to cross. Frank must also be careful to emphasize that he has a limited understanding of the facts of the dispute, and—because he has been retained as a mediator, not an attorney—only a glancing familiarity with the relevant law, and so whatever information he can provide is of limited usefulness. Again, given how disoriented and confused Joleen appears, it is not clear that she will appreciate Frank's disclaimers and put his statements in proper perspective.

As a fourth option, Frank could simply preside in nondirective fashion over the mediation, abstaining from providing any information and telling Joleen that she needs to decide for herself if five hundred dollars is an adequate settlement. Certain mediation models might approve this course, but it plays into long-standing criticisms of mediation as a venue where the powerful and unscrupulous can run amok with impunity. Importantly, if the mediator were to continue mediating and help Joleen sign off on the five-hundred-dollar payment, the mediator should, at a minimum, ensure that Joleen understands that she is giving up certain entitlements that might be recognized in a court of law in order to get out of a dispute that she now finds frightening and unsettling. Although, as the Model Standards state, it is not always possible for a mediator to ensure informed consent, the mediator in this instance should focus on helping Joleen understand what she knows and doesn't know and get clear on the reasons she would settle in mediation, as opposed to pursuing her other options. Working with Joleen on this task may make it hard to preserve absolute impartiality. But in this instance, preserving unimpeachable impartiality would seem to come at too high a price.

CASE 6.2: TUNEMAKER "ATTORNEY"

In case 6.1 the danger was that the unrepresented party was moving toward settlement without adequate information. But what if the problem is reversed? What if the unrepresented party's lack of knowledge leads her to intransigence? Does ethics have anything to say about this problem? Consider this next case in which a defendant who thinks he knows everything doesn't realize how much he could use an attorney!

Tommy Tune is a pop singer who has been sued by the Shante Music Company regarding the ownership rights to certain songs Tune composed and performed while being represented and promoted by Shante.

Tune attended two years of law school before dropping out to pursue his singing career. His singing career has taken off of late, and his confidence regarding his singing abilities seems to be spilling over into other areas. He hired a lawyer to draft an answer to the complaint, but then fired the lawyer when he received the bill. He is representing himself at the mediation and, based on an afternoon he spent at the law library, is convinced that the laws of contract and intellectual property support his claim that he owes Shante nothing.

Shante's counsel sent the mediator, Bob, a copy of its agreement with Tune from the period the songs were generated. From his reading of the agreement, Bob is fairly certain that Tune is dead-wrong on the legal issues. Bob believes that the law obligates Tune to share with Shante some percentage of his profits from the songs; the only question is how much. Based on the revenue figures supplied by both Tune and Shante, Bob believes that Tune may be liable for as much as $150,000. The music company is loathe to become known in the industry as the company that swallows its young and is thus willing to settle for a much smaller amount. The company has asked for $50,000, but Bob suspects it would come down to $10,000 to stay out of the media limelight. Tune has been willing to offer only $1,000.

Shante's counsel appears reasonable. Its offer in mediation is much lower than a judge would likely award after reviewing the contract. Bob believes that Tune is blowing his last chance to make a decent deal because he doesn't have a lawyer.

What should Bob do?

Comments on Case 6.2

Michael Moffitt

This case poses a challenge only because of the combination of two different conclusions Tune has apparently reached.

TUNE'S TWO TROUBLING CONCLUSIONS. First, Tune has concluded that his alternative to settlement (in the commonly accepted lingo of negotiation, his BATNA) is more attractive than Shante's offer. Second, Tune has concluded that he is comfortable reaching the first conclusion without the assistance of legal counsel. And the mediator in this case disagrees with both of Tune's conclusions.

If Tune had not reached both of these conclusions, the mediator would face a far less serious challenge. If Tune's assessment of his BATNA roughly matched the mediator's assessment of Tune's BATNA, settlement would be far more likely and the mediator's job would be far easier. Or if Tune were represented by competent legal counsel, the mediator would surely have fewer qualms about the prospect that Tune might act on his (mis?)perception of his prospects in court. It is the combination of Tune's two conclusions that makes this challenging.

Fortunately, the combination of these two conclusions presents the mediator with several different possible avenues to explore.

THREE BASIC OPTIONS FOR A MEDIATOR. Faced with any potentially troublesome mediation dynamic, a mediator essentially has three choices:

1. Withdraw from the mediation.
2. Do nothing and permit the current dynamic to take its course.
3. Say or do something to try to affect the current dynamic.

Depending on the circumstance, each may be the most appropriate response from the mediator. But in the most complex and challenging circumstances, each of these responses comes with some cost, thus producing a dilemma.

Why Withdrawal Is Not Necessary Here. In some circumstances, the best response for a mediator is to withdraw from the mediation entirely. As a general matter, withdrawal is most appropriate when one of two dynamics is at play:

- The mediation dynamic is such that one or more of the parties is harmed or at risk of being harmed by the continuation of the mediation. For example, continuing a mediation after learning that the parties are in an abusive relationship would risk furthering the victimization.

- The mediator determines that something about the nature of the dispute or the agreement under consideration would be unworthy of the legitimacy that might be conferred on it if it were the product of a mediation. For example, no matter how agreeable the parties are to the proposed terms, a court-affiliated mediator really ought not to continue a mediation to resolve debts associated with illegal drug sales. Or if the mediator suspects that one of the parties is using the mediation to perpetuate a fraud on the other party, the mediator might not want to have mediation associated with the outcome.

In Tune's case, nothing suggests withdrawal. The nature of the dispute—a basic contract claim—does not raise any concerns about the legitimacy of a possible agreement. Furthermore, neither party is apparently harmed in any way by the continuation of the mediation. At most, they might lose some additional time if the mediation persisted and failed to reach settlement. But that hardly rises to the level of considerations that would demand withdrawal. And in all events, the scope of whatever harm might attach to continuation appears to be quite limited, given that the parties are about to reach an impasse anyway. In short, this dynamic does not present the mediator with any reason to call off the mediation.

Implications of Permitting the Dynamic to Continue. If the mediator were merely to say "okay" with respect to both of Tune's conclusions, the scenario suggests that the mediation would produce no agreement and the case would proceed to trial. A crafty student would almost certainly fight the hypothetical presented. ("Well, how can the mediator be so sure about what a court would do?" "Who is the mediator to say what's in Tune's interest?" "Who's to say this isn't part of Tune's negotiating ploy. Maybe he's just saying that now in order to try to get a more favorable deal a little later." And so on.) To be sure, the case for just saying okay becomes far more compelling the more we permit ourselves to ignore or explain away the basic feeling that Tune is making a serious mistake. But doing so removes the most interesting aspects of the scenario.

If we assume that the mediator does believe that both of Tune's decisions are ignorant and unwise, then the mediation principle most threatened by simply remaining silent is informed consent. Virtually every idealized vision of mediation includes the basic assumption that those who participate in a mediation fully understand and consent to the mediation process, fully understand and consent to the substance of any outcome, and fully understand the implications of their alternatives to settlement.

Is it tolerable to sit by while a party reaches a decision without adequate information? The eventual substantive outcome of the case is not the mediator's decision to make, of course. But we should not ignore the cost of doing nothing when a mediator sees a mediation dynamic in which one of the parties is incapable of making an informed decision. At some point, if a party is ignorant enough of the process, the implications of a proposal, or her or his alternatives to settlement, we cannot consider the outcome to have been the product of truly informed consent.

In this case, at the end of the day, if none of the other options available to the mediator were at all attractive, I do not think one could reasonably condemn a mediator who decided simply to let this mediation run its course. It is true that Tune's capacity to assess his decision is more limited than we might prefer to see. He did, however, have at least two years of legal training. (Yes, this might make him *more* dangerous than someone with no legal training, but he does at least have more familiarity with legal issues than the average pro se litigant.) The idea that he might wish to proceed without legal counsel, however unadvisable we may consider it, is not an intolerable judgment on his part. If we permit litigants to represent themselves in the far more complex arena of trial, we certainly cannot categorically reject the idea of a mediator permitting a party to reach a conclusion without legal counsel.

Truth be told, I would not feel great about the outcome if I simply let the mediation unfold on its current trajectory. Not helping the parties to reach an agreement would frustrate me, and I would be concerned about Tune's decision-making process. But I would take this course of action, without concern that I had engaged in an unethical practice, unless I could think of something more appropriate and effective.

Implications of Various Mediator Interventions. Considerable ink has been spilled in an effort to define what "real" mediation is, or what "real" mediators do, with the product being a nearly endless set of categorizations. (Is the mediator in question facilitative, directive, evaluative, transparent, transformative, problem solving, client centered, understanding based, and so on and so on?) I have no interest here in engaging those long-standing debates. In an effort to avoid them conspicuously, let me merely observe that a mediator might engage in a range of different kinds of interventions into the dynamic described in this problem. And each of those interventions has different implications.

Let me oversimplify the possible mediator interventions by suggesting that they might be plotted along a continuum of assertiveness (or, if you prefer, "pushiness" or "passivity" or "interventionism" or whatever other label captures the degree to which the mediator interjects her or his own conclusions into the conversation).

In Figure 6.1, I put words into Bob's mouth for purposes of illustrative simplicity. I have no doubt that a skilled mediator would be more articulate with each of these statements or interventions. I provide them merely as a way to illustrate the range of possible mediator responses to each of Tune's challenging conclusions.

Consider, for contrast purposes, the implications of engaging at the far right ends of these spectra—the most assertive or pushy set of responses. According to the facts of the scenario, each of these statements has the benefit of being truthful. We *do* think Tune has misestimated his BATNA, and we *do* think it is a mistake for him to be making these decisions without representation. Furthermore, each of the statements at the far right may maximize the chance that Tune will reach a different conclusion as to one or both of these issues, thereby increasing the chance that his ultimate decision will be the product of adequate information (informed consent).

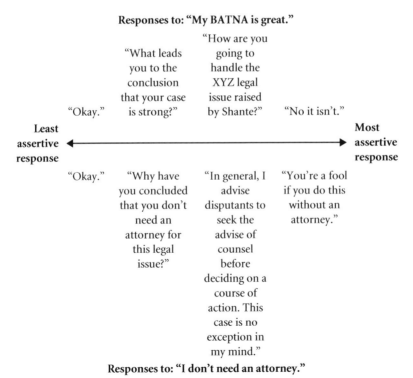

Figure 6.1.   Continuum of Possible Responses to Tune's Statements (or Implicit Assumptions)

The challenge with these most assertive mediator responses is that each of them implicates another fundamental principle of mediation. In one case, self-determination may be impaired, and in the other, the mediator's actions may cause the parties to change their perceptions of the mediator's impartiality or neutrality.

If the mediator tells Tune that he is a fool for making this decision without consulting an attorney, the mediator is at risk of impairing Tune's self-determination in this case. It is not merely that the mediator might affect Tune's eventual substantive decision ("Shall I settle on these terms or not?"). Nor is it that the mediator might affect Tune's decision on why to reach a particular decision ("Shall I spend money on an attorney or not?"). Instead, the mediator making this intervention would be substituting the mediator's judgment for how Tune is making the decision. I suspect we would be horrified if the circumstance were different and a mediator told a disputant, "This is an awfully big decision. You should definitely go and discuss it with your husband before you sign these papers." The principle of self-determination suggests that the decision whether to settle, for what reasons, and through what decision-making process is ultimately for each disputant to determine. The most assertive responses may, in some contexts, threaten aspects of that principle.

As to Tune's other conclusion, if the mediator tells Tune that he has reached an erroneous conclusion about his BATNA, the mediator may risk creating an appearance of partiality. (Depending on the specifics of the circumstance and the jurisdiction in question, it could also constitute legal malpractice or the unauthorized practice of law.) To be clear, I am not suggesting that mediators' impartiality is threatened every time they provide suggestions about likely court dispositions. Many mediators engage in conversations with parties about their perceptions of what a court would do with their cases, and sometimes mediators add their own perspectives on the question. Not all such comments necessarily implicate the mediator's impartiality, though the more assertive these interventions become, the more likely they are to create a perception of bias or favoritism.

In this scenario involving Tune and Shante, I am not convinced that the potential costs to self-determination or impartiality merit interventions at the far end of the assertiveness spectrum. As with the least assertive responses, I do not believe that commonly accepted mediator ethical principles would necessarily condemn a mediator who used maximally assertive responses; but I am not convinced that such responses are necessary here.

SOMETHING IN THE MIDDLE—PUSHING, BUT NOT TOO HARD. The farther left on either of these continua a mediator goes, the more she or he guards against an appearance of partiality and against trampling on Tune's self-determination. The farther to the right the mediator goes, the more the mediator would be aiming to augment Tune's informed consent to the outcome of the mediation (in this case, nonsettlement).

How about something in between? Push (in an effort to augment informed consent) but not too hard (in an effort to preserve self-determination and impartiality). Might that not do an adequate job of protecting all three?

Based only on the information provided in the description of this circumstance, if forced to choose just one intervention, I would probably choose one of the approaches nearer to the "assertive" end of the spectrum, but not at the very far end. Of course, this would depend on my read of the parties, the particulars that led me to the conclusions I had reached about the underlying legal merits, and the timing of the decision. But in an effort to avoid fighting the hypothetical or turning this answer into an unhelpful exercise in saying "it depends," I conclude that I would at least try to push Tune on one or both of the decisions that create the awkward feeling in this case.

If I explored Tune's conclusion about the legal merits of his position and if I encouraged Tune to seek legal counsel, and he persisted in choosing to reject Shante's offer pro se, I do not think I would lose sleep that night. The fact that the parties had not settled would probably bother me at a professional level. Still, I doubt that I would look back on my decision and wish that I had been any more or less assertive, and I do not believe that any articulations of mediator ethics would demand a different response from me.

I am open to the possibility that as a mediator, I am inappropriately drawn to moderate or centrist perspectives. But I sincerely believe that nothing in this circumstance calls for responses at either of the extremes of assertiveness.

The Goldilocks option—not too pushy and not too passive—fits this circumstance best.

Comments on Case 6.2

Dan Dozier

In my view, there is a wide range of permissible conduct in this case and only one central ethical requirement.

THE CENTRAL ETHICAL ISSUE: DETERMINING COMPETENCE. The ethical mediator is obliged to explore Tune's competence to participate and make decisions throughout the mediation process. That means, as the mediator, Bob would need to satisfy himself that Tune knew what he was doing—that he understood the facts of the dispute and understood the range of possible outcomes, including the option that he could be very wrong in his reading of the law. Bob would also need to be confident that Tune demonstrated some appreciation of the consequences of his being wrong. But if Bob came to the conclusion that Tune could understand and appreciate his situation—that he was taking a calculated risk by choosing to roll the litigation dice—he could ethically continue the mediation and encourage Tune and Shante to continue talking to one another for as long as they were willing.

If Tune ultimately chooses to reject Shante's offer, that is his choice. Bob should not attempt to talk him out of it or threaten to withdraw unless Tune "behaves reasonably." Behaving unreasonably is a party's right in mediation so long as the mediator is convinced that the "unreasonable" behavior does not reflect some deeper lack of emotional or mental capacity to process information and make decisions.

If Bob concluded that Tune was incompetent to make his own decisions, Bob should suggest that Tune obtain representation; if he refused to do so, Bob should withdraw from the mediation. To take this step, however, Bob would really have to come to a conclusion that Tune was so deluded as to the facts, the law, and the litigation process he faces that he could not represent himself in the mediation process.

ETHICAL CONSIDERATIONS. Bob should begin his thinking in this case by identifying the sections of the 2005 Model Standards that seem relevant. There are several:

- Section I, which is devoted to the concept of self-determination, provides that "a mediator *shall* conduct a mediation based on the principle of party self-determination [emphasis added]" and defines *self-determination* as "the act of coming to a voluntary, uncoerced decision in which each party makes free and informed choices as to process and outcome."

- Standard VI, Quality of the Process, also advises mediators to be cognizant of circumstances where "a party appears to have difficulty comprehending the process, issues, or settlement options" and to "explore the circumstances and potential accommodations, modifications or adjustments that would make possible the party's capacity to comprehend, participate and exercise self-determination." If a mediator has questions regarding party capacity, she should explore in greater depth the party's ability to participate in the process. This means questioning what the party understands about the goals and purposes of mediation, the issues they are convened to discuss, and the various options available for resolution. The Standards further provide that "if a mediator believes that participant conduct, including that of the mediator, jeopardizes conducting a mediation consistent with these Standards, a mediator *shall* take appropriate steps including, if necessary, postponing, withdrawing from or terminating the mediation [emphasis added]."[12]

GOOD MEDIATION PRACTICE. If a party takes a position that the mediator does not understand—for any reason, including expressing a position the mediator views as irrational or not in that party's interest—the mediator has a duty to inquire as deeply as necessary to try to understand the merits of the viewpoint as well as the supporting reasons. The party's emotional state and motivations should also be taken into account. This duty to inquire is real, it is substantial, and it is ongoing.

Importantly, it is not for the mediator to decide that Tune is "acting crazy" and needs to be "set straight." So long as Tune can articulate a credible rationale for clinging to his position—and so long as he can engage in a rudimentary assessment of the risks and benefits of doing so—he should be supported in his decisions. It is only when a party truly lacks the ability to take in relevant information or assess its meaning that the mediator must ethically intervene and change the course of the discussion.

In this case, the mediator could engage in a colloquy that would allow him to gauge Tune's capacity and delve further into the reasons for his intransigence. For example, the mediator should spend time in private caucus discussions with Tune about the details of Tune's understanding of the law and the issues related to his exposure to damages; how he developed this understanding; whom he consulted about these issues; the consequences if his understanding is incorrect; and whether there are any other reasons, beyond his view of the law, that might be influencing his opinion. These discussions might also include asking Tune to engage in some role-playing exercises to explore the consequences of his position—where the mediator presents different views of the law and explores the issues with Tune.

These discussions might, depending on the nature and timing of the mediation, occur more than once and over a period of time. Were I the mediator, I would be sure to have these discussions when I was meeting privately with Tune, and before I broached the topic, I would first solicit Tune's agreement to engage in this line of inquiry.

In the end, were I in Bob's shoes and if I were satisfied that Tune is competent and able to act rationally on his own behalf, I would feel compelled to continue in my facilitative role—which would entail assisting Tune in advancing his views, even if they appeared to me misguided, ill formed, and possibly self-defeating. If Tune is indeed competent, it would be improper and unethical for the mediator to substitute her or his judgment regarding the value of the settlement and to withdraw from or otherwise derail the discussions.

KEEPING AN EYE OUT FOR THE INTANGIBLES. Tune's hardened stance may be less a product of his legal imagination and more a function of the other intangibles of the case. The mediator should pay close attention to not only the issues in the dispute but the human aspects of the negotiations. The parties' relationships and the emotions aroused between them may be playing a crucial role in Tune's refusal to see reason.

A small example of the need to pay attention to these concerns can be seen in a case I mediated between two nonprofit organizations that often worked together and competed with each other. They were negotiating over a code of conduct that would enable them to compete and cooperate at the same time. The negotiations took place about once a month over roughly six months in various cities around the country. At the last session, where almost all of the issues had been settled, the negotiations got stuck on a minor issue. It was late on a Saturday evening, and I could not understand why the parties were unable to move on this last, small issue. I knew the parties wanted to settle and finish for the evening.

The more I tried to understand what was holding matters up, the harder the issue seemed to get. Finally, a wise attorney for one of the parties suggested that we take a break and go out to dinner together. We did so. When we returned—by then, late in the evening—the issue settled quickly. I learned that human needs—for sustenance, for relief from tension, for human contact of a personal sort—can sometimes spell the difference between coming together or remaining apart. With these parties under these circumstances, it worked.

LETTING THE DISPUTANTS CALL THE SHOTS, EVEN WHEN THEY SEEM TO BE SHOOTING BLANKS. My inclination to avoid pressure—or more directive tactics in the face of disputant missteps (or what I perceive to be missteps)—stems in part from my professional experiences. My own practice as both an attorney and mediator has afforded me front-row seats to the drama of parties' rejecting or accepting offers when I would have done the opposite. In a good number of those instances, the parties walked away from the negotiations satisfied with their decisions.

For example, I worked as a settlement counsel for a party involved in a rather large business dispute. There is no doubt that the client was competent and fully able to represent his own interests; nor is there any doubt that he is a difficult person who bargained, as he put it, "from the gut mano a mano."

This client wanted to settle the case but was very distrustful of mediation because he did not perceive himself to be fully in control of the negotiations. His whole business career was based on one-on-one negotiations without the intrusions of a third party. He was much more comfortable meeting alone with the decision maker on the other side to cut the deal. As the attorney on the case responsible for trying to settle the matter without litigation—a role the client requested I play—I agreed with many suggestions the mediator made regarding how the case could be settled. The client rejected most of those suggestions, as was his right. He strongly believed that he would settle the dispute by meeting privately—without mediators, attorneys, or staff. And he was correct: the case settled on terms the client wanted.

Had the mediator pushed, it is unlikely my client would have responded, except to recoil against the next mediation opportunity.

Editor's Thoughts on Case 6.2 and the Comments

Commentator Michael Moffitt helpfully offers up a fairy-tale analogy to the problem of the very confident Tommy Tune. As Moffitt points out, Tune appears to be going down a dubious path, both by choosing to negotiate without the assistance of counsel and in overestimating the appeal of his BATNA. If Bob takes too passive an approach, he risks failing in his duty to facilitate informed decision making. If Bob takes too directive or intrusive an approach, he risks stifling Tune's self-determination and compromising his impartiality.

Moffitt makes clear that even if the porridge is a tad hot or too turgidly cold, we probably don't have an ethical violation. Bob could let the mediation continue on its current trajectory without worrying that he was violating any of the field's ethical principles. After all, disputants frequently represent themselves in far more complex matters, and they retain the authority to decide not only how they wish to proceed on the substance, but the process by which they come to those substantive decisions. Still, as a personal matter, Moffitt says that if he were Bob, he would take the Goldilocks approach: not too passive to encourage informed decision making, not too pushy to preserve his impartiality and Tune's autonomy. As a practical matter, Moffitt would see himself falling closer to the pushier rather than the passive end of the spectrum, but he would not be at the extreme ("are you crazy, of course you should get a lawyer and settle") outermost point.

Dan Dozier characterizes his approach as highly supportive of party self-determination. He is in favor of "letting the disputants call the shots, even when they seem to be shooting blanks." This inclination, he reports, stems from his work with clients who, in the short term, seemed to be inexplicably rejecting sensible mediator suggestions but were ultimately happy with their choices.

Dozier's inclination toward the laissez-faire, however, has clear limits. Dozier states that Bob's primary obligation is to ensure that Tune has the capacity to make the decisions facing him. He needs to understand the relevant facts and issues and appreciate the consequences likely to ensue if he is wrong about his BATNA. To do that, Dozier suggests that Bob could "engage in a colloquy that would ... delve further into the reasons for his intransigence." He should talk to Tune about "what exactly Tune understands about the relevant law" and how it will be applied in his case and if there are other reasons, beyond the law, that are influencing his decisions.

Dozier draws explicit attention to Model Standards I, Self-Determination, and VI, Quality of the Process, and says that the central inquiry for Bob should be whether Tune is competent to represent himself in mediation. Is there some sort of mental or emotional block that is leading Tune to a deluded understanding of his situation or his options? Figuring this out is Bob's central challenge. But if Bob concludes that Tune has the capacity to take in information and appreciate its implications, then the mediator can continue with few ethical qualms.

Moffitt defines the central question as one of informed consent. He notes that what we aspire to in mediation is decision making that is not simply competent but informed. There is a cost, he warns, when mediators stand by and watch disputants make seriously uninformed decisions that will bind them into the future. At some point, a party's ignorance about the process and her alternatives becomes so serious that it undermines the integrity of the outcome.

Dozier's capstone is competency, Moffitt's informed consent. The one concept focuses on internal capacities, the other on external information. Capacity defines the minimal standards for disputant decision making. Informed consent articulates the aspirational ideal. But both Dozier and Moffitt are pragmatic enough to know that disputant deliberation often falls squarely in between that floor and ceiling—in the Goldilocks space of neither perfectly hot nor perfectly cold, but perhaps good enough to proceed.

CHAPTER SEVEN

Mediating on the Wrong Side of the Law

Although we would like to believe that disputants adhere to the Boy Scouts' creed of honesty and rectitude, sometimes even scouts have trouble making good on their pledge. Most of the time, disputants' bad behavior is confined to rudeness, unwillingness to engage in the process, or a fondness for fanciful and self-serving narratives. But sometimes the bad behavior is worse; sometimes disputants come to us having flirted with criminal activity or with ideas of doing so in the future. When clients' conflicts take us over the border of legality, what do our ethical obligations require?

GUIDANCE FROM THE CODES

The Model Standards urge mediators to take this situation seriously, pronouncing tersely that if mediation is being used to "further criminal conduct," appropriate steps must be taken.[1] Suggested steps range from postponing further discussion to withdrawing from or terminating the mediation. A number of state codes adopt similar language, suggesting that mediators enjoy considerable latitude in deciding whether to slow talks down, impose a cooling-off period, or shut down the mediation entirely.[2] Other states mandate a harsher response. Postponement is not an option. If the parties are using the mediation to break the law, only termination will do.[3]

The Uniform Mediation Act (UMA), crafted by drafting committees from the National Conference of Commissioners on Uniform State Laws and the Section of Dispute Resolution of the American Bar Association to encourage uniformity and consistency in the evidentiary protections accorded mediation communications, provides additional disincentives to continue mediating where the parties appear criminally inclined. The UMA strips the mediator (and the parties) of confidentiality protections if their communications are "intentionally used to plan, attempt to commit or commit a crime, or to conceal an ongoing crime or ongoing criminal activity."[4]

On paper, then, the signaling is clear: mediators should proceed with extreme caution when the parties are using the mediation process to further a criminal scheme, which may mean not proceeding at all. This straightforward injunction, however, leaves some areas unclear. First, what does it mean to "further" criminal activity? Must the mediation be facilitating ongoing or future illegal conduct? Or does the mediator "further" criminal activity when she helps currently law-abiding citizens tie up loose ends that frayed during the disputants' prior unlawful collaborations?

Second, how certain must mediators be that the parties are up to no good before they turn their backs on the conflict? When mediators take a case, they make a commitment to work persistently and with pointed determination to help the parties reach closure. Giving up is a dramatic act. At what point do a mediator's suspicions rise to the level where termination or withdrawal becomes appropriate?

Third, are there other ethical routes besides postponement or withdrawal? The Model Standards say to take appropriate action. Is it ever ethically permissible to continue helping parties who appear motivated to close a legally derelict deal? Putting aside the question of whether it furthers criminality to help past lawbreakers fashion legal agreements using the mediation process, is it permissible to try to talk the criminally inclined into a more palatable arrangement? What, if any, justifications might mediators have to work with "artful dodgers" whose prior schemes haven't always been on the up-and-up? Does the desire to help empower parties legitimately apply to those who play fast and loose with the law?

The answers to these questions cannot be found in the elliptical language of relevant code. The Model Standards and state codes urge that appropriate action be taken when the mediation process is being used to advance illegality, but they don't address the appropriate standard for assessing criminality. Should mediators withdraw when a preponderance of the evidence suggests illegal behavior is afoot? When a reasonable suspicion exists? When the conversation hints that something is not quite right? What level of certitude or burden of proof should be required?

A MEDIATOR'S ATTITUDES AND VALUES

Absent guidance from the codes, mediators will likely reach different conclusions based on their individualized vision of the goals and purposes of the process. Mediators who feel strongly that neutrals should remain nonjudgmental and avoid drawing conclusions on the limited factual evidence typically produced in a mediation will likely require clear and convincing evidence of wrongdoing before considering the drastic step of withdrawal. Suspicion or speculation would not be deemed sufficient to abort the process. Mediators more comfortable with an interventionist and judgmental stance would be comfortable calling a halt on the basis of less conclusive information.

A mediator's attitudes toward the rule of law and understanding of what it means to preside over a quality process and safeguard the integrity of the profession will also come into play. Mediators who venerate legal rules as embodying important social values will be more sensitive to signs of party disregard, whereas mediators with less reverential approaches will be less primed to notice irregularities. If quality and integrity relate solely to the treatment of the parties—the degree to which their autonomy, dignity, and safety are safeguarded—then continuing to mediate despite hints of rule bending need not implicate these values. But if quality and integrity are defined in part by the process's respect for social norms, then even slight evidence of transgression would require a strong response.

Mediator decisions of what to do when disquieting signs of wrongdoing emerge will also be influenced by these value orientations. Will the mediator drop the parties like an ethical hot potato or prolong the discussion in the hopes that the parties can be pushed in more morally acceptable directions? Clearly the mediator's comfort level with shaping the terms of the parties' agreement will play a role. Some mediators find it more comfortable to simply terminate discussions rather than insert themselves directly into a search for options that they (but perhaps not the parties) find more appealing. Others take a more benign view of mediator intervention, acknowledging the encroachment on party autonomy but rationalizing it as justified in light of the parties' tendencies toward illicit conduct.

CASE 7.1: OUTRAGEOUS OFFSHORE

In this case, the parties are contemplating conduct that the mediator knows is illegal. Although their past course of conduct appears unimpeachable, their proposals for future arrangements are troubling. That the mediator should intervene in a dramatic way is clear; exactly what form that intervention should take will hinge on the mediator's preferred level of muscularity and directiveness.

Jenna and Fiona have together built the interior design firm Outrageous Interiors into a successful international business. Beginning with a small investment from each of their parents, the firm is now worth over $5 million. Although financially successful, the two women now hold different visions regarding the firm's future growth. Jenna would like to broaden business to include landscaping and more green activities, whereas Fiona wants to focus exclusively on the firm's niche market in exotic teak chairs—a prospect that Jenna finds environmentally irresponsible and personally repugnant. During mediation discussions, Jenna decides that her environmental passions are more important to her than staying involved in the business: she wants to sell her share in the firm and invest in renewable fuel technology.

The discussions regarding the firm's future trajectory and the fair market value of Jenna's share are difficult. The amount Jenna wants to take out of the deal far exceeds the amount that Fiona is prepared to pay. Negotiations stall, and a decision is made to reconvene the following week with the assistance of Fiona's cousin, a tax planner.

The following week, Fiona and her cousin present a proposal that involves the establishment of an offshore trust in the Cayman Islands. According to the cousin's numbers, with the establishment of the trust, Fiona could—over time—transfer to Jenna the amount she is requesting through credit card payments tied to the trust.

Although you have mediated full time for the past five years, in an earlier life you did trusts and estates and some tax work. You are familiar with the cousin's proposal. You have seen advertisements for these sorts of trusts and handled several cases for clients who had similar arrangements. They are clearly illegal. The plan will increase the amount of money available to Jenna for her share—but only because it will deprive the Internal Revenue Service (IRS) of its rightful percentage of Fiona and Jenna's profits.

Everyone is ready to sign on the dotted line. What do you do?

According to the Model Standards and state corollaries, the answer here is to withdraw as mediator or, at the least, slow things down. As presented, there is no doubt that the party's plan violates federal law, so no question exists regarding the standard of proof to be applied or the quantum of evidence demanded. The mediator has seen these sorts of arrangements before and knows them to be illegal.

The mediator does have latitude in determining whether she wishes to stop things immediately or continue working with the parties. If she decides to keep working, she can pursue one of two different tacks, depending on what level of direct intervention she is comfortable with.

On a less interventionist tack, the mediator could question Fiona's cousin about the legality of the scheme and try to ascertain the cousin's understanding of relevant law and how it relates to the particular trust he is proposing. The mediator could, without revealing his own opinion, suggest to the parties that interpreting overseas trusts in light of prevailing IRS regulations is a thorny business and that it is in all of the participants' interests to ensure that the vehicle they use to resolve their dispute does not create problems for them in the future. To that end, he could suggest that the parties, including Fiona's cousin, conduct further research on the IRS tax regulations or consult another expert, and reconvene at a later date.

On a more interventionist tack, the mediator could tell Jenna, Fiona, and her cousin what he knows about the Cayman Island trusts and explain that in his view, they constitute a breach of American tax obligations. Under this scenario, the mediator could explain that he is obligated to provide a quality process and that any agreement reached must be consonant with U.S. law, including all IRS regulations. Consequently, in order to go forward, the mediator may ask the parties to submit the trust plan to another expert or bring in documentation establishing that the proposed trust is legal and does not constitute a sophisticated form of tax evasion. Of course, this path presents a clear risk that the parties will decide that they'd rather work with a more accommodating mediator who will help them solidify the details of their plan. If so, the mediator here has lost some business. But in the long run, maintaining his reputation and integrity as a mediator who plays by the rules is more important.

Although either approach is acceptable, there may be some benefit to parties if the mediator pursues the more directive tack. If the mediator is confident that the parties' proposal is illegal and is unwilling to proceed while that proposal remains on the table, it may be more efficient to simply present the parties with a choice: jettison this plan and work with me on another, or terminate your relations with me and proceed with this plan on your own or with another neutral. The disputants' best interests might be served by giving them a straightforward choice rather than pursuing a more facilitative path that might consume more resources.

CASE 7.2: SHADY LEAVES

In a murky situation, where the parties' willingness to stay on the right side of the law is unclear, what should the mediator do? Even where it appears that the parties are contemplating no future breaches, should mediators work with past lawbreakers?

Case 7.2, based on a mediation conducted by Julie Macfarlane, tackles these issues. For the purposes of this chapter, I have altered her original case to add an additional level of complexity. The first two commentators, John Bickerman and Jeremy Lack, base their comments on this altered version of the case. The third commentary, by Macfarlane, is based on her actual experience in the mediation.

A mediator has been asked to mediate a business dispute between Don, who runs a small credit operation, and Clive, who borrowed money to fund a small business venture. The business venture failed, and Don now wants his money back. He has begun an action in small claims court but seems anxious to settle the matter in mediation.

After the conclusion of the joint session, it appears obvious that Clive's business venture involved the import and sale of illicit drugs, likely marijuana, but both Don and Clive refuse to confirm the exact nature of the product sold. Don financed the procurement and transport of the drug, just as he has done several times in the past. The latest shipment, however, was uncovered and confiscated by the authorities, leaving Clive unable to repay the debt.

In mediation, the parties quickly begin discussing a trade of services. Clive agrees to paint Don's office if Don agrees to forgive the monetary debt. In addition, Clive suggests that a future business venture with a "solid" rate of return may likely be available if Don allows Clive to pay for the current debt in painting services.

The proposed agreement includes both Don's promise to forgive the amount owed in return for Clive's promise to paint Don's office and Clive's agreement to offer Don the right of first refusal for investment in his next "sure-thing" business venture.

Should the mediator have agreed to continue to work with Clive and Don after learning that the debt repayment issue arose out of a failed drug deal? Also, should she continue to help facilitate their proposed settlement?

Comments on Case 7.2

John Bickerman

Mediators face many challenges in the course of their practice. For some ethical issues, the line between ethical and unethical behavior can be fuzzy. However, there can be no haziness over conduct that crosses the line into sanctioning, participating in, or hiding criminal behavior. Although respecting client autonomy is a touchstone of ethical mediation practice, clear limits to that mandate exist. Indeed, Standard VI(9) of the Model Standards explicitly counsels mediators who are involved in negotiations that are "being used to further criminal conduct" to "take appropriate steps, including, if necessary, postponing, withdrawing from or terminating the mediation."

Just as the attorney-client privilege will not protect a lawyer who engages in activity in furtherance of a criminal enterprise, neither will the less well-recognized privilege of mediation confidentiality absolve a mediator who strays into sanctioning or facilitating illegal conduct.

Faced with Don and Clive's unsavory dealings, a mediator should not offer assistance. She should not work with them to tidy up the problem of the unpaid debt or take a gamble that their future interactions will be legally sound. The mediator should not taint the process by using her skills to help parties clean up the messy overflow from a drug deal gone south. Doing so threatens the mediator's integrity and compromises the field in the eyes of the public.

MEDIATION SHOULD NOT BE USED TO SHIELD CRIMINAL ACTIVITY. The hypothetical sets out a fact pattern that may invite criminal prosecution of the mediator. Here are the facts:

1. Participants to a mediation seek a resolution of a transaction of an unfulfilled contract.

2. The mediator has reason to suspect or knows that the contract at issue relates to the illegal transportation or distribution (or both) of significant quantities of marijuana, a controlled substance. The nontrivial quantities involved and funds at issue would lead a reasonable person to know that the violation is a felony and would subject the participants to criminal indictment and incarceration if they are caught, prosecuted, and convicted.

3. With knowledge or a reasonable suspicion of the illegality of the transaction, the mediator assists the participants in resolving their contract dispute and potentially furthering their illegal activities. The mediator is well aware that the catalyst for the dispute was a failed drug deal, and although the parties are being intentionally vague about the future possibilities for investment, there is a definite possibility that their future business transactions may involve the importation of drugs as well.

Mediators are not potted plants. They have a responsibility to ensure the integrity of the process. While the common understanding of process integrity usually encompasses ensuring that the parties deal honestly with each other and not withhold or unfairly mislead or deceive the other in the negotiations, broader obligations also attach. These facts raise problems for a mediator. A dispute over a loan may be entirely innocent. However, if the mediator has reason to believe that the disputed transaction arises out of past criminal activity, then the mediation should not take place.

Perhaps the crucial reason the disputants have chosen mediation over a judicial adjudication is to keep their past illegal conduct secret. The confidentiality of the mediation process should not be used to shield this behavior. As keepers of the process, mediators are duty-bound to ensure that the mediation process is not used for an improper purpose. "Don't ask, don't tell" has never been part of the mediator's credo. A mediator who is given reason to believe that illegal conduct (even if it's in the past) is being shielded should investigate the underlying facts sufficiently to draw an accurate conclusion or withdraw. If the parties refuse to answer the mediator's questions, she should also withdraw. Using the mediation privilege to further an illegal purpose is contrary to public policy.

The possibility that the parties have foresworn their illegal behavior does not change the analysis. Again, the touchstone for the analysis is that the mediator suspects illegal past behavior. If there is a credible basis for the suspicion, the mediator may be treading on thin ethical ice. Assuming the participants are still in potential legal jeopardy because the relevant limitations statute has not run out, the mediator may still have exposure for being an accessory after the fact. In the same manner that a willing actor provides physical protection against discovery for perpetrators who have committed a crime, the mediator is also providing services to prevent the revelation of a crime. It does not matter that the parties promise not to engage in criminal behavior in the future. The mediator has a reasonable basis to believe that they have committed a crime, which, if discovered, would result in prosecution, conviction, and incarceration.

AVOIDING COMPLICITY IN FUTURE MISCONDUCT. With respect to ongoing criminal behavior, a mediator's course of conduct is even clearer. A mediator has an obligation to understand adequately the ramifications of settlement and the future conduct that will ensue. If conduct seems shady, the mediator ought to proceed with great caution and with the recognition that she may be placing herself in legal jeopardy if future criminal conduct occurs as a result of her successful mediation efforts.

If a mediator learns through her inquiries that the parties will transport a controlled substance for sale or distribution as a wholesaler, then the mediator will be furthering a criminal enterprise. Every state and the federal government would hold possession and distribution of controlled drugs without a license to be unlawful. Distributing quantities as little as one pound of marijuana in New York State would be a Class C Felony. Under federal law, conviction of distribution or intent to distribute one thousand kilograms would carry a mandatory minimum penalty of ten years without parole. Significantly, many prosecutors could bring charges against the mediator as an accessory before the fact or a co-conspirator in the illegal acts.

A mediator will not be protected by professional rules. The Uniform Mediation Act (UMA), which seeks to codify in all states a mediation privilege, exempts from the privilege any communication in mediation that is "intentionally used to plan a crime, attempt to commit, or commit a crime, or to conceal an ongoing crime or ongoing criminal activity."[5] Assuming all of the actors know that the substance of the dispute involves a criminal activity that a successful settlement through mediation will help advance, they would not be shielded by a mediation statute that follows the UMA.

By analogy, lawyers who represent clients are not protected from criminal prosecution if they know that their clients are about to commit a crime. Rule 1.16 of the Model Rules of Professional Conduct for attorneys requires that a lawyer not represent a client if the services provided by the lawyer would further a criminal activity. If this rule were applied to a mediator, no doubt it would prohibit the services contemplated in the hypothetical.

Many states have an exception to their mediation confidentiality statute for crime or fraud. For example, Florida's confidentiality statute mirrors the UMA language, exempting from confidentiality protection communications "willfully used to plan a crime, commit or attempt to commit a crime [or] conceal ongoing criminal activity."[6] These exceptions gain added force by virtue of their incorporation into Florida's court rules regulating the conduct of Florida's certified and court-appointed mediators.[7] Once a prosecutor learns of the facts in the mediation, the mediator and the parties may be in substantially greater jeopardy than if the mediation had never taken place. The mediation communication could provide critical evidence to convict the parties and the mediator of the crimes described above.

DOES THE NATURE OF THE CRIME MATTER? The mediator cannot simply look the other way because she is sympathetic to not prosecuting the underlying crime of distributing marijuana. Would the mediator have a different point of view if the suspicion of past criminal conduct included felony murder? It is hard to imagine any mediator being willing to facilitate the resolution of dispute where the past conduct involved a violent crime.

By proscribing certain activities as illegal, society expresses an interest in deterring criminal behavior. It is proper public policy that individuals who knowingly facilitate criminal behavior in the future or shield past behavior from discovery should be held accountable. Every citizen has a duty to society to obey its laws and ensure that others do as well. It is ethically unsound to allow a mediator to substitute her judgment for that of society's. The rule of law does not stop at the mediator's door.

While civil disobedience certainly has its place in appropriate situations, a central tenet is that those who engage in such activity accept the consequences of their actions. A mediator who condones, furthers, or shields illegal activity out of conscience should be subject to the legal ramifications of that decision, including prosecution and incarceration for her conduct.

Some mediators may be uncomfortable with the bright-line distinction outlined here; they may well argue that mediators should look the other way in certain circumstances. For example, divorce mediators may learn that their participants owe taxes. Although offenses like unpaid taxes may not give rise to criminal prosecution, mediators should not expect that their communications with parties will be protected. While the likelihood of prosecution may be small for the parties (and even smaller for the mediator), the same analysis holds.

Mediators have an ethical duty to maintain the integrity of the process and ensure public confidence in mediation. The discovery of mediations that have been used to shield illicit behavior would harm the reputation of the field. Moreover, the mediator is exposing herself to potential criminal jeopardy if she facilitates a future crime or prevents discovery of one that occurred in the past. There is simply no compelling reason that could justify a mediator assisting parties who have engaged in past illegal activity. The ethical scales argue strongly against such conduct.

Comments on Case 7.2

Jeremy Lack

Is this mediation kosher? Should it be bypassed because it doesn't pass the "smell test"?

It clearly contains aspects that are dubious and would not qualify for an Orthodox Union certificate of kosherness. It raises interesting questions, however, about an individual mediator's tolerance for ambiguity as to the legality of the settlement the parties are reaching, and when a mediator should withdraw from or terminate a mediation. In this hypothetical situation, the mediator has proceeded with settlement discussions after learning that the parties' dispute stems from an earlier commission of a crime and in the face of ambiguity regarding the legality of their proposed solution. Has this mediator already crossed an ethical Rubicon, the point where she learned that the parties have engaged in criminal behavior in the past? Should she have withdrawn at that point, or was it permissible to continue working with these parties? This is a personal consideration for each mediator, and it highlights the importance for each mediator of knowing his or her own comfort levels with ambiguity and his or her own values and ethics. Determining the correct course of conduct may also depend on the codes of conduct or other professional regulations the mediator may be bound by.

The facts of the case are deliberately ambiguous, and the question of when the mediator should withdraw or terminate the mediation needs to be considered both at an early stage of the mediation proceedings and later. Whether to accede to or ratify the settlement agreement itself is not the question, since this will depend on what will have transpired once the ethical issue has first been spotted and how it was dealt with.

MEDIATING WITH PARTIES WHO HAVE ENGAGED IN PAST CRIMINAL CONDUCT. It appears that the disputants informed the mediator at an early stage (in the initial joint session) that they had conspired to commit a crime in the past and that they are now seeking to resolve a debt that one disputant owes to the other as a result of that crime. At this stage, a mediator would be perfectly entitled to terminate or withdraw from the mediation. An agreement to enforce the commission of an unlawful act, or a debt that resulted from it, is arguably tainted in and of itself, and it is not at all clear that a debt arising from an illegal scheme should become more enforceable by virtue of a mediation process. By continuing with the mediation, the debtor may actually be worse off, and the mediator may facilitate the commission of future crimes to repay this debt, since the mediation may turn this unenforceable debt into a legally binding obligation. Taking a moral or legalistic viewpoint, therefore, a mediator could decide to avoid tangling with the problem and withdraw from the case or terminate it at the end of the first joint session.

The mediator would also be perfectly entitled to continue this mediation, however. The mere fact that a past crime was attempted should not prevent the mediator from helping the parties to resolve the matter of their perceived debt even if it is not legally enforceable. If both the parties believe there is a debt to be repaid (even if it is only a matter of honor among thieves), then their subjective perception of an ongoing dispute justifies their perceived need for a mediation and the need to resolve matters between them with respect to the future.

The question becomes ethically challenging only when the mediation itself may facilitate the commission of a crime. A number of codes of conduct explicitly address this question with varying degrees of specificity and leniency.

THE CODES AND FUTURE CRIMINAL CONDUCT. Relevant codes run the gamut from requiring withdrawal to allowing consideration of other options.

The European Code of Conduct for Mediators, for example, suggests that a mediator has broad discretion in these circumstances, by stating that the mediator "may" terminate the mediation if the settlement being reached appears unenforceable or illegal.[8] The guidelines for termination of JAMS go one step further and suggest a more normative standard, by stating that the mediator "should" terminate the mediation in similar circumstances.[9]

The Model Standards appear, on first reading, to require a particularized response to a revelation that the mediation may be used to further criminal conduct, but further parsing reveals a larger space for mediator discretion. The Standards advise that a mediator who believes that a mediation is being used to further criminal conduct "should" take "appropriate steps." But the universe of what may be appropriate remains open. The Standards suggest that appropriate steps may include, "if necessary, postponing, withdrawing from or terminating the mediation."[10] This implies that on occasion, the drastic step of disrupting the talks may not be necessary. In some circumstances, it may be possible for a mediator to continue to conduct the mediation, although she or he should not become an accomplice to the commission of a crime.

The rules of the Chartered Institute of Arbitrators (CIArb), however, appear to be more directive. Although its Guidelines on Termination of Mediation may appear initially to contain the same ambiguity by having discretionary language ("should"), the CIArb's Code of Professional and Ethical Conduct for Members is clear at section 2.1 where it unambiguously states: "A member ... shall withdraw if illegal conduct or substantive unfairness is apparent." A CIArb mediator would thus be compelled to withdraw in this case, and end it earlier if she or he did not wish to run the risk of contravening the organization's code of conduct.

WORKING WITH THE PARTIES TO AVERT A FUTURE CRIMINAL ACT. The facts of the case indicate that the mediator here chose to press on with this mediation, despite the early warning signs that all was not kosher. The mediation has clearly taken place, and the disputants have reached an agreement in which the debtor has agreed to pay off his (possibly unenforceable) debt by (1) painting the creditor's office and (2) providing the creditor with the right to invest in his next "sure-thing" scheme.

If the debtor can repay the creditor by working on a scheme that is legal, there is no problem. The threat in this case is that Don will revert to an illegal money-making scheme and will propose a future investment opportunity that involves drugs or something else illegal. But this is a concern, not a fact. The mediator could condition the provision of continued mediation services on the parties' commitment that any future scheme the parties arrive at involve a legitimate business venture. The parties could explore legitimate business opportunities for the debtor and see if the creditor has any contacts or other above-board business concerns that may be synergistic with what the debtor could do.

It is a matter of the mediator's knowing who she is in mediation, her limits, and her willingness to help the parties fulfill several needs at the same time. A mediator could choose to push for a transformational process, which could be oriented toward rehabilitating the debtor by helping him to get a legitimate job and possible additional legal job prospects. If the creditor does indeed have legitimate business activities, perhaps it is preferable for the mediator to help the debtor get back on his feet and consider other synergies worth exploring here. Even if the reason the mediation has taken place is illicit, some good may yet come of this process. There would not be anything forbidden per se in proceeding with such discussions, helping the debtor to get back on his feet and leave the path of crime forever.

The real difficulty in this case stems from the mediator's torpor and inaction in the face of ambiguity regarding the future scheme. The ethical problem lies upstream—at the point where questions about this scheme began to arise. As a mediator with a legal background, I query how a mediator could have kept a mediation going on for so long if she or he had any doubts about the legality of what the parties were planning. By keeping the mediation going without clarifying this point, the mediator's own moral standing became undermined. This is not a position I would wish to find myself in. I would try to resolve that ambiguity earlier on and prevent it from persisting by clearly establishing my own requirements for continuing the mediation (that the scheme must not involve anything unlawful) and obtaining a definitive answer to the question and the parties' commitment to pursue only legitimate outcomes.

If I were told that the parties were considering the commission of a new crime or that the scheme did entail the commission of a new crime, I would not necessarily immediately terminate the mediation, however. Depending on my subjective sense of the parties and the circumstances, I might try to address why the disputants' needs could not be dealt with in a different way, without a crime being committed. I might continue the mediation if there did indeed appear to be a basis for addressing the debt without the commission of a crime, and I would press for details in the settlement agreement regarding the scheme to ensure its legality. This may be seen as stepping beyond where a mediator should tread, and it may be wrong that I should seek to bring my own values into the outcome or impose them on the parties in any way. But the parties are free to continue their negotiations without me if they do not wish to consider a legally compliant outcome. I may also prefer to keep the mediation going simply to try to prevent the commission of a further crime rather than withdraw and leave this open as a possibility and the disputants to their own devices. This may sound somewhat moralistic and a trifle naive, but it is a personal choice I believe all mediators have and relates to what we wish to achieve as professionals: not simply resolving one particular dispute or reaching one set end point, but going further to help parties address their long-term needs and interests.

Comments on Case 7.2

Julie Macfarlane

The story of Don and Clive is based on a case I mediated a number of years ago, and which I wrote about at that time.[11] I wrote about the case because I wanted to spark a debate about the rights and wrongs of continuing to mediate in a situation where the mediator is aware that the actions that gave rise to the dispute were illegal—in this case, the buying and selling of marijuana for commercial purposes. The two individuals I worked with that day were hardly significant drug barons, but they were engaged in the trading for profit of a prohibited drug.

It is important to note that throughout the (approximately three hours long) mediation, I heard nothing that indicated that these individuals intended to engage in any future illegal activity. In fact, I got the impression that they would not trust one another again in any new transaction, legal or illegal. I am also realistic enough to recognize that they were unlikely to discuss openly with me any future drug deals they might have in mind. For all practical purposes, my work with them focused on finding lawful and nonviolent solutions to the dispute between them. There was a clear acknowledgment that this dispute arose out of an illegal drugs deal. However, their proposals to resolve this dispute did not involve any type of unlawful behavior. This context raises an important distinction that I discuss further below.

At the time, I reflected long and hard about whether I should have assisted them in resolving the matter to their satisfaction or whether I should have withdrawn. For me, both instinct and principled reflection led me to offer my assistance and help the parties conclude their dispute in an entirely lawful manner. Others may disagree, but for me, that was the ethically appropriate course to take.

ARE ALL ILLEGAL ACTIVITIES CREATED EQUAL? First, do the codes of conduct help us answer this question? References to illegal conduct or activities in codes are limited to either exceptions to the duty of confidentiality (see below) or strictures against allowing the mediation process to be used "to further criminal conduct."[12] It is not clear how one would distinguish, in any particular case, between the resolution of the issues in dispute (including the illegal behavior) and "furthering" (appeasing? excusing? condoning? advancing?) the illegal activity itself.[13] The parties were remarkably frank about the facts of the case, both apparently sensing that they would look better if they were the first to out their illegal transaction.

There is an important distinction between furthering illegal conduct and resolving the consequences of such activities. One could argue that any assistance would in effect "enable" the prior illegal activities, but I am not sure that this is a practical place for a mediator to draw the line. It becomes difficult to distinguish which illegal activity to exclude from the purview of mediation and which to allow. If I excused myself from every mediation I conduct in which there was disclosure of, for example, a physical altercation amounting to assault or (commonly) some minor tax evasion on the part of one or other party, I would find myself all too frequently outside the room.

Another difficulty is where to draw the line between thoroughly distasteful illegal activities and those that are just as illegal but more socially acceptable and widespread. Of course, this particular distinction would not be relevant to those who prefer a rule-based analysis. However, in my own practice, I find that because so much of what I do—hopefully, not unreflectively—in mediation is to respond intuitively, the degree of harm caused or potentially caused by the activities is an important consideration for me.

For example, I do not automatically terminate a mediation if I discover past tax evasion. In one case I mediated that revolved around a partnership dissolution, the disputing partners had obviously colluded in the past to disguise actual revenues in order to reduce their tax burden. In a number of employment disputes I have mediated, it has been clear that the employer was not paying all the required taxes and benefits or income was not being declared by the employee. Although tax evaders skirt their duties to replenish the public fisc, for me, the "crime" is not so heinous that I choose to shun these parties or their problems.

Is there a useful distinction to be drawn between illegal activities that cause physical harm or endanger others and those that do not? Or between more or less socially "acceptable" illegal behaviors? Many people have asked me whether I would have continued to mediate this dispute if I had discovered that the drug being traded was crack cocaine or heroin—drugs widely understood as doing more harm to the users and causing more insidious social problems than marijuana. It is certainly possible that if this information was known to me, I would have withdrawn because my personal discomfort—rightly or wrongly—would have been significantly higher.

A MEDIATOR'S MORAL JUDGMENT. This leads me to suggest that we should trust each mediator's intuitive moral compass, which may be realistically responsive to the circumstances of each case, rather than impose a rigidly draconian prohibition on any mediation that tangentially relates to a disputant's past illegal conduct. This should of course make us concerned about the moral compass of each and every mediator, but it at least recognizes that so many of these decisions are made on the spot and using only one's best judgment.[14]

I would also argue that it is intrinsic to the mediator's role that her moral judgment should be not only sensitive to the context of each unique conflict but also as nonjudgmental as possible. How else could we work empathetically with people who are often at their very worst, no matter how righteous their cause? A mediator who is morally rigid or opinionated is a poor touchstone for decisions about refusing (or discontinuing) mediation services. Certainly an individual mediator may consider some activities and behaviors to be immoral that are not constrained by law; for example, common law relationships may be morally offensive to some mediators on religious or other grounds, making it difficult for such individuals to assist a common law couple in resolving their separation details.

Practically speaking, most mediators must adopt an arm's-length approach to the moral circumstances of any conflict in which they are asked to intervene. However, some circumstances may raise, for individual mediators, moral questions that erode their impartiality—for example, where the mediator is repulsed by the behavior of one or other party, such as in a case of admitted sexual abuse or domestic violence. Some might further argue that offering mediation to parties whose immoral behavior has brought them into conflict—a credible view of what had transpired in this case—is inappropriate. I would argue for care in applying all moral judgments in mediation but at the same time assert the right of individual mediators to do so. There is no cab-rank rule in mediation services.[15]

CLIENT SERVICE AND PROFESSIONAL INTEGRITY. In the years I have had to reflect on this case, the argument that comes the closest to persuading me that I made the wrong decision relates to the reputation of mediation in the eyes of the public: in short, that what I did has the potential to bring the profession into disrepute.[16] However, I would also argue that part of our profession's reputation depends on its commitment to assist parties with the real-life problems they find themselves dealing with and to avoid judgment that would remove them from our purview of influence. Having thought about this case over the years, I still believe I made the right decision in proceeding to assist these individual parties. My underlying values or "theory-in-use" emerges as follows.[17]

First, I assume that individuals involved in drug dealing can still contract in good faith. I believe that the motivation to make and to keep a bargain exists for all disputants regardless of their previous experiences with conflict or the circumstances that bring them together. Individuals who have behaved unlawfully or dishonestly in other situations may nonetheless make a powerful personal compact in mediation.[18]

Second, I would draw a clear distinction between cases in which illegal activity has already taken place and led—directly or indirectly—to the conflict, and those in which the parties wish to make an illegal or morally dishonest solution. An entirely different raft of ethical issues are raised by the possibility that the parties will propose illegal outcomes or solutions to their conflict.[19] I routinely inform parties that I will not participate in structuring outcomes that are dishonest or that may have a negative impact on another person not present, whether or not they are unlawful as such. In this case, the solutions agreed to dealt with the debt in a lawful manner.

In this case, where the illegal activity had already occurred by the time I was asked to intervene, I did not understand my intervention as condoning or furthering the illegal drugs trade, but rather helping to resolve the consequences of an already broken agreement (consequences that were clearly about to involve escalation and probably violence). By the time I became involved, their conflict was already a dangerous reality, and my moral view of their previous behavior felt irrelevant. The agreement made in mediation did not enable these parties to continue with their illegal activities (as with any parties, they may or may not choose to do so regardless) since it did not complete or repair an existing arrangement to buy or sell drugs. Instead it dealt with the fallout of a failed transaction.

At the same time, I recognize that my treatment of the case was influenced by my mild reaction to their marijuana trafficking. Had I experienced a strong moral repugnance to their earlier behavior—for example, if they were involved in selling child pornography, or had the drugs been identified as heroin or crack cocaine instead of cannabis—I would probably have felt unable to work with them. Instead, and given the facts as they were told to me, I understood my task as providing an opportunity for structured deescalation rather than moralizing about the circumstances that produced the conflict.

I believe that the potential for private, off-the-record discussions that may alleviate a greater harm is a real strength of the mediation process. I am convinced that these types of ethical and personal judgments can be made only on a case-by-case basis, and I am skeptical about the utility of given distinctions between "acceptable" and "unacceptable" moral or legal activities. This conclusion also points to the importance of being able to solicit feedback—without fear of approbation or prosecution—in order to ensure that personal moral judgments are not made in a vacuum, without the benefit of supportive scrutiny or hindsight.

I have also reflected on how I balanced my obligation to protect the integrity and reputation of the profession with my responsibilities toward these parties. My conclusion is that I experienced my moral and professional responsibility to the parties here—to assist them in resolving their dispute—as a stronger moral imperative than the potential for my intervention to bring the profession or the mediation process itself into disrepute. This suggests to me that my judgment over when, and when not, to offer mediation is responsive first to client needs and only second to the concerns of those who seek to professionalize and promote mediation services. Responsibility to the broader profession for ethical choices implies a different kind of moral consideration than obligations to the parties themselves; an assessment of the possible wider consequences for the profession as a whole may even be quite incompatible with making client-centered decisions over particular ethical decisions in individual cases.

Readers might be interested to know that the parties in this dispute were delighted with the outcome of mediation. I heard from one party again a few months later, who told me that the other individual had fulfilled his part of the agreement. I silently registered some alarm at his apparent enthusiasm about the mediation process—presumably reflecting my own continuing ambiguity—but felt affirmed in my decision to trust that these individuals were still capable of making and keeping a fair and reasonable negotiated agreement. A belief in the potential of our clients to negotiate with one another in good faith and to keep the promises they make in a structured, facilitated process may be an important article of faith for our profession.

Editor's Thoughts on Case 7.2 and the Comments

The commentators in this chapter offer a wide range of responses to the problem of disputants with unclean hands. John Bickerman takes a "just say no" approach, arguing that mediators should refuse to work with disputants who have strayed in the past or are contemplating doing so in the future. He contends that mediators can become subject to charges of conspiracy or aiding and abetting and that such actions cast disrepute on the profession as a whole. Bickerman argues that mediators, as "keepers of the process," must adopt a firm stance, for the reputation of the field hangs in the balance.

Bickerman is also unsympathetic to adoption of a more individualized assessment, where each mediator decides for himself whether the parties' conduct offends his moral sensibilities. Mediators should not, he contends, substitute their judgment for that of society when determining which behavior is wrong and worthy of reproach. A mediator who does engage in civil disobedience and decides to work with some criminals and not others should be prepared to be held accountable if prosecution for complicity with those prior crimes follows.

Jeremy Lack's stance is more tolerant, but he does point out objections that one might have to working with these parties. From a purely legalistic vantage point, he notes that working with the debtor in the mediation may truly disadvantage him by turning an unenforceable debt into an enforceable one. Moreover, he notes that a number of codes, notably the code guiding European mediators and arbitrators, would demand withdrawal.

Still, when Lack considers both past transgressors and parties who may be contemplating future wrongdoing, he would keep his office door open in the hopes that he could push discussions in a more salutary direction. Lack identifies the real problem in the case as the ambiguity that the mediator has allowed to surround the scheme the parties are contemplating.

As the mediator, Lack would make clear that he will continue working with the parties only if they agree that all future interactions will be above board—kosher in the strictest secular sense of the word. The parties would need to understand that he will not stand by and allow them to contract to engage in future drug smuggling. Nonetheless, if Lack learned that Don and Clive were talking about future drug deals, he would not immediately withdraw. Rather he would ply his mediator's skill of asking questions, probing underlying interests, and pushing for a more transformative process. Rather than withdraw and leave the parties to their own potentially recidivist devices, Lack would work to see if the parties could be nudged toward a more law-abiding path.

Julie Macfarlane, who mediated with the real-life characters on whom Don and Clive are based, begins her commentary by noting that in the actual case, no future illegality was contemplated. She makes clear that she would draw the line at working with parties contemplating future illegal conduct, but she felt comfortable helping these individuals work out the knots created by their earlier ill-conceived activities.

Macfarlane questions the applicability of bright-line rules, preferring to leave questions of suitability up to each mediator's own ethical sensibility. This has its risks, she notes, but allows for more flexibility and potentially ameliorative problem solving than does the alternative. Although admitting to some qualms regarding how her conduct fit with mandates to uphold the integrity of the process, she concludes that maintaining a nonjudgmental stance and working to better the situation of the parties in the room present a more compelling charge than do acting in deference to abstract principle and safeguarding the field's professional stature in the eyes of third parties.

CHAPTER EIGHT

Mediating with Lies in the Room

T he previous chapter explored the mediator's dilemma when disputants have or are contemplating illegal conduct. In this chapter, we look at another aspect of disputant misbehavior. What if disputants are lying as a way to get a better deal? If the mediator comes to suspect, or has concrete proof, that one or both disputants are not telling the truth, what is the next step?

PERVASIVE PUFFERY AND WORSE

Anecdotally mediators report that they are no strangers to the tall tale. One group of San Diego court-connected mediators described themselves as "the most lied-to people on earth." This may be hyperbole, but formal and informal investigations confirm the basic sentiment. Don Peters of the University of Florida explored anecdotal reports of mediation chicanery in an informal survey of twenty-three lawyers, five of whom were practicing mediators. When asked to estimate the frequency with which parties or their lawyers lied in mediation, the average estimates ranged from 19 to 43 percent, depending on the nature of the misstatement.[1] These are significant numbers, and although the number of attorneys sampled is small, the responses suggest that the storytelling phase of mediation sometimes involves storytelling of the Hans Christian Andersen variety.

In a more empirically rigorous study of negotiation veracity conducted outside the context of mediation, Art Hinshaw and Jess Alberts surveyed 734 attorneys in the Phoenix, Arizona, and St. Louis, Missouri, metropolitan areas. Research subjects were provided a mock scenario placing them in the role of counsel for a client seeking damages from an ex-girlfriend based on her sexual transmission of a deadly hypothetical disease. Although the client had earlier tested positive for the disease and had told his ex-girlfriend the test results, he later learned that the tests were false and that he is in fact healthy. The client then asks his attorney not to reveal this new piece of information while bargaining with opposing counsel in prelitigation settlement talks. When asked whether they would accede to the client's request for nondisclosure, a request "tantamount to making [a] fraudulent misrepresentation that he [the client] actually has ... [the disease] when he does not,"[2] 19 percent of the respondents said that they would agree with the request and 19 percent said they were not sure how they would respond. The 62 percent who said they would not agree and the 19 percent who were not sure what they would do were asked how they would respond if the client made a more conditional request: avoid disclosure unless directly asked whether the client has the disease. Although seemingly less problematic, this conditional request nonetheless requires the attorney to advance a fraudulent negotiation scheme unless opposing counsel happens to ask the right loaded question. Responding to this query, 13 percent of this subset of respondents said they would agree to the request, and 23 percent replied that they were not sure what they would do.[3] As the authors note, these results provide troubling indicators regarding the way negotiations are routinely conducted. Where a client has made a representation that later proves false, failing to correct the record and inform opposing counsel of the misrepresentation constitutes fraud. It is fraud by omission rather than commission, but it is fraud nevertheless.

Hinshaw and Alberts conclude that attorneys play fast and loose with the truth in negotiations for several reasons, including: confusion regarding what the Model Rules of Professional Conduct require, an overly client-centric understanding of their obligations with regard to disclosure and confidentiality, and a conviction that everyone else is doing it and that negotiation norms allow for such behavior. They call for changes in the text and enforcement of the Model Rules, as well as a greater emphasis on truth telling and ethical decision making in legal education.[4]

Until negotiation norms radically shift, however, we can assume that some mediation participants and their clients will stretch the truth—at times beyond recognition. But the question remains: What should the mediator's response be? The mediation codes don't present a uniform answer, which leaves to each individual mediator wide latitude in separating the acceptable white lie from the intolerable fraud.

GUIDANCE FROM THE CODES

Standard VI(4) of the Model Standards imposes two duties on mediators relating to truth telling and probity. First, it requires mediators to abstain from "knowingly misrepresent[ing] any material fact or circumstance in the course of a mediation." Second, it counsels mediators to "promote honesty and candor between and among all participants."

Mediator Truthfulness

The first requirement seems straightforward, though it could be read to make greater demands than might initially appear obvious. Mediators must avoid making material misstatements. A misstatement is material if a negotiator would attach importance to it in deciding whether to enter into or refrain from entering into the transaction in question.[5] Thus, mediators can't make or repeat statements they know to be both significant to the transaction and untrue. In a proposed sale of a Dutch portrait, a mediator can't report from caucus that the seller said the painting was an authentic Rembrandt when he actually said the painting is a skillful fake. Nor can the mediator report that the painting is a Picasso when he in fact knows it's not and that the seller is trying to deceive the buyer about the painting's provenance. False statements are verboten, whether invented by the mediator or invented by a party and transmitted by a knowing mediator.

But misrepresentation encompasses more than the outright lie. It involves half-truths and sins of omission as well. So if the seller admits in caucus that the painting is a fake but the buyer is operating under the seller or mediator-induced belief that the painting is a Rembrandt, then arguably the mediator's failure to correct the buyer's perception is the equivalent of a misrepresentation. Failure to disclose material facts can give rise to misrepresentation claims in certain circumstances, including where a trust relationship exists and where the nondisclosing party has vital information not readily accessible to the other negotiator.[6]

Imposing a duty to speak on mediators, is, however, a dicey business. Mediators encourage parties to lower defenses and increase information exchange by promising to serve as discrete interlocutors. This translation function does not include serving as fact checker or truth monitor. Moreover, confidentiality strictures preclude mediators from revealing information told to them in confidence. Rather than expect mediators to take it on themselves to set the record straight, it is more realistic to look to them as truth cheerleaders who encourage parties toward probity. The Model Standards implicitly recognize this in including the second admonition: promoting honesty and candor.

Promoting Party Truth Telling

In addition to being truthful themselves, mediators are to "promote honesty and candor between and among all participants."[7] If the mediator is successful in inducing the parties to be honest, then she needn't worry about becoming complicit in fraud or being faulted for failing to air facts that require disclosure.

The difficulty arises when the parties resist such efforts. What if the mediator learns in caucus that one party is lying but does not succeed at cajoling the party to come clean? On the one hand, mediators are duty-bound to keep information learned in caucus confidential. On the other, mediators are to encourage honesty and not engage in misleading nondisclosures themselves. What to do?

Some state codes confront this tension between confidentiality and misrepresentation directly while adopting different suggestions for resolution. For example:

- Virginia's rules for "certified" mediators handling court-based disputes fall on the stern end of the spectrum. They state that if a mediator determines that "the integrity of the process has been compromised by ... gross unfairness resulting from nondisclosure or fraud by a participant," the mediator shall inform the parties and shall discontinue the mediation, but in a way that preserves confidentiality.[8]

- In North Carolina, the ethical rules binding court-connected mediators use similar language but grant the mediator greater leeway. A mediator who suspects that the integrity of the process has been compromised by party fraud or nondisclosure may choose to discontinue the mediation, but again must be careful not to violate confidentiality.[9]

- Alabama states that a mediator may, but need not, withdraw if she believes any agreement reached would be the result of fraud.[10]

- Oregon requires mediators to discontinue their work if it appears a participant's "dishonesty or nondisclosure is so significant that the fairness and integrity of mediation cannot be maintained."[11]

Note that the Model Standards and the analogous state codes leave vague a number of crucial determinations. How big does a lie have to be before "the integrity of the process" is destroyed? What does it mean to say that an agreement is "the result" of fraud? What if one of the ten descriptors the seller assigned his product is untrue? What role did that one-in-ten inaccuracy play in producing an agreement? Should mediators worry only about lies that produce a "grossly unfair" outcome—as opposed to simply an unfair outcome?[12] And how does one tell the difference?

What the codes seem to be saying is that disputants can deviate somewhat from "the truth, the whole truth and nothing but the truth" and mediators can ethically continue with the case. Trivial, nonmaterial mischaracterizations, exaggerations, or omissions are tolerable. But at some point, where the disputant's deception overwhelms and contaminates the deal, the mediator should consider withdrawing.

THE RULES REGULATING ATTORNEY CONDUCT IN NEGOTIATIONS

Although individual mediators draw their lines in different places, they can gain some guidance regarding permissible versus impermissible deception in negotiation from the Model Rules regulating attorney conduct in direct negotiations. Germane to this discussion are two duties mirroring the duties imposed on mediators by the Model Standards: the duty to avoid fraudulent misstatements of material fact and the duty, in some circumstances, to disclose material facts.

No Fraudulent Misstatements of Material Fact

Attorney conduct in negotiation is regulated by Model Rule 4.1, which sets out the limits on attorney disclosures to third parties while representing clients. If we take the Model Rules to be our Beatrice,[13] guiding us from the most venal to the most venial, then clearly the worst sort of lie is one relating to material fact. As noted, a fact is material if a reasonable person would attach importance to it in determining whether to enter into a transaction or the speaker knows (or should know) that the person receiving the misrepresentation is likely to regard it as important.[14] If a fact is material, statements relating to it that are partially true or ambiguous but misleading will also be categorized as an affirmative misrepresentation. And if the speaker knows that a prior statement left the listener with an incorrect perception regarding these facts, then a failure to correct the misperception will also count as an affirmative untruth.

Let's imagine a mediation where the parties are trying to reach agreement regarding the sale of a hotel. The hotel is beautifully constructed and lavishly furnished but is located in a culinary wasteland. The nearest restaurant, a full forty minutes away, is a greasy spoon with a reputation for visits from the county health inspector. Vacationers have only one other option: take their meals in the hotel restaurant, which serves only simple fare: salads, sandwiches, and grilled chicken and burgers.

Imagine that the buyer, who caters to sophisticated urbanites, asks the seller if the hotel would be attractive to "foodies looking for exciting country cuisine." If the seller tells the buyer that there are many Zagat-rated restaurants in the area, then she has engaged in an affirmative misrepresentation regarding a material fact (one important to the buyer), and a mediator who knew the truth about the hotel's eating options would need to start thinking about whether she wants to continue to involve herself in the discussions.

What if the seller were a creative rhetorician and simply responded to the "foodie" inquiry by saying, "A gourmet would be astonished by the food offerings in our little community." Such a reply is ambiguous—but in a deeply misleading way. The buyer might reasonably interpret the seller to be saying that there are so many great restaurants that a gourmet would be amazed by their number and proximity. Even if the seller contends that she meant to truthfully convey a gourmet's likely shock at the paucity of food offerings, the phrasing appears intentionally designed to mislead, and thus a court would likely find it to be fraud despite other possible meanings. When the situation involves either an outright lie or a misleading ambiguity, a mediator who knows the truth needs to assess whether the deception involves a material fact and consider whether withdrawal is appropriate.

Nondisclosure of Material Facts

The Model Rules also clarify that attorneys can run amok by failing to provide information in certain circumstances. The rules make explicit reference to the growing trend in fraud doctrine of imposing a duty to speak where silence would leave a disputant bereft of important information relating to the transaction. Attorney (and client) silence will be treated as an affirmative misrepresentation where a fiduciary relationship is involved, where the nondisclosing party has vital information not accessible to the other, or where special statutory obligations apply. Section 551(2) of the Restatement of Torts states an obligation to disclose "facts basic to the transaction, if the speaker knows that the other is about to enter the transaction under a mistake as to them, and that the other, because of the relationship between them, the customs of the trade or other objective circumstances, would reasonably expect a disclosure of those facts."[15]

So in the same hotel transaction, let's focus on a different aspect of the discussions. In addition to being architecturally magnificent though gastronomically inadequate, the hotel is located on a bucolic river that offers vacationers a quiet and serene spot for fishing, swimming, canoeing, and other water sports. One of the hotel's current advertising themes is that it offers a perfect "backwoods getaway that leaves the hustle and bustle behind."

Now what would happen if the hotel owner mentioned in caucus that one reason he is anxious to sell is that he heard from the town mayor that a lumber company is planning to site a lumber mill a mile up the road from the hotel and he fears that the noise and pollution from the planned mill will destroy the hotel's water offerings? If the owner and his counsel are determined to keep that information from the proposed buyer throughout the mediation, are they acting unethically according to current negotiation norms, and if so, does that behavior "compromise the integrity of the mediation process" such that the mediator should withdraw?

The first questions to ask relate to the nature of the withheld information: Is the information from the mayor regarding the proposed lumber mill a "fact basic to the transaction"? And is it information that "a reasonable person would attach importance to in deciding whether to buy the hotel or not?" To answer these questions, one might want to know more about the quality of the mayor's sources. Was the mayor repeating a vague rumor or relying on reputable sources or verifiable documents supporting the likelihood that a mill will be built? If the mayor was simply repeating unsubstantiated gossip, then perhaps it needn't be passed on. But assuming the mayor's information is solid and grounded in fact, it would seem that the information is material. The hotel is marketed as a quiet water-based retreat. Its serenity and the availability of water-based activities likely go to the future profitability of the hotel, a significant factor in any proposed buyer's decision-making calculus.

The next type of question to ask in determining the seriousness of the omission is to consider whether the relationship between the buyer and the seller and their respective attorneys is such that the buyer should reasonably expect that this information would be conveyed.[16] Traditionally tort law viewed buyers and sellers as existing in arm's-length relationships to one another. Their interests were adverse, and they were not expected to trust one another. Caveat emptor ruled. But increasingly the courts have moved away from a regime of buyer beware to seller beware if crucial information affecting the value of what is being exchanged is not disclosed. Courts have invalidated agreements and awarded damages on nondisclosure grounds in numerous instances—for example:

- Real estate sold proved less valuable to buyers due to defects that could not be readily discovered.[17]

- A personal injury plaintiff was not told of accident-related injuries known to the defendant but not to plaintiff.[18]

- An insurer was not told of summary judgment granted in its favor.[19]

- A university was not told that a professor negotiating an early retirement package had all but accepted a position at another university.[20]

- Adoptive parents were not told in discussions with an adoption agency that the adopted child had received an infant diagnosis of cerebral atrophy and that the birth mother had been diagnosed with chronic schizophrenia.[21]

- A plaintiff had not been told of the existence of or accurate amount of insurance policy limits.[22]

Courts seem to be moving closer to seeing buyers and sellers and other bargainers as entering into trust relationships with one another, requiring disclosure. Thus, it would seem that our hotel seller would be under a duty to disclose the information about the proposed lumber mill in order to avoid a possible misrepresentation charge.

Once it is determined that a party in the mediation has a duty to disclose in order to avoid a fraud claim, then it would seem that codes' ethical injunctions for mediators come into play. Under the Oregon and Virginia codes, if the seller insists on keeping the information from the mayor secret, the mediator should figure out a way to withdraw while preserving confidentiality. Under the North Carolina and Alabama codes, a mediator need not necessarily withdraw, but is ethically permitted to do so and should do so to preserve the integrity of the process provided that she excuse herself using general language and do nothing to reveal the confidential information the seller is determined to keep hidden.

Opinions as to Value, Authority, and the Bottom Line

Once one moves away from material facts, the rules regulating attorney conduct in negotiation become much looser. Rule 4.1 seems to accept that attorneys and their clients will bluff, puff, and bluster and that efforts to persuade the other side that the best and last offer is the one on the table (even when it is not) is a permissible form of deception.

The Comments to Rule 4.1 make clear that a variety of statements cannot be characterized as material facts, and therefore the rule's requirements of truth and reliability do not apply. Opinions and "estimates as to price and value," "party intentions as to acceptable settlement," and the existence of undisclosed principals (except when nondisclosure of those principals constitutes fraud) all fall outside Rule 4.1's purview. Essentially Rule 4.1 awards negotiators a "feel free to distort" pass regarding a great number of the statements one might expect to hear from negotiators in mediation.

Thus, any time a seller of goods or services speculates on the worth of what she is selling, that price tag would be labeled as an opinion or estimate. Even if the number assigned deviates substantially from what the seller truly believes the item to be worth, there is no ethical problem according to Rule 4.1. In addition, while an attorney who flat out lied in a declarative statement of the precise settlement authority conferred would be skirting dangerously close to a Rule 4.1 violation, vaguer comments like, "My client won't go for a number less than six figures" or "I can't go back to my board with a demand like that," need bear little relation to reality. The real walkaway point may be eighty thousand dollars, and the board may have authorized payment of sums vastly exceeding what the plaintiff is asking, but according to Rule 4.1, it is fine for attorneys to suggest in opaque rhetoric just the opposite.[23]

If it is acceptable for attorneys to obfuscate with regard to authority, reservation points, and value estimates, that would suggest that a mediator's duties to safeguard the integrity of the process are not implicated when these sorts of distortions take place. Not everyone is happy with this state of affairs. Indeed, a number of commentators have taken the drafters of Rule 4.1 to task for creating the expectation that attorney negotiations will be suffused with deception.[24] Still, until a normative shift occurs in attorney and client behavior, mediators should not take it on themselves to call the parties on their puffery. Encouraging parties to provide a straightforward assessment of their interests, needs, and bottom lines is one thing. Enforcing such a request is another.

CASE 8.1: WHO OWNS THE DANCE?

In this relatively straightforward case, the parties and their attorneys engage in a number of deceptions, raising questions of what the mediator's ethical response should be.

Julie, a choreographer, and Don, the chief executive officer of a hip-hop performing troupe, are mediating a dispute involving the ownership rights to Julie's most recent work. The piece in question is a duet that Julie choreographed that visually interprets Muddy Waters's blues masterpiece, "I Can't Be Satisfied." Julie and Don had a contract the previous year whereby Don's company was granted co-ownership rights to works "substantially completed during the contract period." There is some question as to whether Julie's piece is "substantially complete" and if so, whether it was created during the contractual term. Julie is willing to have Don's troupe perform the work, but since she contends it does not fall under the terms of the contract, she wants an additional payment of thirty thousand dollars.

Julie and Don's attorneys have both argued that the law surrounding contractual interpretation favors their position. With regard to their personal and business interests, Don's attorney says:

> Look—Julie hasn't made any waves in the art community in a long time. Don's company doesn't need the piece—he has tons of work coming his way. But it is in her interest to have his hip-hop troupe perform anything she does, because it will make her work seem more current. Don's company paid Julie to be a staff choreographer, so we think we have ownership rights to the work, but it's not at all clear that it's going to be a winner. So if we were going to pay her an additional amount, it would be a negligible sum. There is no reason to think this latest work is worth what she is asking. Moreover, we're done working with Julie. We've had good experiences in the past, but we don't feel she's pulled her weight this last year.

Julie's attorney responds:

> Listen, Julie gets plenty of opportunities to show her work. Don is making it seem as if he'd be doing us a favor by associating with Julie—but the truth is, it's the other way around. Julie's work has appeared in three other modern dance companies in town, and in each of these venues, the sales were very good. In fact, we've already been offered thirty thousand dollars from the IN-Sight Dance Company to stage, "I Can't Be Satisfied." And as far as future collaborations, here's where Don and Julie agree: Julie doesn't want to work with Don either.

In truth, each of these attorneys is communicating information about their client's situation that is at odds with the true facts. The reality is Don is working with only one other choreographer whose work has proven too stodgy and traditional for Don's usual audience. Julie is also not as much in demand as she suggests. Since the contract with Don ended, she has not had any commissioned work. Importantly, although she has talked to IN-Sight about staging the work, they have not yet offered her any money.

Additionally, neither Don nor Julie has been entirely forthright about their true feelings. Julie has always enjoyed working with Don's dancers and considers Don's troupe the best in town. When she was scoring "I Can't Be Satisfied," she actually had particular dancers from Don's troupe in mind. In her heart of hearts, she really would like them to stage the work; she just finds it humiliating to acknowledge it. Don too has always liked Julie's works and thinks "I Can't Be Satisfied" is her best yet. He thinks the work is going to garner enthusiastic critical and popular reviews and whichever dance troupe puts it on is going to share in the glory.[25]

What does "promoting honesty and candor" require? As a matter of good practice, the mediator here should encourage Don and Julie and their counsel to be straightforward regarding their true needs and interests. He should explain that it will be difficult to enlarge the roster of mutually attractive options and arrange for complementary trades if they do not reveal the things that really matter to them.

On the other hand, with one major exception little of what the parties have said should sound ethical alarms. Both Don and Julie are presenting their best alternative to a negotiated agreement (BATNA) in more glowing terms than are warranted, and each is downplaying the degree of benefit they would derive from obtaining what the other has to offer. Also, both Don and Julie contend that they have no more use for the other, despite harboring mutual fantasies of future collaboration. This is classic adversarial advocacy in action. Inflating the value of one's offer, undercutting what the other side has put on the table, and disguising one's true preferences fall within the traditional hard bargainer's catalogue of techniques. They may undermine mediation's potential to reach value-maximizing outcomes, but they do not violate any ethical norms.

In the parlance of Rule 4.1, these discussions largely revolve around differing "estimates of value placed on transaction subjects"—namely, Julie's creative work. And the rule specifically says these estimates do not constitute material facts, so even the wildest exaggerations do not run afoul of the rule. Similarly, Don and Julie's declarations that they no longer wish to work together misrepresent their true preferences, priorities, and needs. But these yearnings are aspects of each party's subjective mental state, which fall outside the regulatory ambit of Rule 4.1

The one problematic statement in the negotiations relates to Julie's false claim that she has been offered thirty thousand dollars from IN-Sight. If the mediator knew that statement to be a lie, then the mediator would need to avoid repeating it and think about whether that information triggered any ethical responsibilities on her part to distance herself from the negotiations.

As discussed, Rule 4.1 prohibits attorney negotiators from making misstatements of material fact. If statements about Julie's alternatives to settlement with Don are material to Don's decision-making process, then the mediator would need to think about whether the negotiations have become too ethically tainted to continue. On the one hand, it could be argued that what others think about Julie's work and what they have offered her are ancillary to the contractual question and Don's valuation of the work. Thus, regardless of whether Julie has other offers and the value of those offers, Don can decide whether he wants to continue disputing over whether the work is covered by the contract or whether he wants to offer her some additional sum of money, independent of what she says she has been offered by others. On the other hand, third-party offers have an empirically demonstrable effect on negotiating ranges. They tend to anchor discussions and serve as a floor for seller and buyer alike. Why, sellers ask, should I contemplate an offer less than what others are willing to pay? Buyers who don't have a good answer to that rebuke often slide more coins into the pot. False claims regarding third-party offers thus skew the bargaining range upward, particularly when the buyer is relatively unsophisticated regarding standard negotiation puffery. In addition, the statement here is clear and specific. Julie's counsel did not say, "Julie has many other bidders" or "IN-Sight has shown great interest." Rather, counsel has stated that IN-Sight has offered a precise amount of money for the exact dance piece whose valuation is under discussion. This statement would likely be seen as a misrepresentation of material fact in violation of Rule 4.1 and triggering ethical responsibilities for the mediator.

In this instance, most mediators would likely test reality with Julie and talk to her about the likely consequences if Don finds out that she is not in fact sitting on other offers for her work. At the least, he will feel angry and betrayed—not a good thing if they are working on the staging of her piece. At worst, he may attempt to legally challenge the deal. If Julie is unmoved by these arguments, the mediator may need to consider a delicate way to extricate herself without revealing Julie's deception.

If Julie and Don's puffery stayed at a vague and abstract level, however, the mediator could proceed with no worries. Statements like, "I have no reason to believe 'I Can't Be Satisfied' will be successful" or "I have no interest in working with you in the future" are statements of opinion or intention not typically subject to either legal or ethical scrutiny.

CASE 8.2: AN EMPLOYMENT TERMINATION

In the next case, the parties' deceptions lead directly to the question of resources available for settlement. In the first version, the mediator suspects that the parties are not being honest. In the second version, that suspicion is verified.

Version 1

John and Bernie, partners at a recently formed software engineering company, are being sued by one of their junior associates for wrongful termination. The junior associate is alleging breach of contract and the implied duty of good faith and fair dealing.

The partners insist that their decision was based on merit, but they agree with their attorney's risk analysis that they stand at least a 60 percent chance of being found in breach of their contractual obligations. Comparable jobs in the area are scarce, and plaintiff's preexisting health condition renders her loss of health insurance particularly devastating. The combination of her lost future salary, inability to find comparable employment, and likely high costs of self-insuring could push her damages toward the $600,000 to $800,000 range.

In caucus, the partners tell you that they simply don't have the money to pay anything close to the plaintiff's initial demand of $500,000. They tell you that for the past few years, every dollar they made they reinvested in the business to keep it afloat. Each partner brought a copy of last year's taxes as well as a copy of his bank statements; one showed a balance of $50,000 and the other a balance of $20,000. You note on the W-2 that one partner appeared to have some significant investment income. When you point to that number and ask about the possibility of other accounts not yet disclosed, the partner reports that he did have another stock portfolio, but that it was sold to plough more money into the business. You have questions about whether he is being completely honest about the extent of his assets.

Though the company is well poised for gains in the future, it is still in the process of gaining recognition and attracting clients. Currently it operates on a slim profit margin.

Defense counsel makes the case to the plaintiff that the company and its principals have no money for a substantial payout. They say their best offer can't top $120,000. Based on defense counsel's statements, plaintiff drops the demand to $200,000.

You have concerns about plaintiff's future employment prospects as well as the financial difficulties she is likely to encounter due to her ineligibility for insurance. In addition, you doubt that the defendants have come completely clean as to the true extent of their assets.

What do you do?

Version 2

In caucus, the partners tell you regretfully that as neophyte business owners they had "never gotten around" to purchasing employment practice liability insurance. However, stuck within some of the company's financial documents given you by the partners' counsel to establish the company's meager profit surplus is an e-mail that appears to make reference to a policy. As you look more closely at the e-mail (clearly improperly filed within the documents given to you), you see that the policy is described as "comprehensive"—providing coverage up to $1 million for litigation claims based on negligent and intentionally wrongful acts, including "allegedly discriminatory conduct and breach of contract." Based on your reading of the policy as described in the e-mail and your understanding of the associate's claims, you believe the policy would be available to cover any settlement reached in this case.

What do you do?

Comments on Case 8.2

Dwight Golann

This situation presents two potential problems:

1. In version 1, the defendants may be giving the plaintiff misleading information about their ability to pay a judgment or fund a settlement; in version 2, it seems clearer that they are.

2. The defendants' poverty claims are driving down the settlement numbers to a range that may not truly serve the plaintiff's long-term interests given her lack of health insurance and uncertain employment prospects.

The possibility that the plaintiff may be entering into a grossly inadequate settlement presents a tension between Model Standards I, II, and VI, which support party self-determination, mediator impartiality, and the quality of the process. The defendants' apparent lack of candor poses a conflict involving Standards II, VI, and V: impartiality, quality, and the mediator's obligation to protect confidentiality. These values are in competition with each other in these scenarios, and I must respond in a way that strikes the best possible balance among them.

My judgment as to whether the proposed settlement is so disadvantageous to the plaintiff that it raises concerns about the quality of the process is influenced by my assessments of the plaintiff's capacity and the presence, skillfulness, and intentions of counsel.

VERSION 1 AND THE PLAINTIFF'S LACK OF HEALTH INSURANCE. This is not a hard case for me because none of the factors that would make me concerned that the plaintiff was not able to evaluate the risk of losing income and health insurance appear to be present here. The associate is a professional working in the business world and is therefore presumably an intelligent, educated person. If she has filed a legal claim for more than $500,000, then she almost certainly is represented by a lawyer, who can counsel her about the risk of settling versus pursuing the claim (bearing in mind that even a court victory would probably not restore her job or health coverage).

At the same time, the fact that the plaintiff might leave the mediation in a financially precarious situation would lead me to monitor the situation for certain risk factors. The presence of these factors would set off alarm bells, raising my concern and perhaps leading me to take action over the possibly misleading statements.

Potential Risk Factors. Here are several I may need to consider:

- That the plaintiff may be distraught
- That the disputant does not have a lawyer
- That the lawyer might appear incompetent
- That the lawyer might have conflicting interests

• *If the plaintiff seemed distraught.* Strong emotions and unhappiness are normal in the mediation of employment disputes. It is very unusual for litigants to be able to repair their relationship and thus avoid loss, usually because there has been too much water under the bridge by the time the case gets to mediation (for example, the associate may have been replaced) or the legal process itself has narrowed the parties' perspectives and sharpened their distrust of each other.

Indeed, both plaintiffs and defendants often rely on the legal process to avoid, at least temporarily, feeling or dealing with their feelings of loss. Here, for example, the termination has probably impaired the plaintiff's sense of self-worth, as well as hurt her financial situation. The defendants, for their part, have likely had their practice disrupted and incurred large legal expenses. The parties may have avoided feeling these losses, however, by clinging to the unrealistic belief that they will win vindication or compensation, or both, through the legal process; the plaintiff, for instance, may have thought that she would obtain a large award and perhaps even reinstatement in court. Unfortunately mediation inevitably requires compromise, and as a result, parties rarely achieve either full recovery or vindication and must confront the reality of their loss. As a party does so, he or she is likely to feel strong, perhaps disabling emotions.

If a disputant appeared to be disabled by grief, I would look to her lawyer for guidance. The lawyer usually knows the client better than I do, including both her interests and whether emotion is likely to affect her ability to make an informed decision. If the lawyer or my own observations suggested that a party were disabled by strong emotions I would slow down the process, work with the disputant to deal with her feelings, and/or adjourn the mediation, as counseled by Standard VI(C). Here there are no facts indicating that the plaintiff is disabled by despair, anger, or any other emotion.

• *If the disputant did not have a lawyer.* I have never mediated an employment dispute with an unrepresented party, but if I did, then my rules of thumb would be:

1. Allow more time and lower the pressure for a decision. Advise the disputant to consult a lawyer, and give her an opportunity to do so. If necessary, adjourn the process and work with the disputant. Do so despite the other side's objection—although defendants rarely object in practice.

2. If the disputant does not appear to understand the situation and will not consult a lawyer, ask questions and provide basic information to help her appreciate the risk she is assuming. Be careful, however, not to take on the role of an attorney or lead a disputant to believe that you are doing so.

3. Remember that in the end, the decision, even if a "bad" one, is the party's to make.

• *If the lawyer appears incompetent.* I have seen very few truly bad lawyers. It may be that the cost of commercial mediation screens out incompetents, or perhaps generalist mediators are not able to recognize anything but the grossest errors. In my experience, however, lawyers rarely fail to identify plausible theories or miss clear defenses; rather, the problem is that they assert many far-fetched ones.

For example, I regularly deal with lawyers who greatly overstate the value of their claims or defenses. Most exaggerate the value of their arguments to the point that I would think them nearly incompetent, if sincere. In the large majority of situations, however, I believe that attorneys show false confidence for tactical purposes or to demonstrate loyalty to a client. In other cases, they, and more often their clients, are suffering from cognitive obstacles such as optimistic overconfidence and selective perception. An important part of my role is to help disputants reassess or retreat from unrealistic or impractical positions.

If I do see a lawyer miss what I think would be a good claim or argument, I rarely coach her about it for fear of impairing my impartiality. I will often, however, point out the issue to the other side as a reason to settle the case now. ("Your opponent has not thought of X theory yet, which I think would work better for her than the one she's pursuing. I haven't told her about it because it's not my job to help build up anyone's case. But if the litigation continues, there's a real risk that she will, so perhaps you should try to settle now.") Again, there is nothing in this hypothetical to indicate that the plaintiff's attorney is substandard, although one might wish that she had inquired further into the defendant's assets and demanded additional verification regarding resources available for settlement.

• *If the lawyer has conflicting interests.* My concern would increase if the lawyer appeared to be motivated by inconsistent interests, for instance, a plaintiff lawyer eager for a quick payoff or a defendant attorney determined to string a case out for additional billings. But it is rare for me to feel that a lawyer's personal interests are distorting advice to a client; I usually do not know enough about lawyers' internal motivations for this to appear a factor.

The Defendants' Misrepresentation of Assets. The defendants are apparently misrepresenting their financial resources so as to deceive the plaintiff into agreeing to a lower settlement. I say "apparently" because it does not appear that the mediator (or plaintiff's counsel) has fully explored the existence of hidden assets. Asking more questions might change the mediator's understanding of the problem and would not itself raise an ethical issue, although if questions were posed poorly, the defense might interpret them as evidence of the mediator's lack of impartiality.

I find that when I ask questions even about what appears to be a slam-dunk issue, the answers often change my views to some degree. The hidden assets in this case, for example, may be in a form that would be unavailable to satisfy a judgment. There is no way to know if there is a real issue of concealment until I ask the defendants about it in more detail.

If I came to conclude that the defendants were misleading the plaintiff about material issues, I would follow these principles to balance my conflicting obligations under Standards II, V, and VI:

1. I cannot invade or disregard the obligation of confidentiality.

2. I also cannot aid or abet fraudulent conduct.

3. If it can be done consistently with these principles, I should attempt to avoid embarrassing a lawyer in front of his client, because doing so risks making my job harder (not to mention impairing the prospect of being hired again).

Given the facts presented in this case, I would not suggest to the plaintiff that defendants may be lying, because doing so would violate my obligation of confidentiality under Standard V and perhaps also the agreement covering the mediation and applicable law. In addition, documents about financial resources are generally discoverable, and I see it as the lawyers' job, not mine, to litigate the case. Partly also my stance flows from my lack of knowledge and ability: I don't know how important assets are to the plaintiff's settlement decision, whether she has the willingness or resources to pursue the claim, or the likelihood that she could prove and access the assets through litigation. In general, I don't want to take over the lawyer's job and probably could not do so effectively in any event.

At the same time, I would not help the defendants to conclude a deal based in any material way on a misleading factual statement. I would separate myself from any endorsement of statements they made about their assets to the plaintiff (they do not make any such statement to the plaintiff in the problem, only to me) and would avoid helping the defense lull the plaintiff side into inaccurate assumptions. Nor would I discourage the plaintiff from probing the defendants on this point or refusing to settle until she obtained more information. Avoiding lulling the plaintiff, while at the same time not disclosing data from the defense caucus, poses delicate practice issues of timing, tone, and phrasing.

If I could plausibly argue that withholding the information would imperil the durability of a settlement, I could also raise my concerns about assets privately with defense counsel without imperiling my impartiality or confidentiality.

VERSION 2 AND THE DEFENDANTS' MISREPRESENTATION OF ASSETS. As in version 1, in version 2 there are no special risk factors that would motivate me to intervene simply based on the low settlement being offered to the plaintiff. However, version 2 does add important new data: I have seen a document strongly suggesting that the defendants have misled the plaintiff about their assets, or at least the likelihood that assets exist. Given this evidence, I would probe behind the unsavory appearances. I would ask myself, and perhaps also the defendants, questions such as: Does the mislaid document mean that insurance exists that could satisfy the plaintiff's claims, or is the policy irrelevant to this case? For example, the policy may contain exclusions or have such a high deductible that it is not relevant as a practical matter. Indeed, if the defendants had really paid for a policy covering this risk, I would expect them to have invoked it, if only to cover their defense costs.

Assuming that I did learn that the defendants had a policy covering the risk at hand, I would need to balance the equities. Under the law in my jurisdiction and the terms of the mediation agreement I use, mediation confidentiality is not subject to invasion solely because a party has concealed the existence of an insurance policy that is relevant to the case. Similarly, section 8 of the Uniform Mediation Act(UMA) contains no explicit exception to the obligation of confidentiality—in contrast to section 6, which sets out specific exceptions to the privilege against admitting evidence about what occurred in mediation in a court proceeding. Section 6(c) of the UMA also prevents parties from compelling a mediator to testify about what she has learned. I therefore would not reveal the information without the assent of defendants or their counsel.

If, however, I believed that the defense had lied about a material fact such as the availability of insurance to satisfy a judgment, then I would again be very concerned not to act in such a way as to aid or abet the deception. In terms of the Model Standards, abetting the lie would impair, at a minimum, the quality of the process and perhaps also the plaintiff's exercise of self-determination. It would also potentially impair my own appearance of impartiality and my personal sense of integrity.

Given these circumstances, I would ask the defendants to correct their misstatement; if they did not do so, I would withdraw from the mediation. I would present my concerns in a way calculated to avoid impairing the defendants' perception that I was impartial. I might, for instance, point to durability concerns ("If they sign thinking that you have no assets and then the plaintiff falls on hard times and learns that you do, they'll have a way to get out of the settlement") or the limitations of my role ("Sorry, but given my role as a mediator, I just can't do that").

If I did withdraw, I would seek to do so in a manner that did not reveal the confidence or eliminate the parties' ability to reach a deal premised on more accurate information. After all, the plaintiff may have a strong interest in settling the case quickly, regardless of the existence of insurance.

What is the difference between the two versions? It is the heightened risk in version 2 that fraud is likely to occur in a mediation for which I feel responsible, destroying the quality of the process and involving me in abetting tortious conduct. This risk tips the balance toward a more proactive stance. In version 1, where threats of serious malfeasance seem less likely, I am primarily concerned that if I intervene to bring about disclosure, I will be seen as taking sides or will reveal a confidence.

Comments on Case 8.2

Melissa Brodrick

The ethical dilemma facing the mediator in this scenario raises two kinds of questions, the first obvious, the second more intriguing:

1. What should the mediator do when the quality of decision making for one party in a mediation may be skewed by bad-faith, or even downright dishonest, behavior by the other party?

2. How did the disputants' disagreement end up here, where is "here," and what is the role of the mediator in assessing and acting on "the truth"?

Only by looking at both kinds of questions can I suggest an approach to this mediation.

LOOKING FOR FACTS AND AVOIDING ASSUMPTIONS. In reading the scenario, I find myself looking to determine the facts of the case. What's known to the mediator? We know that termination has occurred and that John and Bernie stand accused of alleged breach of contract and its related implied duty of good faith and fair dealing. What's known, too, is that by one attorney's risk analysis John and Bernie's prospects don't look particularly pretty—at least a 60 percent possibility of being found in breach of their contractual obligations, potentially to the tune of a $600,000 to $800,000 ruling in the plaintiff's favor. One can assume that the prospect of an adverse litigation ruling is a major motivation that brings them to mediation, but this is attorney speculation, not a fact.

Regarding the defendant's assets, we know that bank statements show $50,000 and $20,000 in balances for the partners, though how big the wads of cash are under their mattresses remains to be seen. We might assume, but do not know for a fact, that there are lumps impeding a good night's sleep (or perhaps enhancing it). From the plaintiff's vantage point, we know that she has a preexisting health condition and faces potentially financially debilitating out-of-pocket health care costs and an uncertain professional future. We also know that there has been a flurry of negotiating activity: a demand of $500,000 was countered with an offer of $120,000, which was met with a counterdemand of $200,000.

Is it a fact, though, that anyone is lying here? No, that's a hunch on the part of the mediator, and therein lies the real dilemma.

So let's back it up for a moment to consider the responsibilities of the mediator.

MY ROLE AT THE TABLE. I believe my purpose in any mediation room is to highlight the opportunities present to help parties get clear for themselves about their needs, goals, resources, and options. I believe my purpose is also to help parties recognize the opportunities for understanding the others in the room. I believe I have the potential to help people say what they need and want to say and help them listen in ways that may shift the dynamics of the conflict at hand if they choose to do so. I do this by reflecting, summarizing, asking nonleading questions, and generally staying right in the moment with the parties while substantively getting out of their way so that they can do their own work. Mine is both a simple and complex place at the table.

That said, how did the mediator arrive at this ethical dilemma? Better yet, is it even an ethical dilemma? I don't believe it is the role of the mediator to assess (even if only internally) who in the mediation session is being truthful and who's not. If it is, on what is this based? A gut instinct? The sly look in Bernie's eyes while answering questions? The way John shifts in his seat when talking numbers? It's risky business all around and moves the mediator to the center of the action, or at the least, to a place where she or he may feel compelled to direct the action. I believe that our role as mediators is not to try to discern the truth and direct the conversation and outcome accordingly, but to highlight the opportunities parties have to do their own work together, whatever that might be.

How do those opportunities emerge? Let me suggest something that may seem radical to some. The longer I practice—and it has been twenty-two years to date—the less I find myself in private sessions with the parties. It continues to be a choice the parties are given to exercise throughout my mediations should they want a private session, but it is no longer one that I dictate and, interestingly, not one that parties often request when given the choice. Since I believe this isn't my conversation to have—it's that of the parties—why would I choose to separate them? The more John and Bernie talk directly with the plaintiff, the less they may be emboldened to hide behind shuffling papers and financial numbers that may or may not be truthful ones. The more they talk privately with the mediator, the more they may see the mediator as the conduit for sketchy information, even a pawn, as this dilemma suggests is possible.

Imagine the potential for a different conversation. Face to face, with the permission of their attorneys, the plaintiff chooses to talk of the impact of her termination on so many aspects of her life, giving Bernie and John the opportunity to begin to see her as the whole person she is with the complex life she is living. The partners talk about their sense of the merits of their decision to terminate her, giving the plaintiff an opportunity to ask questions, and get clearer about how they got to this point. Over the time of the mediation, the conversation may shift from positional and transactional to relational. There are people, not defensive stances, in the room. If there is lying in the room, it happens directly between the parties. There's potentially far less of it because the process calls on the parties to answer to each other. And as a colleague said to me once, "No one wants to be a victim. And how many people want to be—or be seen as—victimizers?"

Does this kind of shift from transactional to relational always happen? Of course not. But for John and Bernie and the plaintiff, given the opportunity for a different kind of conversation, there may be one that, regardless of the outcome, is far more meaningful to all of them. And if they reach a resolution, it is one more likely based on a greater understanding of the other and/or a greater clarity about their needs and all of the responsive options available to them, not on the suspicion or reality of untruthful information. If they reach closure and that closure takes the form of moving on to another arena for settlement, well, that decision reflects critical clarity about what they need and is based on the direct conversation at hand.

PERCEPTIONS AND ASSUMPTIONS IN VERSION 2. In version 2, John and Bernie have stated that they never purchased insurance, but the mediator discovers (likely accidentally) during a private session that an employment practices liability insurance policy is in place and may well be available to cover any settlement reached in this case. Once again, how did the parties get here, and once again, what to do?

So "here," now, is information that reveals a contradiction. A lie? Maybe. Maybe the inclusion of the e-mail amid the other documents was a mistake. Maybe it was deliberately placed there by John who is being pressured by his wife who feels so badly about the termination of the plaintiff that she wants the plaintiff to get her due. Who's to know, really, and what does it truly matter? The fact is that what's on the table is on the table. In the belief that we as mediators do some of our best work by holding the mirror up to the parties, I reflect what's there: financial documents and insurance documents. Without judgment. Then I get out of the way. What are they going to do with this now more public information shared in the private session? It is, once again, not my decision to make. What I have really reflected back to the defendants is the simple fact that this information is present and that they have choices in where they go with it.

Maybe this reflection of mine will encourage a consideration by Bernie and John of the use of the insurance policy for settlement. Maybe it will highlight the contradiction of the partners' earlier assertion that they didn't have insurance and motivate them, as a result, to clarify this seemingly suspicious contradiction in a way that builds confidence. I will trust Bernie and John's capacity to do what they feel is needed, just as I trust the plaintiff to respond in kind. If Bernie and John determine that the existence of the insurance policy should not be discussed, that is their choice. But let me be clear: if I am asked by them to lie, I won't agree to do so. They, not I, are then faced with another choice: fire their mediator or move forward in this session with this knowledge.

If, in a joint session, I am asked by the plaintiff about the existence of an insurance policy, I will not lie. In my role, which I hope is clear to all parties at that point, I will reflect once again what's in the room: the question posed by the plaintiff. What follows—a truthful or not truthful answer by Bernie and/or John, a follow-up by the plaintiff to her own question, silence, whatever else—once again will be determined by them.

If the plaintiff poses this question in a private session with me, I will do the same: clarify my role, reflect the question back, possibly ask nonleading questions to invite further thoughts, and summarize what I hear. All of these will be done with the goal of highlighting the opportunities present for her to get clear about her next steps in the process. And if the plaintiff decides to settle in the $100,000 range because the defendants say there is "no more money on the table," I will not intervene. It is the plaintiff's job, not mine, to decide if the money on the table is sufficient and if it is in her interest to settle rather than continue disputing in another forum.

There might be, however, a different sort of scenario. I largely practice in joint session because this is what my clients opt for. If, in this case, the parties had stayed together, Bernie and John would be talking directly to the plaintiff about the company's profit margins and funds available for settlement. If there were documents to share, they would be given directly to the plaintiff. (Note that if they were handed to me, I'd pass them on—without reviewing them—after securing the defendants' permission, since I see myself as a secondary figure in this conversation.) It's once again that both complex and simple place of mine at the table as I get out of the way and one that frees me from the potential ethical dilemma of suspecting or knowing information that the other party doesn't.

STAYING HUMBLE. It is important, I believe, to stay humble in our role. We mediators are not clairvoyants who know what exists within piles of documents on the mediation table any more than we know who is telling the truth during the session. This belief informs my view of this case. If no conversation about the existence of insurance takes place, so be it. The insurance information would be left undiscovered (at least in the way described here), and a potential opportunity for this particular settlement approach lost. I would not view it as my place to disclose or urge disclosure of that information. It is the plaintiff's job to determine if the defendants are operating in good faith and if the offer on the table represents a better conclusion to the dispute than do other alternatives. In addition, the revelation of the e-mail doesn't guarantee settlement, just as leaving this information buried in a folder doesn't foreclose a settlement. We all know there is no telling what the outcome of any mediation will be and what ultimately persuades people to settle when they do.

Over many years, I have come to see how critically secondary to the process we mediators can and should be. In being clear that my role is to be in the moment with the parties before me and to help them be in the moment with each other and with whatever they bring to the table, I can let go of any assumptions and suspicions I may have about the parties and resist the temptation to inform and shape my interventions by these assumptions and suspicions. I can turn the conversation over to the parties again and again, providing critical support for them to do their own work and trust, as I do, that they will choose best for themselves and for their own right reasons. This belief has been affirmed countless times, allowing me in such moments as posed by this ethical dilemma to let go, to recognize that while there are ethical dilemmas for all of us as mediators, this, for me, is not one of them.

Editor's Thoughts on Case 8.2
and the Comments

Mediators aspire to preside over negotiation discussions that are complete, accurate, and honest. They hope the settlements they help construct will be lasting and satisfying to both parties. The employment termination case described here explores the mediator's dilemma both when the mediator suspects the disputants are being untruthful and when the mediator has concrete evidence that she is mediating with lies in the room.

Both commentators caution against assuming a fact-finding or fact-checking role. Melissa Brodrick begins her comments by reviewing what is known and not known regarding the defendant's assets and notes that a mediator can get into trouble acting on mere speculation about who is being honest and who isn't. Her understanding of the mediator role does not include drawing inferences about the accuracy of the disputants' narratives; rather, she is there to highlight opportunities to clarify and make choices about their needs, goals, and resources. She is also there to highlight opportunities for disputants to better understand each other and make choices based on these understandings. She believes that what happens with these opportunities is ultimately the responsibility of the parties to the dispute.

Dwight Golann also notes that he will not intervene in the bargaining on a hunch that a defendant is being cagey about resources available for settlement. He also will not intervene to save the plaintiff from settling at what may turn out to be an imprudently low number because none of the hallmarks of impaired decision making are present. Golann notes that where disputants are distraught, unrepresented, or represented by incompetent counsel, he may intervene in an effort to prompt better, more informed, and deliberate decision making. Here, the facts don't indicate that plaintiff requires such prompting.

In version 2 of the case, where it becomes obvious that the defendants are not being honest, the commentators propose different solutions. Golann suggests that he would question the defendants about the wisdom of concealing this information and talk to them about the vulnerabilities their nondisclosure introduces into the deal. If, after this frank discussion, the defendants are intransigent, Golann says he would withdraw while preserving confidentiality.

Brodrick, maintaining her role as a secondary figure, would not withdraw. But she also indicates that her practice, as guided by her clients, takes place primarily in joint session. Keeping the parties together and refusing to function as the intermediary in a shuttle diplomacy process reduces the likelihood that the mediator will have information that the parties lack. Were a document slip such as the one described in this case to occur, she notes, the other party, not the mediator, would be privy to the insurance policy, and the mediator would be witness to, not guardian of, the secret information. That, Brodrick observes, is where she feels the value of the mediator rests: as witness, not director, however subtle or not so, of the parties' decision-making process.

CHAPTER NINE

Confidentiality

Most mediators include in their introductions some discussion of mediation as a safe space. They urge parties to unburden themselves without fear that their secrets will be betrayed. "Trust us," mediators tell their clients, for this is a private place where confidences are kept and respected.

For many, the duty to keep confidences is mediation's most compelling and straightforward ethical imperative. Both practical and philosophical reasons ground this claim. On the practical level, protecting party statements from disclosure is thought essential to the success of the process. Without an airtight confidentiality seal, it is feared, mediation's alchemy will fail, and zero-sum disputing will not transmute into settlement gold. As a matter of moral propriety, mediators cannot credibly present themselves as faithful and impartial information brokers unless they honor the private nature of the facts and feelings entrusted to them.

Confidentiality in the mediation context encompasses two related but separate concepts. The first involves keeping disputant disclosures secret in all respects. The second involves protection from forced disclosure of mediation communications in subsequent legal proceedings. In these introductory remarks, I also discuss the usefulness of tailoring parties' expectations regarding disclosure.

CONFIDENTIALITY AS THE DUTY TO KEEP DISPUTANT DISCLOSURES SECRET

Most hortatory ethics codes at the national and state levels use broad language to describe a mediator's duty to keep disputant confidences secret. The Model Standards exhort mediators to "maintain the confidentiality of all information obtained ... in mediation, unless otherwise agreed to by the parties or required by applicable law." In addition, the Model Standards make clear that information conveyed by one party in caucus should not be disclosed to the other party (or anyone else) without that speaker's permission.[1] This language is mirrored in numerous state standards and codes.[2]

Essentially these standards address the mediator's obligation to respect disputant interests in keeping communications private. In some sense, this aspect of confidentiality can be seen as a natural extension of mediation's commitment to party self-determination. The parties—and the parties alone—choose when information transmitted to the mediator may be communicated to a broader circle. Regardless of the mediator's sentiments regarding the uses to which a party's information should be put, it is the party herself who ultimately controls that use. Consequently, even if a party's statement in caucus that she would accept considerably less than her stated walkaway price may be helpful in bringing the case to closure, a mediator may not, according to these standards, divulge that concession to the other party without permission.

Standards that speak globally about a mediator's duty to maintain confidentiality preclude mediators from talking about their cases in both formal and informal settings. This means that mediators are not to gossip about their day's work with spouses, neighbors, or the bartender at the local watering hole. They can't call up the local newspaper and dish about the nasty fight that brought a prominent state official into the mediation room. And they must refrain from debating the wisdom of a disputant's settlement agreement with the local judge at the state bar's annual Christmas party.

CONFIDENTIALITY AS AN EVIDENTIARY PRIVILEGE

The second concept implicated when we talk about confidentiality is the privilege to avoid testifying in court. Numerous state evidentiary codes frame confidentiality as a privilege that protects mediation communications from use in subsequent legal proceedings.

The Uniform Mediation Act (UMA), adopted currently in eleven states,[3] declares that communications made in mediation are "privileged" and "not subject to discovery or admissible in evidence in any judicial proceeding or legislative hearing."[4] This broad exemption is then followed by a slew of exceptions.[5] Yet like the state standards that set out mediators' duties to keep disputants' statements private, the main focus of the UMA is to cradle mediation in a thick, though not impermeable, cloak of secrecy.

Virtually every state that has not adopted the UMA has enacted some legislation conferring evidentiary protection on mediation statements.[6] Some, like California and Alabama,[7] provide a near absolute exemption from disclosure, while others contain exceptions designed to allow parties or the mediator to testify in discrete situations.[8]

Existing legislation assumes that strong confidentiality protections are necessary to spur mediation's continued growth. Because this belief is so widely held and so tightly wound into the fabric of our regulatory structures, it is important to examine its foundational premises.

INTERESTS ADVANCED BY PROTECTING MEDIATION COMMUNICATIONS FROM DISCLOSURE

Creating a regime that offers strong confidentiality protections is thought to be important for three main reasons. First, it is thought to strengthen the level of trust that mediators can establish with disputants (and between the disputants themselves).[9] Disputants need to have confidence that the revelations they choose to make in a collaborative search for solutions will not later be used against them. When disputants unveil their true wants, vulnerabilities, and stripped-down expectations, they need to know that this strategic undressing will not later become the basis for their adversaries' advantage. The inflated demands and puffed-up case assessments that parties advance in regular negotiation sessions provide them bargaining cover. If we ask them to strategically disrobe, they must be able to count on the fact that only the mediator gets to see them "naked." Disputants are willing to call for a cease-fire, lay down their arms, and work toward an end to hostilities. But if the battle resumes, they want to be sure that the weapons relinquished during the truce have not found their way over to enemy lines.

The second reason relates to mediators' promise to function as impartial intermediaries. Confident that the mediator will not take sides regardless of what happens, parties feel free to confess the less appealing aspects of their situation. Maybe they will acknowledge that their behavior in the dispute hasn't always been civil. Maybe they will concede that they have played a role in generating unhappiness on the other side. Maybe they will admit that they haven't entirely lived up to their end of the bargain. And maybe they will reveal that they could take a little less or give a little more than they have previously allowed.

If a mediator later repeats any of these admissions, it is likely that the party who made them will feel that the mediator has taken sides against him. Even if the disclosure is compelled by subpoena or court order, the fact of compulsion is unlikely to dispel the impression of partiality. A party who witnesses a mediator giving testimony "against" him would probably conclude that the mediator was biased from the start.

The third reason is that threat of mediator disclosure can cast a pall over the integrity of the process as a whole. Mediators promise to protect party privacy, and parties rely on those promises. If promises are broken, parties would be justified in wondering what other aspect of the process is a forgery. If a mediator vows to keep confidences and then offers up a party's secrets, perhaps the vows to remain impartial and promote party autonomy are shibboleths as well.

All of these concerns were eloquently captured by a California mediator seeking to quash a subpoena demanding her testimony. In that case, the wife was seeking to set aside her mediated marital settlement agreement on the grounds of fraud and duress. The husband sought the mediator's testimony to refute those claims. The mediator, in resisting the subpoena, wrote:

> Confidentiality and neutrality are the life and breath of mediation. A party must be guaranteed that statements made by him or her

will not be admissible in a later action, for without this guaranty the party will never speak frankly and honestly. Similarly, a party must be guaranteed that the mediator is neutral, for without this guaranty the party will not continue in the voluntary mediation process....

To require testimony of a mediator is to require that the mediator take sides in a dispute, because the subpoena is served only when one party wants the mediator to testify on his or her behalf. If a mediator takes sides, it is a breach of trust and makes a lie of the promises that are made by mediation.[10]

To maintain trust, encourage forthright disclosure, and preserve parties' faith in the process, confidentiality is urged as inviolate. Yet adopting an impenetrable barrier to disclosure poses ethical quandaries of its own. Sometimes revealing what has gone on in a mediation becomes critical to advancing other worthwhile goals. It is to a consideration of these countervailing goals that we now turn.

INTERESTS ADVANCED BY DISCLOSURE OF MEDIATION COMMUNICATIONS

Disclosure of what transpired in a mediation is generally urged in one of two circumstances: to right an already existing wrong and to prevent a wrong from occurring. Both instances relate to doing justice, in the sense of correcting an existing injustice or preventing an injustice from materializing in the future. Let's look first at the concern with preventing harm.

Preventing Future Harm

The majority of state and federal legislation conferring confidentiality protection on mediation communications create an exception for statements that reveal a threat of future harm.[11] These statutes or court rules suspend confidentiality protections if parties are planning to commit a crime,[12] are poised to inflict serious physical harm,[13] or are otherwise posing a significant and immediate risk to others.[14]

The UMA explicitly states that no privilege is available for communications that constitute "a threat or statement of a plan to inflict bodily injury or commit a crime of violence" or are "intentionally used to plan a crime, attempt to commit or commit a crime, or to conceal an ongoing crime or ongoing criminal activity."[15]

In a variant on the general concern for preventing harms to mediation participants and third parties, many states authorize disclosure when a mediator has grounds to think that a child is being abused, abandoned, or neglected.[16] Concern for the welfare of vulnerable persons also motivates a provision of the UMA that renders admissible evidence of child or elder abuse in mediations involving state agencies charged with their protection.[17]

Implicit in these carve-outs is a concern that mediators not stand idly by while parties engage in behavior that is damaging or destructive to themselves or others. Although safeguarding party confidences is an important value, preventing harm—especially serious physical harm—emerges as an equally, and in some instances predominant, concern.[18]

But it's important to note how careful legislatures and drafting committees have been to cabin the circumstances in which disclosure is permitted. Usually mediators must be acting to prevent a credible risk of serious bodily injury,[19] and some states require the risk of harm to be imminent.[20]

Although worried that overly rigid confidentiality rules might hamstring mediators from doing the right thing, lawmakers also fret about chipping away too freely at the privacy protections mediation would otherwise enjoy. Create too many exceptions, and mediation's supposed safe harbor becomes more theoretical than real. This concern is especially true when considering the exceptions geared toward addressing past wrongdoing.

Righting Past Wrongs

The problem with an unpierceable confidentiality shield is that it may, in some instances, protect those who have abused the mediation process. If we lace confidentiality's protective cloak too tight, parties who have been disadvantaged as a result of others' bad behavior will never be able to prove their case.

Imagine the worst-case scenario: the bullying mediator who threatens and coerces an intimidated disputant into signing off on a bad deal. Or the innocent disputant who swallows the tall tales of her adversary and finds her credulousness repaid by deceit. How are these parties to prove that they were victims of duress, fraud, and other legally significant misconduct if they cannot tell what happened during the mediation? How are they to extricate themselves from their bad deals if they cannot point to the defects in the process that led them there?

Most state evidentiary codes acknowledge this problem and provide misused parties some tools to work with in the battle to redress prior bad behavior. Recognizing that mediation's integrity is seriously compromised by mediator misconduct, many state legislatures have created a confidentiality exception for aggrieved parties bringing claims against their mediator.[21] Some states expand the exception to suits brought against alternative dispute resolution (ADR) programs as well.[22]

The UMA takes an expansive approach to malpractice, excluding from protection information relevant to professional misconduct claims lodged against mediators, parties, party representatives, or nonparties.[23] Thus, if an individual sues her attorney for malpractice or breach of fiduciary duty, the mediator may discuss what transpired in joint session or caucus as long as the discussion is relevant to the allegations or related defenses.

Concern with the integrity of the bargaining process has led a few states to open up testimony about the mediation when a party claims that the resulting agreement was based on fraud, duress, or some other process defect. Louisiana, for example, maintains that "all oral and written communications and records made during mediation ... are not subject to disclosure," except where the agreement generated is being challenged. If the parties seek a judicial hearing on the meaning or enforceability of their mediated agreement, a court might consider "testimony concerning what occurred in the mediation proceeding" if they deem such testimony "necessary to prevent fraud or manifest injustice."[24] Other states also permit testimony tending to show that one party was misled by lies, intimidation, or other trickery.[25]

The UMA assigns significant weight to the concern that parties in mediation not be duped or shanghaied into disadvantageous agreements, but requires parties seeking to open up the mediation process to show that their fairness concerns are compelling.

The UMA places two procedural hurdles in the path of parties seeking to introduce evidence of mediation conversations for the purpose of rescinding or reforming the mediation agreement. First, they must convince a court or arbitrator in camera that the evidence is not otherwise available. Second, they must establish that the need for the evidence substantially outweighs the interest in protecting confidentiality.[26]

So under the UMA, a party wishing to repudiate her mediated purchase of a mule on the grounds that the seller advertised in mediation that the animal was a horse would be able to open up certain conversations and documents for judicial scrutiny. The buyer could offer into evidence documents used in mediation to establish the pedigree of the "horse," but only if the court found that no other evidence exists establishing the other side's efforts to pawn off the mule as a horse. In addition, the court would have to find that the plaintiff's interest in proving the horse deception is more important than the public's interest in maintaining mediation confidentiality.

Although the mule-laden plaintiff could introduce incriminating documents and offer testimony herself, she could not force the mediator to discuss in open court the content of her mediation discussions. Careful not to impinge too heavily on the mediator's ability to remain neutral, the UMA drafters chose to grant mediators substantial latitude in determining whether they will testify in suits challenging a mediation agreement. Parties can be compelled to testify about mediation communications when claims of fraud, duress, or unconscionability are being asserted, but mediators are explicitly exempted from compulsion.[27]

The decision whether to participate in a judicial inquiry into the purity of the mediation process is, under the UMA, left up to mediators' individual consciences. They can assist courts in their efforts to uncover who was duped and who simply is suffering buyer's remorse, but they need not.

TAILORING PARTIES' EXPECTATIONS OF CONFIDENTIALITY

Deciding whether to stay silent or to disclose, like many of the other ethical conundrums in this book, involves carefully weighing and balancing the competing interests and values at stake. Much will depend on context and the particular harms at issue.

Notably, the Model Standards point out that "parties may make their own rules" with respect to confidentiality and that mediators may contract with parties to accept disclosure of certain information should it arise in the course of mediation discussions.[28] Given the pervasive lifting of confidentiality protection to prove past misbehavior or the likelihood of future harm, mediators would do well to reconsider their blanket assurances of confidentiality "no matter what."

The thrust of the Model Standards and corollary state codes is that mediation is a private process, shuttered from the invasive gaze of the outside world. However, the louvers are not invariably closed tight. Legal requirements may force disclosure, and the parties may agree up front that certain information will be considered to be in the public domain. When public policy concerns or mediator practice dictate that certain subject matter be aired, it is important that parties be informed of those carve-outs from the start. In that way, parties retain the capacity to act in a purely self-determining fashion. They can choose to reveal information to the mediator in the hopes that it will assist in settling the case—knowing that the mediator may make the information available to others. Or they can keep the information secret. Either way, they have acted pursuant to their own best judgment, and there will be no unpleasant surprises.

What mediators most fear when confronting confidentiality dilemmas is the prospect of breaking faith with the disputants they have sworn to help. Mediators don't want to be in the position of disclosing exactly that information they earlier agreed to keep confidential. But this is a difficulty that can be addressed through foresight and careful communication at the front end of the process.

Some mediators try to avoid disappointing client expectations of privacy by educating parties about the legal restrictions that dilute confidentiality protections and fostering more modest expectations. For example, one might say: "I will endeavor to keep secret everything that is said in mediation. There are a few circumstances, however, where I might be called on to reveal confidences, and I will do so. I will do so if it appears that one of you—or a third party—is at serious risk of harm and disclosure is necessary to protect against that harm. Also, a court may call on me to discuss what went on here if one of you challenges the validity of the agreement we ultimately reach."

Disputants should know that in some jurisdictions, legal rules require disclosure. Even where the legal requirements are unclear, ethical norms may push toward openness. If mediators can antici-pate situations where they will be legally or ethically compelled to reveal mediation statements to third parties, they should discuss that possibility with their clients. Setting out the exact scope and limits of what confidentiality supplies is the best way for mediators to avoid being caught between conflicting loyalties.

Conflicting loyalties and a tug of war between maintaining confidences and preventing fraud and abuse are at the heart of the case that follows. Note the importance of separating out the legal from the ethical analysis and the way in which some of the tensions could be resolved by a carefully crafted introductory statement.

CASE 9.1: DUTIES OF CARE—MEDIATING WITH A CROOKED DOCTOR

Six months ago, you mediated a dispute that had arisen between two physicians who had purchased office space together. Dr. Santo and Dr. Friedrich had jointly signed a ten-year lease agreement for a suite in an office building. They pooled their funds to furnish the office area and secure certain medical equipment that both used in their practices.

After two years, Santo decided he wished to pursue opportunities elsewhere. A dispute arose regarding his obligations under the lease and how his interest in the office furnishings and medical equipment should be valued.

You agreed to mediate and helped Santo and Friedrich reach a cordial resolution. Friedrich took on the remainder of the lease and agreed to pay Santo $15,000 for his interest in the jointly purchased medical equipment. Friedrich also agreed to purchase Santo's patient list and all associated goodwill for the sum of $40,000—based on Santo's representations that he dealt only with private insurance and that his practice generated approximately $150,000 annually. To support his representations, Santo distributed a packet of documents, including his latest tax returns as well as a statement from his accountant asserting that billings from private insurance had generated between $150,000 and $170,000 annually for the past three years.

Your role in the mediation was facilitative. Essentially you simply helped both parties better identify their true interests. At one point, Friedrich asked you whether you thought Santo would accept $5,000 for the medical equipment and you replied that based on your discussions in caucus, you thought he would require at least double that amount. Neither party asked for your opinion or evaluation of the sale of the patient list.

Three months after the mediation and two months after Santo's departure, Friedrich discovered documents suggesting that Santo's income stream was largely generated by defrauding Medicare and Medicaid. A close review of Santo's medical files revealed billings for a host of procedures that Santo's medical assistant told Friedrich had never been done.

Friedrich is furious and seeks to rescind the contract, alleging fraud and deceit. He has also urged the court to invalidate the contract on the grounds that he "was coerced into signing by the mediator." The suit for rescission is proceeding in court, and Friedrich has called you as a witness. He wants you to tell the court what Santo said in caucus about the value of the practice. Santo has counterclaimed for enforcement of the contract, arguing that the defenses of fraud and coercion are inapplicable. Santo seeks to have you testify that no coercion took place.

How do you respond to the demand that you discuss what happened at the mediation? What is the ethically correct course of conduct?

Before we begin to discuss what is ethically required or advisable, it is first helpful to separate out the ethics of the case from the legal realities.

The Legal Realities

LEGALLY, CAN YOU TESTIFY ABOUT WHETHER YOU COERCED DR. FRIEDRICH TO SIGN THE AGREEMENT? As noted, states are sensitive to the dilemma that may confront some mediators who are accused of professional negligence but are precluded from defending their prior conduct by confidentiality constraints. To ease the burden, a number of states allow mediators to open up the black box of mediator-party dialogue in the name of self-defense. However, these "self-defense" exceptions usually apply only if the mediator is actually herself being sued.[29] The UMA is typical in allowing disclosure only "to prove or disprove a claim or complaint of professional misconduct or malpractice filed against a mediator."[30]

Here, Friedrich is certainly suggesting that you mediated badly. Mediators aren't supposed to coerce anybody into signing anything, and that is exactly what he says you did. But he isn't suing you for professional negligence or malpractice. He is describing your conduct as coercive in order to challenge the validity of the contract he signed. Consequently the specific exceptions that would authorize you to testify about your conduct in a malpractice action brought against you don't apply.

Friedrich's claim that the agreement is unenforceable due to duress might trigger other statutory exemptions to confidentiality, though this seems unlikely. Statutes in Alaska and Louisiana allow disclosure of mediator testimony in a subsequent legal proceeding if a court determines that testimony is necessary to prevent "manifest injustice."[31] Maryland also allows a mediator to disclose mediation communications to "the appropriate authorities" if necessary to "defend against a claim or defense that because of ... duress ... a contract arising out of mediation should be rescinded."[32]

As noted, the UMA would allow testimony to prove a claim for rescission—though it is not clear that it would allow testimony for the purpose of defeating such a claim. In any event, the UMA only *allows* mediator testimony in cases challenging enforceability; it does not compel it.

LEGALLY, CAN YOU TESTIFY REGARDING DR. SANTO'S STATEMENTS ABOUT THE WORTH OF HIS PRACTICE? The same statutory exceptions to confidentiality for fraud or the prevention of manifest injustice would seem to allow your testimony regarding Santo's income claims. Santo said in mediation that his billings from private insurance amounted to $150,000. As it turns out, much of his income appears to derive from phantom billings to Medicare and Medicaid. Kansas, Louisiana, and Maryland all authorize disclosure to prevent him from capitalizing on his fraudulent statement.[33]

Like the UMA, however, these states do talk about the testimony being "necessary" to prevent fraud. It could be argued that your testimony, while helpful, is not truly necessary to prove the existence of Santo's misrepresentation. The documentation supplied by Santo's accountant establishes the income claims being made at the mediation. Thus, it is unlikely that Friedrich would be able to establish that your testimony is necessary, and the testimony would likely be inadmissible under the UMA and other state statutes as well.

The Ethical Side

SHOULD YOU TESTIFY REGARDING DR. FRIEDRICH'S CLAIM THAT HE WAS COERCED? If state law permits you to testify regarding your conduct at the mediation, the question remains whether you are ethically justified in doing so. At first blush, the answer may appear to be yes. After all, Friedrich hit you with a low blow. He has publicly stated—in legal papers yet—that you coerced him into signing an agreement. This is patently untrue. He asked you what you thought of a proposal, and you provided him with your best estimate of where the other side was with the numbers. You didn't tell him what to do with your guesstimate. That is hardly coercion. So isn't it ethically proper to face this accusation directly and refute it?

Although it might be emotionally tempting to do so, the better course ethically is to refrain from giving testimony. It is unlikely that Friedrich's accusation, unjust as it may be, is likely to result in any significant harm. Courts are typically unsympathetic to claims that a mediated agreement should be overturned due to mediator coercion.[34] If the mediation involved a vulnerable party and went twelve hours with no food or rest breaks, the court might be tempted to take a closer look.[35] But none of those facts is at play here. It is likely that the court would reject Friedrich's claim as unsubstantiated, regardless of whether you testify.

In addition, even if the court did overturn the agreement, it cannot be said that any terrible wrong will have been done. In truth, the agreement was based on fraud, so voiding the agreement will produce the right result, albeit for the wrong reason.

The only real harm that would materialize in the unlikely event that the court did void the agreement would be reputational. But this harm is insufficiently weighty to justify breaching client expectations of privacy. Clients don't frequently consult legal rulings when seeking information about prospective mediators, so it is uncertain whether the opinion's existence would affect your practice in any way. And even if a client did learn of the opinion, its negative effect could be easily blunted by pointing out that the court heard only one side of the story. You could explain that the truth differs from the narrative told by Friedrich, but that you didn't want to violate client confidences by testifying about what really happened.

Behaving ethically doesn't require saintly self-abnegation. But it does require temperance and restraint, even in provocative circumstances. Friedrich seems to have thrown down the gauntlet, and it is natural to want to defend against professional calumny. But unlike a mediator malpractice or negligence suit, Friedrich's effort to unwind the agreement by casting aspersions on your methods does not threaten your continued professional survival. It is unlikely to succeed, and even if it did, the adverse judgment is unlikely to have much effect on your practice. Consequently the duty to honor your prior confidentiality pledge outweighs your interest in defending your professional honor. Ironically, keeping silent remains the best way to preserve your reputation as an ethical mediator.

SHOULD YOU TESTIFY REGARDING DR. SANTO'S FRAUDULENT STATEMENTS IN MEDIATION? Again, the primary question to ask is whether the interest in righting the wrong that has occurred in mediation outweighs the interest in maintaining confidentiality. Certainly Santo lied about the value of his practice, and Friedrich has suffered a loss as a result. He has purchased a client list that cannot generate legitimate billings at the volume that he was led to believe exists.

It is troubling to imagine that mediation has become the vehicle by which Santo perpetrated his fraud, and it is tempting to want to assist in undoing the agreement. If your testimony were the only means by which the court could be informed of Santo's misrepresentations, the balance of equities would tip substantially in favor of doing so. However, your testimony is not truly necessary. Friedrich could seek admission of the documents relied on in mediation, including the accountant's statement regarding the volume of income generated by Santo's practice. That packet establishes for the court the representations Santo made in mediation; your testimony would only confirm what the court already knows. In this circumstance, providing supporting—but essentially redundant—information to the court cannot justify breaching the party expectations regarding confidentiality.

But consider how the landscape changes if your testimony were the only means of proving that Santo had lied during the mediation. In that circumstance, the interest in righting a past wrong and preventing mediation from becoming a vehicle for abuse grows while the interest in honoring party confidences remains static. Although this is ultimately a matter for each individual's conscience, it would seem ethically permissible to provide evidence of Santo's false and misleading statements in order to ensure that improprieties committed in the mediation process don't saddle Friedrich with a deal far different from the one he bargained for.

CASE 9.2: THE TOXIC PLAYGROUND

The hard case that follows suggests that educating parties and fostering modest expectations might be the most proactive strategy for addressing confidentiality dilemmas.

In a large and controversial land use dispute involving proposed construction of a new playground, a mediator has caucused with all parties. Following the most recent caucus, a safety engineer working for one defendant takes the mediator aside in the hall and tells him that she is wracked with guilt and concern over a document that she just came across. The document, which was not requested or disclosed in discovery, indicates that her employer inadvertently buried radioactive materials from a different job at the site of the proposed playground. The engineer tells the mediator that she may lose her job if this becomes public, but that she "just had to tell someone." She strongly discourages the mediator from discussing this issue with anyone else.

You are mediating. What do you do?

Comments on Case 9.2

Bruce Pardy

My land use dispute suddenly has turned into an environmental nightmare. Children may be put at risk. Unfortunately, I have received that information in confidence. As mediator, what should I do?

CONSIDERATIONS: THE MEDIATOR'S ROLE. In this situation, it would be easy to forget my place. After all, I appear to be running the show. I control the mediation process, caucus privately with the parties (and thus become a confidant for all simultaneously), and provide the sole source of neutral assessment and advice (assuming this is an evaluative mediation). So why should I not act directly and forcefully to protect innocent children? Because doing so misconstrues the nature of my job.

My Limitations. As mediator, I have an extremely limited role to play. Mediation is a voluntary, private conversation. Its fundamental premise is that parties can resolve their dispute any way they see fit.[36] They have freedom to contract their way out of the conflict, and the nature of their agreement is limited only by the general principles of contract law. Mediation is a conciliatory, cooperative process that takes place within an adversarial legal system. In such a system, the dispute belongs to the parties. They may choose to resolve it coercively (by going to court or entering into arbitration) or voluntarily (by negotiating their own outcome). If they choose the latter, mediation is for the sole purpose of helping them to invent a settlement, whatever its terms.

In the process of assisting with this resolution, the mediator is merely a guest. He serves the interests of the parties as potential collaborators, not as adversaries. The mediator is there to make agreement more likely, not to place additional problems in the way.

Therefore, I am at the table only by invitation and have a role only so long as all parties consent. Since for the parties the entire process is voluntary,[37] the only value I can bring to the dispute is my influence over the nature of the parties' interaction. Therefore, as mediator, I have no power to coerce or to insist on a course of action with which the parties do not agree. Instead, my only tool is persuasion—my ability to influence the nature of the conversation among the parties and the content of the agreement that they might reach.

In these respects, the role of a mediator is distinctly different from that of judge, arbitrator, and lawyer.[38] These other roles have responsibilities that transcend the dispute between the parties. Judges apply the law, as do arbitrators. Lawyers represent clients and are restrained by that duty, but also have obligations to the court and by virtue of their status as members of the bar. But mediators have no independent duties to the court, the public, or unrepresented third parties. Mediators are not decision makers. They are not free to pursue their own convictions about right and wrong. The role of a mediator is not to exercise his or her judgment on the proper resolution of the problem, but to help the parties exercise their own judgment. They have no mandate to impose upon the parties their own conceptions of justice or to pursue their own formulation of the public good. To do so is to attempt to play two conflicting roles: facilitator of an agreement and protector of an interest potentially in conflict with that agreement. Rational parties do not retain mediators who are inclined to play this double role (assuming that intent has been disclosed, as it should be, before the mediation begins). They have no reason to give up control of their own dispute or to make resolving the dispute more difficult than it already is.

Therefore, my only tool is persuasion. I will attempt to persuade participants to take a course that will provide an effective and lasting resolution. If that advice is rejected, I have no power to insist.

A Mediator Is Not a Fact Finder. Mediation is not a truth-gathering exercise.[39] Unlike judges and arbitrators, a mediator does not weigh evidence, assess credibility, or find facts. Instead, the parties have control of the substance of the conversation. They decide what is real and what is important.

Therefore, when I am told there are radioactive materials under the site of the proposed playground, my job is not to believe or disbelieve. In my role as mediator, the significance of the conversation with the safety engineer is that there may be information relevant to the matter in dispute that has not been disclosed. My mandate is to continue to mediate—to facilitate a conversation that includes, if possible, full voluntary disclosure of all relevant information.

Confidentiality. Much of the commentary on confidentiality in mediation concerns disclosure to the world beyond the walls of the mediation room. As a general rule, all parties to mediation, including the mediator, owe a duty of confidentiality to the others unless there is explicit agreement to the contrary. Therefore, I am not at liberty to disclose the engineer's information to anyone outside the mediation.

But that is not the most pressing issue in the playground scenario. Instead, the question is the nature of the confidentiality obligation within the mediation. When a mediator speaks privately with a participant, is information automatically privileged? First principles and the Model Standards of Conduct for Mediators suggest that the answer is yes. Standard V(B) of the Model Standards states, "A mediator who meets with any persons in private session during a mediation shall not convey directly or indirectly to any other person, any information that was obtained during that private session without the consent of the disclosing person."[40]

This approach makes sense because participation in mediation is voluntary. Information is owned by the person who possesses it, and no one is under a legal compulsion to disclose. If the parties are already engaged in litigation, disclosure may be compelled at discovery, but that is a court requirement, not one created by the mediation. Therefore, participants are in a position to determine what they will disclose and under what circumstances. (Of course, if the mediation is to be productive, the parties usually need to agree that they will disclose all relevant information. In many circumstances, settlement may be unlikely if they do not. But even so, disclosure is a voluntary, negotiated act, not one that can be coerced by the mediator.)

Since the engineer has specifically requested that I not share her information with anyone else, I may not do so without her consent.

Interests of a Third Party Not Represented at the Mediation. A mediator does not have the authority to protect the interests of unrepresented third parties or force the parties to take those interests into account.[41] He must not attempt to impose extra responsibilities on the parties or skirt his duties to the parties in the name of protecting such interests. No rational party involved in a dispute would consent to the participation of a mediator who considered that to be part of his mandate. Having learned of a possible danger to children who might use the playground, am I at liberty to disclose the existence of radioactive materials at the site? In other words, can the interests of a third party who is not represented at the mediation override the duty of confidentiality? Unless there is an explicit statutory provision providing otherwise, the answers are "no" and "no."

National mediator codes in the United States and Canada confirm this approach. For example, the Model Standards suggest that where a mediator becomes aware of domestic abuse or violence or that the mediation is being used to further criminal conduct, the mediator should take "appropriate steps." The appropriate steps contemplated by the relevant sections are postponement of, withdrawal from, or termination of the mediation. These are the appropriate choices. Violating the duty of confidentiality is not among them.[42] The mediator is not a law enforcement official. His clients are the parties to the negotiation. His obligation is to provide neutral, confidential facilitation. None of this changes when the mediator hears something he does not like.

Mediation Ethics. Ethics are moral principles that help determine right from wrong. They are not determined by committee. That is, the declaration of a committee may reflect a consensus opinion about what is right and wrong, but the committee may itself be right or wrong about its opinion.

While codes and model standards developed by committees are helpful guidelines to assist mediators in deciding what to do in particular situations, the question of ethical behavior is one that ultimately rests with each individual mediator. Much effort has been expended in recent years in attempting to professionalize the practice of mediation, but unlike lawyers, judges, and arbitrators, who have gatekeepers to restrict who may join their ranks, "mediator" is not truly a professional designation. A person who helps his neighbors resolve their conflict about repairing the back fence is a mediator, and no training or official designation is required. Even more than lawyers, judges, and arbitrators, mediators should be guided by their own moral compasses. When they encounter situations they believe are contrary to their ethical beliefs, the proper decision is to step down. Otherwise they will mediate in the presence of a conflict of interest between their duty to the parties to facilitate resolution and their personal moral convictions.

Withdrawing from the mediation has little or no effect on the welfare of the parties, while disclosure of confidential information obviously breaches the very obligations the mediator has promised to fulfill.

WHAT I CAN DO. I cannot coerce, but I can attempt to persuade. I will attempt to persuade the safety engineer to disclose the existence of the document to her employer. She may ask if she has a legal duty to do so. If I am a mediator, then at that moment I am not a lawyer, and I do not know. My best answer is that she should retain her own lawyer for independent legal advice. If she refuses and the document remains hidden, I would withdraw from the mediation, not because there is danger in the playground (that I do not know), but because there is information that has not been disclosed that is relevant to the dispute and whose absence affects the efficacy of the mediation process.

If the engineer informs her employer of the document and he does not disclose the document to the other parties, I will attempt to persuade him to do so. Creating possible danger to children should be relevant to the party in and of itself, but so is potential liability and the weakness of a resolution made without disclosure of key information. If the employer refuses, then I would withdraw from the mediation, again because of the lack of disclosure of key information, which undermines the mediation process and my performance within it.

If the employer discloses the document to the other parties, then I would attempt to persuade the parties that their best collective interests are served by ensuring that the property is not hazardous—that they should wish children to be safe, but also that their potential liability and the durability of their settlement depend on the quality of their due diligence. If, in spite of my best efforts, the parties decide collectively to bury the information and proceed as though it does not exist, then I would withdraw from the mediation—this time because I have a conflict of interest between my own ethical standards and my role as mediator.

Comments on Case 9.2

Charles Pou

This scenario—although unlikely to arise in everyday practice—poses a classic hard choice. An individual mediator's response likely will reflect his or her vision of how confidentiality fits into a hierarchy of ethical, community, social justice, and other values we hold dear and seek to promote.

Mediators have duties to society, their profession, their clients, and themselves. As a general rule, I, like nearly all other mediators, would do everything possible to avoid disclosing information received in confidence during mediation; for me, mediator confidentiality, along with the concept of self-determination by the parties, ranks at the top of the hierarchy of critical values in mediation. If confronted with a clear, hard choice between my obligation as a mediator to protect confidences and my concern for the health of future generations, I'd seek to act in a way that harmonizes the mediation process's integrity with competing statutory, investigative, justice-related, or public welfare goals.

In this case, I'd initially try to use all my persuasive skill to encourage and aid the informant to find and take a course of action that will prevent harm. If that effort and all others were to fail and there were a reasonable certainty that

- Radioactive material is present, and
- It poses a real harm to public safety or health, and
- No one else is likely to say anything,

then my concern over the significant possibility of serious harm to innocent third parties would lead me to search hard for a rationale and means to effect disclosure.

I'd tell my informant that I was seeing no way to avoid my duty to disclose and wanted to work with her to find an approach that meets as many of our interests and obligations as possible. I'd point out to her that I might seek the assistance of the judge presiding over the litigation by requesting an in camera hearing and then taking the appropriate course, guided by the court's decision and other factors.[43] If we could not find a mutually satisfactory approach, I'd check my gut and, I hope, follow the course that will allow me to look in the mirror the next morning and succeeding mornings, possibly including the in camera hearing option. As I think about it, I really could not proceed in a business-as-usual mediation mode if I believed that a deal I was helping to close would likely result in innocent children getting seriously ill.

CONFIDENTIALITY AS A CRITICAL VALUE IN MEDIATION. I believe the grounds generally advanced for strictly limiting disclosure by mediators to be compelling ones:

- Confidentiality enhances participants' frank and open communications in, and effective use of, ADR processes. Without assurance that their confidences will not be disclosed, parties would be far less willing to discuss freely their interests and possible settlements.

- A mediator's disclosure of private recollections or documents could affect his or her perceived neutrality, be misconstrued as showing bias, and seriously disadvantage a participant.

- In practice, even one or two cases where expectations of confidentiality are seriously undermined could precipitate a damaging loss of trust in mediation generally and even inhibit future participation in ADR processes.

For these reasons, mediators generally are expected to avoid disclosure as an ethical duty, a legal obligation, or both. The Model Standards of Conduct for Mediators, probably the most widely recognized mediator ethics code,[44] require that a mediator "maintain the reasonable expectations of parties with regard to confidentiality." While acknowledging that the parties' confidentiality expectations depend on the circumstances of the mediation and any agreements they may make, these standards state that a mediator "shall not disclose any matter that a party expects to be confidential unless given permission by all parties or unless required by law or other public policy."

FACTORS POTENTIALLY AFFECTING CONFIDENTIALITY EXPECTATIONS. In addition to general ethical duties, the rules governing mediator confidentiality (and parties' reasonable expectations) will almost always be shaped by specifically applicable legal standards—for example, the applicable state law, federal statute, or court or agency rule governing the case.[45]

Thus, mediator confidentiality obligations may vary considerably, since statutes or rules take many different approaches:

- Even today, many agencies, courts, and jurisdictions have no law or rule governing confidentiality.

- Some statutes endorse the notion that mediation processes should be "confidential," without defining the term or saying much about potential exceptions.

- Others, like the UMA, create a "privilege" that protects against disclosure primarily in legal proceedings. Under the UMA, a mediator would ordinarily be precluded from testifying in court, but might not be prohibited from disclosing mediation communications in some other nonjudicial contexts.

- Still others—like the Administrative Dispute Resolution Act that is applicable at the federal agency level—operate as a flat prohibition against unauthorized disclosure by a mediator (subject to limited exceptions).

Whether the law or another explicit public policy requires, prohibits, or affects disclosure by the mediator will be a jurisdiction-specific issue. In the scenario at hand (or any other), a conscientious mediator would presumably seek to ensure his or her understanding of the various applicable authorities and their impact. Having done so, the mediator's approach might well depend on his or her interpretation of the Model Standards or on standards and procedures set forth in the governing statute or in the agreement to mediate for that case.

Here, at least one party has clearly stated her expectation that sensitive information be kept confidential and has refused the mediator permission to disclose—although some might see the act of telling the mediator as indicating an implicit desire to avoid the harm that may come with silence. Thus, disclosure would presumably be prohibited by the Model Standards, and possibly applicable law and the agreement to mediate.

Some ethics codes (though not the Model Standards) provide explicit guidance as to when a mediator might be ethically justified in breaching a party confidence. Certain codes, for instance, allow disclosure in the narrow circumstance when disclosure is necessary to prevent "death or serious bodily injury" or "substantial financial loss" from a crime or fraud one party has committed or intends to commit.[46]

There is accord between, on one hand, codes that carve out a contravening obligation of disclosure in situations where the mediator believes continued secrecy threatens serious physical harm and, on the other, existing statutory, common law, and ethical duties that bind attorneys and nonattorneys alike, regardless of whether they are serving as a mediator. For example, many states impose mandatory reporting requirements on members of the healing professions; that is, they require physicians, social workers, and, in some jurisdictions, mediators to notify public health authorities if they have grounds to suspect child or elder abuse. Additionally, judicial decisions in a number of states require individuals to take reasonable measures to warn or protect third parties from a foreseeable threat of serious violence. Whether the risk posed here is substantially certain or imminent enough to trigger any of these common law or statutory duties is doubtful. Although it is likely (if the document truly reveals the presence of toxic chemicals) that some children at some point in time would suffer some type of harm if the land deal goes through as contemplated, my understanding is that this type of diffuse, future risk is usually not sufficient to trigger disclosure duties under existing legal or ethical rules.

Still, even if we conclude that the specific confidentiality rules at issue don't authorize disclosure under these facts, it is troubling to think that ethically, no authorization exists to disclose information for the sake of the larger public good.[47] After all, mediation's aspiration is to generate outcomes superior to litigation. Open, forthright discussions among parties who have been coaxed into more trusting attitudes are thought conducive to optimal outcomes. Here—in terms of public safety—the mediation would result in a potentially disastrous conclusion.

It does not strike me as self-evident that a contravening obligation to disclose presents itself—neither legal (for example, child abuse); common law (disclosure necessary to avert a substantial risk of death or serious bodily harm); nor ethical (for example, lawyer's duty to report information to prevent death, serious bodily harm, or substantial financial loss).

PRACTICAL ADVICE. So what options might a mediator have between the extremes of breaching a legal, ethical, or contractual duty to keep silent and possibly averting potential serious long-term public harm? Mediators hoping to avoid, or deal with, such difficult dilemmas might benefit from some of these ideas:

- Since expectations regarding confidentiality are important, the mediator should discuss these expectations with the parties, both at the outset and as soon as potential questions begin to arise—hopefully, before any party has disclosed "dangerous information."

- Some mediators seek to shape expectations by including a clause in their mediation agreement that addresses cases like these. They may include a sentence similar to the following: "If I discover any information that in my judgment threatens to pose a risk of serious harm to any of the mediation participants present or third parties, I will feel free to disclose that information in order to prevent such harm from materializing." While such a clause may dampen the parties' comfort level with the process, it would afford advance notice, give the mediator some room to maneuver if troubling information is revealed, and allow parties to look elsewhere or negotiate something different with the neutral if they found such a clause objectionable.

- Assess the information in question. Much depends on determining the credibility and seriousness of the risk. If it is not wholly dubious, the mediator might—by asking questions or otherwise—raise the possibility that the soil be tested, or try to slow the mediation and get answers to determine exactly the type of risk that is being posed. After all, confidentiality is a critical value in mediation, and I wouldn't want to move toward disclosure unless the harm I was seeking to avert was clear and substantial.

- Some statutes (including the UMA and federal Administrative Dispute Resolution Act) contain procedures for communicating privately with a judge to obtain direction as to how to handle requests for mediator disclosure of sensitive communications that are arguably protected.[48] Even absent such a formal request, in a situation where major ethical or other concerns suggest disclosure may be appropriate, a mediator might seek to employ such a process to obtain a declaratory judgment, order, or judicial advice.

- Mediators and ADR programs for which they serve should regard their disclosure of a dispute resolution communication as an absolute final resort. Ordinarily they should not disclose such a communication unless required by law and unless no other person is reasonably available to disclose the communication.

CONCLUSION. Even confidentiality—which is in many ways the most objective and clearly defined of a mediator's ethical duties—may involve a good deal of subjectivity as a mediator weighs obligations and options, susses out for himself what is ethical, and then acts accordingly. If a neutral were to preserve confidentiality in this "nuclear playground" case and members of the public later learned of it, they would likely be outraged; the mediator, the credibility of mediation processes generally, and innocent children would all likely suffer long-term harm. Thus, if the information presented to the mediator is in fact credible and the mediator goes through the process described above and finds no alternative to disclosure, I would conclude that this is one of those exceedingly rare cases in which his duty to disclose would outweigh mediation-based values like confidentiality.

Editor's Thoughts on Case 9.2 and the Comments

Both commentators in this toxic playground case recognize the importance of keeping party confidences. And both are deeply troubled by the prospect that keeping quiet about the possibly lethal presence of chemicals might sicken future generations of children. But after jointly recognizing the problem, each commentator formulates a different set of responses that give divergent weights to the conflicting values at stake.

Bruce Pardy stresses the importance of remaining humble about the place of the mediator in the dispute. "I am a guest," he reminds us, invited in to the disputants' party for a limited purpose. Taking a modest view of the terms of the invitation, Pardy points out that his own judgments about the toxic chemicals and what should be done to protect future children cannot play a prominent role in the progress of the negotiation. Pardy notes that he can deploy his powers of persuasion to advocate for disclosure and problem solving around the issue of the chemicals. But persuasion is the only tool he finds available.

Pardy's modesty flows from his unitary vision of the mediator's duty. Mediators, he argues, owe a duty to the parties and no one else. The parties turn to the mediator with the expectation that he will work toward an agreement that will effectuate their jointly determined interests. Mediators, in Pardy's view, "have no independent duties to the court, the public, or unrepresented third parties." They work for the parties and the parties alone. Perhaps, given the facts, we might wish that the children of the neighborhood had a representative at the table, but they don't, and the mediator cannot assume that role. In Pardy's view, part of the covenant mediators make with disputants is that their best interests, and no one else's, will remain paramount.

Charles Pou is working with a slightly different conception of the mediator's obligations. In his view, mediators "have duties to society, their profession, their clients, and themselves." Rather than defining the challenge as keeping the faith with the only stakeholders whose claims really matter—the parties—Pou sees the difficulty as one of "harmonization"—how one balances the "mediation process's integrity with competing statutory, investigative, justice-related, or public welfare goals."

Pardy and Pou cite different texts in supporting their different notions of the problem. Pardy notes that the Model Standards do not explicitly endorse disclosure, even in the face of possible threats of domestic violence. Pou notes that many jurisdictions embrace a duty-to-warn rule when third parties are at imminent risk of serious harm and notes that at least some ethics codes impose a similar obligation on the mediator. And their choice of text reflects larger assumptions. Pardy assumes that no party would hire a mediator if she thought that the mediator was keeping a third eye out for the intangible interests of the greater good, whereas Pou surmises that most people would "be outraged" if they learned that a mediator stood by and allowed a public health danger to ripen under his watch.

Interestingly, given their philosophical differences, Pou and Pardy don't come out so very far apart when it comes to their practical responses to the case. Both would initially call on their rhetorical powers to advocate for disclosure. Pardy says he would point out to the engineer and her boss that they should want to address the problem, not only because it is right but because it is sensible from a business perspective. Ultimately if the land is tainted, the other party will discover this and attempt to unravel the deal as a result. At the very least, the unraveling process will consume time, energy, and money. In the worst-case scenario, it could lead to a hefty damage assessment.

Pou would also begin by talking to the engineer. He would point out the ethical dilemma as he sees it and invite her to brainstorm with him some range of solutions that would meet her privacy concerns while preventing harm. To move things along, he would share with her his thoughts about contacting the presiding judge (assuming the case is in active litigation) and suggesting an in camera hearing.

After an initial resort to soft methods, Pou and Pardy's next responses diverge. For Pardy, the next step after persuasion is withdrawal; disclosure to anyone is simply not an option. Pou's next step, if persuasion fails, is to bring in the presiding judge and ask him to help make a judgment. Unlike Pardy, Pou feels an obligation to prevent a bad outcome, and that obligation, in his view, might warrant disclosure of the engineer's secret.

CHAPTER TEN

Confidentiality Continued

Attorney Misconduct or Child Abuse

s introduced in the previous chapter, the duty to maintain party confidentiality may create agonizing choices when countervailing values push toward disclosure. Mediators may feel compelled to reveal mediation communications either to rectify an existing wrong or to prevent future serious harm. This chapter continues exploring this tension, focusing on the problems of attorney misconduct and mandatory or permissive reporting of child abuse.

THE MANDATE TO DISCLOSE OTHER ATTORNEYS' MISCONDUCT

Attorney mediators seeking to preserve inviolate confidences made throughout the process will face difficult choices if confronted with attorney misconduct. Rule 8.3 of the Model Rules of Professional Conduct for attorneys (Model Rules) not only allows attorneys to report other lawyers' bad behavior but affirmatively requires it. The reporting requirement is triggered if both of these hold:

1. An attorney knows that another lawyer has committed a violation of the rules of professional conduct.

2. The violation raises a substantial question as to that lawyer's honesty, trustworthiness, or fitness as a lawyer in other respects.[1]

Crafted to encourage self-policing, Rule 8.3 falls short of demanding clear proof of wrongdoing. Rather, attorneys are to report when it would be reasonable to form a "firm opinion" or "firm belief" that it was more likely than not that the suspected misconduct had occurred.[2] In terms of the gravity or severity of offense, the rule's "substantial question" language makes clear that only serious violations catalyze the rule's whistle-blowing mandate. Responding to discovery with an aggressively ungenerous interpretation of what is called for—leading to the withholding of arguably relevant documents—would not rise to the level of misconduct contemplated. Comingling or expropriating client funds, forging signatures, or lying to the court certainly would.[3]

Sometimes referred to as the "snitch rule," Rule 8.3 is unpopular. Attorneys resist the tattling mandate. Few file complaints against erring colleagues or opponents. Responding to this reluctance, some state actors have piled on incentives. The Illinois Supreme Court, for example, suspended one attorney's license for a year for failing to report another attorney's conversion of client monies. Although the client herself had given instructions that no formal complaint be issued, the court nonetheless determined that public discipline of the nonreporting attorney was both warranted and appropriate.[4]

The Illinois court's draconian interpretation of Rule 8.3's dictates is anomalous and unlikely to spark a trend. Sanctions against nonreporting attorneys remain rare. Still, the existence of a reporting duty threatens to lift the veil on communications that most mediators pledge will remain secret. When attorneys are functioning as neutrals and learn of misconduct on the part of counsel, which ethical mandate should they consider most pressing?

CASE 10.1: AN ATTORNEY'S WRONGFUL TERMINATION CLAIM

Ted is mediating a wrongful termination claim brought by Austin Tower against his former employer, the Liggett Law Firm. Austin was discharged six months ago after four years as an associate at the firm. Austin was told that he was being discharged for poor performance, but his evaluations until discharge had been excellent.

Austin claims that he was discharged because he discovered that the senior partner, Mr. X, was overbilling a corporate client on a large piece of litigation that he and Mr. X were both involved in. Austin claims that he spoke with another partner about his discovery and urged the partner to take action. He cited recent case law censoring attorneys who had failed to report colleagues' misconduct and threatened to go to the authorities himself if the firm did not take action. The following week, Austin was shown the door.

In caucus, Austin shows you copies of his original time sheets and client invoices that demonstrate that Mr. X had charged the client for twenty hours that Austin had not billed. In addition, Austin brought in copies of Mr. X's computer calendar records and e-mails for a four-week period that showed that Mr. X had billed the client for several days during which he was traveling and working on other cases. Austin has not notified the state disciplinary board about Mr. X's behavior, nor has anyone else at the firm.

In mediation, the Liggett Law Firm agrees to pay Austin a healthy severance package and assist him in his efforts to land a job at another law firm. In return, Austin agrees to drop the lawsuit. The mediation discussions center on both Austin and Mr. X's feelings of betrayal. The overbilling allegations are not explored in any detail. Austin maintains that Mr. X was dishonest in handling the client's account, and Mr. X. continues to rebut the allegations and assert no wrongdoing occurred.

Mediator Ted is licensed to practice in the state, although he has not served in any role other than a neutral in the last two years. What should Ted do?

Technically the Model Standards and most state codes would allow disclosure on the grounds that it is "required by applicable law." Regardless of the vigor with which disciplinary boards and state courts pursue nonreporting attorneys, the reporting mandate remains on the books, commanding allegiance.[5]

As a matter of practice, however, most attorney mediators place their duties of confidentiality above their professional self-policing obligations. Some mediators resolve this difficulty by alerting parties prior to the mediation that they have reporting requirements that will take precedence over the duty to maintain confidentiality. Many, however, do not go into detail regarding specific reporting requirements for fear of undermining trust and rapport with the parties with an overly legalistic opening presentation. Attorney mediators tend to resolve this tension by subordinating their obligations as members of the bar to their obligations as third-party neutrals and fiduciaries to the disputants who are entrusted to their care.

This is probably as it should be, but the tension can engender moral distress. Here, the alleged overbilling is troubling but does not rise to the level of wrongdoing that would justify a breach of disputant trust. First, on the facts as given, questions remain regarding Mr. X's behavior. Is it possible that Mr. X did work on the client's case while on a trip primarily motivated by another's case? Could the bill to the client represent a clerical error rather than intentional churning? Even if the bills are inflated, is the harm sufficiently serious that disclosure is required?

A large corporate client is probably paying more than it should for a law firm's services. Perhaps the invoice for four weeks where overbilling occurred is twenty-five thousand dollars when it should have been twenty thousand dollars. This is not right, but it likely does not rise to the level of harm that would lead a disciplinary board to impose sanctions for nonreporting. Moreover, a mediator must consider not simply whether the wrongdoing is sufficiently serious to trigger the reporting requirement, but also whether the harm is so great that it justifies breaking faith with the parties.

In this instance, maintaining impartiality and preserving party confidences outweigh any duty Ted has as an attorney to police the profession. He might, in caucus, talk to firm members about Mr. X's behavior, mentioning the risks they run in condoning this behavior. He could point out that Austin is merely one attorney who takes the mandates of Rule 8.3 seriously, but that if wrongdoing continues, there will be others. But Ted should not take it on himself to contact the authorities given how dramatically that would vitiate his neutral stance in the dispute.

Although disclosure is not currently called for, the scales could easily tip in the other direction. What if Ted comes to learn that Mr. X has bilked an elderly client out of her life savings? Or that a chronic practice of overbilling has wrongfully deprived clients, corporate and individual alike, of tens or hundreds of thousands of dollars? If the theft were ongoing and no one else was contemplating disclosure, the need to staunch the wrongdoing would outweigh the harm associated with flouting disputant expectations.[6]

The more heinous, damaging, and chronic the misbehavior, the more compelling the duty to report. The proper balance to be struck between maintaining mediation confidentiality and reporting attorney malfeasance is not static. Although most mediators lean toward preserving confidentiality, the balance of equities could switch if the attorney behavior is grievous enough. As in every other mediation dilemma, context matters.

MEDIATORS' REPORTING DUTIES FOR CHILD ABUSE

Tensions between confidentiality obligations and statutory reporting duties similarly arise in the poignant arena of child neglect and abuse. Embattled spouses attempting to work out child care arrangements after their divorce are encouraged to be candid about their hopes, expectations, and fears regarding the restructuring of family relations. Yet a mediator who pledges absolute confidentiality may find herself running afoul of state-imposed reporting obligations. What can mediators safely promise without rendering such promises illusory?

The answer hinges on a number of considerations. First, what does state law require? In some states, mediators are mandatory reporters, while in others, they are permissive reporters, meaning they may, but are not required to, notify state authorities when they suspect abuse. In Kansas, Louisiana, Virginia, and Wisconsin, mediators are explicitly listed within the category of professional roles saddled with a mandatory duty to report.[7] Eighteen other states list as a mandatory reporter "any person" who reasonably suspects abuse, a categorization that could capture mediators within its broad sweep.[8]

A mediator who straddles more than one profession may find herself statutorily burdened because she possesses a license to practice law, psychology, or other branch of the healing arts. Only a weak technical argument can be made that statutory duties that attach to one profession (for example, social work) do not transfer to different professional roles. Attorneys, medical personnel, and mental health workers are likely assigned reporting tasks because they provide services to, elicit private information from, and have the opportunity to closely observe parents and children in a wide variety of circumstances. Families in crisis are likely to interact with clinical care workers and attorneys—and mediators. The functions, goals, and strategies of each profession are too intertwined to allow technical parsing. The more prudent approach is to assume that psychologists and attorneys whose reporting duties attach by virtue of their law license or psychology degree retain their reporting duties while mediating.[9]

If this is so, how should mediators balance their commitment to offering a confidential process with their duties to alert authorities when they reasonably suspect abuse? How should they approach this balancing act in a mandatory reporting jurisdiction? Should the approach change if the duty is merely permissive? Our commentators on the next case address this difficult question.

CASE 10.2: DIVORCE AND POSSIBLE CHILD ABUSE

John and Mary are in the middle of a heated divorce, and they have chosen Alex to help them mediate both the property and custody issues. During his introduction, Alex went through his standard explanation of the process. He explained his role as facilitator and the parties' role as ultimate decision makers based on their own assessments of what works for them and their children. When it came time for Alex to talk about confidentiality, he kept it brief. He said, "Local rules protect statements made in and prepared for mediation. Such statements are not discoverable or admissible in a court of law."

The first session proceeded amicably as the couple talked about what they would like to do with the house. Today's session is devoted to child custody issues, but the conversation is not proceeding so smoothly. John is seeking 50 percent custody, while Mary is contending that John's parenting skills do not warrant an equal division of parenting time. Mary has accused John of being overly strict, rigid, and controlling. John has ridiculed those charges, claiming that Mary's permissive approach requires that he "pick up the slack" when the children are with him. After that remark, Mary explodes: "Oh, for God's sake, 'picking up the slack.' Let's face it: your disciplining of the children is nothing short of abuse." John vociferously denies Mary's characterization, saying that he does not use any corporal punishment that his grandma did not use with him. Mary then details three episodes where John hit their eldest son with a belt on his back, leaving bruises.

Alex's jurisdiction allows disclosure of suspected abuse to Child Protective Services, but does not require it. What should Alex do?

Comments on Case 10.2

Art Hinshaw

Child abuse allegations present family mediators with difficult professional decisions. Among other considerations, many decisions surrounding the reporting of child abuse directly impact mediation's core values: mediator neutrality, party self-determination, and mediation confidentiality. An initial act of minimizing or legitimizing abuse allegations may appear hostile to either or both parties, thereby compromising the mediator's appearance of neutrality. Moreover, once a report is made, an accused party is likely to believe the mediator is biased, the parties lose their self-determination as the state's Child Protective Services agency will determine what happens next, and expectations of mediation confidentiality are dashed. With such serious consequences to the parties and the process, why would a permissive reporter mediator consider reporting suspected abuse?

PRELIMINARY CONCERNS. Before answering this question, the mediator's recital of mediation's confidentiality protections must be addressed. In the hypothetical, the mediator has made an overly broad statement that mediation communications are protected and not admissible in court. His explanation is lacking in many ways, but by focusing only on the general rule of confidentiality, he gives the parties a mistaken impression that there are no repercussions for anything said during the mediation. Without belaboring the point, mediators should accurately describe the limits of mediation confidentiality by including exceptions to the general rule of confidentiality in their introductory statements. Because a full discussion of the contours of mediation confidentiality would be too lengthy for a mediator's opening remarks, mediators are well advised to give a more detailed explanation in their premediation correspondence with the parties and incorporate an accurate shorthand explanation of mediation confidentiality in their retainer agreements or their agreements to mediate that the parties sign. An accurate depiction of mediation confidentiality is an important element of obtaining the parties' informed consent to breach mediation confidentiality in the appropriate circumstances.

PROMOTING THE CHILDREN'S BEST INTERESTS. In divorce and child custody matters, mediation's primary purpose is to provide a personalized approach to renegotiating familial relationships to meet the needs of everyone affected by the dissolution, including the parties' children. This concern for children corresponds with the state's foremost and compelling interest in the safety and welfare of children. For example, the Model Standards of Practice for Family and Divorce Mediation specifically advise mediators to "assist participants in determining how to promote the best interests of children."[10] And some state custody mediation statutes require family mediators to act in the child's best interest. Failing to act in a clearly abusive situation obviously is not in a child's best interest. Furthermore, threats of violence or harm and disclosures of ongoing criminal activity are routinely excluded from confidentiality protections afforded to other mediation communications. Communications related to child abuse easily fall within these categories, and mediator disclosure of such statements is appropriate.

Nothing in mediation policy prohibits the reporting of a reasonable suspicion of abuse. On the contrary, the goals of mediation policy suggest that permissive reporters of abuse should report reasonable suspicions of child abuse. When child abuse comes to light in mediation, it is in neither the child's best interest nor society's best interest to take the chance of allowing abusive behavior to continue.

EVALUATING THE LIKELIHOOD OF ABUSE. Once the issue of child abuse arises, the mediator's task becomes one of minimizing the reporting decision's impact on mediation's core values. This is the case in both making the decision to report and, if a report is forthcoming, making the report to the authorities.

The hypothetical clearly depicts three instances that may, if Mary is being truthful, constitute child abuse under state law. Fortunately for our mediator, Mary has given him the perfect opportunity to correct the erroneous explanation of mediation confidentiality in his opening remarks. At this point, he should explain the various exceptions to the general rule of confidentiality that might apply in this situation, including the possibility that he may report suspected child abuse to the authorities pursuant to the state reporting statute. This discussion not only salvages the mediator's mistake, it also serves as a method of gaining the parties' informed consent to breaches in mediation confidentiality. Furthermore, it enhances their self-determination as one or both may choose to confirm or dispel any suspicions of abuse, move the discussion to other topics, or even decide to terminate the mediation, the ultimate act of self-determination.

Mary's detailed description of the three episodes of physical harm to her eldest son suggests abusive conduct, but at this point there is not enough information to warrant a report to the authorities. Presuming that the mediation proceeds following the disclosure discussed above, the mediator should inquire into the issue of abuse while maintaining his neutrality, which is not an easy task.

To determine if there is enough evidence to support a reasonable belief that abuse has occurred, the mediator should attempt to better understand the revelation of possible abuse by focusing the conversation on the alleged acts and actions without labeling them as abuse. While Mary may be speaking the truth, she also may be engaging in hyperbole just to make a point, or she may be engaging in a strategy of bad-faith bargaining to gain negotiation leverage. However, the mediator must remember he is not conducting an investigation into whether the abuse occurred; he simply wants to determine whether there is a reasonable suspicion of abuse.

If the further discussion of the three episodes supports a reasonable suspicion that abuse has indeed occurred, a report is warranted. At this point, the mediator has to temper two important tasks: safely terminating the mediation session and subsequently making a report to the authorities while protecting the core values of mediation as much as possible.

ENDING THE SESSION AND MAKING THE REPORT. Once a decision to make a report has been made, the session should be terminated because doing otherwise may lead the parties to believe that their self-determination remains intact, when, in fact, it is severely limited. When there are safety concerns for the children that will involve other institutions in deciding who gets to make parenting decisions, mediating the terms and conditions of parenting is deceptive and inappropriate.[11] Moreover, once informed of the forthcoming report, at least one of the parties is likely to regard the report as a hostile action, affecting both the mediator's appearance of neutrality and the accused party's desire to participate any further in the mediation.

An important part of terminating the session, barring any compelling circumstances, is informing the parties that a report will be made.[12] Doing so without sounding accusatory is both important and very difficult. Moreover, the mediator's failure to adequately discuss the contours of mediation's confidentiality protection in his introductory remarks makes the need for disclosure of the upcoming report critical. This is sure to be an uncomfortable conversation, but is absolutely necessary. Failing to report the alleged abuse simply because of a failure to disclose the possibility of reporting suspected child abuse shows poor professional judgment and could make the situation much worse. If the child is subsequently abused, completely ignoring the best interests of the child in an attempt to cover up an erroneous explanation of mediation confidentiality could lead to malpractice liability.[13]

While there are many ways to inform the parties that a report will be made, the first thing this mediator should do is acknowledge his initial mistake in describing confidentiality's contours, refer back to his correcting comments, and then discuss the state's reporting statute. In this example, he cannot claim a requirement to make such a report, but he can say that the state's child protection policies and law encourage reports to be made when a "suggestion" of child abuse arises in the mediation.[14] At this time, the mediator should let the parties know that no one has been charged with a crime because the alleged abuse has not been proven. Furthermore, the mediator may also help the parties understand how to pursue their legal rights and responsibilities in light of the report and the upcoming investigation. Alternatively, the mediator may educate the parties about the institutions that will become involved once the report is made and what actions they are likely to take as part of the investigation. In some cases, mediators may ask the parties if there is any information that they would like to have included in the report of suspected abuse, such as a rebuttal to an accusation of abuse.

When making the report itself, mediators need a clear understanding of which information retains its status as confidential mediation communications. A mediator's goal in complying with both the reporting requirement and mediation confidentiality statutes should be to provide enough information to maximize the possibility of child protection while minimizing the breach of confidentiality. Thus, only information that assists Child Protective Services in making its determination of whether the child needs state protection is to be disclosed. As a result, mediators should limit their disclosures to mediation communications that support their suspicion of abuse. Appropriate disclosures include

- The identity of the child
- The identity of the child's parents or persons responsible for the child's care
- The suspected perpetrator's name and relationship to the child (if any)

- A description of the abuse or neglect
- The identity of other people who have knowledge of the abuse

Information outside these parameters should be disclosed only if the parties agree.

CONCLUSION. When child abuse issues arise in mediation, there is no question that mediators are under tremendous pressure to address the issue professionally without causing unnecessary harm to everyone the mediation process touches. When confronted with such situations, mediators should remind themselves that the primary goal in mediation is to improve outcomes for all parties affected by the mediation, which include taking the "best interests of the children" into account. If a mediator is presented with credible allegations of physical abuse, like those presented in this hypothetical, it is all but impossible for the mediator to follow that directive without reporting the suspected abuse.

Comments on Case 10.2

Gregory Firestone

EXPLAINING THE SCOPE AND LIMITS OF CONFIDENTIALITY AND PRIVILEGE. Mediators have an obligation to advise parties of the extent and limits of confidentiality and privilege protections for mediation communications. Unfortunately, many mediators oversell the concept of confidentiality by failing to properly do so at the outset of mediation. This is what may have occurred when Alex discussed the confidentiality of mediation by stating, "Local rules protect statements made in and prepared for mediation. Such statements are not discoverable or admissible in a court of law." While Alex's explanation of confidentiality appeared to have addressed the privileged nature of mediation communications (that the communications are inadmissible in court), he failed to inform Mary and John as to whether these communications would be held confidential to the world. Alex also failed to notify Mary and John that exceptions to confidentiality and privilege likely exist by either statute or case law. Lastly, if Alex planned to voluntarily report child abuse, he also failed to advise them of his intention to report such allegations should these concerns arise in mediation.

The Model Standards of Practice for Family and Divorce Mediation[15] (Divorce Mediation Standards) state, "Prior to undertaking the mediation the mediator should inform the participants of the limitations of confidentiality such as statutory, judicially or ethically mandated reporting."[16] Interestingly, the same obligation is not included in the Model Standards of Conduct for Mediators (Model Standards).[17] Under the Model Standards, the mediator's ethical obligation is more limited: "A mediator shall promote understanding among the parties of the extent to which the parties will maintain confidentiality of information they obtain in a mediation."[18] Thus, under the Model Standards, a mediator must promote only an understanding as to the parties' obligation to maintain confidentiality, whereas under the Divorce Mediation Standards, a mediator apparently must explain the limits of confidentiality as the limits relate to all mediation participants, including the mediator.

Alex failed to provide a clear and understandable explanation of the extent of confidentiality and privilege protections that apply, and if he intended to report child abuse, he also failed to notify them of his intent to report any allegations of child abuse. As such, his explanation of confidentiality provided to John and Mary was inadequate. As a result, Alex now faces a difficult decision as to what to do next. Before discussing that decision, however, let's consider another important question: Must the mediator inquire further about the allegations?

INQUIRING INTO THE ALLEGATIONS. Does the mediator have an obligation to inquire about the allegations of child abuse to determine if the alleged abuse is likely child abuse? While a mediator does not automatically have a responsibility to inquire in all cases whether abuse might have occurred, if a statement is vague, some mediators might feel compelled to inquire as to whether the alleged abuse, if true, is likely child abuse. Hitting a child with a belt that leaves momentary redness or a temporary bruise is probably not child abuse, while the same act would likely be child abuse if such an act results in bruises that last for days.

Although a mediator need not feel compelled to make such an inquiry in all cases, a mediator in this case might be tempted to inquire as to the extent and duration of the bruises, not only perhaps to determine if the mediator feels that a report is necessary but also to determine if the parties are able to adequately consider the interests of their children. In the event that the mediator has concerns that the parties have problems such as domestic violence, substance abuse, or significant mental illness that largely compromise their ability to protect their children's interests, then mediation may not be an appropriate method of dispute resolution for this family, or the mediator may need to conduct the mediation in a somewhat different fashion.

Under certain circumstances, such as domestic violence, where significant safety concerns or power imbalances often exist, termination of the mediation may become necessary. Further inquiry about the abuse allegation might help a mediator to identify whether any safety concerns exist (for the child or anyone else) and whether mediation could be ethically modified to address these concerns.

Because the scenario provides that the mediator is not a mandated reporter—which is, in fact, the case in some jurisdictions—the mediator is not required to report child abuse. However, the mediator's own personal ethics might affect his ultimate decision. If the mediator believes that he should make a report, he now faces an ethical dilemma because he failed to disclose this exception to confidentiality at the beginning of the mediation.

HONORING PARTY EXPECTATIONS CONCERNING CONFIDENTIALITY. Typically mediator ethics provide that absent parties' consent, mandatory reporting, or court order, a mediator shall not voluntarily disclose mediation communications.[19] Given that the mediator did not indicate any exceptions to the confidentiality of mediation at the start of the mediation and that the mediator is not a mandated reporter, I suggest that the mediator need not immediately breach the promise of confidentiality by reporting child abuse in this case. If possible, the mediator should attempt to maintain the parties' reasonable expectations of confidentiality based on the mediator's opening comments and seek another way to address the problem. As the drafters of the Uniform Mediation Act (UMA) state in its prefatory note, "Candor during mediation is encouraged by maintaining the parties' and mediators' expectations regarding confidentiality of mediation communications."[20] If mediators do not honor the parties' reasonable expectations concerning the confidentiality of mediation communications, we can expect that parties will likely learn to participate less openly in mediation, and opportunities for empowerment, mutual understanding, collaborative problem solving, and resolution will be diminished.

Because Standard IX of the Divorce Mediation Standards provides that "a family mediator shall recognize a family situation involving child abuse or neglect and take appropriate steps to shape the mediation process accordingly," Alex is not necessarily precluded from continuing to mediate this divorce. According to Standards IX(B) and IX(C), if Alex has appropriate training and believes the case is still suitable for mediation, he may continue to mediate the divorce as long as he continues to "comply with applicable child protection laws." Standard IX(C)(1) further states that "the Mediator should encourage the participants to explore appropriate services for the family." Thus, if Alex has sufficient training in this area and believes that the case can still be mediated, he could first explore whether the allegations of abuse can be adequately addressed in a manner that does not breach Alex's confidentiality obligations.

The mediator could certainly discuss the matter with the parties and explore whether they would waive confidentiality protection to the extent necessary to allow the mediator to make a report. In doing so, the mediator could indicate that making such a report does not mean that the mediator believes the allegations to be true, only that the mediator believes that when a reason to suspect child abuse exists, making such a report is in the best interest of the child. After such a discussion, regardless of whether the parties waive confidentiality, the mediator should inquire as to whether either party feels that the mediator is no longer impartial. If the mediator is no longer viewed as impartial or if the mediator feels that he can no longer be impartial, then the mediator should withdraw from the case.[21]

Additionally, the mediator could suggest that the parties discuss the issue of child abuse allegations with their respective attorneys and seek their attorneys' advice. A possibility exists that one of the attorneys might recommend reporting the abuse. For example, the wife's attorney might advise the wife that if she did not report child abuse, a court later might determine that she shared responsibility for any possible child abuse because of her failure to notify the authorities and protect her child. For that reason, or out of concern for the child's safety, the wife's attorney may encourage her to report the child abuse to the authorities.

The mediator could also ask the wife and husband if either of them had considered directly reporting the child abuse. The mediator could encourage them to consider their various options and to think about what the consequences would be for each alternative.

If the parties agreed that parental differences regarding discipline of the children needed to be addressed in mediation, the mediator might help the parties explore options for obtaining parenting assistance that, if they wished, could be included in any resulting mediation agreement. Options to enhance a child's well-being could encompass parenting classes; mental health evaluation, treatment, or consultation; custody evaluation; voluntary parenting assistance from child protection agencies; supervised visitation; parenting coordination; and a medical or psychological examination for the child.

Another option would be for the mediator to advise the parties that the mediator would be willing to mediate the case only if a guardian ad litem (GAL) or court-appointed special advocate (CASA) participated in the process. The GAL or CASA could determine if mediation would adequately meet the needs of the children and, if so, be a voice for the children's interests in mediation. By including a GAL or a CASA, the mediator could remain neutral and impartial because the child advocate would be responsible for addressing the child's interests. If the GAL or CASA felt that the case involved child abuse concerns, then this person would likely report the matter to the court and/or child protection agency in that jurisdiction. In the event that a court determined that child abuse did occur, it might be possible to later mediate the case as a child protection mediation that could address many of the parenting and child support issues involved in a divorce. The primary difference is that the child protection agency investigating the child abuse as well as the attorney prosecuting the case on behalf of the child protection agency would also likely participate in mediation along with the parents and the GAL or CASA. The parents could still be empowered to participate in the child protection mediation and could seek to negotiate the issues pertaining to their child, and the agreement likely would be subject to court review.[22]

If the mediator suspected that the child might be at risk and believed that none of the above options adequately addressed the mediator's concern for the child's safety and well-being, the mediator might decide to directly report the matter to the child protection agency even if the parties believed such statements were confidential and did not waive confidentiality. Reporting possible child abuse

might serve to protect the child and allow the mediator to avoid violating his own personal ethical standards. However, the mediator will
have violated standards of professional conduct for mediators cited
earlier—Model Standards, Standard V(A), and Divorce Mediation
Standards, Standard VII—and performed a disservice to the field of
mediation and to public confidence in mediation, because the mediator would have breached the confidentiality of mediation without
being required by law to do so or obtaining party consent. This would
be very unfortunate since such circumstances could have easily been
avoided with a clear explanation of mediation confidentiality at the
outset of mediation. If mediators are seen as misrepresenting the
confidentiality protections of mediation and behaving unethically,
fewer families will seek to use mediation. In such an event, more
divorces may be subjected to the traditional litigation process, which
often fails to adequately meet the needs of children.[23]

SETTING APPROPRIATE EXPECTATIONS. In his effort to move the
mediation along and avoid a detailed discussion of confidentiality exceptions, Alex has perhaps acted unethically because he has
failed to provide the parties with sufficient information to determine
how openly they should speak in mediation. While self-determination
is one of the primary ethical principles governing mediation, misleading reassurances about the confidentiality of mediation serve
only to compromise the parties' ability to exercise self-determination
in making an informed decision regarding participation in and
communication during mediation.

Numerous exceptions to mediation confidentiality and privilege
exist in case law and statutes. For example, in the UMA, exceptions exist to the mediation privilege for certain communications
involving open records laws; threats to inflict bodily harm or commit
a crime of violence; planning, attempting to commit, or concealing a
crime; malpractice and professional misconduct; and child abuse
and neglect.[24] In addition, if a "court, administrative agency, or
arbitrator" determines, after an in camera hearing, that "there is
a need for the evidence that substantially outweighs the interest in
protecting confidentiality," additional exceptions apply. Importantly,
while the mediator has a privilege under the UMA, the mediator may
use the privilege to block only two of the UMA privilege exceptions.[25]

Even in states that have adopted mediation confidentiality
statutes other than the UMA, statutory protections typically provide

exceptions to the confidentiality and privilege of mediation communications, or case law often sets out circumstances where the court can compel parties and mediators to testify regarding mediation communications. For example, the Florida Mediation Confidentiality and Privilege Act[26] provides that mediation is both confidential and privileged and yet lists five exceptions to these confidentiality and privilege protections in addition to the ability of the parties to waive confidentiality and privilege protections.[27] In addition, many other possible exceptions exist. For example, if the parties move to another state while still divorcing and, as a result, the matter is now before a court in a different state with less statutory protection for mediation communications, no guarantee exists that the court in the different state would honor the mediation confidentiality and privilege protections from the state where the mediation had actually occurred.

Be Clear Up Front. Mediators must be clear in explaining to the parties the extent of confidentiality and privilege protections that apply to the mediator, parties, and nonparty participants. The easy way to do so is to explain, in a manner consistent with the law of the jurisdiction, that "mediation is confidential to the extent provided by law, and some exceptions exist to these confidentiality protections." In the case of John and Mary, the mediator should have made clear that while mediation communications enjoy broad protection in court, that protection is not absolute. Under some circumstances, courts may compel disclosure. Moreover, he should have made clear that the courtroom is not the only setting where mediation communications may be revealed and should have explicitly mentioned the mediator's policy concerning child abuse and neglect reporting if he intended to report any allegations of child abuse or neglect. For example, the mediator could have stated, "One example of an exception to the confidentiality of mediation involves any statements concerning child abuse or neglect, which would not be confidential for the purpose of reporting child abuse or neglect."

Since Mary and John may not grasp these concepts easily at the outset of mediation, a good practice would be to provide them with a written confidentiality agreement that delineates the extent of mediation confidentiality and privilege protections and explains that exceptions exist to the confidentiality and privilege protections for mediation communications. The parties could then read the confidentiality agreement and, if they agreed, sign the agreement indicating that they understood and agreed to the provisions in the confidentiality agreement. By doing so, the mediator could address laws and rules that govern confidentiality as well as the mediator's own possible preferences concerning such matters as the voluntary reporting of child abuse. In addition, the mediator could invite John and Mary to agree to additional confidentiality protections, especially in a jurisdiction where mediation communications are inadmissible in court, but not confidential to a wider audience, as is generally the case in states where the Uniform Mediation Act has been adopted. The mediator could also explain the confidentiality agreement to John and Mary in plain language to ensure that they accurately understand and agree to the limits of confidentiality.

The Effectiveness of Clarity. In my experience, when the mediator is clear about the limits of confidentiality, the parties are still willing to participate openly in mediation and are not surprised when the mediator in a mandatory report jurisdiction notifies them that the mediator must report suspected child abuse. Many times, if appropriate, parties will agree to continue with the mediator and understand that the mediator's report does not reflect a loss of impartiality, but rather an obligation to follow the mandates of state reporting laws. In my twenty-five years of divorce mediation practice, I have always informed parties of the limits of confidentiality and privilege and provided the mandatory reporting requirement of child abuse and neglect as an example of an exception to the confidentiality of mediation. When allegations of child abuse or neglect have arisen, I have complied with mandatory reporting laws. While announcement of my intent to report the allegation affected the mediation process, parties were never surprised by my announcement. In most cases, they did not feel the disclosure requirement affected my impartiality and were willing to continue mediation if the matter was still appropriate for mediation.

CONCLUSION. Alex's failure to provide Mary and John with an adequate explanation of the confidentiality of mediation communications in his opening statement placed him in a difficult position where he ultimately might have to choose between violating his personal ethics (to protect the child) and his professional mediation ethics (to honor the parties' reasonable expectations concerning the confidentiality of mediation and not disclose mediation communications unless permitted by the parties or required by law). Before choosing to breach either ethical code, Alex should first explore whether any ethical ways exist to resolve the problem in a manner that satisfies both his personal and professional ethics. Hopefully, Alex will learn that providing the parties with a more accurate and complete explanation of the extent and limits of mediation confidentiality protections at the outset of mediation will greatly lessen the chances that he will face such an ethical dilemma in the future.

Editor's Thoughts on Case 10.2 and the Comments

Both Art Hinshaw and Gregory Firestone point out that the mediator in this hypothetical created his own ethics maelstrom by promising more in the way of confidentiality than he felt comfortable delivering. Both note that the mediator's breezy allusion to the protective function of local rules does not adequately discuss the limits of that protection. Furthermore, the blanket assurance that all mediation statements are nondiscoverable and inadmissible simply does not reflect the more nuanced and complex state of the law in many jurisdictions. Many state codes, including the UMA, allow testimony regarding mediation communications to come into court in a number of specialized circumstances. And legislative protection from judicial scrutiny says nothing about a mediator's reporting obligations to other government authorities, which is the disclosure at issue in John and Mary's case. Firestone also distinguishes between confidentiality and privilege and stresses the importance of providing the parties with clear guidance regarding both types of privacy protections.

Acknowledging that the mediator oversold the degree to which mediation discussions can really be sealed from public view, our commentators stress different features of the botched sale. Firestone focuses on promise keeping. He critiques the mediator for irresponsibly presenting mediation communications as immunized from leakage but suggests that the mediator, having done so, should strive, if at all possible, to avoid defeating the parties' expectations. Although the mediator may need to break faith with his earlier pledge of silence, such a breach should be a last resort. Firestone details a number of possible avenues to pursue before possibly dead-ending at disclosure.

Hinshaw focuses his analysis elsewhere: on the choice the mediator faces, given that he is practicing in a permissive, rather than mandatory, jurisdiction. He urges confirming one's suspicions before reporting. He believes that keeping quiet after Mary's statement could compound the mediator's earlier error. He advises the mediator to make a reasonable inquiry into the incidents that allegedly make up the abuse, determine if a report is required, and, if so, notify the parties that a report will be made to the proper authorities. Failing to report, if a report is warranted, would, in Hinshaw's view, reflect poor professional judgment and might, if it turns out that the child is actually being harmed, lead to malpractice liability.

Both commentators stress that Mary's statements should not be taken at face value. Further inquiry into her characterization of John's actions is necessary. Hinshaw notes that Mary could be exaggerating (or lying) in order to discredit John and gain leverage, while Firestone notes that Child Protective Services would likely view belt swatting that resulted in giant black and blue marks differently from hitting that caused the skin to redden but left no bruise or injury. Firestone adds that careful questioning should be considered not only to ascertain whether a report should issue, but also to determine if other professionals should be brought into the conversation. Firestone suggests that delving into the parents' habits of punishment could be helpful to determine if they are capable of thinking through and advancing their child's best interests. If parental judgment is skewed by mental illness, substance abuse, or other problems, then they may be incapable of advancing or protecting their children's interests and well-being, and it may be inappropriate to continue mediating. Questions about parental judgment might also push toward appointment of a guardian ad litem who would speak for and work to protect the child throughout the mediation.

Hinshaw's primary message is that the mediator—though not required by law to file a report—should not dismiss reporting out of hand as a matter of professionalism. In his view, mediation exists to help parties find solutions that best advance their interests—and in divorce cases, the needs and interests of the children must remain a primary concern.

Firestone, though concerned that mediators communicate their reasonable suspicions of child abuse in appropriate cases, hones in instead on the issue of mediator care and diligence when it comes to explaining the scope and limits of confidentiality protection. Firestone critiques mediators who make overly broad statements regarding mediation's "safe space" and directs mediators to both explain orally and commit to writing the situations when a mediator may voluntarily or by legal compulsion disclose what went on in mediation. Because some concepts surrounding confidentiality can be complicated, Firestone urges the mediator to set them out in plain language and ask the disputants to sign in writing that they read the confidentiality explanation, understand it, and agree to its terms.

Although the question of whether a mediator should make an abuse report in a discretionary jurisdiction does, as Hinshaw points out, challenge mediation's core values, Firestone contends that most of the ethical trauma can be alleviated by providing a realistic and carefully accurate picture of confidentiality's gaps before the mediation session gets started. While careful practice won't drain confidentiality dilemmas of all of their knottiness, it will help keep mediation's most central values—neutrality, self-determination, and confidentiality—intact.

References for Gregory Firestone's Comments

Firestone, G., & Weinstein. (2004). In the best interest of children: A proposal to transform the adversary system. *Family Court Review, 42,* 203–215.

Hinshaw, A. (2007). Mediators as mandatory reporters of child abuse: Preserving mediation's core values. *Florida State University Law Review, 34,* 271–309.

Milne, A. L., Folberg, J., & Salem, P. (2004). The evolution of divorce and family mediation: An overview. In J. Folberg, A. L. Milne, & P. Salem (Eds.), *Divorce and family mediation* (pp. 3, 8). New York: Guilford Press.

Saposnek, D. T. (1998). *Mediating child custody disputes.* San Francisco: Jossey-Bass.

Taylor, A. (2002). *The handbook of family dispute resolution.* San Francisco: Jossey-Bass.

CHAPTER ELEVEN

Conflicts of Interest

As we've discussed, mediator impartiality is crucial to ethical practice. Disputants must be able to trust that mediators approach their cases with no preconceived idea of how the settlement negotiations should go. They must be confident that the mediator isn't rooting for one side or hopeful that a particular outcome will prevail. Not only must mediators actually conduct their mediations with no bias in favor of (or against) one set of disputants, the mediation setting must appear clear of any taint of bias. That is, mediators must avoid playing favorites or even mediating in a context in which the temptation to play favorites appears strong. Proscriptions against conflicts of interest are designed to avoid inappropriate alliances between mediator and disputant, as well as the appearance of inappropriate alliances.

Alliances can be created in many ways. They can be based on preexisting personal, professional, or financial relationships with the parties or others close to the parties. Thus, if a mediator's tennis partner of the past ten years asks her to mediate a dispute she has with her employer, the mediator should think about whether her athletic bond with the partner precludes her from handling the case.

Similar considerations exist if a business associate or former client solicits mediation services. These personal and business relationships may compromise a mediator's ability to mediate impartially. At the least, these relationships create a perception problem: they make it seem as if the mediator will favor the people she knows, even if no such favoritism occurs.

A perceived affinity for one side can also result from involvement with the subject matter of a dispute. For example, consider the plight of the mediator who is a vegetarian and passionate animal rights advocate who is asked to mediate a dispute involving the business practices of the butcher down the street. Or the mediator who volunteers her time at the Planned Parenthood clinic in her community and finds herself called on to mediate a dispute between parents and the school district regarding the sex education class being taught to seventh graders at the local middle school. The mediator may face a conflict of interest because her volunteer work in the area of reproductive freedom biases her toward a particular outcome regarding the way sex education is taught in schools.

What does this mean in terms of a mediator's ability to accept work that comes through the door? Does this mean mediators can accept cases only from complete strangers involving topics that have never touched their lives? This approach seems too extreme, and, in fact, mediation guidelines allow mediators to participate in cases where they have preexisting relationships with other participants and the issue in dispute, so long as they take several steps.

DEALING WITH PERSONAL OR PROFESSIONAL TIES

Guidance for handling potential conflicts is provided in Standard III of the Model Standards. The standard urges a number of steps. First, a mediator must think hard about the nature of the bonds that exist. Do they create a situation that might lead a reasonable person to question the mediator's impartiality? This "reasonable person" inquiry means that a mediator need not worry if she has had an interaction with a mediation participant that was trivial or ephemeral. If the mediator and a disputant once shared tips about choosing cantaloupes in the produce section or volunteered for an hour at the same soup kitchen, it is unlikely that a reasonable person would conclude that these prior meetings create a problematic conflict of interest. That is, a reasonable person would not think those transient and shallow connections would lead a mediator to consciously or unconsciously try to benefit such an attenuated acquaintance.

But can the same be said for a business associate or the spouse of the mediator's long-time tennis partner? A reasonable person would likely grow concerned about those relationships because they might tempt a mediator to provide those individuals with "favored nation" status. So the "reasonable person" inquiry is designed to separate out those relationships too unimportant to create a threat or appearance of bias from those where the possibility of bias appears real and pressing.

If the inquiry reveals that a significant connection does indeed exist with a mediation participant, like the tennis-playing bond or business relationship, then the mediator should disclose this to all disputants and secure their consent to continuing. However, whereas in most situations disputant consent is sufficient to allow the mediation to proceed, consent is not enough in some situations according to many codes. In the Model Standards and most state codes, mediators are asked to make an additional finding. They must ask, "Might this conflict of interest be reasonably viewed as undermining the integrity of the mediation?" If so, mediators are instructed to withdraw from the mediation even if the parties themselves wish to proceed.[1]

The idea that some alliances between mediators and participants are so profound that they can't be cured by party consent undercuts the weight mediation usually gives to party autonomy. Disregarding party consent removes from parties the ability to determine who can mediate their dispute and under what circumstances. It assumes that parties are not able to judge when a mediator is too encumbered by personal, professional, or financial ties to preside properly over their discussions. In this area, as in many others, party autonomy chafes against the desire to ensure a fair and equitable process. And because this remains a contested issue in mediation, some codes allow parties to make the ultimate judgment about whether their chosen mediator can continue in the case, while others require the mediator to exercise her own judgment as to whether the conflict contaminates her ability to mediate impartially or creates too unsavory an appearance of bias.[2]

Conflict-of-interest concerns require mediators to think hard about past relationships and ask the following questions:

"Do I know these mediation parties or their intimates, and if so, what is the nature of our relationship? Is it trivial and superficial or important and profound?"

"Will our past contacts and current feelings toward one another sway my behavior?"

"Even if our relationship has no effect on how I actually conduct the mediation, would observers, finding out about my connections with the participants, naturally conclude that I must have preferred one side over the other?"

Mediators must also be wary about forging ties with disputants during the mediation. Once a mediator has contracted to mediate with the parties, she should avoid establishing a personal, professional, or financial relationship with them. It would be ethically suspect for a mediator in the middle of a construction defect case, for example, to ask the defendant construction company to stop by and provide an estimate for a kitchen remodel. Similarly, mediators should avoid suggesting social outings with disputants or making investments in their business ventures. Some state codes go so far as to prohibit a mediator from accepting gifts from grateful disputants at the close of the final session.

DEALING WITH TIES BASED ON SUBJECT MATTER ALLIANCES

Standard III suggests a similar approach should be taken with regard to subject matter alliances. Mediators must engage in the same series of steps:

1. Conduct an internal interrogation as to whether a reasonable person would think that her relationship to the subject matter of the mediation raises questions about her ability to remain impartial.

2. If so, disclose fully to the parties her experience with and relationship to the mediation's subject matter.

3. Secure all parties' consent.

4. Engage in a final inquiry as to whether, despite party consent, her relationship to the dispute topic fatally compromises her impartiality such that it would be foolhardy to proceed.

The avid vegetarian who has engaged in advocacy work with the animal rights community would likely raise a reasonable disputant's eyebrow were she to accept a case involving the local butcher's professional practices. The reasonable person would certainly question whether she could remain impartial when dealing with a professional practice that she finds, on its face, repugnant. The same is true for the Planned Parenthood volunteer called in to mediate over the school district's sex education classes.

Because a reasonable person would almost certainly have questions about the ability of both mediators to remain impartial, they must disclose their advocacy and volunteer work and provide the parties an opportunity to pursue other mediators.

Even if the parties decide that they are unbothered by their mediator's animal rights or Planned Parenthood connections, the mediator must still ask herself whether her involvement in these causes, and her own personal attachments, would undermine the integrity of the mediation. According to the Model Standards and mirroring state codes, the mediator knows better than the parties whether her subject matter ties will have a negative influence on the course of the mediation, and it is her job to make the final determination as to whether the mediation should go forward.

CASE 11.1: TENNIS CENTER NEGLIGENCE?

Maureen has enjoyed a successful career as a mediator for the past fifteen years. She works primarily with individuals and insurance companies. Consequently, she knows and is on good professional terms with many of the senior claims adjusters at the largest insurance companies in town. Indeed, the senior adjuster at Rate Farm, the largest local company, is one of her biggest fans and has referred many cases to her. When other insurance adjusters call and ask for a recommendation, he always suggests Maureen.

When out of the office, Maureen is an avid tennis player. Every Friday night, she plays round-robin tennis at the Youth-Adult Tennis Center (YATC). In fact, she is so enthusiastic about the game generally and YATC in particular that she has pledged ten thousand dollars to set up a scholarship fund for underprivileged children who want to take lessons.

Maureen has been asked by her "fan," the senior adjuster at Rate Farm, to mediate a case being brought against YATC by Polly Plaintiff. Polly had been playing in a doubles tournament at YATC when she tripped over some maintenance equipment that had been left in the far corner of the court. Polly has sued YATC, alleging negligence in the failure to properly store the equipment and to maintain a safe recreational environment. Rate Farm is YATC's insurer and the likely payer if a negligence claim is successfully established.

Should Maureen take the case?

Maureen's involvement in this case raises considerable ethical red flags. Obviously she has a strong professional relationship with senior claims personnel at Rate Farm. The senior adjuster has worked with her often, and the facts suggest they like and respect each other. More important for the ethical analysis, he refers cases to her, so his esteem yields her a direct financial benefit. So long as he thinks well of her, she receives from him a substantial book of business. His power of referral could lead her, consciously or unconsciously, to want to please him. It could cause her to push discussions in a direction favorable to Rate Farm.

Similarly, Maureen appears to have a strong personal connection with YATC. She plays there often and feels sufficiently strongly about its educational mission to donate money to its scholarship program. Might her warm feelings for YATC and its mission impair her ability to mediate impartially and fairly in connection with Polly's claims?

Taking and Continuing the Case

Maureen's relationships with Rate Farm and YATC trigger responsibilities on her part. Because a third person would view the facts of Rate Farm's referrals and Maureen's use of and contributions to YATC as raising conflict-of-interest concerns, Maureen must disclose these facts to Polly and ask whether Polly remains comfortable proceeding under the circumstances.

Even if Polly consents, however, Maureen should still ask herself whether she can ethically continue with the case. Given the strength of her relationships with both Rate Farm and YATC and given that they are allied in this matter, she should consider whether those relationships fatally undermine the integrity of the process.

It is common for mediators to enjoy repeat business and continue to work for particular clients and referral sources. What arguably pushes this situation over the line is that Maureen has also given money to one of the defendants whose interests are congruent with her referral source. Given that congruence of interest, the temptation to look kindly on a resolution with favorable consequences for Rate Farm and YATC, like a small or zero pay-out, may be irresistible. At the very least, it may look to a third party as if it must have been irresistible. For this reason, Maureen should think hard about whether she can continue to mediate in this particular case, regardless of what Polly says.

Postmediation Activity

A mediation's conclusion does not signal the end of conflict-of-interest concerns. Postmediation interactions may also raise questions about a mediator's impartiality. Imagine that Maureen's mediation settled with a modest payment to Polly by Rate Farm and a signed statement acknowledging YATC's continued insistence that the injury reflects no negligence on its part. Imagine also that two days later, the center invites Maureen to become a board member, a paid position that brings with it free tournament tickets, unlimited court time, and additional benefits. Should Maureen accept the position?

Although Maureen may have comported herself perfectly throughout the mediation, her acceptance of YATC's proffered honor, coming so close on the heels of her work on Polly's case, creates the suggestion that the board nomination is a reward for providing the center a favorable outcome. As the Model Standards counsel, "Subsequent to a mediation, a mediator shall not establish another relationship with any of the participants in any matter that would raise questions about the integrity of the mediation." Factors to be considered include "time elapsed following the mediation, the nature of the relationships established, and services offered."

Here, the offer to serve on the board came only two days following the mediation, and board membership carries with it significant rewards. In light of these facts, Maureen would do well to decline the offer in order to preserve the appearance of impartiality and remain beyond ethical reproach.

Keeping Subject Matter Bias in Mind

Note that Maureen might need to engage in an intrapsychic "conflicts check" even if she has no direct relationship with YATC and Rate Farm. She is, after all, a tennis buff. Her involvement with the subject matter of the dispute, that is, her intense love for and participation in the game, may incline her to have warm feelings for entities like YATC seeking to spread the gospel of tennis to players of all ages. At the same time, her love of the game may lead her to sympathize with enthusiasts like Polly, injured through the actions of those who don't treat the tennis environment as reverentially as they should. It is not clear how Maureen's tennis proclivities cut. It is not even clear if they create any bias at all. Still, the Model Standards would require Maureen to interrogate her own conscience to determine if her involvement in the game inclines her toward a particular direction when working with tennis clubs and players and whether that inclination requires, at the least, disclosure, and perhaps withdrawal.

Conflicts of interest cases take many shapes. Cases 11.2 and 11.3 deal with relationship and subject matter conflicts, respectively.

CASE 11.2: A BOUTIQUE RELATIONSHIP

John Parker is the managing partner in a small boutique firm, the Parker Law Group. He works with five other partners who collectively specialize in age, race, and gender discrimination cases. Two years ago, John's colleague Bill Brown mediated a race discrimination case involving Alfra Fertilizer, stemming from claims that the company discriminated against its African American and Hispanic salespeople in hiring, retention, and promotion. Bill was involved in frank discussions regarding Alfra's hiring practices as well as discussions with Alfra's insurer regarding its procedures and philosophy with respect to evaluating litigation risk and claims management. The mediation was successful, an agreement was reached, and the claim dismissed.

Roughly ten months later, Penny, another Alfra Fertilizer saleswoman, has contacted John Parker and Bill Brown. She has heard good things about them as a team (they frequently partner on cases), and she would like them to represent her in an age discrimination suit against Alfra. Alfra remains insured by the same company that was involved in the mediation ten months ago.

What are the conflict-of-interest rules?

What should Bill Brown do? What should John Parker do?

Comments on Case 11.2

Bruce E. Meyerson

Can a lawyer undertake legal representation against a party after recently serving as a mediator in a dispute involving that very same party?[3] If the lawyer who served as mediator avoids direct involvement, can other law partners in the firm take the case? In my view, were Bill Brown to take this case, he would run afoul of at least three provisions of the Model Standards applicable to mediators and one provision of the Model Rules applicable to attorneys. Although the rules provide a bit more leeway for the Parker Group to participate in Penny's litigation, assuming Bill Brown is adequately screened and adequate notice is given, the law firm would be on sounder ethical ground if it declined.

THE MODEL STANDARDS. With respect to matters that may arise after a mediation, Standard III(F), which relates to conflicts of interest, states that "subsequent to a mediation, a mediator shall not establish another relationship with any of the participants in any matter that would raise questions about the integrity of the mediation." If Brown were to undertake Penny's representation against Alfra Fertilizer, he would violate this standard and establish an adverse relationship with a party with whom he had participated previously as a mediator.

Model Standard III(F) also states that mediators who do establish postmediation relationships with parties should consider the "time elapsed following the mediation, the nature of the relationships established, and services offered." Because Brown's mediation occurred only ten months previously and involved similar issues (employment claims) directly relevant to issues likely to arise in the subsequent litigation, his representation of Penny would, at a minimum, create a perceived conflict of interest and most likely an actual conflict of interest.

Considerations of the mediator's ongoing duties to preserve confidentiality and avoid appearing partial inform my analysis as well.[4]

Standard V (Confidentiality) provides that a mediator "shall maintain the confidentiality of all information" obtained in the mediation. If Brown served as Penny's attorney, it would seem virtually impossible, given the nature of the contemplated litigation, for him to maintain the confidentiality of the information provided to him in the prior mediation. Moreover, how could Brown credibly maintain that he remained impeccably unbiased throughout his mediation when he later emerges as Penny's counsel?

Concerns regarding the appearance of impropriety also affect Parker. Even assuming Brown did not participate in the representation, he would potentially breach his duties under the Impartiality and Conflicts of Interest Standards through his association with his partner, John Parker, in the Parker Law Group, since both standards advise against giving "the appearance of a conflict of interest during and after a mediation."[5] There is little doubt that Alfra could reasonably perceive that Brown was not impartial during the mediation if ten months later, his partner undertook representation adverse to Alfra in a substantially similar dispute.

THE MODEL RULES. The ethical framework for this situation is regulated not only by ethical standards applicable to mediators, but also by ethical standards applicable to lawyers. In this case, the Parker Law Group is contemplating representation in a matter that is adverse to a party that participated in mediation in which one of the firm's attorneys served as the mediator. This situation implicates Rule 1.12 from the American Bar Association Model Rules of Professional Conduct, which provides that a lawyer should not represent anyone in connection with a matter in which he participated personally and substantially as a mediator. Although Rule 1.12's use of the term *matter* is vague, courts have disqualified lawyers from representing a party in a case substantially related to a dispute in which they previously served as a mediator.[6] Although the first mediation is technically a different matter from the second representation, courts would most likely view the circumstances in Penny's litigation as sufficiently related to Brown's earlier mediation with Alfra Fertilizer that Rule 1.12's prohibition applies.

Rule 1.12 also speaks to the other ethical dimension to this problem, namely, whether any conflict that applies to Brown also extends to his partner, Parker. The rule contemplates this situation by permitting lawyers in a law firm to undertake representation even if another is disqualified, provided that the disqualified lawyer is screened in a timely way from the representation and receives no fee from the representation. In order to avoid the imputation of the conflict, the Parker Law Group would have to screen Brown from the litigation, ensure that he receives no fee, and give notice to the parties and the appropriate tribunal.

CONCLUSIONS ABOUT AVOIDING CONFLICTS. If Brown were to undertake this representation, he would violate both the letter and the spirit of the Model Standards provisions on Conflicts of Interest, Impartiality, and Confidentiality.

Parker's involvement is also problematic. Even assuming Brown did not participate in the representation, Parker's assumption of a representational role could nonetheless raise questions about Brown's earlier impartiality as a mediator. Alfra could reasonably perceive that Brown was not impartial in the mediation ten months earlier and would likely view the Parker Law Group's involvement in current related litigation as proof of that suspicion. Although as a technical legal matter, one could parse the Model Rules in permissive fashion to allow Brown to take Penny's case, this would be a risky move given existing case law. In addition, though the model rules would permit Parker to serve as Penny's lawyer, provided Brown is screened, he receives no fee from the representation, and notice is given to the parties and appropriate tribunal, given the small size of the firm, the apparent close working relationship between the two attorneys, and the similarity of the litigation to the earlier mediation, such a move on Mr. Parker's part would be suspect. The better ethical choice for Brown and the Parker Law Group would be to decline representation.

Comments on Case 11.2

Wayne Thorpe

Both John Parker and Bill Brown should decline the case, although applicable rules and law could provide some argument to the contrary. The issue here is whether Brown's former status as a mediator with Alfra Fertilizer carries any ethical obligations for Parker or Brown in the subsequent litigation against Alfra for age discrimination.

In analyzing these issues, we need to look at laws and rules applicable to both mediation and legal ethics. These ethical problems serve to spotlight the potential difficulties for practicing lawyers who also serve as mediators. Although the various rules of ethics for lawyers and for mediators do not absolutely bar lawyer mediators from litigating against disputants from prior mediations, both the Model Standards of Conduct for Mediators and the American Bar Association Model Rules of Professional Conduct put us on clear notice that lawyer mediators who seek to litigate against such parties may encounter conflicts. These conflicts are particularly problematic when the two matters are substantially related or when the mediator has learned of relevant confidential material during his or her prior mediation with the now adverse party.

THE MODEL STANDARDS. Model Standards applicable to conflicts of interest and confidentiality suggest that it will be problematic for either Bill Brown or John Parker to take the new case. With respect to Standard III(A), which provides that conflicts of interest may arise after a mediation based on the mediator's involvement in the subject matter of the dispute, the question here is whether the issues raised in the legal proceeding against Alfra Fertilizer overlap sufficiently with the issues discussed in the prior mediation as to raise a question regarding Brown's prior impartiality during the mediation. To borrow language from the Model Rules regulating lawyers discussed below, are the two matters so "substantially related" as to be problematic? The two cases involve different claimants with different histories, but they will likely focus on similar hiring practices and human relations personnel and turn on some similar legal issues. The manner in which Alfra has investigated, defended, and assessed the two matters could also be similar. On the other hand, Parker or Brown might be able to take the case if the new litigation implicates entirely different personnel following different policies and internal company guidelines.

Parker and Brown could also have problems taking the case with respect to Model Standard III(F), which provides that "a mediator shall not establish another relationship with any of the participants in any matter that would raise questions about the integrity of the mediation." The similar subject matter between the initial mediation regarding racial discrimination and subsequent litigation regarding age discrimination, compounded by the relatively short passage of time between the two, would, at a minimum, suggest an extremely cautious approach.

Our hypothetical also tells us that "frank discussions" took place with Alfra regarding its hiring practices and with Alfra's insurer regarding its evaluation of Alfra's litigation risk and claims management. These discussions would present difficulties for Parker and Brown with respect to Model Standard V, which requires mediators to keep disputant confidences, unless otherwise agreed to by the parties or required by applicable law. Of course, Brown might argue that no confidences were shared during this mediation and that the philosophies behind Alfra's hiring practices were the types of generic, nonmaterial facts he routinely hears in mediations of this type and should not interfere with his or his client's ability to establish this new attorney-client relationship. But Alfra might legitimately insist that while these may be confidences that mediators commonly hear, they are not the sort of confidences that Alfra would expect to be shared with someone opposing the company in a related lawsuit ten months later.

As you evaluate these arguments, consider them through the eyes of Alfra Fertilizer and ask if the arrangement produces at least a perceived conflict of interest. Alfra will surely reevaluate Brown's neutrality in the clear light of hindsight. Similarly, Alfra will likely begin to doubt the confidentiality of what occurred in the mediation with Brown. These are the sorts of concerns that can meaningfully undermine the public's confidence in a system that lets a lawyer mediate for them one day and sue them in a similar case on another.

THE MODEL RULES. The following sections from the American Bar Association Model Rules of Professional Conduct suggest a similar caution:

- Rule 1.12 provides that a "lawyer shall not represent anyone in connection with a matter in which the lawyer participated personally and substantially as a judge or other adjudicative officer or law clerk to such a person or as an arbitrator, mediator or other third-party neutral, unless all parties to the proceeding give informed consent, confirmed in writing." This rule, of course, applies expressly to mediators' subsequent representations adverse to parties in their mediations; it limits the extent of disqualification to matters in which the lawyer "participated personally and substantially."

- Rule 1.6 provides that a lawyer shall not reveal confidential information.

- Under most circumstances, Rule 1.9 prohibits a lawyer from representing a client in a matter adverse to a former client if the new matter is the same as or substantially related to the former matter. However, in this rule, the "substantially related" test is limited to subsequent representations adverse to former clients—and thus by its terms, it plainly does not apply to former mediation parties.

The Rules Applied to Attorney Brown. On the surface, these provisions seem easy enough to apply here: Brown did not represent Alfra as an attorney in the former matter. He was a mediator who represented no one, and hence Rule 1.9 does not apply. Under Rule 1.12, disqualification occurs only if the newly offered representation is in the same matter as the mediated case. In our hypothetical, this is not the case. Thus, in theory, it is quite clear that these two rules do not present a problem here.

There are two important qualifications, however. First, Rules 1.9 and 1.12 were adopted by the ABA in February 2002. Previously Rule 1.12 applied to judges and arbitrators but not to mediators. ABA Model Rules are adopted by the states at the legislators' discretion and, accordingly, not all jurisdictions have elected to include mediators in the scope of 1.12. As of this writing, eight jurisdictions continue to exclude mediators and third-party neutrals.[7]

Second, cases decided under the prior version of the Model Rules applied the "substantially related" test under old Rule 1.9 to prior mediations, even though the literal language of former Rule 1.9 explicitly applied only to prior representations and not to prior mediations. Those cases express grave concern about the perceived violation of confidences by the mediator (or settlement judge) turned opposing counsel.[8] Given this analysis, it is not clear that the modification of Rule 1.12, even where it has gone into effect, will be enough to satisfy the courts. Rule 1.6 prohibits revealing confidential information and may cause concerns for courts handling disqualification issues.

The Rules Applied to Attorney Parker. Finally, there is the question of whether Parker should be disqualified by imputation based on the probable disqualification of Brown. The Model Standards of Conduct for Mediators do not address the issue explicitly, and indeed they would have no application to Parker, who is not a mediator here, but only a law partner to the mediator, Bill Brown.

The ABA Model Rules, however, explicitly address the imputation issue. If Model Rule 1.12 applies, Parker would not be disqualified, even if Brown is disqualified. If, however, under current or former Rule 1.9 (former representation) or Rule 1.6 (confidentiality), Brown is disqualified, then under Rule 1.12, his law partner Parker would be unable to pursue representation.

The new ABA Model Rules take a somewhat liberal approach to avoiding lawyer disqualification after serving as a mediator, in terms of both the standard to be applied—personal and substantial participation in the matter versus a "substantially related" matter—and in freely permitting screening to avoid imputed disqualification of law firm colleagues. As a liaison from the ABA Section of Dispute

Resolution to the Ethics 2000 Commission, which produced the 2002 version of the Model Rules, I advocated for both viewpoints. These were the views of the section, and I wholeheartedly agreed with them. With the passage of time and twenty-twenty hindsight, I am not as sure today as I was then of the correctness of this approach. Since adoption of these rules, I have heard reactions of parties concerning mediator conflicts, and I have given more weight to their concerns about confidentiality and neutrality in a mediation where a mediator subsequently appears in the guise of opposing counsel in a similar case. At an appropriate future time, I hope that the ABA will consider the experience of parties, lawyer advocates, and lawyer mediators with this new approach and evaluate whether revisions or modifications are called for.

Editor's Thoughts on Case 11.2 and the Comments

Both commentators Bruce Meyerson and Wayne Thorpe suggest that Bill Brown and John Parker should refuse the offered representation. They cite virtually identical provisions of the Model Standards and Model Rules of Professional Conduct and interpret those provisions with a similarly sensitive eye to appearance problems.

Thorpe gives a bit more deference to a strict textual reading of the Model Rules that might provide some conceptual crawl space for taking Penny's case. Still, after giving those arguments their due, he nonetheless concludes that it would be far safer to let someone else assume the role of counsel in a discrimination case against Alfra.

Noting that the Model Standards advise against postmediation relationships that cast doubt on the integrity of the mediation and the impartiality of the mediator, Meyerson contends that taking Penny's case would compromise both. He suggests that Alfra couldn't help but feel that Brown was biased in the earlier mediation if they were to find that he or his law partner was serving as litigation counsel in a subsequent discrimination case. And in Meyerson's view, it would be "virtually impossible" to maintain Alfra's reasonable expectations of privacy. Brown was privy throughout the mediation to information about Alfra's hiring practices, as well as its insurer's methods for evaluating claims and assessing risk. How could he keep that information confidential while serving as a zealous advocate for an aggrieved Alfra employee? Thorpe makes the same point, directing readers to imagine how Alfra would feel reading Brown's name on counsel papers after having treated him ten months earlier as a confidential listener.

Meyerson takes the stronger position when he considers the impact of the Model Rules on Brown and Parker's decision. Although noting that Rule 1.12 precludes representation only when the representation involves the "same matter" as the former mediation, Meyerson says that language would not serve as a bar to court intervention. Penny's case may not be the "same matter" as the prior litigation, but it is certainly uncomfortably close. They are both discrimination claims and may involve similar facts and similar legal issues. Based on case law interpreting similar rules, Meyerson concludes that a court would find the disputes sufficiently related to invoke the spirit—if not the exact letter—of Rule 1.12. Thorpe, reading the rule more narrowly, suggests a technical argument could be made that Penny's age discrimination is sufficiently dissimilar from the racial bias claims at issue in the prior mediation that Rule 1.12 doesn't apply; but he too nonetheless counsels restraint. As a matter of prudence and propriety, Thorpe suggests that law partners should forgo this offer of new business.

Thorpe confesses, as a member of the drafting committee for the 2002 Model Rules, that committee sentiment leaned toward liberalizing conflicts rules. Adopting too strict an approach has the potential to chill the law practice of competent attorney mediators. If these mediators face the loss of lucrative representational opportunities because they participated in a two- or three-hour mediation with one of the parties, they may decide that they can no longer afford to function in a mediative capacity. This might drive talented and effective attorneys out of the mediation profession. On the other hand, as Thorpe notes, excessively lax rules potentiate boundary crossing. Mediation parties want to be sure mediators are not trolling for legal business and can be trusted to put their clients' interests ahead of their own business development. It may be that revision of the Model Rules is in order. In the meantime, taking a cue from our commentators, conflicts questions involving representation adverse to a former mediation party should be approached by asking, "What would the former mediation party think?"

Clearly, the extent and intimacy of a mediator's personal and professional contacts can raise conflict-of-interest questions. As case 11.1 demonstrated, mediators must search their collective conscience to determine whether they can avoid favoring disputants with whom they have a relationship. The next case examines a slightly different aspect.

CASE 11.3: SYMPATHY FOR THE TENANT?

What difficulties arise when the mediator has worked with and on the subject matter implicated in the disputants' conflict? Mediators live in the world and engage with issues. What should they do when the cultural, political, or social issues that have aroused their interest and engagement in other contexts turn out to be front and center in the dispute before them?

Before moving into mediation full time, Carol worked as a legal aid lawyer in an impoverished section of the city. Many of her cases involved landlord-tenant disputes, and many of her clients were poor urban dwellers who were at risk of being evicted from the shabby public or low-rent housing projects they inhabited.

Carol's current mediation reminds her of this former work. One party is a single mom working in a minimum wage job who has fallen behind on her rent payments. She is apologetic about her late payments, but she says that the apartment is in execrable shape. The stove hasn't worked for five weeks, and the hot water heater works sporadically at best. Carol knows that a spotty hot water heater will mean cold water showers in the middle of winter for the mother and her six-year-old daughter: the thought makes her shiver. The landlord reminds Carol of many of the men she faced on the other side in the legal aid job. He is well dressed, with a sharp leather jacket, well-shined boots, and several gold chains dangling around his neck. Like so many of the other landlords Carol litigated against, he is making a good living, delaying repairs, spending little money on his properties, and squeezing the tenants as much as they can stand. Carol doesn't understand how he and the others sleep at night.

Both the landlord and the mother are unrepresented. The mother clearly doesn't want to move. Thirty minutes into the mediation, she is ready to pay the back rent with 20 percent interest. She is even willing to forget about the stove and hot water heater (in caucus, she says she has a friend who she thinks might be able to fix it at little cost). Carol is fairly certain that the apartment, with its problems with the heater and the stove, would be found by a judge to be in violation of the implied warranty of habitability. And Carol is worried about the mother and her daughter because it's only December, and January and February are the coldest months.

Should Carol have taken this case? And what should she do at this juncture, forty-five minutes into the mediation?

Comments on Case 11.3

Roger Wolf

Carol's challenge here is a formidable one. She needs to make sure that she can conduct this mediation in an impartial manner, while also ensuring that she provides a quality process to the beleaguered tenant. Carol's own sense of what is fair—both procedurally and substantively—may be inordinately shaped by her past work as a tenants' rights attorney, and that is a question that she will need to look at very closely. Carol will need to walk a difficult path, trying to stay neutral and giving adequate but not undue account to the fairness concerns that animated her past life as a lawyer. She will need to consider both whether she should really be mediating this case and whether she can ethically continue to do so.

TAKING THE CASE. To begin, Carol should have disclosed to both parties at the outset that she had been a legal services lawyer and has represented many low-income tenants against landlords so they could have decided at the outset if they were comfortable with her mediating the case. That would have been the safest thing to do.

Standard III of the Model Standards mandates that a mediator "avoid a conflict of interest or the appearance of a conflict of interest" and make a "reasonable inquiry to determine whether there are any facts that a reasonable individual would consider likely to create a potential or actual conflict of interest for a mediator."[9] At one time Carol was significantly involved in the subject matter of this dispute, landlord-tenant relations, and Standard III cautions against mediating where one has substantive involvement in the issues under discussion.

I wouldn't have thought this would have posed a problem for two reasons:

- Carol never had any involvement with these two individuals and their particular problems.
- Carol's involvement with landlord-tenant matters generally is dated.

At some point, the passage of time buys a clean slate. However, something about this case—maybe the landlord's attitude or the helpless nature of the tenant—revived those old juices in Carol, and it is clear that her ability to continue to conduct the mediation in an impartial manner is at risk.

SHOULD CAROL CONTINUE? Standard II places the burden of determining whether a mediator can conduct the mediation in an impartial manner solely on the mediator. If Carol doesn't think she can continue to conduct the mediation in an impartial manner, then she must withdraw.[10] Carol doesn't even need to consult the parties. At this juncture, if I were Carol, I would take some time to mull the case over, focus on why it bothers me so much, figure out if I can provide quality mediation process, and see if I can proceed in an impartial manner. Carol should review her notes and reconvene either in separate sessions with the parties or meet together jointly.

PROMOTING QUALITY. What should bother Carol the most is that given the posture of the mediation, forty-five minutes into it, the tenant will actually be worse off having gone through mediation than she would be had she gone to court. That suggests to me that Carol has not done enough to ensure the quality of the mediation process. The tenant is so ill informed about her rights and so passive that she is letting the landlord intimidate her, and she is not exercising her rights to self-determination. Standard VI(A)(10), Quality of the Process, encourages a mediator to "explore the circumstances and potential accommodations, modifications or adjustments that would make possible the party's capacity to comprehend, participate and exercise self-determination." Carol, it seems, has not done this.

Considering what has happened so far in the mediation, one problem may be that Carol has not explored sufficiently with the tenant the consequences of her decision to pay back rent plus 20 percent interest and not get any of the repairs done that caused her to withhold her rent in the first place. Also, Carol needs to make more effort to focus the tenant on whether she feels she has enough information about her options and, if not, how she might get the necessary information so that she can make a more informed decision.

If Carol feels comfortable proceeding, she should meet separately with the tenant and consider saying: "I wanted to check with you to see if you felt that the agreement you and the landlord were considering addressed the interests and concerns you had when you came to mediation." The hope is that the tenant will either say "no" or "not really," which will then let Carol start exploring what her concerns are and get her refocused on how she might make a proposal that addresses those interests or how she might get the information she needs to be more informed of her rights and choices.

If the tenant says "yes," Carol might continue: "My notes reflect that you did not pay rent because of the conditions you described in your apartment. The agreement that you are thinking of entering into with the landlord makes no mention of those concerns or how those conditions will be corrected. Was that your intention?" Both of those questions aim to provide an opportunity for Carol and the tenant to "explore the circumstances and potential accommodations, modifications or adjustments that would make possible the party's capacity to comprehend, participate and exercise self-determination."[11]

REMAINING IMPARTIAL. By exploring the impediments blocking the tenant's ability to assert her interests, Carol is addressing the underlying causes of her inability to remain impartial. If the tenant does become more involved in the process, comprehends her options and interests, and exercises some self-determination, she will propose solutions that reflect her interests. Carol can then begin to explore these interests with the landlord in a joint session or separately. If, alternatively, after exploring the issues raised, the tenant still chooses to sign the proposed agreement, Carol can rest easier knowing that the tenant's choice is an informed one. Carol may still have doubts regarding the quality of the result (which links in my mind to justice), but she should feel satisfied that her own standards regarding the quality of process have been met and would be able to move forward in impartial fashion to help tenant and landlord conclude their dispute in the way they deem appropriate.

If the tenant chooses to reject the landlord's proposal after meeting with Carol, should Carol worry that the landlord will question her impartiality? Yes, a bit, but the worry is a minor one. Carol's response to the landlord would be to remind him that a mediator's job is to ensure that all parties understand and are satisfied with the agreement before they sign it. She might say:

> Just as I wouldn't want you, Landlord, to sign an agreement that doesn't meet your needs, similarly I don't want the tenant to do so either. When I met with the tenant, I asked her if the proposed

agreement met the interests and concerns she had, and she said, "No," so I explored with her what her concerns were, and the proposal I've conveyed to you is the result of that conversation with her. Where would you like to go from here?

My best guess is that the landlord would be satisfied with Carol's explanation and would accept that his best interests are served by an agreement that stands the test of time and meets the tenant's needs as well as his own.

Although working with this landlord has prompted some internal reflexes that Carol thought had long faded away, I believe if Carol acts deliberately and with care, she can remain open to both disputants and work to fashion an agreement that satisfies minimal standards of fairness while not unduly compromising her own impartiality.

Comments on Case 11.3

Susan Nauss Exon

Mediator impartiality is a guiding benchmark for mediation; the mandate to remain impartial is included in every set of general civil mediation standards of conduct that I have examined.[12] But universal acknowledgment that impartiality is important does not ensure uniform treatment. Actual definitions vary from state to state.

Standards range from the very unhelpful to the reasonably instructive. On the one end of a spectrum are standards that demand impartiality but fail to supply any guidance as to what that means. On the other end of the spectrum are standards that provide some clarification. For example, impartiality according to some definitions requires mediators to act with "freedom from favoritism, bias or prejudice," avoiding even the appearance of partiality.[13] Others delineate that mediator impartiality encompasses reactions not only to who disputants are, but also to what they say and do. According to these standards, mediators are to maintain impartiality with respect to the participants' "personal characteristics, background, values and beliefs, or performance at a mediation, or any other reason."[14]

Given the array of understandings embodied in the standards, questions about impartiality are not easily answered by reference to these texts alone. Much room is available for individual interpretation, discretion, and internal interrogation. Gut responses may matter. Mediators should ask themselves, "Can I approach each party with equal openness, curiosity, and respect? Can I remain impartial with regard to the information I receive? Can I function in an evenhanded fashion throughout the process and remain neutral as to the final result?"

THE DILEMMA FOR THIS TENANT-ORIENTED MEDIATOR. In the case before us, the first questions Carol should ask herself are: "Should I have taken this mediation? Based on my prior experience as a legal aid attorney, can I remain impartial toward the parties, the process, the substantive information, and the final result? In other words, will my prior experience representing poor urban dwellers skew my questioning? Will my substantive knowledge of landlord-tenant law help or hinder my ability to remain evenhanded?"

Responding to these initial questions, an established, responsible mediator should be able to accept the case, assuming a conflicts check reveals that the mediator does not know either party and has never been involved in a landlord-tenant dispute with either one. But even if Carol has had no prior dealings with this landlord, she seems to have some troubling negative predisposition. If this landlord truly reminds her of unsavory characters from her past practice, her impartiality is compromised at the very outset unless she can put these biases aside and enter the mediation with an open mind. Carol must remove all thoughts of her prior advocacy role for tenants. She must be able to embrace a diversity of people and views and welcome an opportunity to assist two disputants.[15] Who knows? Not every landlord-tenant dispute is alike, and, based on the information that the parties share with the mediator, initial appearances may change.

POSSIBLE ACTIONS. Carol should maintain flexibility regarding her substantive knowledge of landlord-tenant law. The parties are not represented by counsel so Carol can help diffuse the conflict by educating the parties regarding relevant legal principles so that they will understand what type of settlement will comport with the law. Once the parties acknowledge the legal parameters, they can then craft some type of settlement that is suitable to their needs. Carol should allow the parties the autonomy necessary to formulate their final settlement.

A Different Start. From a pragmatic standpoint, the mediation might better have begun like this. Since the landlord and tenant are not represented by counsel, Carol could have inquired initially about the basic dispute. On learning that the dispute involved a landlord and tenant and that the tenant was behind on rent payments, Carol could have incorporated some education into her introductory remarks. For example, she could have educated the parties about the meaning of contract law, for example, abiding by the terms of the lease agreement. That means the tenant should make timely rental payments, and the landlord should provide a habitable apartment. Once Carol educated the parties about basic landlord-tenant law and completed other preliminary comments, she could have asked for opening remarks by each party and begun to gather additional information.

As I see it, the problem with Carol's behavior here is that she did not provide some basic education at the beginning of the session, and it is now forty-five minutes into the mediation. Had she provided a basic outline of the legal requirements binding both the landlord and the tenant, she might not now be facing the uncomfortable situation of feeling protective and biased in favor of the tenant.

Fleshing Out Both Sides. By forty-five minutes into the mediation, Carol has learned that the stove and hot water heater are in disrepair, yet the tenant wants to stay. In caucus, Carol needs to flesh out why this particular apartment is so important to the single mother. Is it within walking distance to her daughter's school? Is that particular school important because it has an after-school program that provides coverage while the mom is at work? Are there no other affordable apartments that meet mom's needs? Does she have a close support system with other tenants in the building? Is the apartment close enough to mom's place of work so she does not need to have a car with its added expense? Why does she want to stay there when the apartment is almost uninhabitable? These and numerous other questions are available to help Carol gain an understanding of why the apartment is so important to this single mother.

In a separate caucus, Carol should inquire why the landlord has not fixed the appliances. Has the tenant reported the malfunctions? In an attempt to instill a reality check, Carol could mention that the coldest months of the year are coming. How would the landlord like to have a place with no stove or hot water? Does the landlord's home have a working stove and hot water? What is necessary to make an apartment habitable for him? Should the same standard apply to his tenants?

Self-Examination About Impartiality. At this juncture, Carol needs to take a deep breath and ask herself whether she is becoming too allied with the tenant against the landlord. The mediator needs to remind herself that she is serving as a third-party neutral, not as a legal aid attorney today. She should not advocate for either party.

Carol also needs to ask herself whether she is going beyond empathy—the ability to understand a party—to become sympathetic with the tenant. While empathy is a necessary skill for mediators, feelings of sympathy are not.[16] If the mediator becomes so sympathetic that she steps into one party's shoes, she will have a difficult time serving as a third-party neutral to the process and the parties. The mediator needs to show that she understands the tenant's views yet not place herself in the tenant's position.

If Carol is becoming biased toward the parties and situation, she needs to ask herself whether she will be more of a help or hindrance for both parties. Will she focus only on information to aid the tenant? If she believes she cannot remain impartial, should she withdraw? If she does withdraw, how long will it take to get another mediator and another session scheduled? This is an important question because the lack of a stove and hot water will persist for the tenant.

Another consideration related to the partiality problem is Carol's subject matter expertise, which can be very helpful to the parties. Can she put aside her feelings of partiality and begin to ask questions in a targeted way so that both parties understand the ramifications of the situation and what is needed to create an enforceable settlement agreement? Asking questions, rather than telling the parties what to do, should help Carol remain impartial. In addition, fleshing out the parties' interests in separate caucuses might help Carol convey ways to rectify the imbalance she sees and create a valid settlement agreement while meeting everyone's individual needs.

Carol's partiality dilemma also is affected by other concerns. In addition to impartiality requirements, many standards require a mediator to ensure procedural fairness, informed decision making, and a balanced process. Six state standards explicitly require or encourage substantive fairness or justice of the final result.[17] This creates an obvious tension. As soon as a mediator attempts to ensure a balanced process by helping a weak party, she has compromised her impartiality. And if she moves beyond her role as neutral and works to ensure justice, she likely will be bolstering one party's position, thus violating her duty to mediate impartially. Ensuring informed decision making may sound innocuous, but conveying knowledge to one party of her substantive rights gives that party powerful bargaining leverage and shifts the dynamic at the table. It could be seen as a breach of the duty to remain impartial. Standards requiring mediator impartiality while simultaneously requiring the mediator to ensure informed decision making, a balanced process, or some other type of fairness demand a high-wire act that often cannot be sustained.

In Carol's situation, should she encourage the landlord to fix the appliances? Should she inform the landlord that failure to do so probably violates the implied warranty of habitability and threaten to tell the tenant about her rights if the landlord refuses to respect them? If the mediator wants to ensure justice and a balanced process, the answer to these questions is a resounding yes. Yet if the mediator takes such action, her impartiality is subject to question.

Supporting a Fair Result. I believe that mediators should support a fair result in limited situations, so long as such matters are approached carefully. If skillful questioning does not shift the discussions, I would recommend Carol discuss the concept of habitability with the tenant. She should do so using a set of targeted questions. She should ask, "Is the apartment habitable?" If the tenant answers yes, then Carol should try to work out a payment schedule to bring her rental payments current. If she answers no, then Carol should ask what would make it habitable for her. Additionally, Carol could ask the tenant whether she is receiving the value that the rent is intended to cover. Then it would be time to convey this information to the landlord and give him a reality check.

AN ONGOING TENSION. The tension between the various mediation values suggests questions that affect more than the landlord-tenant dispute scenario. Carol's concern for tenants' rights based on her prior advocacy certainly complicates her ability to steer a middle course. But remaining neutral is a problem endemic to all disputes where power imbalances, uninformed decision making, and grossly unjust outcomes are present. If fairness is paramount, then we should jettison the blanket requirement of impartiality. If different dispute contexts dictate different practice models, then we should be comfortable with the notion that different mediators will assign these values different weights. And if a consensus emerges that one value should be preeminent in all cases, then the standards should say this explicitly. If fairness receives trump card status, then the standards would make clear that in this landlord-tenant hypothetical, mediator impartiality could permissibly give way to justice in an effort to ensure the tenant receives hot water and a functional stove.

The dilemma posed in this commentary, and particularly the tension among the various mediation values, suggests questions not only for the mediator in this landlord-tenant hypothetical but for the mediation field as a whole. Scholars, practitioners, legislators, and regulators should explicitly acknowledge the tensions within the standards that regulate mediation practice and address how these tensions might be managed better. The answers will help not just the mediator in this landlord-tenant quandary, but all other mediators being pulled in a host of contradictory directions.

Editor's Thoughts on Case 11.3 and the Comments

This case poses two questions. First, should the mediator have taken this case, given her prior involvement with the subject matter of the dispute? Second, given her emerging feelings of protectiveness and concern for the tenant, how should she proceed?

Roger Wolf begins his commentary by conceding that in retrospect, the mediator should have disclosed her background as a legal aid attorney up front. Although the legal aid work was in the past, it's clear that the emotional instincts from that time remain. With the clarity of hindsight, he concludes, disclosure might have been the better choice.

Still, Wolf says, and Susan Exon agrees, that it was reasonable to take the case, given that none of the legal aid work involved either this particular tenant or this particular landlord.

In terms of going forward, both Wolf and Exon are uncomfortable with the tenant's passivity and her inclination to settle on terms that don't meet the needs that propelled her into mediation. Wolf would question the tenant regarding why she'd be willing to live without heat and hot water now when she wasn't several weeks ago and seek to understand why she is willing to capitulate on issues that she previously considered well worth fighting for. In doing so, he feels the mediator is acting in accord with Standard VI, which encourages mediators who doubt a party's ability to participate in mediation to "explore the circumstances and potential accommodations, modifications or adjustments that would make possible the party's capacity to comprehend, participate and exercise self-determination." Although typically understood to refer to parties laboring under psychological or physical disability, Wolf interprets the standard to encompass a mediator's latitude to remedy informational deficits and encourage a more assertive stance.

Susan Exon also indicates that she would want to explore the potentially troubling dynamic taking place between the landlord and tenant. She suggests that one possible scenario would involve an initial educational session, followed by caucus with both parties in succession. In caucus, the mediator would explore why the tenant is willing to stay in an apartment with no heat or hot water and why the landlord has not made the necessary repairs. As part of a larger exercise in self-interrogation, Exon would encourage the mediator to think about whether she has crossed over the line between empathy and sympathy and whether she has taken on an advocacy role for the tenant.

Exon notes that the hypothetical raises a larger question that demands the attention of the mediation field generally. As she sees it, there is an incontrovertible tension between the duty to remain impartial and the duty to encourage fair outcomes. She suggests that further refinement of the standards is necessary to clarify the right path for mediators, such as Carol, who find themselves torn between competing, and compelling, ethical mandates.

CHAPTER TWELVE

Mediating Multiculturally
Culture and the Ethical Mediator

W hether your mediation practice takes you on a circuit of local postal codes or globe-trotting overseas, it is likely that you will find yourself mediating with parties from a different culture. In most instances, the questions you confront will be functional and practice oriented: How do I manage the process with parties whose cultural affiliations lead them to perceive language and behavior so differently? How can I help them reach an agreement despite their culturally distinct approaches to the issues they face?

Occasionally, though, the clash of cultures will lead to ethical conundrums. Although all ethical problems are challenging because they present compelling values in ineluctable tension, cross-cultural ethical dilemmas are particularly agonizing because they seem to require a choice between deeply felt cultural traditions. Amid current heightened sensitivities attending charges of Western cultural domination, the act of choosing in this context seems particularly fraught.

Before delving into the specifics of intercultural negotiation, it is important first to clarify some fundamental terms and concepts.

What do we mean by culture? How does culture affect negotiation? And how might intercultural mediation spawn head-scratching ethics questions?

CULTURE AND DISPUTING

Ask ten people what *culture* means, and you will likely get eleven answers. The term is notoriously difficult to define and takes on different shadings depending on the purposes the definition is intended to serve.

A Current Definition of Culture

In the late nineteenth century, British social critics spoke of culture when they sought to distinguish aristocratic forays into the "high arts" from the baser pursuits of the masses. Matthew Arnold, in his 1869 polemic, *Culture and Anarchy,* referred to culture as the "best which has been thought and known in the world."[1] In contrast to materialistic or mechanistic concerns, he viewed culture as those endeavors that would "help men live in an atmosphere of sweetness and light . . . where they may use ideas . . . freely-nourished and not bound by them."[2]

Later definitions dropped the distinction between "high" and "low" artistic or intellectual production and sought to expand understandings of culture to include the wide variety of ways that people create, consume, and transmit meaning in the world. This capacious view of culture's dominion gained traction throughout the twentieth century and is reflected in the sweeping field of academic study termed cultural studies, which encompasses anthropology, sociology, linguistics, and semiotics. According to current understandings, culture is the "deep-grammar"[3] or "mental software"[4] that we use to communicate with and "decode" others.

This broad view of culture surfaces in legal definitions as well. The United Nations Educational Scientific and Cultural Organization, a body devoted to promoting diversity and multiculturalism, defines *culture* as "the whole complex of distinctive spiritual, material, intellectual and emotional features that characterize a society or social group. It includes not only the arts and letters, but also modes of life, the fundamental rights of the human being, value systems, traditions and beliefs."[5]

Clearly culture today encompasses all those habits of action and thought that link us to the larger communities around us. Thus, culture is not simply what we do; it is the lens through which we see the world. It not only primes our choices but shapes how we view the choices of others.

Cultural Aspects of Disputing Style

Cultural lenses tint virtually every scene we encounter. What if we are in a negotiation and a representative from the opposing firm takes off his jacket and rolls up his shirt sleeves? Do we think, "Oh, that's nice, he feels comfortable being informal with me. We must be getting somewhere." Or do we fret, "Hmmm, how disrespectful. He doesn't even think enough of me to stay business-like in his attire. I must be losing ground here." Hailing from a formal, hierarchically driven culture or from one focused less on status and more on function will shape our response to such a change in our negotiating partner's dress.

Experts in intercultural negotiation have identified a series of cultural features that influence disputing style. These features reflect different cultural conceptualizations of identity, language, and structure. If disputants bring to the mediation table dramatically differing expectations of how individuals fit into group hierarchies and communicate within and between them, mediation becomes more of a challenge. Often stylistic differences require the mediator to constantly explain, reinterpret, and reframe. In some situations, the parties' norms will be so different from both the mediator's and each other's that helping forge agreement will prove ethically problematic. Here briefly are some poles along which cultures tend to divide:[6]

• *Sense of identity: Individualistic or collectivist?* Negotiators in individualistic cultures feel less attached to social groups and more inclined to focus on personal goals and preferences.[7] They are likely to view negotiation solely as a resource-distribution exercise, focusing on the end result of who gets how much and when. Negotiators in collectivist cultures view themselves as more interdependent and bound by a larger web of social relations and obligations. They place greater emphasis on the relationship-building aspect of negotiations. Decisions to compromise, hold fast, agree, object, or explain are all made with an eye to how decisions will affect goodwill, sympathy, and trust between the parties.

• *Rules: Universalist or particularist?*[8] Universalist cultures (often also individualistic) believe rules should be applied consistently. Membership in a particular school, profession, family, religious institution, or ethnic group is seen as irrelevant to how rules should be understood and implemented. If a rule is fair for one group, it is fair for all. By contrast, particularists would trade uniformity for sensitivity to context. They believe members of in-groups deserve special consideration, precisely because of the relationships involved. For particularists, every situation is different, and different situations call for different rule application.

• *Status and power: Low power distance or high power distance?* Low-power-distance cultures deemphasize status and hierarchy, focusing on individual performance and function. These cultures tend to promote democratic decision making; the distance between individuals at the top or the bottom of an organizational hierarchy is not viewed as justifying radically differential treatment. In high-power-distance cultures, individuals at the low end of the scale "expect and accept that power (e.g. wealth, prestige, access to education and other benefits that enhance power) [is] distributed unequally."[9] In these cultures, age, seniority, rank, and title figure prominently in the distribution of rewards and burdens.

• *Use of language: Low context or high context?* High-context cultures assume that speaker and listener share a common heritage or background and that language builds on a set of unspoken but acknowledged understandings.[10] Speakers in this culture communicate indirectly through implication and suggestion, assuming that the message is partially transmitted to the recipient through a shared history and context. By contrast, speakers in low-context cultures rely on direct, concrete speech to convey meaning. They believe that the message embodied in any communication can be found exclusively in the detail and logic of the words used. That is why they stress clarity and precision.

• *Structure and time: Monochronic or polychronic?* Monochronic cultures (like the United States, Germany, and Northern Europe) view time as a precious resource to be guarded and preserved. In these cultures, individuals are comfortable proceeding through tasks in linear fashion, finishing one project before taking up another. Efficiency is highly valued and entails advance planning, agenda setting, and strict adherence to schedules. Personal needs are adjusted to fit existing work timetables.[11] Polychronic cultures view time as a more flexible resource that should be subordinated to people's changing needs. In addition, projects do not necessarily proceed in lockstep fashion. Multitasking, juggling, and zigzagging between projects are acceptable approaches to managing professional obligations and the many intrusions that disrupt them.

• *Attitude toward uncertainty: Low uncertainty avoidance or high uncertainty avoidance?* Low-uncertainty-avoidant cultures have a higher tolerance for ambiguity and risk. This propensity creates space for innovation and experimentation. Low-uncertainty-avoidant cultures celebrate new ideas and are open to alternate approaches and deviations from the norm. Rules tend to be informally expressed, open textured, and subject to variable interpretations. High-uncertainty-avoidant cultures, on the other hand, view new or ambiguous situations with anxiety. These cultures celebrate structure, tradition, ritual, and formally expressed rules. Comfort is found in "doing things the way we've always done them."[12]

Although it is useful to learn to identify such traits and features that may broadly characterize a particular culture, it is also important to avoid cultural essentialism—the urge to reduce that culture and its members to one monolithic pattern. Cultural characteristics are not immutable or universal, and individuals often belong to not one national culture but a series of overlapping communities, each with its own norms and values. Family units, professional communities, religious sects, and even tightly knit recreational groups foster their own sets of expectations and understandings. An Argentinean accountant may engage in behaviors that can be identified with the larger Latino culture, but he may also follow a cultural script dictated by his family, church, accounting firm, and local soccer league. These other behaviors may be consistent or inconsistent with those traits we see as "typically South American."

When analysts speak, for example, of collectivist or high-power cultures, they are using shorthand. What they mean to say is that a higher percentage of individuals in that culture (as opposed to other cultures) are likely to behave pursuant to collectivist or high-power assumptions. Of course, there will be outlier individuals on either tail of the bell curve. While generally Mediterranean cultures tend to employ a more flexible, expansive view of time and deadlines, no one should go into a negotiation with a Spanish or Italian team with the expectation that previously agreed-to timetables will have no meaning. Better to view the descriptors presented above as cultural proclivities that may or may not be actualized in any given setting. Keep the information above in mind when mediating multiculturally, but do not become rigid or stereotypical in your thinking.

HOW CULTURAL DIFFERENCES COMPLICATE MEDIATION

It doesn't take much imagination to see potential challenges in mediating between two individuals from different cultures. Consider a buyer-seller dispute: pair a collectivist, high-context, high-power-distance, high-uncertainty-avoidant buyer with an individualist, low-context, low-power-distance, low-uncertainty-avoidant seller. Their dealings may falter on linguistic misunderstandings alone.

Of course, individuals within a culture do vary, and it is dangerous to overgeneralize. Still, if we can indulge in some broad-based stereotypes, we may assume that the seller from the individualist culture (say, the United States, Germany, or some other Northern European or North American region) will be inclined to want to begin the encounter by getting down to business. She will not be shy in saying what she needs to complete this sale, and she will be aiming to memorialize the deal in a detailed document that considers all contingencies and explicitly provides for remedies if the buyer fails to perform. The buyer (say from China, Japan, or other Asian country), working with different conceptions of what a negotiation should look like, would likely be more comfortable beginning with small talk, perhaps showing the seller the sights about town and breaking bread in an informal way before beginning number-crunching in earnest. Uncomfortable with blunt self-assertion, the buyer will likely shy away from direct requests for a particular price or clear dismissal of the seller's demands. Rather, he will talk circuitously about his financial budget and other constraints. Also, he will want to frequently check back with his associates at the home office to be sure that his instincts are in sync with the rest of his department. If the seller is of a lower rank in her company than the buyer is in his, that may lead the buyer to view her with less respect, whereas the seller may feel that such rank differentials are irrelevant.

Differences in how buyer and seller approach language, relate to status differentials, identify as embedded in relational networks, and experience time may breed confusion and turmoil. The seller may become impatient with the buyer and conclude that his unwillingness to say yes or no to particular numbers means he's not really ready to deal. The buyer may conclude that the seller is rude and abrupt and that her obsession with discussing what will happen in the event of a breach means that she is operating in bad faith. The buyer may begin with a bias against the seller because her tenure with her company is not as lengthy as his and her position as a bargaining partner may seem to imply disrespect for his experience. Extensive rapport-building chitchat about non-deal-related topics may seem vital to the buyer, but wasteful to the seller.

FOUR STEPS IN DEALING WITH CULTURAL DIFFERENCES

Hal Abramson, an experienced cross-cultural mediator whose commentary appears later in this chapter, has suggested that mediators adopt a four-step approach to cross-cultural negotiations.[13] When mediators are working with disputants from different cultures, he advises they (1) understand their own culture, (2) research the other culture, (3) bridge any cultural gap, and, when appropriate, (4) consider withdrawal. Mediators always retain the option of withdrawing if the parties' preferred outcome violates their own ethical sensibilities, and they should take that option seriously in difficult cases.

If the buyer and seller discussed above decided to pursue mediation, a mediator who worked through these steps would likely be helpful in surmounting culturally generated confusion and moving closer to an agreement.

Step One: Understand One's Own Culture

This first task involves self-interrogation. The mediator must first evaluate her own cultural expectations and biases. Continuing the buyer-seller story, for example, a North American mediator (say, from

Manhattan) is likely to sympathize with the individualist seller. She too might see the negotiation purely as a resource distribution exercise that should be handled with maximal economy and parsimony. She might encourage both parties to be clear, direct, and straightforward; to share interests, needs, and bottom-line reservation points. And she might find a detailed, precise agreement preferable to a vague, open-ended one. But preferences are not requirements. If the mediator scrutinizes her own background, she will come to understand that her negotiating style is heavily culturally determined. She will see that predilections for meandering versus strictly cosseted meetings, for vague versus meticulous drafting, or for formal versus informal manners of speech are equally valid choices, and that it would be improper for her to favor one cultural style over another.

Step Two: Research the Other Culture

Because in our example the buyer is from Asia, the mediator should inquire into Asian practices and gather as much information as possible about prevailing cultural norms of the area. In the course of doing this, the mediator will learn that the buyer is following a well-established cultural script and that the buyer's obliqueness and concern for what peers back at the home office say about the deal are not necessarily ploys to drive up the price. Rather, they reflect the more communal, relationship-oriented values that predominate in the buyer's homeland. Once the mediator gains a better understanding of the buyer's view of relationships, language, negotiating pace, and structure, she can function more effectively as interlocutor.

Step Three: Bridge Any Cultural Gap

At this point, the mediator can attempt to bridge the cultural divide by helping educate each party about the other's culturally driven behavior and help them approach one another with a more open and accepting mind. The mediator might explain to the impatient seller that the buyer is working with a different set of goals for the negotiation. She might help the seller see that the buyer's elliptical use of language fits into his larger notion of keeping relations harmonious. She might question the seller's assumption that the buyer doesn't really want to settle and explain that team negotiating is common in other areas of the world. She might ask the seller whether she might be comfortable slowing the discussions down, engaging in more purely social activity, and relying on a final document that might not be as thorough or detailed as she would ordinarily like. The mediator would also approach the buyer and talk to him about how he is interpreting the seller's abrupt response to his offers. She might explain the more task-oriented approach of North American negotiators and see if the buyer might be able to respond to the seller's need for clarity and forward movement by streamlining the process.

Step Four: Consider Withdrawal

Working with culturally diverse parties, a mediator needs to consider whether the end result comports with her own sense of ethics and professionalism. In the buyer-seller example, it would not seem that the stylistic differences presented by the North American seller and Asian buyer call the mediator's professionalism into question. It is possible that the parties' cultural differences may have so corroded trust and belief that the mediator is unable to repair the damage. Misunderstandings may have reached such a pitch that the mediator is unable to excavate common ground. But these failures implicate a mediator's skill and effectiveness, not her ethics.

In some multicultural disputes, however, the culture clash leads to ethical problems. In some cases, the question is not whether the mediator can locate common ground, but whether the ground that one or both parties insist on occupying is terrain the mediator feels comfortable sharing. What happens when a clash of cultural values leads to a potential outcome that the mediator finds ethically troublesome? Case 12.1 explores this question.

CASE 12.1: HANNAH AND YOAV'S BROOKLYN DIVORCE

Hannah and Yoav grew up in an ultra-Orthodox Jewish community in Brooklyn where arranged marriages are common. Following this tradition, they wed when they both turned eighteen. In the thirteen years since the wedding, Hannah and Yoav have followed Jewish law (the Halakhah) assiduously, observing every ritual of Orthodox Jewish life.

As is common in this community, Yoav has not held a steady job throughout the marriage. Most of the time he can be found in *shul* studying the Torah. He has relied on Hannah to be the primary wage earner. In the early years of the marriage, Hannah worked as a grade-school teacher, but ten years ago, Yoav gambled away the family's savings. To boost her salary, Hannah began working for her father, who owns several nursing homes throughout the country. As a highly positioned and well-paid member of the family enterprise, Hannah was required to travel extensively and was exposed to a more secular world. Over time, she found herself questioning many of the practices of her community and found herself attracted to a life less circumscribed by religious rules and mores. At the same time, Yoav proved himself unwilling to confront and manage his gambling addiction. When Hannah sought help from the neighborhood rabbi, he simply told her to pray to God and continue being a "good wife."

Disillusioned with her community and despairing of her marriage, Hannah asked her husband for a divorce. He refused. Jewish law provides that only the husband may initiate a divorce. The husband alone is authorized to grant a *get*, the certificate that ends the marriage.[14] If a husband withholds his consent, his wife is considered still bound to him by Jewish law. She cannot remarry, and any children she might bear in a subsequent marriage would be considered *mamzerim* (literally, bastards) and heavily stigmatized. A woman whose husband refuses to deliver a *get* is known as an *agunah*, "a chained woman."

Hannah does not want a huge fight with Yoav and would like to obtain a *get* through mediation, if that is possible. Although she feels alienated from the ultra-Orthodox community and feels certain she will not return, she does not want to stigmatize or taint the prospects of any future children she might have. In addition, she appreciates her parents' support and does not want to damage them further among their peers. Pursuing a secular rather than Jewish divorce would heighten the scandal. Yet she is sufficiently offended by Yoav's recalcitrance and the unhelpfulness of the rabbis that a secular divorce remains very much on the table. Hannah has consulted an attorney and has learned a bit about how divorces are obtained in New York family courts.

Yoav is furious and afraid. He has never supported himself. He says the only way he will grant Hannah a *get* is if she promises to give him $500,000, which is almost the entire amount that Hannah has saved by working with her father and scrimping on personal expenses over the past decade. Hannah feels the request is extortionate. She worked hard for that money and does not believe Yoav contributed anything positive to the marriage. She is willing to give him some money, but not the entire amount. When she learns that a secular court would not award him more than $250,000, she names that number as her walkaway point.

In mediation Yoav makes the case that any future children Hannah might have will never be able to have a "Jewish life" because of her selfish decision to pursue a civil divorce. Hannah is entirely unsure if she will have children, but the argument has some force with her. She has authorized you to offer Yoav $375,000—50 percent more than he would be entitled to in a New York family court. You believe that Yoav will probably take it.

Do you go forward facilitating this agreement?

Before proceeding, it is first necessary to clarify in what sense this is a multicultural dispute and consider what ethical issues are raised.

Jewish Orthodoxy Versus Secular Culture

We can consider this a multicultural dispute because Yoav is negotiating solely within the confines of Orthodox Jewish culture, whereas Hannah has only one foot in that world. Increasingly, she has begun to locate her values, expectations, and goals in the secular world.

Ultra-Orthodox Jewry and secular culture are different in many ways. Most important for our purposes, they differ regarding gender roles and equality between the sexes. Obviously these differences figure prominently in Hannah and Yoav's notion of what constitutes a fair and correct division of property in the wake of divorce.

According to ultra-Orthodox tenets, men and women possess different intellectual, emotional, and spiritual capacities that incline them toward different life tasks. Women are thought to be particularly well suited to domestic activities, whereas men are thought to be naturally predisposed toward spiritual pursuits. Education in those Jewish communities is sex segregated, designed to prepare women to raise children within the faith and keep a kosher home, while men are trained for a life of Torah study.[15]

A primarily patriarchal ordering of rights and responsibilities finds expression in the Halachic rules governing marriage and divorce. In granting husbands unilateral control over divorce, Jewish law gives men an invaluable bargaining chip and an almost insurmountable advantage at the negotiating table.[16] Secular liberal democracies are founded on different assumptions that grant men and women equal status (at least theoretically) in the public as well as private sphere.

The culture clash here relates both to power distance and gender roles. Ultra-Orthodox Jewish culture can be viewed, at least in the matter of divorce, as a high-power-distance culture in which both women and men accept that power is distributed unequally by gender. The culture of most secular liberal democracies adopts a lower-power-distance approach to marriage and divorce in insisting that men and women enjoy equal power to enter into and dissolve their marriages.

Self-Identification with Different Cultures

Yoav is immersed in and accepts the cultural values of his Orthodox Jewish community, including the male prerogative to exercise and exploit the unilateral power to divorce. Hannah has rejected these cultural values and has adopted a lower-power-distance approach. Her cultural alignment is with the larger secular community where her professional interactions occur.

The ethical issue for the mediator arises because Hannah is considering entering into a settlement that affords her a smaller percentage of the marital pie than would a secular court. Yoav is using the power conferred on him by Orthodox Jewish law and tradition to extract a more favorable postdivorce settlement than would be his due were the case decided by a New York judge. Is this use of Orthodox patriarchy in the mediation problematic? Is Hannah being disadvantaged in a way that the mediator should not condone? Is the outcome here one that the mediator should repudiate by speaking out against it or terminating the mediation?

Validating Hannah's Choice

Although reasonable people could differ on this point, a strong argument can be made that the mediator should feel ethically comfortable helping Yoav and Hannah settle, even if Yoav is walking away with 75 percent of the marital assets.

Why is this? First, it is important to remember that one of the primary advantages of mediation is that disputants can conclude their disputes according to their own values, norms, and preferences and not anyone else's. So if a disputant chooses to give more or accept less than a judge, legislator, arbitrator, or anyone else might deem prudent, that is her right and privilege. Of course, if the agreement is too one-sided, a mediator may, and should, worry about whether fear, despair, or ignorance is driving the willingness to settle for what others would see as a bad deal. And when dealing with cultural differences, it is important to consider whether cultural norms so disable one party as to render negotiations dangerous. In that situation, a mediator may want to think about withdrawing or recommending that the disempowered party seek assistance or information from a support person.

As we have seen, cultural norms support some behaviors and demonize others. In addition, as in Yoav and Hannah's case, they offer substantive bargaining chips to some individuals and withhold them from others. In light of the advantages that cultural norms can confer, mediators are well advised to consider whether the bargaining table is too tipped in one party's favor to yield an ethically acceptable outcome.

Here, for a variety of reasons, the mediator may view Hannah's choice as sufficiently free and self-determining that the mediator should feel comfortable proceeding. First, Hannah does not feel confined by the ultra-Orthodox rules governing divorce. She has already made a choice to step out of that community and live her life according to a different set of standards. For this reason, she enjoys a certain liberty of choice. She can choose to bargain with Yoav regarding his consent to the Jewish divorce, or she can pursue a secular divorce in the New York courts. She has a variety of options, and each is real and viable.

Pursuing a Jewish divorce holds certain advantages for her; it will remove the possibility of exclusion and stigma for any future children she may have and spare her parents unnecessary embarrassment. But Yoav's consent will cost her an additional $125,000. Hannah appears to be a strong, capable, well-informed negotiator. She understands the entitlements that secular law would confer and understands the costs of pursuing them. She is well positioned to determine whether the personal advantages that obtaining a Jewish divorce confers are worth the additional money she will need to pay. If she chooses to pay it, she will still be financially stable and can look forward to rebuilding her nest egg using her existing skill set.

Finding Balance

Taken too far, the notion that "parties should be able to do what they want in mediation" has the potential to yield monstrously unfair outcomes. Although we should be wary of imposing our cultural norms on others, most of us would draw a line at outcomes that seem (to our admittedly Western, democratic eyes) abusive or exploitative. Whereas a purely relativistic stance renounces universal standards of right and wrong, a less extreme view maintains that it is possible to embrace and reject cultural practices pursuant to a consistently applied set of standards and principles.

In sum, mediating multicultural disputes forces mediators to confront the twin dangers of cultural imperialism and cultural relativism. Taken too far, either stance can cause harm. Refusing to work with disputants because of their culturally determined norms communicates that those norms, and the culture that produced them, are inferior. This message undercuts the values of tolerance and inclusion to which the dispute resolution field aspires. On the other hand, viewing any cultural practice as permissible simply because it has gained acceptance in some part of the world may place vulnerable disputants in jeopardy and violate individual mediators' cherished moral commitments.

It is important to find some balance between a cultural provincialism that finds fault in difference and a radical relativism that insulates from ethical judgment all culturally driven practices. In Yoav and Hannah's case, the liberty Hannah enjoys to choose between cultural norms and evaluate the benefits she can derive from each makes the mediator's balancing act easier. The mediator can affirm Hannah's financial sacrifice without worrying that she has fallen into a trap set for her by a culture unsympathetic to female autonomy and agency. But what if, due to the disputants' cultural affiliations, the choices are more constraining?

In the next case, starker options make finding the balance more difficult.

CASE 12.2: ZIBA AND AHMED'S IRANIAN-AMERICAN DIVORCE

Seventeen-year-old Ziba and her forty-four-year-old husband Ahmed have come to you for mediation services. Ziba and Ahmed have been married for four years. They have two sons, ages three and two. Ziba wants a divorce, but, like her husband, is anxious to remain part of the local mosque and surrounding community. In order to ensure that the divorce is handled in accord with Quranic principles and meets the approval of their peers and community elders, Ziba and Ahmed met with their imam to learn how their marriage contract may be properly resolved in accord with local interpretations of Islamic law.

Their imam advised them that while a husband can ask for and obtain a divorce for any reason, he is obliged to support his children until they reach the age of majority, regardless of who has primary custody. If the wife remains in the husband's home to observe a mandatory waiting period of seclusion, then he must provide for her needs during that time. In addition he is obliged to pay the amount stipulated in the marriage contract that must be paid if the marriage comes to an end. Ziba and Ahmed's marriage contract calls for a payment of forty thousand dollars.

The imam also tells Ziba that she cannot receive a divorce without Ahmed's consent. And if she initiates the divorce, she will lose her right to the marriage contract payment, although Ahmed's financial obligations toward the children still stand. As far as custody of the children goes, local understandings of Islamic law presume that young children should stay with their mother, but that once sons reach their seventh birthday, custody reverts to the father.[17]

Ziba is miserable in the marriage. Ahmed is controlling and rigid in his notions of what Ziba can do. He monitors her movements, allowing her outside only to shop for groceries and run errands for the house. In addition, he has taken a second wife (in accord with his privileges pursuant to Islamic law) and has begun to pay less and less attention to both Ziba and their children.

Angry and humiliated, Ziba insists she must have permission for the divorce from her husband and without it cannot move on with her life. Ahmed says that he will not grant her request unless she forfeits her marriage dissolution payment and any other financial support for herself and agrees to give up custody of each child at age five. Ahmed says that by asking for a divorce, Ziba is demonstrating that she is an unfit mother and that his sons should thus revert to his care at the earlier age. Ahmed says that it is fitting that his sons should be taken into his care and raised by his female relatives.

At the mediation, Ziba capitulates and tearfully says she will waive all rights to financial support and agree to his requests regarding the transfer of custody at the given ages so long as Ahmed grants her request for a divorce. Although Ziba has agreed to relinquish her children two years earlier than traditional Islamic law would warrant, privately negotiated deviations from default rules are not uncommon. Ahmed is very unhappy with the prospect of divorce and strongly feels Ziba's behavior compromises her ability to parent. He has stated to you in private that the only reason he is not demanding immediate transfer is that he doesn't think Ziba will agree and doesn't believe he would receive support from his community. He is confident, however, that the agreement as contemplated is broadly supportable and within the norms of the Iranian community in which they live.

As mediator, do you help the parties with their divorce?

Comments on Case 12.2

Carrie Menkel-Meadow

Whose culture? Whose laws? Whose ethics? Yours or mine?

Ziba and Ahmed's divorce mediation raises very difficult issues of cross-cultural mediation. My response to the dilemma presented here is easy for me, but likely to be seen as very controversial and unacceptable by many other mediators. I will explain why.

Self-determination (by both the parties and the mediator), capacity and consent to any agreements, "true" understanding of possible alternatives, and my own legal and social justice concerns all militate against my deferring to the parties' claimed desire to use religious law and principles to resolve their dispute.

SUITABILITY FOR MEDIATION? CLASH BETWEEN RELIGIOUS/COMMUNI-TARIAN AND LEGAL SYSTEMS. Many ethnic, religious, and other affiliated communities have their own systems of rules, laws, and customs that they may seek to "enforce" through private mediation. Some have argued that mediation is particularly appropriate in such settings where communities seek to enhance their shared community values by their own systems of dispute resolution, away from the state or other cultures that they do not recognize or that do not recognize them (Freshman, 1997). If Ziba and Ahmed had contacted me with their desire to use Shari'a law, I would likely have made a referral to a specialized religion-based mediation center. I would not take their case. Here's why:

First, Ziba, now seventeen, has, according to the facts, been married for four years. That means she was thirteen when she married. The facts as given do not specify whether her marriage took place in the United States or in another country, but by no measure of "full faith and credit" would I regard a marriage made at thirteen to be a legal marriage in the United States. And wherever they live in the United States, a state court will have to finalize their "legal" divorce. Most states require evidence of a marriage certificate to certify the marriage when the divorce is judicially approved. A marriage certificate of a girl of thirteen would not be valid in virtually all states of the United States. Thus, in my view, the marriage is not "legal" under American domestic law (and American law is still required to make the divorce legally binding here) and legally could be annulled. In addition, it is also possible that, given the absence of a legal marriage, Ahmed might even be guilty of statutory rape under American law. Ziba could possibly file charges against him if she wanted to (or she might choose to use this information to prevent him from further abusing her or to "bargain" for her "rightful" financial and custody rights).

As a lawyer mediator with some experience in domestic relations (in litigation and in mediation), I would tell Ziba and Ahmed this together in a joint premediation session, as well as in any separate caucus that I would have with both parties. I would give legal advice and counsel to both of them at the same time and tell them what American law provides. I would, in the presence of both parties, tell Ziba that if she consulted an American lawyer, she would likely be entitled to financial support, as well as custody of both of her children. Other mediators might fear doing this because of possible domestic abuse or other negative actions that Ahmed might take when he sees his wife being so advised, but in my view, as long as she is living in the United States, she has the right to legal information according to the rules of this country.

WHOSE SELF-DETERMINATION? While I fully acknowledge all of our profession's norms and platitudes about self-determination (Standard I, Self-Determination, Model Standards of Conduct for Mediators, 2005), I do not believe that a thirteen-year-old girl had the capacity to "self-determine" when she married Ahmed, and thus the whole premise of the termination of the marriage is in question (for me). In addition, as long as we are looking at the platitudinous standards (which seldom help resolve really difficult questions), I would decline this case also for several other reasons:

- I am obviously not "impartial." I am judging the validity of the marriage and giving advice to one of the parties that at least one, if not both, of them is likely to view as "partial" (Standard II, Impartiality, Model Standards of Conduct for Mediators).

- I do not have the "competence" to mediate a case involving Shari'a law since I know not much about it, except as a legal educator and scholar.[18] I do know that its teachings are actually subject to much controversy, change, and interpretation, and I do not entirely trust what the parties tell me their mullah has told them (Abu-Odeh, 2006; Model Standards of Conduct for Mediators, Standard IV, Competence).

- I do not believe that a mediation that would sanction or permit these results would be one with the requisite "quality of process" (Standard VI, Quality of the Process, Model Standards of Conduct for Mediators), which, in my view, requires "safety" of the parties (including the affected children), full presence and participation of the parties, party competency (including non-interference by third parties), and "mutual respect" among all participants.

- I have a conflict of interest (Standard III, Conflicts of Interest, Model Standards of Conduct for Mediators) because I have spent a great deal of my legal career as a feminist advocate for equality in marriage, self-determination, and the rights of women to no-fault divorce, as well as to adequate child and spousal support, and thus could not possibly be seen as neutral or impartial by Ahmed (and maybe by Ziba as well). In addition, I am committed in print (Menkel-Meadow, 2001), as well as in my practice, to tolerance and appreciation of diversity, in culture and religion, but I am a secular humanist, who, while acknowledging the importance of plural systems of law and culture, could not myself "preside" over a mediation that used a set of norms and customs that institutionalizes deep structures of inequality, even if seemingly "consented to."

I have turned down other cases in which parties are subject to deeply unfair or unequal rules or bargaining endowments (some cases of employment settings, some cases of unequal legal representation) or other matters where, in my view, mediation would lead to outcomes for which I would not want to be ethically responsible (Menkel-Meadow, 2004).

More complex issues actually underlie these "easy" answers from the Model Standards. One is that, as the hypothetical is intended to reveal, mediations like this pit significant cultural differences against each other: the couple's desire to use Shari'a law, which does not grant Ziba the same rights as domestic laws would, versus the mediator's own sense of legal entitlements and "justice." In cases of radically different cultural understandings, whose cultural understandings should govern? Isabelle Gunning has written eloquently on this point, in several relevant contexts, first in how "Western" feminists should deal with the religious or ethnic practice of "female genital mutilation" in the face of "international" standards of human health and safety (Gunning, 1991–1992, 1995) and, second, in seeing mediation as a site for self-empowerment for groups that are not recognized by or likely to be disadvantaged in formal court proceedings. The problem of cultural relativism or cultural hegemony is very significant in many modern mediations where parties choose to avoid formal law and legal systems and elect to apply other sources of social norms that they (and their mediators) may or may not share. There are no easy answers to the question of "whose culture" should govern.

PROCEED ON A BASIS OF DECLARED "SELF-DETERMINATION"? I suspect that many mediators would proceed with the mediation on the theory of party "self-determination," as long as they were comfortable with the conclusion that Ziba has "chosen" to be bound by Shari'a law. For these mediators, the cultural decision is for the parties, and as long as the parties "agree" on what cultural norms they want to apply to their dispute, the mediator's role is simply to ensure the process is fair and the agreement is freely consented to. In this case, some mediators might ask who am I to judge what these parties want; in the interest of self-determination, they have chosen to be governed by their own religious norms.

I could not, given my own "ethical culture" (Menkel-Meadow, 2001), act or be "complicit" in an agreement that I felt was legally, morally, or ethically wrong (and under these facts, I think all are true for me). Ziba did not knowingly consent to her marriage; she is dominated by Ahmed in the marriage and wants out so badly she is willing to bargain away her own maternity in order to be free of him.

Mediators have cultural and ethical commitments too, and in my view, no mediator (and certainly not this mediator) should participate in a mediation that she thinks will lead to a morally, legally, or ethically "unconscionable" result. What is unconscionable is, of course, subjective, personal, and nonuniversal. Thus, mediators must disclose their own relevant cultural, legal, personal, ethical, religious, political, or other commitments that will clearly affect how they facilitate dispute resolution.

One shorthand way to think about this is that the standards are for mediators too—and that includes self-determination. Mediators must also have the ability to determine when their "self" (including identity, integrity, professionalism, or other commitments) cannot be realized in a particular mediation.

WHAT IF THE PARTIES DO NOT REALLY SHARE A CULTURAL UNDERSTANDING? As difficult as the above "cultural" issue is, there is even more difficulty if the parties themselves do not share cultural understandings or agreements about what norms to apply. Although not at issue as the hypothetical case is framed, suppose that early on or during the course of the mediation, it becomes clear that Ziba has actually been "coerced" into accepting Shari'a principles and, once informed of her rights under American domestic law, she would prefer to have those legal norms applied to her case. How mediators should "mediate" cultural differences between the parties in mediation is enormously complex. The norms by which mediation agreements are to be reached are often themselves the subject of negotiations and mediations, and mediators need to be able to mediate which norms will govern the mediation, even across cultural differences. Sometimes parties can agree on outcomes without explicitly acknowledging what principles got them there, but in general, where there is not some agreement about the governing norms or principles, the agreement may be in trouble if it requires enforcement, justification to third parties, or acceptability and legitimacy for the parties.

In this case, Shari'a law and American equitable distribution, community property, and no-fault divorce principles clearly conflict with each other, and if the parties cannot agree on what norms to apply to their divorce, mediation may not be the appropriate forum. In my view, a culturally competent mediator must at least raise with the parties what their differences are, what are the sources, cultural, religious, legal, or personal, of their differences, and offer sensitive conversations about how those differences might be handled. Of course, "cultural differences," like all other issues in mediation, may in fact differ in the eyes of the beholders, and different perceptions about whether there are in fact "cultural differences" may lead to an even deeper level of analysis, and disagreement (Gadlin, 1995).

THE RELEVANCE OF LAW. The astute reader of this commentary would have noticed that I have used legal analysis to locate my own cultural differences with the parties. "Under domestic/state/American law," Ziba would be entitled to no-fault divorce, possibly both child and spousal support, and certainly a legal right to pursue custody of her children. Thus, this mediator is using law to center (at least part of) her judgments about the case (and "judgments" they are). As

I have controversially stated in other venues, mediation is often (and in this case would be) "the practice of law" (Menkel-Meadow, 1996). Even if the parties chose to be governed by Shari'a law, in the United States, a legal divorce must be approved by a state court, and thus American law is implicated in the decision. While it is now a controversy in many legal systems, including the United Kingdom, the United States, and Canada, about whether formal state courts should recognize Shari'a law in family law determinations, in the United States, Shari'a law has not yet been recognized in formal court determinations.

Every year in the United States, thousands (maybe even millions) of couples use private mediation, often with nonlawyer mediators who may be unfamiliar with applicable legal principles, using whatever principles they can agree on, to resolve issues of separation, financial support, child custody, and property division. In many, if not most, cases, if there is a settlement or private agreement, courts will approve the divorce in a general, pro forma (but legal) way and will not usually inquire into the equities of the parties' agreement unless an issue is raised formally with the court. There is no regular court review of private divorce agreements, even when the court must sign a formal decree of legal divorce. Nevertheless, family relations and status are still a matter of state law in the United States (indeed a very contested question of law, as the same-sex marriage political and legal battles make clear), and for me, in this case, as in all others I mediate, "the law is relevant, if not determinative" (Friedman & Himmelstein, 2008). Thus, I will not mediate a case where there is relevant law for the parties to consider in evaluating their possible outcomes, rights, and alternatives, and the parties are unaware of those legal entitlements or endowments.

I *would* ask the parties here if they have discussed their legal rights with counsel, and if they have not, I would ask them if they would like referrals to do so. In this case, if Ziba and Ahmed said they were not interested in American law, I would tell them anyway (advising them together in joint session and then asking if they wanted to meet with me individually to discuss further).

For many mediators, this would be overstepping the boundaries of the mediator's "neutral" role, would involve the mediator in legal information provision or more accurately, legal advice giving, and would likely lead to the perception that the mediator was "partial" to one side (advising Ziba of what she could gain by pursuing American secular law). Yet for me, this legal advice and information would be absolutely essential for any determination I might want to make about whether the parties could in fact consent knowingly and willingly to an agreement under Shari'a law that eschewed legal entitlements that the parties might otherwise have.

Mediation is a process, not a separate justice system that automatically dismisses or renders inapposite "the law." At the same time, if a party is fully knowledgeable about the legal entitlements or arguments the law may provide, that party (indeed, both parties) may well decide to reach agreement or settle on the basis of other values (or nonlegal principles), seeking to apply his or her own sense of justice or fairness within his or her own relationship or community. Law or legal principles are not always determinative, and parties may and often do seek to do "real," if not "legal," justice between themselves. If, as a mediator, I am convinced they fully understand what they are doing, the parties may agree to depart from what the law might grant them. Laws are passed by legislatures for "the general public" and are interpreted by judges in particular situations. Mediation offers the parties a more democratic, nuanced, individualized, and self-empowering opportunity to interpret the law for themselves, as long as they agree and as long as the agreement is not legally voidable (by being unlawful).

However, as a lawyer mediator I will not participate in or "preside" over an agreement that is "unlawful" under applicable law. In this case, the secular law of divorce is still necessary to grant the parties a legal divorce in a state court of appropriate jurisdiction.

CONCLUSION. In this case, beyond the question of "whose culture" and "whose law" is the (for me) ethical question of "whose justice." Mediation is a process; it has no substantive commitments except knowing consent of the parties (and is backed up by the legal system's enforcement of legally acceptable contracts that can be enforced in courts) and an aspiration to do individualized and legitimate justice for the parties *as they see it.* For me, however, a mediator is also a party to a mediation, and thus the agreement that is reached must also be one that I can be accountable and responsible for as a participant in the process. *My* sense of *ethics, culture,* and yes, even *justice* is also at stake, for I am a party too.

I would honestly and completely tell the parties everything I have just told you, the reader, and would (1) advise them to seek legal advice and counsel about what is necessary for a legal divorce in my community; and (2) withdraw and ask them to find another mediator if they insist on applying a set of norms I am not competent to enforce, even as I have views about whether they do justice or not. This, of course, raises the next difficult issue of whether I am at all responsible for an outcome reached by someone other than myself (another mediator who agrees to let the parties use the agreement they have framed in the hypothetical, which you can see I think is unfair and unjust to Ziba). But that is a question for another day.

Comments on Case 12.2

Harold Abramson

The challenge posed by Ziba and Ahmed's divorce differs from difficulties customarily encountered in cross-cultural disputes.[19] Often in domestic or international mediations, a cultural gap exists between the parties. But here the parties are culturally aligned, and the gap lies between the mediator and the parties.

The goal, as I see it, is clear: to ethically bridge the gap between the mediator and the parties while avoiding culturally imperialist behavior. No mediator wants to be charged with cultural imperialism when mediating private international disputes. And yet mediators run this risk whenever they resist doing what the parties want done. The challenge is to "give the parties what they want" without doing violence to universally held norms or one's own deeply held personal values.

For myself, after much soul searching, I decided that were I the mediator, I would go forward and assist Ziba and Ahmed in their efforts to conclude their divorce. But I reached that determination only after rejecting all the alternatives. Ziba and Ahmed don't afford a Western mediator any easy answers. All roads point toward moral discomfort. As difficult as this was, I tried to put my own personal values aside and look instead to see whether working with this couple would violate universally accepted international principles of human rights. My inquiries suggest that the answer is no; norms surrounding gender equity diverge dramatically throughout the world. This is one of the disturbing facts of multiculturalism, and as a mediator, I am wary of using my own personal views as the yardstick for how the parties should structure their affairs.

A second consideration influencing my decision flows from examining Ziba's other options. They didn't look promising to me. I thought by continuing to work with the couple, I could help them get the best deal possible. Contrary to the usual sunny rhetoric of win-win, here I would aspire toward "the least bad" outcome—an outcome that involves the least amount of moral violence and coercion for all involved. Here is how I got there.

THE CHALLENGE FOR THE MEDIATOR: A CROSS-CULTURAL DISPUTE. The thorny aspect of this cross-cultural conflict can be presented succinctly. Both parties agree broadly to a rule that, when they apply it, results in a mediated agreement that is unfair according to the mediator's Westernized values and may even violate Western domestic law.

Consider the way Ahmed's power over granting a divorce was being used to extort a one-sided agreement, at least from a Westernized point of view. A Western mediator would likely view as unfair an agreement where unemployed Ziba waives needed financial support and relinquishes rights to her children once they turn five. Under Westernized common law and statutory laws, such a one-sided agreement also is likely to be invalid and unenforceable due to Ahmed's extortionate behavior and the duress suffered by Ziba who wants the divorce.[20]

This culturally shaped family mediation starkly raises an old issue in new packaging: Should a mediator withdraw when the mediator encounters a rule, practice, or emerging agreement that the mediator thinks is unfair? In this dispute, the new packaging entails an objectionable foreign cultural rule and its impact on the resulting mediated agreement. Without this cultural overlay shaping the parties' behavior and resulting agreement, I suspect that many Western mediators would withdraw from the mediation. With the cultural overlay, however, it is less clear what a mediator ought to do.

A FOUR-STEP APPROACH. Cross-cultural mediators live under the constant threat of being charged with cultural imperialism. Mediators do not want to be guilty of parochial ignorance and arrogance when objecting to what might be a cultural practice. They want to avoid claiming that they are right and the parties wrong. In order to reduce this risk, cross-cultural mediators should approach mediations with a healthy respect for cultural pluralism and a clear understanding of the other cultural practice.

In analyzing what a mediator might do in this case, I will follow the four-step approach that the editor of this book introduced on my behalf at the outset of the chapter. This sequence is designed to guide mediators along an ethical path that can also help to avoid the cultural imperialist charge. The mediator should:

1. Understand his or her own cultural practices

2. Research the other cultural practice to be sure that the mediator understands its terms and its rationale

3. Bridge any cultural gap between the mediator and parties by posing questions to the parties to be sure that the parties are making informed, voluntary, and uncoerced decisions

4. Withdraw if the mediator concludes that the practice violates an internationally recognized norm or compromises the mediator's impartiality or the mediation process

Understand One's Own Culture. Consciously or not, mediators inescapably read a dispute through their own culturally shaped lens. Consequently, they need to develop a degree of cultural competency and self-awareness in order to distinguish universal behavior from their own cultural views. Developing this self-awareness requires doing some research. I have found it helpful to read articles and books that compare communication in different cultures and describe U.S. culture for foreigners; it is especially fascinating to learn how others view one's own culture. For mediator ethics in the United States, the Model Standards of Conduct for Mediators provide the primary cultural lens through which mediators see their disputes. So I began this journey by reacquainting myself with the Model Standards and especially the values that they reflect.

As discussed in Chapter Five in this book, the Model Standards do not hold mediators accountable for the substantive fairness of the mediation agreements they help orchestrate. Rather, they require mediators to focus on process fairness and assume that when process fairness is ensured, substantive fairness will follow. To this end, the Standards require mediators to foster party self-determination and competency, mediator impartiality, and scrupulousness of process. But they steer clear of discussions of fairness, equity, and substantive justice.[21]

The code reflects the mediation culture in the United States: a studiously process-oriented culture that exempts mediators from the burden of judging the fairness of the parties' desired outcome. Still, while mediators need not subject proposed agreements to a fairness litmus test, principles of party self-determination, impartiality, and quality process still offer much for mediators to ponder, as this hypothetical illustrates.

A mediator might view Ziba's custody and financial giveaways as so problematic as to call into question the likelihood that she is acting voluntarily, consistent with the mandate of self-determination. The one-sidedness may tug at the mediator's sympathies, causing the mediator to ally with Ziba and creating partiality. In the face of these types of problems, the Model Standards instruct the mediator to "take appropriate steps including . . . withdrawing from or terminating the mediation."

Therefore, ample justification exists for a mediator to consider withdrawing. But in a dispute laden with non-Westernized practices and behavior, the mediator should take additional steps before deciding whether to withdraw. The mediator needs to research the other culture and try to bridge any cultural gaps. These additional steps are essential if the mediator wants to avoid the charge of cultural imperialism.

Research the Other Culture. A mediator cannot help bridge a cultural gap without learning and understanding the cultural practices of the parties. Sources may be difficult to locate, and their messages recondite and conflicting. Still, the mediator needs to endeavor to become acquainted with the terms of a cultural practice as well as its rationale. The inquiry may be discomfiting because the relevant practice may seem abhorrent to a mediator of a certain background and upbringing. However, the inquiry is crucial, and the mediator must be open to the possibility that an offensive practice may turn out to be tolerable when understood in context.

For example,[22] seeking to understand a practice of arranged marriages involving payment may seem offensive. After all, the practice was condemned in the United Nations Report of the Committee on the Elimination of Discrimination Against Women.[23] Why seek to understand this approach to women and family? Because you might find it helpful to learn one commentator's justification for the practice: "The payment of mahr (dower), which involves payment or preferment, is a central feature of the marriage contract in Islam and, as a measure intended to safeguard [a woman's] economic position after marriage [the mahr is offered to the bride]."

It may feel equally repugnant to remain open to a practice that gives men a right to a greater share of property, a practice also apparently condemned in the Convention on the Elimination of All Forms of Discrimination Against Women (Article 16[h]). But you might find it helpful to hear the same commentator's explanation on this point: in Islam, men have financial obligations to others that are not shared with women, so men need a disproportionate amount of assets to meet those other obligations. Of course, neither this nor the earlier rationale provides the final word, but they do offer leads on further research that a mediator might want to pursue.

For this hypothetical case, a mediator would need to learn the cultural explanation for a practice that confers on Ahmed the exclusive power over approving a divorce and therefore the potential to extract a one-sided divorce settlement.

My preliminary research uncovered some initial insights.[24] The Egyptian government, in commentary on an international treaty relating to women's rights, explained that the restrictions placed on women's ability to terminate marriage are designed to balance out their rights to full financial support within the marriage and the payout they receive at the marriage's end. That is, according to Shari'a, women enter into marriage free of any requirements to contribute financially but then must yield to male preferences regarding how long or whether the marriage is to endure. In short, Shari'a aims toward symmetry, balance, and equality between the sexes, although Westerners may not be comfortable or agree with the manner in which burdens and benefits are distributed.

Bridge Any Cultural Gaps. With some understanding of the cultural context of the practice, the mediator is ready to proceed with a sophisticated self-determination inquiry. As a threshold matter, I assume that the parties have legal counsel. I also assume that the parties were encouraged to seek counsel from a trusted family member or friend so that each party has the benefit of a support system that each party trusts.

As the mediator here, I would give Ahmed and Ziba an opportunity to express their reactions to the rule and consider its rationale, benefits, and drawbacks. Then I might follow up with clarifying and reality-testing questions. This is not a simple inquiry, and of course it is often easier to describe what to do than to actually do it. But it is an essential inquiry if mediators want to seriously pursue party self-determination. One of two basic scenarios might emerge: Ziba accepts the rule or she objects to it.

Under the first scenario, in which Ziba accepts the rule, if she does so understanding the disadvantageous trade-offs that it can produce when dissolving the marriage, at least she is making an informed choice to live with its consequences. Her formal acceptance under these circumstances, however, should not go uninspected. It is important to inquire into the circumstances surrounding the "choice" to accept. As critics of cultural pluralism point out, the term *choice* connotes options: "It is one thing to embrace a way of life when none other is available, an entirely different one to cling to it when alternatives present themselves."[25]

Therefore, I would test her acceptance by tempting her with options. For example, Ziba does have an alternative if the mediation is taking place in New York State, which has a state law designed to diminish the ability of a husband to extort an unduly favorable settlement under a religious rule that gives the power to divorce to the husband.[26] The mediator might inquire whether the parties or attorneys are aware of the applicable law. Through their attorneys, the parties would learn that New York law authorizes a court to consider whether Ahmed exploited a barrier to remarriage when the court determines the distribution of marital property and appropriate maintenance. Therefore, Ziba would have an option for ameliorating the influence of the rule and a choice to make. She could agree to Ahmed's onerous demands. But she could also turn to or threaten to turn to the secular courts to reduce her unequal bargaining power. This may not seem like a real choice for someone who wants to preserve her standing in her own religious community. But it gives Ziba an opportunity to choose which value is more important to her: preserving her standing in her community or improving the terms of divorce.

I found this part of my deliberations unsettling because it seemed disconcertingly easy to justify Ziba's rights waivers by casting them as deliberate demonstrations of her idiosyncratic will. Having knowingly accepted the rule and chosen to follow it, Ziba would probably continue to pursue the religious divorce regardless of the alternatives the secular courts might offer. This substantive result may be unfair by Westernized standards, but not necessarily unfair based on the values Ziba adopted. My limited role as a mediator who perseveres to honor the principle of party self-determination becomes clear in this situation. In the end, all mediators can do is conduct a process where the parties can make an informed choice, regardless of how personally painful the choice may be to one of the parties and how unfair the result may seem to the mediator.

The second scenario is that Ziba—albeit perhaps a dedicated member of her religious community—objects to its rule and its consequences. In that case, the conflict of values between her and the mediator disappears. Then the mediator can no longer be accused of imposing his or her own values on the parties, since one of the parties now asserts those values. With this agreement, Ziba effectively shields the mediator from the charge of cultural imperialism, although not from the charge of partiality. The mediator no longer needs to bridge a cultural conflict between the mediator and the parties. The mediator can now return to the familiar territory of trying to bridge a gap between the parties.

Withdraw? Even in the face of the parties' consent or apparent consent, the mediator may still find the agreement so personally abhorrent as to want to withdraw. But how can a mediator withdraw and avoid the charge of cultural imperialism?

Walking this tightrope requires attention to two inquiries. First, does the cultural practice violate internationally recognized norms? Second, even if it doesn't, is it possible to remain impartial when intensely disapproving of the norms the parties are embracing?

My search for universal international norms relating to Ziba and Ahmed's case led me to scrutinize international treaties touching on the rights of men and women in the domestic sphere. If most countries, including Iran and surrounding nations, had ratified these treaties, then I could comfortably conclude that the norm of gender equality was universally recognized, even by the countries to which Ziba and Ahmed were culturally aligned. Unfortunately, I found no such universal agreement.

The United Nations General Assembly has adopted two statements: the Convention on the Elimination of All Forms of Discrimination Against Women and the Universal Declaration of Human Rights. Both declare in ringing language that men and women have equal rights in marriage and its dissolution. But when I checked the fine print, I discovered that Iran has never ratified the Convention, and the Universal Declaration was simply enabling legislation that did not require endorsement or acceptance of any sort. Even worse, many Middle Eastern countries, including Iran's close neighbors, took explicit exception to the convention's gender equality language, opting out of those provisions that violated "norms of Islamic law" or were "incompatible with the provisions of the Islamic Shari'a."

Rather than unanimity in the realm of gender equality, I found disarray. My forays into international law revealed no principled source of internationally recognized standards that could be the basis for withdrawing from the mediation. Different cultures view women's rights to enter into and exit marriage differently. Given this (discomfiting) fact, I pondered whether there was any other principled basis for withdrawing—specifically the second inquiry about my ability to remain both impartial and intensely disapproving of the norms the parties were embracing.

Obviously if I found myself hopelessly partial—biased against Ahmed—then withdrawal would be appropriate. Standard II of the U.S. Model Standards requires mediators to maintain impartiality, and if my feelings about Ahmed's demands eliminate my ability to respond evenhandedly, then I should not continue. Standard VI's discussion of a "quality process" may also be implicated. Of course, if my decision to withdraw is based on my own cultural value, then I might remain vulnerable to the ultimate charge of cultural imperialism—the charge that I'm claiming "my culture is better than your culture."

Despite my desire to be respectful toward Ziba and Ahmed's claimed cultural stance, withdrawal was the direction I was going in until my research assistant innocently asked about next steps: "Would what would happen after withdrawal be better than the mediator continuing?" she inquired. What would Ahmed and Ziba's BATNA (best alternative to a negotiated agreement) be if the negotiation in the mediation were prematurely halted? This inquiry prompted me to consider Ziba's opportunities without mediation. What if no fairer venue exists for her? In that case, depriving her of the mediation opportunity contributes to her disadvantage. If I withdraw, Ziba loses access to help by a third party with expertise in dispute resolution, who might be culturally sensitive to this unequal power dynamic and might be able to help her negotiate further details within the parameters of the agreement. If I continue with the mediation, on the other hand, I might be able to help Ahmed and Ziba negotiate valuable details that might benefit the children, including addressing such issues as visitation and education plans.

This was the most difficult decision moment for me. After trying to research Ziba's BATNA and much cogitating,[27] I thought I still would withdraw if faced with this dilemma. I would not want the mediation process (or me) to be associated with such an unfair mediated result. I would want to avoid conferring the imprimatur of mediation on a process and result that violated such a core value of fairness, even when my definition of fairness was shaped by distinctively Westernized values. This was my conclusion until I realized that I was so determined to withdraw that I had become blinded to the significant benefits of continuing for the parties. I am now inclined to continue to mediate.[28] If both parties want to continue with me and the mediation, I think I should try to mediate the best agreement the parties are willing to enter into, so long as the agreement is not illegal.

CONCLUSION. When crossing borders, mediators are crossing into new ethical territory. Ethical issues can arise due to differences in culture between the mediator and the parties. In order to navigate this new territory, mediators need to be aware of their own culturally shaped behavior and perspective and be open-minded and nonjudgmental when learning about other ways of behaving. And mediators should diligently search for ways to bridge any gaps between the mediator and the parties before confronting the difficult possibility of withdrawing. By conscientiously following the steps outlined in these comments, mediators should be able to avoid the charge of cultural imperialism, except when they consciously decide to be imperialistic.

Editor's Thoughts on Case 12.2 and the Comments

Both Abramson and Menkel-Meadow acknowledge the difficulty of this case and come to dramatically different conclusions regarding what they would do. Although superficially it seems as if they "went to the same movie theater but saw a different show," a closer look reveals their analyses to be more similar than initially apparent.

First, both Abramson and Menkel-Meadow note that the Model Standards provide ample justification for withdrawal. Both make reference to the provisions regarding impartiality and ensuring a quality process and note that their discomfort with Ziba's anguished rights waivers would call into question their ability to proceed on these grounds. At the same time, both commentators note that the Standards beg the larger questions of how mediator partiality to familiar (in this case, Western) norms can be ethically squared with multicultural practice and whether the primary self-determination commandment takes adequate account of the coercive environments in which disputants may be situated.

Both Abramson and Menkel-Meadow note that many mediators would proceed on the grounds that the parties have chosen the governing norms and that respect for party self-determination justifies mediator acquiescence to that choice. However, Abramson questions whether choice in the absence of adequate options passes muster, and Menkel-Meadow affirmatively denies that Ziba's financial and custody giveaways could be viewed as "freely chosen," even when measured by the "thinnest" notions of self-determination's requirements.

Though discomfited by Ziba's predicament, Abramson states that he would proceed with the case, while Menkel-Meadow maintains that she would have to turn it away. Each of these thoughtful mediator scholars reaches a fork in the road where a singular path calls. In assessing the road to take and the road not taken, they are prodded by different visions of mediator autonomy in the process.

For Menkel-Meadow, one primary consideration appears salient. She believes that the opportunity for self-determination exists for mediators as well as parties. Mediators hew to a moral code that guides their everyday thoughts and actions. Just as mediation offers parties an opportunity to express their deepest normative commitments, so too must the process respect and give voice to mediator values. Abramson takes a more self-abnegating view. He holds that mediators should strive to avoid withdrawal or termination based solely on their own personal assessment of the parties' values. Rather, withdrawal can be justified only when grounded in the parties' rejection of universally held international norms. If what the parties are inclined to do violates a United Nations proclamation or a treaty to which the majority of the world is a signatory, then withdrawal is amply justified. If it simply makes the individual mediator queasy, withdrawal is suspect.

Given Abramson's inclination to stifle his visceral offense and consider Ziba and Ahmed's options, it is perhaps not surprising that he comes to the conclusion that he, and mediation, can produce a happier outcome than would likely be achieved in a different forum. Abramson takes a dim view of Ziba's BATNA and so decides that the most ethical course is to hang in there and see if he can help bring about as salutary a conclusion to the marriage as is possible under the circumstances. Menkel-Meadow says that if she played any role with the couple, she would discuss with them Ziba's entitlements under American law and would then refer the case to someone whose "ethical culture" did not recoil against the structural inequities built into the Shari'a law that both Ziba and Ahmed honor. Menkel-Meadow notes that ethical issues attach to the question of whether she is at all responsible for an outcome that another mediator facilitates but concludes, "That is a question for another day."

References for Carrie Menkel-Meadow's Comments

Abu-Odeh, L. (2006). Family law reforms: The central Arab states. In S. Joseph (Ed.), *Encyclopedia of women in Islamic cultures.* Leiden: Brill.

Freshman, C. (1997). Privatizing same-sex marriage through alternative dispute resolution: Community enhancing versus community enabling mediation. *UCLA Law Review, 44,* 1687.

Friedman, G., & Himmelstein, J. (2008). *Challenging conflict: Mediation through understanding.* Chicago: ABA Press.

Gadlin, H. (1995). Conflict resolution, cultural differences and the culture of racism. *Negotiation Journal, 33,* 35.

Gunning, I. (1991–1992). Arrogant perception, world traveling and multi-cultural feminism: The case of female genital surgeries. *Columbia Human Rights Law Review, 23*(4), 189–248.

Gunning, I. (1995). Diversity issues in mediation: Controlling negative cultural myths. *Dispute Resolution Journal, 1,* 55–93.

Menkel-Meadow, C. (1996). Is mediation the practice of law? *Alternatives to the High Cost of Litigation, 14,* 57.

Menkel-Meadow, C. (2001). And now a word about secular humanism, spirituality and the practice of justice in conflict resolution. *Fordham Urban Law Journal, 28,* 1073.

Menkel-Meadow, C. (2004). What's fair in negotiation? What is ethics in negotiation? In C. Menkel-Meadow & M. Wheeler (Eds.), *What's fair: Ethics for negotiators.* San Francisco: Jossey-Bass.

CHAPTER THIRTEEN

Ethics for ADR Provider Organizations

S̶o far we have been considering the ethical dilemmas that individual mediators may face in their day-to-day practice. But focusing on the conundrums of individuals does not exhaust the range of ethical inquiry. Rather, alternative dispute resolution (ADR) provider organizations, such as courts, government agencies, and private providers, also encounter ethical tensions in their everyday operations, and these tensions require careful thought and attention.

For private ADR providers, the primary danger is that the need to be profitable may push toward ethically suspect practices. Providers aiming toward a high volume of business will likely generate higher revenues than those who adopt a more leisurely schedule that allows ample time for premediation review, client consultation, and investigation. Implementing rigorous evaluation and grievance procedures is also ethically desirable but carves away at the business bottom line. Rewarding "repeat players" with favorable settlement outcomes may increase business but violates basic norms of impartiality and avoiding conflicts of interest.

Public providers, such as courts and government agencies, face related challenges as well as resource constraints, and for them the ethical mandate to ensure a quality process is, if anything, even greater. In the private sector, disputants consciously choose the ADR marketplace. In a court-connected program, disputants often do not enjoy the luxury of choice. Rather, they have filed a court complaint and then find themselves required, or strongly "encouraged," to give mediation a try. A provider's obligation to guarantee procedural and substantive fairness is inversely related to the disputants' ability to make process choices: the less choice a disputant enjoys, the higher the ethical responsibility of the provider to ensure a quality process.

CODES AND STANDARDS FOR PROVIDERS

The idea that institutional, as well as individual, dispute resolution providers may require ethical guidance emerged in concert with the growing reliance of state courts and public agencies on dispute resolution referrals. As courts and agencies began to assemble their own rosters of mediators and administer increasingly active dispute resolution programs, it became clear that organizational decisions regarding training, recruitment, marketing, and quality control had ethical ramifications.

In 1991, the Law and Public Policy Committee of the Society for Professionals in Dispute Resolution issued a report examining the policy implications of court-sponsored mandatory mediation programs.[1] That same year, the Center for Dispute Settlement, the Institute of Judicial Administration, and an eighteen-member advisory board collaborated on the National Standards for Court-Connected Mediation Programs, which set out aspirational goals relating to access, informed consent, case selection, attorney roles, service quality, evaluation, and grievance procedures. Several years later, the Center for Public Resources (CPR)-Georgetown Commission on Ethics and Standards of Practice (CPR-Georgetown Principles) developed a set of best practices for provider organizations, both public and private. Those standards were circulated in draft form for public comment in 2000 and adopted in final form in 2002.[2]

Both the National Standards and the CPR-Georgetown Principles exist as aspirational ideals only. As the Standards' drafters explained, the goal is to "inspire court-connected mediation programs of high quality," not to suggest language that would later be rigidly adopted in legislation or court rule.[3] The Principles too serve a guidance, but not a regulatory, function.[4] Still, while lacking the force of law, their identification of ethical flashpoints reveals areas where ADR providers must exercise special care in the initiation, expansion, and modification of their programs.

COMPARING THE NATIONAL STANDARDS AND THE CPR-GEORGETOWN PRINCIPLES

The National Standards and the CPR-Georgetown Principles apply to overlapping but different target audiences. This difference in scope and application results in divergent emphases; the two codes focus on different ethical problems and propose different solutions.

CPR-Georgetown Principles: Disclosing Conflicts and Curbing the Profit Motive

The CPR-Georgetown Principles seek to provide guidance to each ADR provider organization, defined broadly as "any entity or individual which holds itself out as managing or administering dispute resolution or conflict management services." The Principles are thus meant to apply to for-profit firms handling disputes outside the ambit of the legal system, as well as public courts that set up their own referral or in-house mediation programs.[5] Thus, the Principles devote considerable attention to establishing protection for consumers who may be disadvantaged by a provider's efforts to increase its market share.

For example, the Principles contain a provision devoted to conflict-of-interest concerns. The Principles address the possibility that, just as individual mediators may have personal or professional relationships with disputants that compromise their ability to stay neutral, provider organizations may develop institutional relationships that threaten the neutrality of the procedures they administer. Anticipating that private organizations may come to rely on repeat players for a predictable source of revenue, the Principles seek to ameliorate this threat by requiring transparency and informed consent. Just as individual mediators must reveal ongoing relationships with one or both parties, the Principles require disclosure of "the existence of any interests or relationships which are reasonably likely to affect the impartiality or independence of the Organization."

Barring provider organizations from cultivating return customers subverts basic business practice, but the Principles are clear that if an organization enjoys a "contractual stream of referrals, a de facto stream of referrals or a funding relationship between a party and the organization," those relationships must be disclosed. Furthermore, mediation should not proceed unless all parties consent.[6]

National Standards: Educating Litigants About the Mediation Process

The National Standards are meant to apply to "any program or service, including a service provided by an individual, to which a court refers cases on a voluntary or mandatory basis, including any program or service operated by the court." They thus treat only programs handling cases that were originally filed with a court. Private providers handling disputes where the parties consciously pursued ADR from the outset do not fall within their ambit.

Courts are not for-profit entities that cultivate repeat business, so conflict-of-interest concerns do not dominate the National Standards.[7] Rather, this document reflects the drafters' appreciation that some litigants, especially those appearing pro se, may be surprised to find themselves in mediation after initiating an adversary process. Moreover, many will be unsure of what mediation is and what will be demanded of them in the process. The National Standards thus place the court in an educational role. Courts that send cases to mediation must inform attorneys and parties of at least seventeen different types of information, ranging from the fees and program intake procedures to the mediator's lack of authority to impose a decision and the availability of formal adjudication if a resolution is not reached informally.[8]

Ensuring Access to Mediation Services

Central to both the CPR-Georgetown Principles and the National Standards is a concern with access, though each focuses on a different barrier. The Principles attend to the financial barriers that might prevent poor individuals from accessing ADR services. They advise provider organizations to "take all reasonable steps" to provide access at "reasonable cost to low-income parties."[9] The comment to that provision makes clear that the requirement can be satisfied in a number of ways, including requiring affiliated neutrals to provide their services at below-market rates or on a pro bono basis.[10]

The Standards, geared as they are for court-connected cases, make clear that mediation services must be made accessible to a linguistically and culturally diverse community. In addition, physical or mental disabilities cannot be grounds for exclusion. The Standards state that mediation services should be available to disputants "on the same basis as are other services of the courts," meaning that program administrators must be sensitive to the myriad barriers facing immigrant and non-English-speaking communities, as well as those who are disabled.[11]

Ensuring Quality and Disputant Choice

Both the CPR-Georgetown Principles and National Standards assert that providers should, to the extent possible, ensure the quality of the mediation that occurs under their auspices. But both also impose a sliding scale of responsibility based on the locus of choice and control. The Principles state that a provider organization should take "reasonable steps" to maximize the quality and competence of its services, but they note that provider organization responsibilities decrease "as ADR parties' knowing involvement in screening and selecting the particular neutral increases."[12] The Standards similarly impose a sliding scale, noting that courts are fully responsible for the mediators they employ or to whom they refer cases but have no responsibility for the quality of "outside programs chosen by the parties without guidance from the court."[13]

DEFINING QUALITY: MEDIATOR SKILL AND COMPETENCE. Both the Principles and the Standards state that provider organizations should strive toward maximizing the quality of the services they offer by referring cases to mediators with sufficient skill and competence. But the Standards are more detailed in defining what quality services might entail and impose more rigorous obligations on provider organizations than do the Principles. The Principles are vague when discussing how mediator skills might be assessed. They note that because mediation is a multidisciplinary field with no specific entry qualifications or exams, mediation competence is traditionally associated with "some combination of training, experience, skills-based education, apprenticeships, internships, mentoring and supervised experience" and that "the appropriate combinations must be linked to the practice context."[14] Moreover, the Principles explicitly adopt a "rule of reason" regarding provider obligations to ensure quality, explicitly noting that "this obligation will vary with the circumstances of the organization."[15] Indeed, the Principles permit providers to limit their quality obligations through a "clear and prominent disclaimer" directed to the parties and public at large.[16]

The Standards provide greater detail as to what skillful mediation requires. They list nine skills necessary for competent performance, including the ability to understand the negotiating process and the role of advocacy, the ability to convert parties' positions into needs and interests, and the ability to help parties assess their nonsettlement alternatives.[17] In addition, the Standards specify that "where parties' legal rights and remedies are involved, awareness of the legal standards that would be applicable if the case were taken to a court or other legal forum" is an important component. Like the Principles, the Standards reject the notion that any particular academic degree should serve as a prerequisite to mediation practice. The Standards also note that "courts should not set up barriers that inappropriately exclude competent mediators and should encourage diversity among service providers, including gender, racial and ethnic diversity."[18]

DEFINING QUALITY: BEYOND SKILL AND COMPETENCE. Clearly both the Principles and the Standards focus on mediator skill and competence as indicia of provider quality. But hiring skilled mediators alone does not discharge provider obligations under either code.

The Principles obligate a provider organization to ensure that ADR processes provided under its auspices are "fundamentally fair and conducted in an impartial manner."[19] Fundamental fairness is measured in part by the degree to which mediation rosters reflect the demographics of the community, but in part by criteria unrelated to the characteristics and competence of the mediators. These criteria include whether

- Parties are able to select their own neutrals
- Parties enjoy adequate legal representation and fair hearing procedures
- Sufficient time has been allocated for the sessions, and the amounts charged are reasonable and reasonably allocated[20]

The Standards also concern themselves with questions of fairness extending beyond the skill level of the mediator hired. For example, the Standards state that courts should be sensitive to the dilemma of unrepresented litigants who may inaccurately believe they have no choice but to settle during the mediation. The Standards require courts to "take steps to ensure that pro se litigants make informed choices about mediation" and to "take special efforts to alert [pro se litigants] to settlement alternatives."[21] When referring cases to mediation, courts must consider as well whether such referrals will have a positive or negative impact on "the parties, the court, or others."[22] Specifically, the Standards suggest that certain considerations may militate against referral, including when the behavior at issue warrants public censure, repetitive rule violations require uniform treatment, or disputants and/or counsel "are not able to negotiate effectively." [23]

Although the Standards allow mandatory mediation, they specify that certain conditions should be in place before compulsory attendance is imposed. Specifically, mandatory mediation is appropriate only where the service is publicly funded and where disputants are free of inappropriate settlement pressure, have ample opportunity to participate, are well informed as to what they can expect, and are permitted to bring their attorneys into the process.[24] Moreover, even where referral remains appropriate, the Standards suggest courts devise special procedures for vulnerable disputants (for example, victims of domestic violence)[25] and ensure that disputants mandatorily referred to mediation understand that they are under no obligation to compromise or concede their claims.[26]

MONITORING MEDIATOR PERFORMANCE: EVALUATIONS AND GRIEVANCE PROCEDURES. Although neither the Principles nor the Standards suggest that providers can guarantee mediator performance, they do suggest that procedures should be put in place to weed out bad apples. The Standards recommend that courts ensure that providers monitor their mediators' performance to determine whether they are meeting existing performance expectations.[27] This monitoring function can be achieved through peer review, supervisor observation, client surveys, feedback from referring judges, and outcome data. If mediators fail to meet performance expectations, the Standards require courts to take concrete action to address the problem. A court may initially offer a helping hand by providing additional training, supervision, or assistance from a comediator. Ultimately, however, if no improvement results, the court must have in place procedures for removal from the court roster or the cessation of referrals. In addition to this monitoring and removal function, courts must establish complaint mechanisms that allow mediation parties to pursue their own grievances regarding the mediator's handling of the process.[28]

Interestingly, recent scholarly inquiry into the grievance procedures of five court-connected programs reveals surprisingly modest activity.[29] Over a thirteen-year period, in regions with jurisdiction over roughly nine thousand mediators, fewer than two hundred grievances were filed.[30] Of these grievances, sixty-seven were dismissed. Disciplinary action was taken against fewer than one hundred mediators.[31] When action was taken, most often the errant mediator was asked to take additional training, pursue mentorship from experienced mediators, or accept an oral or written reprimand.[32] Only six mediators were actually removed from a court roster, and five of those removals occurred in one state (Maine).[33] Although court-connected programs are moving forward in establishing mechanisms for complaint, it does not appear that most disgruntled mediation parties are taking advantage of those developments.

In addition to continually assessing the quality of service being offered by individual mediators, the Standards ask courts to engage in programmatic evaluation to determine if the goals of the overall program are being met. Toward this end, courts should collect quantitative and qualitative data, addressing both disputant perceptions of legitimacy and fairness as well as settlement rates and cost efficiencies.[34]

The Principles also explicitly address the need for grievance procedures and note that such procedures must be fair to both disputants and the neutrals whose conduct is being questioned.[35] Provision VI of the Principles states that provider organizations should promulgate information about the nature and availability of such procedures in a "clear, accurate and understandable manner." Comments to this provision make clear that the grievance mechanisms should relate to the conduct of the neutral or the provider organization's rules and regulations and should not serve as a back-door route for challenging the substance of the agreements reached.[36]

Confidentiality

Both codes treat confidentiality as an important topic and allow significant latitude in approach. Neither set of provisions seeks to determine the appropriate level of protection or acceptable conditions for disclosure. Under both the Principles and the Standards, private providers, courts, and their referral organizations are free to adopt whatever policies make sense given their programmatic goals; however, these policies must be clearly stated and communicated to mediators and parties alike.

For example, the Principles accept that confidentiality protections may derive from party agreement, organizational fiat, or established law.[37] Recognizing that contractual or statutory restrictions will dictate what sort of mediation information remains private and what will be admissible should future litigation ensue, the Principles require providers to formulate policies and ensure those policies are made known to neutrals and parties.[38]

The Standards also state that courts should draft clear confidentiality policies consonant with the laws of the jurisdiction.[39] These policies should explicitly clarify which mediators and cases are protected, the holders of the privilege, the scope of protection, and any exceptions that may exist.[40] Commentary to the Standards advises that "in weighing the benefits of confidentiality protections against the potential costs of nondisclosure of information in order to determine their policies regarding confidentiality, courts should take care to preserve the integrity of the mediation process. At a minimum, policies regarding confidentiality in mediation should provide no less protection than policies regarding confidentiality in settlement conferences."[41]

Ethics for Participating Mediators

A final mandate imposed by both the Standards and the Principles involves the adoption of an ethical code to guide the individual practice of affiliated neutrals. The Principles state that provider organizations, absent a controlling statutory or professional code of ethics, should require their mediators to adopt a reputable internal or external code of ethics.

The Standards also exhort courts to adopt an ethical code that will guide the practice of those who mediate under their auspices. This code should address at a minimum these six topics:

- Impartiality
- Conflicts of interest
- Advertising by mediators
- Disclosure of fees
- Confidentiality
- Role of mediators in settlement

In creating such a code of conduct, courts should bear in mind the twin goals of promoting honesty, integrity, and impartiality while maintaining an effective operation. As the Standards point out, ethically upstanding conduct on the part of individual mediators is not simply a good in itself; it redounds to the effectiveness and smooth functioning of the court program.

CASE 13.1: PHYSICIAN MEDIATORS

In this case, a for-profit firm is making money hand-over-fist. But it is not clear that this financial health reflects a sound ethical core.

A group of three psychiatrists from the local hospital have just graduated from a three-year course in conflict management. With their extensive background in health care and newly found knowledge of mediation, they decide to leave their positions at the hospital and form a company offering mediation services to medical professionals whose patients are unhappy and contemplating filing malpractice or licensure complaints. They decide to call the company Talk That Heals (TTH). They hire ten bright, well-educated physicians, refugees from the medical profession, and train them in their own distinct model of "medically oriented mediation." The training is forty-five hours and is followed by an internship period where each trainee comediates five cases with a more experienced mediator.

TTH's mediators hail from four subspecialties: obstetrics, surgery, psychiatry, and pediatrics. When a case involving one of these four areas of practice comes into the office, the case manager assigns the case to the mediator with the appropriate background and experience.

The company model typically results in outcomes that are highly favorable to the complained-against medical personnel. Word of mouth spreads among the local medical community, and the business thrives. Whenever a physician or psychiatrist gets wind that a patient is unhappy and contemplating formal action, he or she suggests a preliminary mediation. Soon TTH mediators are completely booked; some mornings they are handling two cases at once, spread out over a number of conference rooms. Although the TTH business model requires disputants to submit premediation briefs, frequently the papers go unread. The mediators are just too busy to attend to them. Sometimes, they confess to one another, they are so overwhelmed with work they have trouble keeping the names, facts, and faces straight.

This scenario raises some obvious concerns:

- To what extent is TTH responsible for the quality of the mediation performed under its auspices?
- Is the company model biased in favor of the medical professionals who constitute its primary referral source?
- Is the company hiring mediators who are themselves biased due to professional affinity and their knowledge that medical personnel keep the TTH income stream flowing?
- Should the company inform prospective disputants that their mediators are drawn exclusively from the ranks of former clinical providers? And is there any responsibility to inform disputants about the nature of the outcomes reached?
- Does the way THH handles the flow of business raise any red flags for the individual mediators and THH as their employer?

TTH's Responsibility for the Quality of Its Mediation Services

Because TTH is a private provider unconnected with the courts, we would look to the CPR-Georgetown Principles as the starting point of analysis. Although the Principles state that TTH should take "all reasonable steps to maximize the quality and competence of its services," they remain intentionally vague as to what those "reasonable steps" might involve. A combination of "process training and experience, substantive education and experience" is presented as relating to competence, but greater specification is lacking. Still, it must be said that TTH's forty-five-hour training and internship is standard in the field. A recent article offering training suggestions for program administrators suggested that a twenty-four-hour core course focusing on elemental, universally applicable skills, followed by a twenty-hour specialization enhancement, would be optimal for programs handling specialized types of cases.[42] Certainly many public and private ADR organizations offer education and training in similar doses. Whether the dose is sufficient to potentiate "quality mediation" remains up for debate. TTH both hires individual mediators and assigns them to each case. Parties play no role in the selection process. Consequently, under the Principles, TTH must assume full responsibility for "maximizing the likelihood of individual neutral competence and quality."[43]

Is TTH's Mediation Model "Fair"?

We know little about TTH's training model, except that it results in substantive outcomes that are highly favorable to medical practitioners. This aspect of TTH's model may be ethically problematic, though it is not necessarily so. One might interpret the fact that the model generates outcomes that do not require significant provider payouts to mean that medical practitioners are engaging in negligent conduct but are escaping the full measure of their culpability. According to this view, complaining consumers are being deprived of the payments that they would justifiably receive had they taken their cases to a court; from this perspective, TTH's model minimizes wrongs that would otherwise merit significant remediation. Under this interpretation, TTH's service may violate Principle III, which states that provider organizations must ensure that ADR processes provided under their auspices are "fundamentally fair."

But there is another way to look at what TTH is doing. First, it may be that the claims being brought against medical personnel are not legally cognizable and would not fare well in court. Thus, the fact that TTH'S outcomes favor medical personnel financially may simply reflect the weak legal foundation on which these consumer grievances rest.

It is also possible that TTH's model results in outcomes favorable to medical personnel because the model skillfully manages patient discontent in a way that allows medical personnel to empathize, apologize, and otherwise soothe existing psychic wounds. It may be that the outcomes in terms of monetary payout are small, but that medical consumers emerge feeling satisfied that their basic needs have been met. Outcomes favorable to medical providers may also favor disgruntled patients who no longer feel disrespected or ill served. It may be that comparing mediated outcomes with expected judicial determinations provides an inadequate measure of what's "fair."[44]

A Biased Roster?

But even if we accept that the TTH outcomes are "fair" in terms of meeting both clinician and consumer needs, it is still important to consider whether its mediators are biased in favor of medical personnel. ADR provider organizations are under an obligation to ensure that mediations conducted under their auspices are conducted in an impartial manner, and if the former obstetricians, surgeons, and psychiatrists who are employed by TTH relate better and feel more sympathetic to clinicians than to aggrieved patients, then TTH is failing to meet that basic responsibility. It is notable that the Principles' comment relating to fairness and impartiality states, "Key indicia of fair and impartial processes ... include ... rosters of neutrals that are representative of the community of users." TTH's roster includes neutrals who are representative of only one set of users: medical professionals. It does not place on its panel individuals whose expertise lies in understanding the experience of medical consumers—a gap that TTH would do well to remedy.

Even if TTH concludes that its mediation roster is appropriately constructed and that each mediator is evenhanded beyond reproach, its recruiting and revenue patterns require disclosure. Provision V of the Principles requires organizations to disclose interests or relationships that might create the appearance of or are likely to induce actual bias. These include "any significant financial, business, organizational, professional or other relationship ... including a ... de facto stream of referrals." The warm relationship TTH enjoys with local medical professionals creates a "de facto" stream of referrals perpetuated by the consistently favorable set of outcomes that TTH brokers. At the very least, TTH should inform every disputant that the majority of its business derives from medical providers, thus giving nonmedical disputants the opportunity to opt out or choose another mediation service.

Since the Principles also recommend that provider organizations "take all reasonable steps to provide clear, accurate and understandable information" about the "training and qualification requirements" for neutrals, it might be advisable for the organization to disclose the medical socialization of its neutrals. Technically it's not clear that the neutrals' past employment creates the "reasonable appearance that the organization is biased against a party or favorable toward another." Indeed, the fact that TTH's neutrals are former medical workers creates the possibility that the neutrals, not the organization itself, have a conflict. Still, to the degree that the Standards rely on disclosure and party consent as a curative for structural features that are ethically problematic, it makes ample sense to let disputants know the background of the mediators they are being assigned.

Quality and Mediator Work Conditions: Allowing Sufficient Time and Energy for Each Case

Finally, the sheer volume of work that TTH is accepting raises questions regarding whether the organization is taking "all reasonable steps to maximize the quality ... of its services."[45] TTH mediators are so busy they are double-booking, not reading premediation submissions, and struggling to keep names, faces, and key facts straight. At a minimum, mediators must be able to set aside the time and mental energy sufficient to establish rapport, ascertain underlying interests, help explore each side's best alternative to a negotiated agreement (BATNA) and worst alternative to a negotiated agreement (WATNA), and nudge the parties toward mutually beneficial outcomes. If mediators are working with multiple disputants simultaneously, unable to engage in predispute information gathering, and too befuddled to remember party names, it is unlikely that they are performing at even minimally competent levels.

If individual mediators fall below reasonable standards of care, this has both legal and ethical ramifications for provider organizations. The CPR-Georgetown Principles state that organizations have an ethical responsibility to see that individual mediators subscribe to reputable codes of conduct. The Model Standards, perhaps the most reputable code we have, state that mediators shall conduct a mediation in a matter that promotes diligence and that a mediator should aim to mediate only when prepared to "commit the attention essential to an effective mediation."[46]

To the degree that TTH mediators declare fealty to the Model Standards, or local codes with similar requirements, and then fail to measure up, that failure implicates TTH and casts doubt on its organizational integrity. TTH administrators would do well to stop taking in so much work and instruct its mediators to devote their full and undivided attention to each case singly, on its own merits. Presubmission briefs must be read, cases should be scheduled seriatim, not simultaneously, and the mediators at a minimum should be able to remember who they are mediating with and the facts and issues at stake. Putting a break on the profit motive and paying special attention to training and recruiting methods should help TTH improve its practices.

CASE 13.2: A RECURRING LANDLORD-TENANT PATTERN

This case features a public provider. The problem here lies not in the temptation to cut ethical corners in pursuit of higher profit margins; rather, it is that existing legal norms fit uneasily with these disputants' basic needs, and the fast pace of the mediation program makes it difficult, if not impossible, to address those needs in a comprehensive fashion. The two commentators discuss whether the structure of the mediation program as constituted poses ethical problems and, if so, what to do about it.

You run a mediation program staffed by law students in the local small claims court. Technically mediation is not mandatory, but most small claims litigants, after they are told by the presiding judge to "go outside and try and work things out with our trained mediators," don't believe they have much of a choice. They obediently follow the mediators out to the nearby hallway tables, and they generally continue to participate until an agreement is reached or the bailiff comes to take them back to court.

The judges in your program like the trains to run on time, and they worry if it appears that cases are not being processed quickly. They give the mediators approximately twenty to thirty minutes to work. If no settlement has been reached after that time, they send the bailiffs to retrieve the case. Essentially they go off the bench at 4:00 P.M. sharp and don't want to wait around for cases that are still being worked out in mediation.

Lately, the law student mediators have begun to report on a recurring case scenario. Landlords from multiple housing complexes have been filing eviction notices against tenants under the same grounds. In each case, the tenants have signed leases to rent a "single-family residence" but have brought in extended family to live under the same roof. The landlords cite housing agreements and county zoning restrictions to argue for eviction. They say the apartments are constructed to house two to five individuals and should not be used to provide a primary residence for more than that number. The tenants admit to bringing in grandparents, aunts, uncles, and cousins, but say that back home in Jamaica, that is a common practice. The tenants seem genuinely puzzled as to why they are in court.

Because the zoning ordinances and apartment rules are clear, the cases typically end in one of two ways: the tenants either capitulate in mediation or they go to court, where they lose.

Your mediators are growing uneasy about this type of case, especially since it seems that the endings are always predictable.

What, if anything, should you as the administrator do? Is there an ethical problem here?

Comments on Case 13.2

Phyllis Bernard

This hypothetical presents the everyday reality for many mediators in small claims courts throughout the nation, particularly in mediating landlord-tenant disputes. Specific details about the tenants' national origin or ethnicity may differ, but the fundamental issue—severe imbalance of power between parties—remains constant. There are times when mediation, as commonly described and practiced, does more harm than good. The administrator here needs to seek something different, beginning with heretical questions: Why mediate? Is mediation appropriate?

The law student mediators are asking themselves core questions that many professionals avoid. They sense that the integrity of the process is compromised by the time pressures imposed by the judge. The students were taught that the process has value because it provides the tenants an opportunity to exercise their right of self-determination. A candid consideration of the ethics of system design will lead them to a more challenging question: In this context, is mediation's promise of self-determination real or illusory? If, functionally, it is the latter, then why mediate at all?

One could argue that the tenants' right to self-determination is an illusion given the exigencies of an eviction, the landlord's need to apply the law equally to all tenants (or risk claims of housing discrimination), and that tenants are almost always unrepresented by counsel, while landlords either have counsel or are so knowledgeable about evictions they do not require counsel.

DEBUNKING THE DEFAULT ARGUMENT. Proponents of mediation as an all-encompassing theory or proponents who merely see mediation as a way to palliate reductions in judicial budgets often converge on the same default argument: even if mediation does not result in a truly voluntary, evenly negotiated resolution, the process provides a venue for parties to understand the "strengths and weaknesses" of their case.[47] Mediation can be a tool for party education and self-evaluation. When woven into a coherent system designed to permit parties to act on that new knowledge, this argument has the ring of truth.

However, the time pressure placed on the program's mediators prevents attaining even this de minimis goal. It takes more than twenty to thirty minutes to bridge the conceptual gap between city ordinances designed for modern urban settings and family structures rooted in millennia of cultural norms. The overly crowded court docket and hallway setting functions in the way that hardball negotiators use artificial time restraints to pressure acceptance of terms the opposing party would ordinarily refuse given sufficient time to consider their legal rights and options. These landlord-tenant mediations are not bound by the technicalities of courtroom procedure, but they are bound by the clock.

This is not the unstated exchange that mediation theory argued for, whereby tenants who bypass the formalities of the courtroom gain additional freedom to speak, listen, and make choices. Instead, tenants confront the landlord in a setting that takes away the limited legal protections of the small claims court while not replacing it with anything meaningful. Tenants leave confused and frustrated, not understanding the outcome any better than they did before. Mediation has not added value to the legal process. To the contrary, this truncated process has probably validated critics' view of mediation as second-class justice for minorities.[48]

CAN POWER BE REBALANCED IN LANDLORD-TENANT MEDIATIONS? The program's law student mediators may privately believe that the severe time constraints and lack of adviser resources for the tenants contribute to a coercive mediation environment.[49] Granted, the 2005 Model Standards of Conduct for Mediators require the third-party neutral to inform parties to seek professional advice, especially when legal rights may provide the only mechanism to rebalance power.[50] But to what end? Logic dictates that tenants who cannot afford to pay rent probably cannot pay for legal or other professional counsel. More frequently than not, working-class tenants appear pro se in evictions; conversely, the landlord has developed expertise sufficient to handle the matter unrepresented by counsel, or the landlord is represented.[51]

The institutional limitations create an ethical dilemma that calls for solutions at the macrolevel, not the microlevel. Resolution cannot be achieved by the individual third-party neutral on a case-by-case basis while remaining true to the mediator's ethical duty to be impartial. Indeed, the conscientious mediator who questions the "fairness, equity, and feasibility" of the process may, in many states, be challenged as tipping the scales in favor of one party over the other—perhaps interfering with the parties' right to self-determination.[52]

SOLUTIONS ON A MACROLEVEL. If mediation is to play a role, the program administrator must explore how and where mediation can be used most effectively and ethically. This opens several options, broadening the focus of problem solving to view the full system of inputs and public perceptions of justice.

Recharacterize the Process. The truncated information exchange can continue largely as is, but without being called mediation. As described, the process offers no meaningful expectation of promoting voluntary decision making by the parties in the exercise of their informed right of self-determination. The process is so short that it likely serves no role beyond simply providing tenants more information about why they are being evicted. It does not provide sufficient time for the give-and-take of facilitated bargaining. Finally, on the face of it, it appears that city ordinances may offer little or no margin for compromise except through the good graces of the landlord. Such a process could be more appropriately titled "prehearing conference" or "consultation." But to allow this to be described as mediation subverts and tarnishes the process, which ought to imply a facilitative, balanced, safe harbor for mutual decision making.

Build in a Second Session. If time permits—that is, if the time line for eviction allows rescheduling—the initial session at the courthouse would be continued to another day and time. Scheduling a second session would allow fuller exposition and exploration of the issues.

Granted, so long as the local ordinances remain unchanged, the result may again be eviction. However, parties would have had a greater opportunity for mutual education, which may alter future behavior. Although the final result may be eviction, the manner in which the landlord handles it may affect the landlord's relationship with other tenants. Regardless of statements about confidentiality, human nature virtually ensures that other tenants are indirect constituencies to the mediated eviction.

Another reason to allow rescheduling is that if the second mediation provides a setting and tone more respectful than a bustling courthouse hallway, the mediation allows the tenants a degree of face saving that can result in a smoother vacation of the property with reduced likelihood of property destruction and personal altercations.

Enlist Support Persons for Tenants. If the court-connected mediation rules permit, the participation of nonattorney party assistants, local housing advocates, churches, and other organizations with strong links to the immigrant community could help rebalance power at the mediation table without giving legal advice. Through consultation with the court clerk, tenants could receive written notice of their right to bring nonlegal assistance to the mediation, listing contact information for organizations willing to assist. Such notice would be affixed to each eviction notice.[53]

The tenants' underlying issues concern not only the stability of their family but also the larger community, and they ultimately affect property values. Tenants' extended family constitutes their primary support system. When intact, the family facilitates child rearing, food, and caregiving. These functions are essential for success at work and in school. Without them, the family and the neighborhood deteriorate.

Can representatives of the immigrant community provide support without additional court funding? Conceivably, yes. In fact, this may be inevitable because inadequate funding of the court system probably created the predicament the student mediators currently encounter. If a larger small claims court budget is not forthcoming, then at a minimum, court administrative processes should be revised to permit and encourage the participation of tenant supporters using their organizational resources. Court rules may also need revision to immunize such persons from claims that they have engaged in the unauthorized practice of law.

Modify the City Ordinances to Better Meet Party Needs. The city ordinances themselves may need to be revisited, offering the public at large and interested parties the ability to make necessary changes in line with the evolving needs of the city, its neighborhoods, and its values.[54] The mediation program could provide facilitation services for public dialogues considering the fuller range of concerns, such as education of tenants about wear and tear on rental property; how tenants can mitigate such damage; the possibilities of negotiating higher rents to cover actuarially determined increases in the landlord's liability when renting to larger numbers of occupants; and how such evictions will increase the rates of homelessness, straining public and private resources, if extended families are not allowed to live together.

CONCLUSION. For far too long, mediation has been (mis)marketed as a "kinder, gentler" way to achieve a "win-win" resolution to thorny human problems. Mediation has been presented as nearly fungible with or even preferable to judicial proceedings. Unfortunately, few marketing materials, even for court-connected programs, acknowledge the harsh realities these law students have observed: mediation works well when power between the parties is balanced; it works poorly when the power is severely unbalanced. The deeper issues in the landlord-tenant dispute are too great and complex to be solved in episodic sessions where the power of the disadvantaged party is minimized through further isolation.

The most effective power must come by bringing to the table the wider network of stakeholders who understand the connection between stable family life, community life, and property values.

Comments on Case 13.2

Susan M. Yates

This scenario presents two types of issues. One type appears in the typical day-to-day problems of mediation programs concerning how cases are referred to mediation and how much time is allowed for mediation. Those relate to fundamental ethical issues such as self-determination and the quality of the mediation process. The other type of issue, which may not be so typical of mediation programs, revolves around what to do, if anything, about these particular recurring landlord-tenant cases. Even if these cases are not so typical, they do carry underlying ethical issues that may arise in any program, including self-determination, impartiality, conflicts of interest, confidentiality, and quality of the process. Fortunately, some options exist for tackling these issues.

DAY-TO-DAY PROBLEMS OF REFERRAL AND ALLOWED TIME. I would start by tackling the more straightforward group of issues: the referral and time allowance issues.

Observation. If I had not personally been doing so, I would start by observing the student mediators to ensure that they were conducting mediations that were voluntary (once the parties got into them) and of good quality, both required under the Model Standards.[55] If there were any performance issues, I would address them with debriefings and role-plays for individuals and with class time to work on any issues that were widespread.

The Mandatory Referral Issue. Regarding mandatory versus voluntary referral, the manner in which the cases are being referred to mediation is not a great concern to me. For most people, mediation is still such an unknown that the only way to know for sure if they want to do it is to give it a try. The potential harm in requiring an attempt at mediation is generally outweighed by the potential benefits, as long as precautions are taken once the parties meet with the mediator. I agree with the National Standards for Court-Connected Mediation Programs, which state in Standard 5.1 that mandatory referral may be appropriate when mediation is free to the parties, there is no pressure to settle, and the mediation program and mediators are high-quality.[56]

As long as the student mediators are ensuring to the best of their ability that the parties understand that participating in mediation and resolving their cases are voluntary, and as long as the mediators are providing quality mediation services, the fact that the parties are not being offered an opportunity to decline to mediate prior to the mediation does not overly concern me. Certainly voluntary participation is only one component of self-determination, but it is an essential component.

Time Allocations. The limited amount of time provided for the mediation seriously concerns me. Mediators have a responsibility, under both the Model Standards and the National Standards, to provide a quality mediation process. Despite the time allocation, I would recommend this program adopt a facilitative model of mediation in which the parties are assisted in reaching their own agreements. Even if an evaluative model would have been faster, I would suggest using the facilitative approach for a number of reasons, in part because students do not have the legal experience to be evaluative mediators and I do not think that would be an appropriate role with so many unrepresented parties in the program. Furthermore, facilitative mediation is the way to teach students valuable problem-solving skills they will not learn elsewhere in the curriculum. I would not suggest a transformative model because the goal here is to settle cases, typically among strangers, not to reform relationships.

Twenty minutes is almost never enough time except in the extremely rare case where the parties have already agreed among themselves and do not really need a mediation. A half-hour may be enough time for some cases as the semester goes on and the mediators become more experienced. As the students progress, they learn how to make a well-honed opening statement, ask incisive questions, and get to the heart of the parties' needs and interests much more quickly. Still, even as the mediators become more skilled, the parties simply need time to tell their stories, hear the other side, make offers, hear counteroffers, and come to terms. That rarely can happen in half an hour, much less twenty minutes.

Working to Expand the Mediation Sessions. To address these referral and timing issues, I would start by discussing these issues with the students and getting them on board with how to address them. Next I would meet with the judges to flesh out whether there is any more I need to know about their interests other than that they want to be off the bench by 4:00. If possible, I would bring a judge who is enthusiastic about the program to talk to the other judges about its benefits; however, my main goal would be to listen to the judges talk about their goals and then explore how we might help them work toward those goals.

We might offer to study the resolution rate of cases mediated under the current time frame as compared to the resolution rate of a pilot program of cases that had an hour to mediate and see what the difference is. We might talk with the judges about the characteristics of cases that take longest if they go to trial and see if there is a way for law students to identify them by case files ahead of time and refer them to mediation at the beginning of the call, or even earlier on another day. I might offer to show them a simulated mediation, one of the most popular ways to educate judges about mediation. If they have not seen a small claims mediation, this would help to show how it is different from other mediations the judges might have seen and from settlement conferences. In this conversation I would work to design a new way to meet the judges' need for being off the bench at 4:00 and also increase time for the mediators to work with the parties.

With that established, I would work to build a new understanding with the bailiffs as well. I do not know whether they are feeling pressure from the judges to bring back the parties, whether they may be concerned about the voices that are sometimes raised in the mediations, or if they are simply doing their jobs by bringing the parties back on time. I would meet with them to identify their needs and interests. If I had identified a judge who was interested in looking at the program in a different way, I might invite that judge to the meeting with the bailiffs to improve credibility.

How does this relate back to ethics? The most fundamental principle of mediation is self-determination, and if parties are to exercise self-determination, mediators need to function in an atmosphere that is as free as possible from outside pressure to engage in mediation involuntarily, push for settlement, or rush the parties through the process. It is my job as their program administrator to help them continue to provide quality mediation services and act to correct that environment when I see that the mediators and the parties are in danger of these pressures.

LANDLORD, TENANTS, AND FAIRNESS. The other major issue—the recurring evictions of tenants under complicated rules and zoning ordinances forbidding extended family in housing units that the landlords successfully argue are designed for two to five residents—raises further issues about what is fair and how that relates to a mediator's responsibilities. I would engage my students in a discussion about fairness in mediation and the broader discussions of what lawyers' responsibilities are and what they feel their individual responsibilities are.

In the long run, I would argue that mediators are not required to ensure fair outcomes. Indeed, if this type of case was a rarity, it probably would not attract much attention. However, when these cases unfold similarly over and over, I would say that the mediator does have some opportunities rather than responsibilities. As program administrator, I have responsibility for the program's integrity as well. Again, I would turn to the Model Standards for guidance on the ethical issues.

Self-Determination. The essence of self-determination is not just a free choice but a free informed choice.[57] The case says that the tenants are "genuinely puzzled" about why they are in court. Puzzled is certainly the opposite of informed. There is some guidance in the Model Standards about what to do in this situation. Standard I, Self-Determination, states, "A mediator cannot personally ensure that each party has made free and informed choices to reach particular decisions, but, where appropriate, a mediator should make the parties aware of the importance of consulting other professionals to help them make informed choices." While it would be inappropriate for student mediators to hand out business cards for lawyers, I think it is appropriate for mediators to ask questions about what parties know and how they are going to get informed if they do not know enough. I also think this standard gives me latitude on behalf of my program to work with this issue, which I discuss below.

Impartiality. Model Standard II, Impartiality, says, "A mediator shall decline a mediation if the mediator cannot conduct it in an impartial manner." This is part of why I start by observing mediations. I want to be sure that the mediators are not being swayed by either party. This could happen in either direction: because the tenants could inspire sympathy or because the landlords are represented and could be overpowering.

Conflicts of Interest. It can be challenging to adhere to Standard III, Conflicts of Interest, which says, "A mediator shall avoid a conflict of interest or the appearance of a conflict of interest during and after a mediation. A conflict of interest can arise from involvement by a mediator with the subject matter of the dispute or from any relationship between a mediator and any mediation participant, whether past or present, personal or professional, that reasonably raises a question of a mediator's impartiality."

One of the realities of mediating in a setting like most small claims courts is that there will be potentially sympathetic parties, like the tenants, and there will be repeat players, like the landlords. In this situation, the mediators report that they are concerned about the tenants, but it is the landlords who are consistently winning the cases, so it appears that there is no conflict of interest that is having an effect on these cases. Nonetheless, it is important to ask if anyone would raise a question if the tenants were consistently winning. As program administrator, it is important to keep the playing field balanced for all involved.[58]

Confidentiality. The Model Standards include, in Standard V, Confidentiality, Section A, a rather stark statement about confidentiality: "A mediator shall maintain the confidentiality of all information obtained by the mediator in mediation, unless otherwise agreed to by the parties or required by applicable law."

How, then, do I even come to know about these issues? Part of the answer lies in subsection (A)(1): "If the parties to a mediation agree that the mediator may disclose information obtained during the mediation, the mediator may do so." Programs should obtain a clear written exception from parties so that mediators may communicate about their cases within their programs. There also should be a court rule that provides this exception for program monitoring, mediator development, and ongoing mediator education.

A part of subsection (A)(3) applies here also: "If a mediator participates in teaching, research or evaluation of mediation, the mediator should protect the anonymity of the parties and abide by their reasonable expectations regarding confidentiality." I have always taken that as a reminder that while we may be permitted to talk about cases, there is still no need to provide any identifying information about the parties when we do so.

Interestingly, in some ways, these confidentiality issues are moot. The landlords' reasoning behind the legal cases, the views of the tenants about who lives in the apartments, and the outcomes of those cases are a matter of public record because they have all been discussed in open court.

Quality. One part of section A of Standard VI, Quality of the Process, keeps ringing in my ears: "A mediator shall conduct a mediation in accordance with these Standards and in a manner that promotes diligence, timeliness, safety, presence of the appropriate participants, party participation, procedural fairness, party competency and mutual respect among all participants." It is the "party competency" phrase that is important here. Are the tenants competent to mediate in this case? Do they have sufficient information?

But just as I ask that, I am reminded of subsection (A)(5): "The role of a mediator differs substantially from other professional roles. Mixing the role of a mediator and the role of another profession is problematic and thus, a mediator should distinguish between the roles. A mediator may provide information that the mediator is qualified by training or experience to provide, only if the mediator can do so consistent with these Standards."

What can I really do?

A PLAN. Having considered all the ethical issues, I believe it would be possible to try to stop these cases from getting to the courthouse by approaching this as a larger, community-based mediation. My suspicion is that this is a situation where neither side wins because even a landlord "win" is a loss; there still is the cost of going to court, conducting the eviction, and having to find new tenants. My goal would be to gather lawyers and parties on both sides; any additional representatives on each side, such as community organizations or business groups; and perhaps some cultural representatives.

I would start with background work by my students. I would have them do research on the legal issues from each side, the cultural issues, and the neighborhood where these cases have occurred. I would contact the potential participants, starting with the landlords, because they have been winning and would seemingly have the most to lose by participating in any other process. I also would talk with the judge in charge of the court mediation program. This other mediation would be outside the court program, but I would not want the judge in charge of that program to be unaware of what was going on in relation to the program.

The goal of this mediation would not be to resolve a particular case, but to accomplish whatever larger goals the parties established. They might want to educate the public, particularly the affected communities, about building codes; they might want to educate one another about their different cultures; they might want to reach some new agreement about how many people could live in apartments; or they might want to agree that the landlords will place rental advertising in outlets serving the Jamaican community or provide employment opportunities for tenants to work on the buildings in return for reduced or free rent.

It is impossible to predict what would come of the larger mediation, or even if the parties would respond positively to the offer. It would, however, be a practical solution to the ethical problem of parties who seem not in a position to function with self-determination, are not completely competent to mediate, and do not have access to legal assistance on a case-by-case basis, without creating more ethical problems of lack of impartiality, conflicts of interest, or breaking confidentiality.

CONCLUSION. To paraphrase that great H. L Mencken quote, "The cure for the evils of democracy is more democracy," the cure for mediation is more mediation. By that I mean that the way to address ethical issues like those described here is to rely on the ethical underpinnings of the field. We should use the skills of identifying and addressing underlying needs and interests of judges and others in the court system, while also addressing the needs of the parties in each mediation process. Finally, when appropriate, we should use mediation approaches for larger groups than simply those that come to our programs one case at a time.

With all that said and done, I am optimistic that there would be a way to ensure that mediations are allotted more reasonable amounts of time—certainly never only twenty minutes—based on our program results and ongoing conversations with the judges. In terms of the landlord-tenant cases, even if there were no changes in the relationship between these groups of landlords and tenants or no large mediation, the mediators would still be able to continue to mediate these cases. They would need to continue to be extremely careful about self-determination, impartiality, conflicts of interest, confidentiality, and quality.

Whether it is a day-to-day issue or an unusual case, the basic ethical standards for the mediation field and for court mediation programs offer guidance about how to assess issues and plan a programmatic response. Combined with the skills and outlook of a mediator, there is useful guidance available.

Editor's Thoughts on Case 13.2
and the Comments

The problems of the court-connected mediation program that the commentators described lead both to conclude that a broader vision is called for. Susan Yates would pursue informal discussion with the judges, bailiffs, and other court personnel to see if more time could be wrung from the schedule to allow mediators a better opportunity to do their job. In addition, although not convinced that a program administrator's job includes being the "fairness watchdog," she would leverage her position to see if the disconnect between tenant needs and local zoning restrictions could be negotiated. Phyllis Bernard also views the short time allotted for mediation discussions as problematic and expresses concern that this sort of mediation does not "add value" to the legal process. Troubled by the imbalance in power between unsophisticated tenants and repeat-player landlords, Bernard would bring in nonlawyer assistants to help tenants navigate the court system. She too would support a community-wide mediation that moved beyond individual disputes to address the gap between the law on the books and an ethnic minority's cultural traditions.

It is interesting to note that both commentators contend that the cure for mediation is more mediation. That is, the problems created by the court's too-fast track and the tenants' lack of knowledge and power can best be handled through mediation's interest-based, problem-solving method. Yates would engage court personnel to determine if there is a way to lengthen the standard mediation session while keeping to the judges' preferred schedule. Bernard would see if there is a way to schedule a second session, outside the strict timing parameters of the court, to allow more relaxed and productive discussion. Although Bernard speaks more forcefully about the need to avoid "second-class justice" for the tenants in this program, both she and Yates would bring together stakeholders—community advocates, landlord trade groups, or agencies tasked with reducing homelessness—and encourage them to think creatively about how the mismatch between housing law and the ethnic community's needs can be best addressed.

If there is a substantive distinction between the two commentaries, it lies more in what is implied than in what is said. Yates, like Bernard, urges a macro, large-scale mediation designed to keep the recurring issue of tenant evictions from coming into the courthouse. Yet if such a mediation did not occur or proved unsuccessful in effecting a change in zoning rules or rental patterns, these cases could, she argues, continue to be mediated. Mediators could handle these cases as long as more time were allowed and the mediators took care to comport themselves according to the dictates of the Model Standards.

Bernard's tone is less sanguine. Without structural change, she questions whether the mediators in the program can do more than pay lip-service to ideals of party self-determination and informed decision making. She notes that law student mediators could advise the tenants of the importance of consulting with lawyers but suggests that if the program is not reorganized so that the court takes responsibility for bringing in third-party advisers, it is unlikely that the tenants will get the help they need. If the program continues in its current form, Bernard suggests, then critics of mediation could gain another footnote for their brief against ADR as discounted as-is justice for the less moneyed classes.

Appendix

MODEL STANDARDS OF CONDUCT FOR MEDIATORS

AMERICAN BAR ASSOCIATION

AMERICAN ARBITRATION ASSOCIATION

ASSOCIATION FOR CONFLICT RESOLUTION

AUGUST 2005

The Model Standards of Conduct for Mediators
August 2005

The *Model Standards of Conduct for Mediators* was prepared in 1994 by the American Arbitration Association, the American Bar Association's Section of Dispute Resolution, and the Association for Conflict Resolution.[1] A joint committee consisting of representatives from the same successor organizations revised the Model Standards in 2005.[2] Both the original 1994 version and the 2005 revision have been approved by each participating organization.[3]

Preamble

Mediation is used to resolve a broad range of conflicts within a variety of settings. These Standards are designed to serve as fundamental ethical guidelines for persons mediating in all practice contexts. They serve three primary goals: to guide the conduct of mediators; to inform the mediating parties; and to promote public confidence in mediation as a process for resolving disputes.

Mediation is a process in which an impartial third party facilitates communication and negotiation and promotes voluntary decision making by the parties to the dispute.

Mediation serves various purposes, including providing the opportunity for parties to define and clarify issues, understand different perspectives, identify interests, explore and assess possible solutions, and reach mutually satisfactory agreements, when desired.

---

[1] The Association for Conflict Resolution is a merged organization of the Academy of Family Mediators, the Conflict Resolution Education Network and the Society of Professionals in Dispute Resolution (SPIDR). SPIDR was the third participating organization in the development of the 1994 Standards.

[2] Reporter's Notes, which are not part of these Standards and therefore have not been specifically approved by any of the organizations, provide commentary regarding these revisions.

[3] Proposed language. No organization as of April 10, 2005 has reviewed or approved the 2005 Revision.

Note on Construction

These Standards are to be read and construed in their entirety. There is no priority significance attached to the sequence in which the Standards appear.

The use of the term "shall" in a Standard indicates that the mediator must follow the practice described. The use of the term "should" indicates that the practice described in the standard is highly desirable, but not required, and is to be departed from only for very strong reasons and requires careful use of judgment and discretion.

The use of the term "mediator" is understood to be inclusive so that it applies to co-mediator models.

These Standards do not include specific temporal parameters when referencing a mediation, and therefore, do not define the exact beginning or ending of a mediation.

Various aspects of a mediation, including some matters covered by these Standards, may also be affected by applicable law, court rules, regulations, other applicable professional rules, mediation rules to which the parties have agreed and other agreements of the parties. These sources may create conflicts with, and may take precedence over, these Standards. However, a mediator should make every effort to comply with the spirit and intent of these Standards in resolving such conflicts. This effort should include honoring all remaining Standards not in conflict with these other sources.

These Standards, unless and until adopted by a court or other regulatory authority do not have the force of law. Nonetheless, the fact that these Standards have been adopted by the respective sponsoring entities, should alert mediators to the fact that the Standards might be viewed as establishing a standard of care for mediators.

STANDARD I. SELF-DETERMINATION

A. A mediator shall conduct a mediation based on the principle of party self-determination. Self-determination is the act of coming to a voluntary, uncoerced decision in which each party makes free and informed choices as to process and outcome. Parties may exercise self-determination at any stage of a mediation, including mediator selection, process design, participation in or withdrawal from the process, and outcomes.

1. Although party self-determination for process design is a fundamental principle of mediation practice, a mediator may need to balance such party self-determination with a mediator's duty to conduct a quality process in accordance with these Standards.

2. A mediator cannot personally ensure that each party has made free and informed choices to reach particular decisions, but, where appropriate, a mediator should make the parties aware of the importance of consulting other professionals to help them make informed choices.

B. A mediator shall not undermine party self-determination by any party for reasons such as higher settlement rates, egos, increased fees, or outside pressures from court personnel, program administrators, provider organizations, the media or others.

STANDARD II. IMPARTIALITY

A. A mediator shall decline a mediation if the mediator cannot conduct it in an impartial manner. Impartiality means freedom from favoritism, bias or prejudice.

B. A mediator shall conduct a mediation in an impartial manner and avoid conduct that gives the appearance of partiality.

1. A mediator should not act with partiality or prejudice based on any participant's personal characteristics, background, values and beliefs, or performance at a mediation, or any other reason.

2. A mediator should neither give nor accept a gift, favor, loan or other item of value that raises a question as to the mediator's actual or perceived impartiality.

3. A mediator may accept or give de minimis gifts or incidental items or services that are provided to facilitate a mediation or respect cultural norms so long as such practices do not raise questions as to a mediator's actual or perceived impartiality.

C. If at any time a mediator is unable to conduct a mediation in an impartial manner, the mediator shall withdraw.

STANDARD III. CONFLICTS OF INTEREST

A. A mediator shall avoid a conflict of interest or the appearance of a conflict of interest during and after a mediation. A conflict of interest can arise from involvement by a mediator with the subject matter of the dispute or from any relationship between a mediator and any mediation participant, whether past or present, personal or professional, that reasonably raises a question of a mediator's impartiality.

B. A mediator shall make a reasonable inquiry to determine whether there are any facts that a reasonable individual would consider likely to create a potential or actual conflict of interest for a mediator. A mediator's actions necessary to accomplish a reasonable inquiry into potential conflicts of interest may vary based on practice context.

C. A mediator shall disclose, as soon as practicable, all actual and potential conflicts of interest that are reasonably known to the mediator and could reasonably be seen as raising a question about the mediator's impartiality. After disclosure, if all parties agree, the mediator may proceed with the mediation.

D. If a mediator learns any fact after accepting a mediation that raises a question with respect to that mediator's service creating a potential or actual conflict of interest, the mediator shall disclose it as quickly as practicable. After disclosure, if all parties agree, the mediator may proceed with the mediation.

E. If a mediator's conflict of interest might reasonably be viewed as undermining the integrity of the mediation, a mediator shall withdraw from or decline to proceed with the mediation regardless of the expressed desire or agreement of the parties to the contrary.

F. Subsequent to a mediation, a mediator shall not establish another relationship with any of the participants in any matter that would raise questions about the integrity of the mediation. When a mediator develops personal or professional relationships with parties, other individuals or organizations following a mediation in which they were involved, the mediator should consider factors such as time elapsed following the mediation, the nature of the relationships established, and services offered when determining whether the relationships might create a perceived or actual conflict of interest.

STANDARD IV. COMPETENCE

A. A mediator shall mediate only when the mediator has the necessary competence to satisfy the reasonable expectations of the parties.

 1. Any person may be selected as a mediator, provided that the parties are satisfied with the mediator's competence and qualifications. Training, experience in mediation, skills, cultural understandings and other qualities are often necessary for mediator competence. A person who offers to serve as a mediator creates the expectation that the person is competent to mediate effectively.

 2. A mediator should attend educational programs and related activities to maintain and enhance the mediator's knowledge and skills related to mediation.

 3. A mediator should have available for the parties information relevant to the mediator's training, education, experience and approach to conducting a mediation.

B. If a mediator, during the course of a mediation determines that the mediator cannot conduct the mediation competently, the mediator shall discuss that determination with the parties as soon as is practicable and take appropriate steps to address the situation, including, but not limited to, withdrawing or requesting appropriate assistance.

C. If a mediator's ability to conduct a mediation is impaired by drugs, alcohol, medication or otherwise, the mediator shall not conduct the mediation.

STANDARD V. CONFIDENTIALITY

A. A mediator shall maintain the confidentiality of all information obtained by the mediator in mediation, unless otherwise agreed to by the parties or required by applicable law.

1. If the parties to a mediation agree that the mediator may disclose information obtained during the mediation, the mediator may do so.

2. A mediator should not communicate to any non-participant information about how the parties acted in the mediation. A mediator may report, if required, whether parties appeared at a scheduled mediation and whether or not the parties reached a resolution.

3. If a mediator participates in teaching, research or evaluation of mediation, the mediator should protect the anonymity of the parties and abide by their reasonable expectations regarding confidentiality.

B. A mediator who meets with any persons in private session during a mediation shall not convey directly or indirectly to any other person, any information that was obtained during that private session without the consent of the disclosing person.

C. A mediator shall promote understanding among the parties of the extent to which the parties will maintain confidentiality of information they obtain in a mediation.

D. Depending on the circumstance of a mediation, the parties may have varying expectations regarding confidentiality that a mediator should address. The parties may make their own rules with respect to confidentiality, or the accepted practice of an individual mediator or institution may dictate a particular set of expectations.

STANDARD VI. QUALITY OF THE PROCESS

A. A mediator shall conduct a mediation in accordance with these Standards and in a manner that promotes diligence, timeliness, safety, presence of the appropriate participants, party participation, procedural fairness, party competency and mutual respect among all participants.

1. A mediator should agree to mediate only when the mediator is prepared to commit the attention essential to an effective mediation.

2. A mediator should only accept cases when the mediator can satisfy the reasonable expectation of the parties concerning the timing of a mediation.

3. The presence or absence of persons at a mediation depends on the agreement of the parties and the mediator. The parties and mediator may agree that others may be excluded from particular sessions or from all sessions.

4. A mediator should promote honesty and candor between and among all participants, and a mediator shall not knowingly misrepresent any material fact or circumstance in the course of a mediation.

5. The role of a mediator differs substantially from other professional roles. Mixing the role of a mediator and the role of another profession is problematic and thus, a mediator should distinguish between the roles. A mediator may provide information that the mediator is qualified by training or experience to provide, only if the mediator can do so consistent with these Standards.

6. A mediator shall not conduct a dispute resolution procedure other than mediation but label it mediation in an effort to gain the protection of rules, statutes, or other governing authorities pertaining to mediation.

7. A mediator may recommend, when appropriate, that parties consider resolving their dispute through arbitration, counseling, neutral evaluation or other processes.

8. A mediator shall not undertake an additional dispute resolution role in the same matter without the consent of the parties. Before providing such service, a mediator shall inform the parties of the implications of the change in process and obtain their consent to the change. A mediator who undertakes such role assumes different duties and responsibilities that may be governed by other standards.

9. If a mediation is being used to further criminal conduct, a mediator should take appropriate steps including, if necessary, postponing, withdrawing from or terminating the mediation.

10. If a party appears to have difficulty comprehending the process, issues, or settlement options, or difficulty participating in a mediation, the mediator should explore the circumstances and potential accommodations, modifications or adjustments that would make possible the party's capacity to comprehend, participate and exercise self-determination.

B. If a mediator is made aware of domestic abuse or violence among the parties, the mediator shall take appropriate steps including, if necessary, postponing, withdrawing from or terminating the mediation.

C. If a mediator believes that participant conduct, including that of the mediator, jeopardizes conducting a mediation consistent with these Standards, a mediator shall take appropriate steps including, if necessary, postponing, withdrawing from or terminating the mediation.

STANDARD VII. ADVERTISING AND SOLICITATION

A. A mediator shall be truthful and not misleading when advertising, soliciting or otherwise communicating the mediator's qualifications, experience, services and fees.

1. A mediator should not include any promises as to outcome in communications, including business cards, stationery, or computer-based communications.

2. A mediator should only claim to meet the mediator qualifications of a governmental entity or private organization if that entity or organization has a recognized procedure for qualifying mediators and it grants such status to the mediator.

B. A mediator shall not solicit in a manner that gives an appearance of partiality for or against a party or otherwise undermines the integrity of the process.

C. A mediator shall not communicate to others, in promotional materials or through other forms of communication, the names of persons served without their permission.

STANDARD VIII. FEES AND OTHER CHARGES

A. A mediator shall provide each party or each party's representative true and complete information about mediation fees, expenses and any other actual or potential charges that may be incurred in connection with a mediation.

  1. If a mediator charges fees, the mediator should develop them in light of all relevant factors, including the type and complexity of the matter, the qualifications of the mediator, the time required and the rates customary for such mediation services.

  2. A mediator's fee arrangement should be in writing unless the parties request otherwise.

B. A mediator shall not charge fees in a manner that impairs a mediator's impartiality.

  1. A mediator should not enter into a fee agreement which is contingent upon the result of the mediation or amount of the settlement.

  2. While a mediator may accept unequal fee payments from the parties, a mediator should not allow such a fee arrangement to adversely impact the mediator's ability to conduct a mediation in an impartial manner.

STANDARD IX. ADVANCEMENT OF MEDIATION PRACTICE

A. A mediator should act in a manner that advances the practice of mediation. A mediator promotes this Standard by engaging in some or all of the following:

  1. Fostering diversity within the field of mediation.

  2. Striving to make mediation accessible to those who elect to use it, including providing services at a reduced rate or on a pro bono basis as appropriate.

  3. Participating in research when given the opportunity, including obtaining participant feedback when appropriate.

  4. Participating in outreach and education efforts to assist the public in developing an improved understanding of, and appreciation for, mediation.

    5. Assisting newer mediators through training, mentoring and networking.

B. A mediator should demonstrate respect for differing points of view within the field, seek to learn from other mediators and work together with other mediators to improve the profession and better serve people in conflict.

Notes

Chapter One

1. Homer, The Odyssey Abridged (3rd ed.) book 12, lines 213–224 (Ian Johnson trans. 2006).

2. In this text I use the terms *values* and *principles* interchangeably to refer to the moral commitments that underlie ethical practice. Precedent exists both for treating the terms virtually synonymously (see Norm Daniels, *The Articulation of Values and Principles Involved in Health Care Reform*, 19 J. of Med. and Philosophy 425–433 [1994]) as well as treating principles as a means by which values are operationalized (see *Values and Principles in European Union Foreign Policy* 10 [Sonia Lucarelli & Ian Manners eds. 2006] defining values as "notions laden with an absolute positive significance for the overall order and meaning we try to give our world" and principles as "normative propositions that translate values into general … standards for policy action").

3. See L. Susskind, *Environmental Mediation and the Accountability Problem*, 6 Vt. L. Rev. 1 (1981) and J. Stulberg, *The Theory and Practice of Mediation: A Reply to Professor Susskind*, 6 Vt. L. Rev. 85 (1981).

4. See R. S. Landau, The Fundamentals of Ethics 112–175 (2010), for a clear and accessible discussion of both utilitarian and deontological theories.

5. This means that duties provide a reason in favor of a specific action, but this reason can be outweighed by other duties that may be stronger in the particular situation.

6. From W. D. Ross, The Right and the Good 42 (P. Stratton-Lake ed. 2009).

7. See Code of Professional Conduct for Labor Mediators, 29 C.F.R. app. sec. 1400. 735-20 (2010). See also 29 C.F.R. sec. 1400 (2010) (stating, "In 1964, a Code of Professional Conduct for Labor Mediators was drafted by a Federal-State Liaison Committee and approved by the Service and the Association of Labor Mediation Agencies at its annual meeting. It is expected that mediators in the Federal Mediation and Conciliation Service will make

themselves familiar with this Code and will conduct themselves in accordance with the responsibilities outlined therein").

8. See Preamble to Model Standards of Conduct for Mediators (2005).

9. See Note on Construction in the Model Standards (2005).

10. A Guide for Federal Employee Mediators (A Supplement to and Annotation of the Model Standards of Conduct for Mediators) (Federal Interagency ADR Working Group Steering Committee) (2006).

11. The state codes frequently clarify that violation of their adopted standards will result in removal from the roster of court-connected mediators but not legal liability.

12. See, for example, Georgia ADR Rules Appendix C, Ethical Standards for Neutrals, Standard IV, Fairness (2010): "A mediator may refuse to draft or sign an agreement which seems fundamentally unfair to the party."

13. The Association of Family and Conciliation Courts, Model Standards of Practice for Family and Divorce Mediation (2000); University of Minnesota Center for Restorative Justice and Peacemaking, Guidelines for Victim-Sensitive Victim-Offender Mediation; Restorative Justice Through Dialogue (2000); ADA Mediation Standards Work Group, ADA Mediation Guidelines (2000), housed on the Cardozo Law School's Kukin Program for Conflict Resolution Web site at www.cojcr.org/ada.html.

14. Ala. Code of Ethics for Mediators, Standard 3(b) (1997).

15. Model Standards of Practice for Family and Divorce Mediation, Standard VI(B) (2000).

16. See S. *Exon, How Can a Mediator Be Both Neutral and Fair? How Ethical Standards of Conduct Create Chaos for Mediators,* J. Disp. Resol. 387 (2006).

17. See L. L. Riskin, *Understanding Mediator Orientations, Strategies and Techniques: A Grid for the Perplexed,* 1 Harv. Negotiation L. Rev. 7 (1996).

18. See L. L. Riskin, *Decision Making in Mediation: The New Old Grid and the New New Grid System,* 79 Notre Dame L. Rev. 1–53 (2003).

19. Riskin, in addition to identifying facilitative and evaluative approaches, also identified broad versus narrow styles. The broad style took an expansive view of the parties' issues that encompassed a wide array of psychological and relational goals. The narrow style, conversely, adheres to a more constricted, legalistic view of the issues to be explored and the topics to be discussed. See Riskin, supra note 17, at 22, figure 1. For the purposes of simplicity, and because the narrow and broad terminology have achieved less traction in the field, we limit our discussion here to the evaluative and facilitative approaches. See id. See also L. L. Riskin, *Mediator Orientations, Strategies and Techniques,* 12 Alternatives 111 (1994).

20. L. L. Riskin, supra note 18, at 111–114 (1994).

21. Id. at 14.
22. Id. at 11.
23. See J. Hyman & L. Love, *If Portia Were a Mediator: An Inquiry into Justice in Mediation*, 9 Clinical L. Rev. 157 (2002).
24. See R. A. Baruch Bush & J. P. Folger, The Promise of Mediation (2nd ed.) 13–14, 233–234 (2005).
25. Id. at 85–86.
26. See J. Winslade & G. Monk, Practicing Mediation 31 (2008).
27. Id. at 32.
28. J. Winslade & G. Monk, Narrative Mediation: A New Approach to Conflict Resolution 43 (2000).
29. J. Winslade & G. Monk, Narrative Mediation: A New Approach to Conflict Resolution 43 (2000).

Chapter Two

1. See C. Beck & L. Frost, *Defining a Threshold for Client Competence to Participate in Divorce Mediation*, 12 Psychol. Publ. Pol'y & L. 4–5, 9–10 (2006).
2. M. Radford, *Is the Use of Mediation Appropriate in Adult Guardianship Cases?* 31 Stetson L. Rev. 611, 649 (2002); Beck and Frost, supra note 1, at 4.
3. See generally T. Grisso, Evaluating Competencies: Forensic Assessments and Instruments (2nd ed. 2003); R. J. Bonnie & T. Grisso, *Adjudicative Competence and Youthful Offenders*, in Youth on Trial: A Developmental Perspective on Juvenile Justice 73 (T. Grisso & R. Schwartz eds. 2000) (identifying three values underlying legal competency evaluation in the criminal justice context: autonomy, dignity, and efficiency).
4. Model Standards of Conduct for Mediators, Standard VI(A)(10), reads, "If a party appears to have difficulty comprehending the process, issues, or settlement options, or difficulty participating in a mediation, the mediator should explore the circumstances and potential accommodations, modifications or adjustments that would make possible the party's capacity to comprehend, participate and exercise self-determination."
5. See ADA Mediation Standards sec. I(D)(2) (stating that "an adjudication of legal incapacity is not necessarily determinative of capacity to mediate"). See also Divorce Mediation Standards, Standard III (requiring that "a family mediator shall facilitate the participants' understanding of what mediation is and assess their capacity to mediate before the participants reach an agreement to mediate"). See also id., Standard XI (mandating that "a family mediator shall suspend or terminate the mediation process when

the mediator reasonably believes that a participant is unable to effectively participate or for other compelling reason").

6. See S. H. Crawford et al., *From Determining Capacity to Facilitating Competencies: A New Mediation Framework*, 20 Conflict Resol. Q. 385–401 (2003) (urging use of support people to facilitate a party's ability to participate in mediation when that party has diminished capacity). See also T. Hedeen, *Mediation as Contact Sport? Issues of Fitness and Fit Arising from Georgia's Wilson v. Wilson*, 15 Disp. Resol. Mag. 24 (2009).

7. The term *mentally retarded* is gradually being phased out and replaced with the designation *mild mental handicap or disability*. In addition, the phrase *intellectual disability* is beginning to replace the term *mental retardation*. See *American Association on Intellectual and Developmental Disabilities, Intellectual Disabilities: Definitions, Classifications and Systems of Support* (11th ed. 2010).

8. *Normal Development: 9 Years Old,* Pediatric Advisor 2006.2: Normal Development: 9 Years Old, www.cpnonline.org/CRS/CRS/pa_devninyr_pep.htm (Sept. 7, 2010).

9. Kimberly L. Keith, *Child Development—The Nine Year Old,* http://childparenting.about.com/od/childdevelopment/a/nineyearoldhom _3.htm (Oct. 15, 2010); See also L. Bates & C. Haber, Your Nine-Year-Old: Thoughtful and Mysterious 49 (1990).

10. The name has been changed to protect the client's privacy.

11. American Psychiatric Association, Diagnostic and Statistical Manual of Mental Disorders (4th ed. 2000).

12. AAIDD, *Definition of Intellectual Disability,* www.aaidd.org/content_100 .cfm?navlD=21.

13. These questions are a variation of those developed by the Center for Social Gerontology for use in determining whether an adult with diminishing capacity can participate in a mediation about impending guardianship proceedings. See S. D. Hartman, Adult Guardianship Mediation Manual 64–66 (1996).

Chapter Three

1. See M. Nussbaum, Upheavals of Thought: The Intelligence of Emotions (2000); R. S. Lazarus, Emotion and Adaptation (1991).

2. See P. Goldie, The Emotions: A Philosopher's Exploration (2000).

3. See J. P. Forgas, *Affective Influences on Attitudes and Judgments,* in Handbook of Affective Sciences (R. J. Davidson et al. eds. 2003).

4. R. Fischer & D. Shapiro, Beyond Reason (2005).

5. See Lazarus, supra note 1, at 6–7.

6. Id. at 39.

7. See C. J. Freshman, *The Lawyer-Negotiator as Mood Scientist: What We Know and Don't Know About How Mood Affects Negotiation,* 2002 J. Disp. Resol. 1 (2002).

8. See Lazarus, supra note 1, at 221–223.

9. See A. Ellis, *The Philosophical Basis of Rational-Emotive Therapy,* 8 Psychotherapy in Private Practice 97–106 (1991).

10. This list of cognitive distortions is drawn from Albert Ellis and Aaron Beck, the architects of cognitive behavioral therapy. See generally A. Beck et al., Cognitive Therapy of Personality Disorders (2004); A. Ellis, New Directions for Rational Behavior Therapy (2001).

11. See L. Cosimide & J. Tooby, *From Evolution to Behavior: Evolutionary Psychology as the Missing Link,* in The Latest on the Best: Essay on Evolution and Optimality 296 (J. Dupre ed. 1997).

12. See H. Lerner, Fear and Other Uninvited Guests: Tackling the Anxiety, Fear, and Shame That Keep Us from Optimal Living and Loving 55 (2004).

13. See Stress-Related Disorders Sourcebook 5–6 (A. Sutton ed. 2007).

14. Id. at 57.

15. See A. Ohman, *Fear and Anxiety, Overlaps and Dissociations,* in Handbook of Emotions 709, 718 (M. Lewis et al. eds. 2008).

16. See G. Bonanno et al., *Sadness and Grief,* in Handbook of Emotions 797–810 (M. Lewis et al. eds. 2008).

17. Id. at 798.

18. See H. Welling, *An Evolutionary Function of the Depressive Reaction: The Cognitive Map Hypothesis,* 21 New Ideas in Psychology 147–156 (2003).

19. See G. V. Bodenhausen et al., *Sadness and Susceptibility to Judgmental Bias: The Case of Anchoring,* 11 Psychological Science 320–323 (2000).

20. See J. Storbeck & G. L. Clore, *With Sadness Comes Accuracy; With Happiness, False Memory: Mood and the False Memory Effect,* 16 Psychological Science 785–791 (2005).

21. See Depression Sourcebook 30–31 (S. J. Judd ed. 2008).

22. See S. Nolen-Hoeksema et al., *Rethinking Rumination,* 3 Perspectives in Psychological Science 400–424 (2008).

23. See Depression Sourcebook, supra note 21, at 30–31.

24. See F. Flach, The Secret Strength of Depression 31–40 (1995).

25. P. D. Kramer, Against Depression 45 (2005) (positing that, "in depression, a person understands matters one way and feels them another, or sustains multiple understandings, of which the darkest are the most compelling").

26. See id. at 22 (stating that "depression skews the proportions of good and bad recalled in self and others. The I has always been needy and useless; they have always been justified in their rejection of the damaged, sinful, demanding self").

27. See M. Lewis, *Self-Conscious Emotions: Embarrassment, Pride, Shame and Guilt,* in Handbook of Emotions 742–756 (M. Lewis et al. eds. 2008).

28. Id. at 742–743.

29. This case is a vastly reworked version of a case presented in L. Engel & T. Ferguson, Imaginary Crimes: Why We Punish Ourselves and How to Stop 25–26 (1990).

30. See id. Family members often accuse themselves of various imaginary "crimes": outdoing ("if we perceive ourselves as happier, more successful, more popular, or more capable of enjoying life than our parents, brothers or sisters"), love theft ("If we believe that we received the love and attention another family member needed in order to thrive, we may judge ourselves guilty of the imaginary crime of love theft"), and abandonment ("this is the crime of wanting to separate from our parents, to make our own choices, to move away from the family home, and to establish a separate and independent life"). Id. at xv–xvi.

31. In fact, research on hypothetical scenarios remarkably similar to the one under discussion was presented by R.A.B. Bush & J. P. Folger, The Promise of Mediation: Responding to Conflict Through Empowerment and Recognition 33–40 (1994) as evidence that many mediators focus on quality of outcome and subtly influence the outcome in the direction of their own opinion about a good quality outcome, to the detriment of party self-determination. See also R.A.B. Bush, The Dilemmas of Mediation Practice: A Study of Ethical Dilemmas and Policy Implications (1992).

32. See R.A.B. Bush & J. P. Folger, The Promise of Mediation 13–14, 233–234 (2nd ed. 2005); R.A.B. Bush & J. P. Folger, The Promise of Mediation: Responding to Conflict Through Empowerment and Recognition (1994).

33. For a more thorough explanation of the theory and practice of the transformative model, see e.g. id.; R.A.B. Bush et al., *Changing the Quality of Conflict Interaction: The Principles and Practices of Transformative Mediation,* 3 Pepp. Disp. Res. L.J. 67 (2002); D. J. Della Noce et al., *Clarifying the Theoretical Underpinnings of Mediation: Implications for Practice and Policy,* 3 Pepp. Disp. Res. L.J. 39 (2002); D. J. Della Noce et al., *Identifying Practice Competence in Transformative Mediators: An Interactive Rating Scale Assessment Model,* 19 Ohio St. J. on Disp. Resol. 1005 (2004); J. P. Folger

et al., *Transformative Mediation and Third-Party Intervention: Ten Hall-marks of a Transformative Approach to Practice,* 13 Mediation Q. 263 (1996).

34. Certified mediators in Virginia are bound by a particular set of statutes and a code of ethics; it is considered good practice even for mediators who choose not to be certified to follow these rules.

35. Code of Virginia sec. 8.01–576.4 (2010).

36. In fact, Virginia's Standards of Ethics and Professional Responsibility for Certified Mediators state in section E, Self Determination:

    1. "Mediation is based on the principle of self-determination by the par-ties. Self-determination requires that the mediator rely on the parties to reach a voluntary agreement."

    2. "The mediator may provide information about the process, raise issues, and help explore options. The primary role of the mediator is to facili-tate a voluntary resolution of a dispute."

    3. "The mediator may not coerce a party into an agreement, and shall not make decisions for any party to the mediation process."

37. Virginia recognizes the possibility that a variety of models may be employed by practitioners within the state. Hence, consistent with the overarching policy supporting party self-determination, the Virginia Standards of Ethics require mediators to disclose their approach to mediation to the parties and inquire about the parties' expectations in this regard: "The mediator shall also describe his style and approach to mediation. The parties must be given an opportunity to express their expectations regarding the conduct of the mediation process. The parties and mediator must include in the agreement to mediate a general statement regarding the mediator's style and approach to mediation to which the parties have agreed."

38. Failure of a mediator to advise participants in mediation of "the four legals" is grounds for setting aside a mediated agreement. Code of Virginia sec. 8.01–576.12 (2010).

39. Virginia's Guidelines on Mediation and the Unauthorized Prac-tice of Law are helpful in delineating the highly contextualized distinction between legal information and advice (available at www.courts.state.va.us/courtadmin/aoc/djs/programs/drs/mediation /resources/upl_guidelines.pdf[2000]).

40. Code of Virginia sec. 8.01–576.12 (2010): "The fact that any provisions of a mediated agreement were such that they could not or would not be granted by a court of law or equity is not, in and of itself, grounds for vacating an agreement."

41. In fact, to suggest that a mediator might know exactly what he or she would and would not do in any abstract sense is to suggest that the mediator has already made a decision about what the desired outcome is and is simply strategizing to get the parties to make that decision. See D. M. Kolb & Associates, When Talk Works: Profiles of Mediators (1994).

Chapter Four

1. K. Fischer et al., *The Culture of Battering and the Role of Mediation in Domestic Violence Cases,* 46 SMU L. Rev. 2117 (1993).
2. J. Johnston and L. Campbell, *A Clinical Typology of Interparental Violence in Disputed-Custody Divorces,* 63 Amer. J. Orthopsychiatry 190, 193–198 (April 1993).
3. See Fischer, supra note 1, citing various inventories, including: L. Marshall, *Development of the Severity of Violence Against Women Scales,* 7 J. Fam. Violence 103, 114 (1992); D. Follingstad et al., *The Role of Emotional Abuse in Physically Abusive Relationships,* 5 J. Fam. Violence 107, 114 (1990); R. M. Tolman, *The Development of a Measure of Psychological Maltreatment of Women by Their Male Partners,* 4 Violence and Victims 159, 162 (1989).
4. L. Girdner, *Mediation Triage: Screening for Spouse Abuse in Divorce Mediation,* 7 Mediation Q. 365, 374 (1990). See also S. K. Erikson & M. S. McNight, *Mediating Spousal Abuse Divorces,* 7 Mediation Q. 377, 379–380 (1990) (recommending that mediation is inappropriate when the abuser discounts the victim and refuses to acknowledge how his behavior affects her; abuse is ongoing between the mediation sessions; either client is carrying a weapon or attempts to mediate while drinking or using drugs; or either party continues to violate the mediation ground rules). N. Ver Steegh, *Yes, No, and Maybe: Informed Decision Making About Divorce Mediation in the Presence of Domestic Violence,* 9 Wm. & Mary J. Women & L. 145 (2003).
5. Both the Model Standards and the Divorce Mediation Standards authorize mediators to terminate mediation if they believe that the violence destroys the possibility of constructive dialogue. Standard IV(B) of the Model Standards counsels a mediator who is made aware of domestic abuse or violence among the parties to take "appropriate steps," including withdrawing from or terminating the mediation. The Divorce Mediation Standards require family mediators to receive training about domestic abuse and screen out cases that are not suitable because of safety, control or intimidation issues. Divorce Mediation Standards, Standard X.
6. Christopher Moore, The Mediation Process: Practical Strategies for Resolving Conflict 377–379 (3rd ed. 2003).

7. Of course, one piece of knowledge relevant to deciding in mediation is what will happen if the dispute proceeds to litigation. Information about the law applied and the facts that will become salient under that law are useful in developing informed speculation about the likely outcome. But certainty as to how a case will be treated by a judge or jury is elusive. See Lela Love's commentary in Chapter Five on Cases 5.3 and 5.4.

8. R. Delgado, *Fairness and Formality: Minimizing the Risk of Prejudice in Alternative Dispute Resolution,* 1985 Wisc. L. Rev. 1359 (1985).

9. Id. at 1397–1398.

10. See In Litigation Do the "Haves" Still Come Out Ahead? (H. M. Kritzer & S. Silbey eds. 2003).

11. See, e.g., Fla. Rules for Certified and Court-Appointed Mediators, Rule 10.370(c) (2006); Tenn. Sup. Ct. Rules, Rule 31, sec. 10(b)(3) (2007); Rules of Conduct for Mediators in Court-Connected Mediation Programs for Civil Cases sec. 3.857 (Calif. 2007). See Paula M. Young, *A Connecticut Mediator in a Kangaroo Court? Successfully Communicating the "Authorized Practice of Mediation" Paradigm to "Unauthorized Practice of Law" Disciplinary Bodies,* 49 S. Tex. L. Rev. 1047, 1120–1121, 1204–1219, n. 341, n. 725–823 (2008) (discussing at length the state codes' prescriptions regarding mediator provision of legal information). See also Chapter Five, this volume, for further discussion about the permissibility of educating disputants regarding the risks and benefits of settlement.

12. See P. T. Coleman, *Power and Conflict,* in The Handbook of Conflict Resolution 108–130 (M. Deutsch & P. T. Coleman eds. 2000), in which Coleman discusses four perspectives on power: "Power Over," "Power With," "Powerlessness and Dependence," and "Empowered and Independent." See also D. T. Saposnek, *The Dynamics of Power in Child Custody Mediation,* in The Handbook of Mediation: Bridging Theory, Research and Practice 260–276 (M. S. Herrman ed. 2006); C. Moore, The Mediation Process 389–396 (2004); and M. Lang & A. Taylor, The Making of a Mediator 163–166 (2000).

13. See Lang & Taylor, supra note 12, at 119–149, building on the reflective practice approach of Donald Schön.

14. For a fuller discussion of this approach, see *Toolbox of Strategies for Collaborative Agreement,* in F. S. Mosten, Collaborative Divorce Handbook 77–104 (2009).

15. With similar orthodoxy played out in an opposite way, traditional commercial mediation was premised on an exclusively caucus model to quell client emotions by preventing disruptive and unproductive client interaction. Perhaps this is due to more frequent involvement of lawyers in commercial settings with the selection of mediators favored by lawyers who use a

more directive and evaluative style and who generally are former judges and litigators.

16. See C. Moore, The Mediation Process 369–377 (2003); see also F. S. Mosten & D. Mercer, Advanced Mediator Moves, Association for Conflict Resolution Family Section (2005).

17. See S. Goldberg & M. Shaw, *The Secrets of Successful (and Unsuccessful) Mediators Continued, Studies One and Two,* 23 Negotiation J. 393–418 (2007).

18. See Mosten, supra note 14, at 72.

19. The attorney engagement could be "full service" as counsel of record for the entire case or "unbundled" (also known as limited scope representation or discrete task representation) for mediation consultation only. See F. S. Mosten, Unbundling Legal Services 112–113 (2000); F. S. Mosten, Complete Guide to Mediation chaps. 15–18 (1997); H. Abramson, *Problem Solving Advocacy in Mediations: A Model of Client Representation,* 10 Harv. Negot. L. Rev. 103 (2005).

20. I generally recommend that experts be invited to attend mediation sessions rather than "refer out" parties. The mediator can then also hear the expert input and facilitate discussion based on shared information. Bringing in the expert also spares the mediator from assuming a more evaluative role, which can hamper neutrality and mediator effectiveness.

21. California mandates the right of a "victim" in domestic violence to have a resource person and/or private sessions during court-ordered mediations. Private mediators can encourage voluntary use of this same protection in situations less extreme (but still unbalanced). See Mosten, Complete Guide to Mediation, supra note 19, at 145–160.

22. See R. A. Baruch Bush & J. P. Folger, The Promise of Mediation (rev. ed. 2005).

23. For a toolbox of more than 215 conflict resolution strategies, contact Forrest Mosten.

Chapter Five

1. Model Standards of Conduct for Mediators, Standard I(A)(2) (2005).

2. See L. P. Love & J. W. Cooley, *The Intersection of Evaluation by Mediators and Informed Consent: Warning the Unwary,* 21 Ohio St. J. on Disp. Resol. 45 (2005).

3. See American Medical Association, Code of Medical Ethics, Opinion 2.03 (2001).

4. American Psychological Association, Ethical Principles of Psychologists and Code of Conduct, General Principles, Principle A (2010).

5. National Association of Social Workers, Code of Ethics, Preamble (2008).

6. American Bar Association, Model Rules of Professional Conduct, Preamble(1) (2010).

7. See L. Susskind, *Environmental Mediation and the Accountability Problem,* 6 Vt. L. Rev. 1 (1981); J. B. Stulberg, *The Theory and Practice of Mediation: A Reply to Professor Susskind,* 6 Vt. L. Rev. 85 (1981).

8. Susskind, supra note 7, at 14.

9. Id.

10. Id. at 58.

11. Stulberg, supra note 7, at 114.

12. Id. at 97.

13. Id. at 116.

14. See O. Fiss, *Against Settlement,* 93 Yale L.J. 1073 (1984); No Access to Law (L. Nader ed. 1980); *The ADR Explosion: The Implications of Rhetoric in Legal Reform,* 8 Windsor Y.B. Access Just. 269 (1988).

15. See R. L. Abel, *The Contradictions of Informal Justice,* in The Politics of Informal Justice Volume 1: The American Experience (R. L. Abel ed. 1982); M. Fineman, *Dominant Discourse, Professional Language, and Legal Change in Child Custody Decisionmaking,* 101 Harv. L. Rev. 727 (1988).

16. See B. McAddo & N. A. Welsh, *Look Before You Leap and Keep on Looking: Lessons from the Institutionalization of Court-Connected Mediation,* 5 Nev L.J. 399 (2004); N. A. Welsh, *The Thinning Vision of Self-Determination in Court-Connected Mediation: The Inevitable Price of Institutionalization?* 6 Harv. Negot L. Rev. 1 (2001) (lamenting increasingly directive behavior of court-connected mediators and reduced emphasis on party self-determination).

17. Ala. Code of Ethics for Mediators, Standard 3(b) (2010).

18. Ark. Alternative Dispute Resolution Commission, Requirements for the Conduct of Mediation and Mediators, Standard B (2004); Fla. Rules for Certified and Court-Appointed Mediators, Rule 10.420(b)(4) (2006).

19. See Ga. Alternative Dispute Resolution Rules, app. C, Ethical Standards for Neutrals, Standard IV(A) (1995).

20. N.C. Standards of Professional Conduct for Mediators, Standard V(E) (2010).

21. See Smith v. Mitsubishi Motors Credit of America, Inc., 247 Conn. 342, 349 (1998).

22. Fla. Rules for Certified and Court-Appointed Mediators, Rule 10.370(c) (2006).

23. Tenn. Sup. Ct. Rules, Rule 31, sec. 10(b)(3) (2007).

24. See Department of Dispute Resolution Services of the Supreme Court of Virginia, Guidelines on Mediation and the Unauthorized Practice of

Law (2000), www.courts.state.va.us/courtadmin/aoc/djs/programs/drs
/mediation/resources/upl_guidelines.pdf.

25. See N.C. Bar Association Dispute Resolution Section, Task Force
on Mediation and the Practice of Law, Guidelines for the Ethical
Practice of Mediation and to Prevent the Unauthorized Practice
of Law (1999), http://disputeresolution.ncbar.org/media/1387275
/guidelinesForEthicalPractice.pdf.

26. See ABA Section of Dispute Resolution, Resolution on Mediation and
the Unauthorized Practice of Law (2002), www.abanet.org/dispute
/resolution2002.pdf (stating, "In disputes where the parties' legal rights
or obligations are at issue, the mediator's discussions with the parties may
involve legal issues. Such discussions do not create an attorney-client
relationship, and do not constitute legal advice, whether or not the
mediator is an attorney").

27. See S. R. Cole et al., Mediation: Law, Policy and Practice, sec. 10:5 (2nd ed.
2009), citing Florida Bar v. Furman, 451 So. 2d 808, 812–814 (Fla. 1984).

28. P. M. Young, *A Connecticut Mediator in a Kangaroo Court? Successfully
Communicating the "Authorized Practice of Mediation" Paradigm to
"Unauthorized Practice of Law" Disciplinary Bodies*, 49 S. Tex. L. Rev.
1047, 1083–1085,1120–1127 (2008). Out-of-state attorney mediators who
give advice in mediation are also at risk. Moreover, attorney mediators
are subject to traditional liability rules attaching to all professionals and
can be found negligent if they have failed to exercise the skill and care of a
reasonable attorney in similar circumstances.

29. Rules of Conduct for Mediators in Court-Connected Mediation Programs
for Civil Cases sec. 3.857 (Calif. 2007) (stating, in full, that "subject to the
principles of impartiality and self-determination, and if qualified to do so,
a mediator may (1) discuss a party's options, including a range of possible
outcomes in an adjudicative process; (2) offer a personal evaluation of or
opinion on a set of facts as presented, which should be clearly identified as a
personal evaluation or opinion; or (3) communicate the mediator's opinion
or view of what the law is or how it applies to the subject of the mediation,
provided that the mediator does not also advise any participant about how
to adhere to the law or on what position the participant should take in light
of that opinion").

30. R. A. Baruch Bush & J. P. Folger, The Promise of Mediation: Responding to
Conflict Through Empowerment and Recognition 213–214 (1994).

31. See J. Winslade & G. D. Monk, Practicing Narrative Mediation: Loosening
the Grip of Conflict 133 (2008).

32. Id. at 68.

33. E. Waldman, *Identifying the Role of Social Norms in Mediation: A Multiple Model Approach,* 48 Hastings L.J. 703 (1997).

34. L. L. Fuller, *Mediation—Its Forms and Functions,* 44 S. Cal. L. Rev. 305, 308 (1971).

35. Fair Labor Standards Act of 1938, 29 U.S.C.A. sec. 206(d)(1), as amended by the Equal Pay Act of 1963.

36. The facts of this hypothetical are derived loosely, in substantially watered-down form, from newspaper accounts of the allegations lodged in a class action lawsuit filed by the Equal Employment Opportunity Commission against Mitsubishi Motor Manufacturing of America. See *Mitsubishi Settles for 34 Million: Automaker and EEOC Agree on Terms in Largest Sexual Harassment Case in History* (1998) at http://money/cnn.com/1998/06/11/companies/mitsubishi.

37. This assumes that the chosen ends and means are lawful and not contrary to public policy. Where parties seek to use the mediation process to further unlawful activity (for example, pay an obligation by supplying illegal drugs), the mediator would not allow such a violation of the integrity of the process.

38. See J. Feerick et al., *Standards of Professional Conduct in Alternative Dispute Resolution,* 1995 J. Disp. Resol. 95 (1995) (addressing a similar issue).

39. If the Tongan attorney is not a member of the bar, the mediator can urge the party to get a licensed attorney.

40. L. L. Riskin, *Understanding Mediator Orientations, Strategies and Techniques: A Grid for the Perplexed,* 1 Harvard Negot. L. Rev. 7 (1996).

41. E. Waldman, *Identifying the Role of Social Norms in Mediation: A Multiple Model Approach,* 48 Hastings L.J. 703 (1997).

42. A pro se is a party who appears unrepresented in court.

43. J. Nolan-Haley, *Informed Consent in Mediation: A Guiding Principle for Truly Educated Decisionmaking,* 74 Notre Dame L. Rev. 775, 787 (1999).

44. Model Standards of Conduct for Mediators, Standard I (August 2005). It is noteworthy that the original 1994 version of the Model Standards did not contain a provision for informed choice as to outcome. Most state mediation ethical codes contain similar provisions for party self-determination.

45. European Commission Justice Directorate, European Code of Conduct for Mediators, sec. 3.3 (2004).

46. Nolan-Haley, supra note 43, at 819.

47. Id. at 820.

48. See S. N. Exon, *How Can a Mediator Be Both Impartial and Fair? Why Ethical Standards of Conduct Create Chaos for Mediators,* 2006 J. Disp. Resol. 387 (2006).

49. Model Standards of Conduct for Mediators, Standard VI(A)(4) (2005).

50. See id. Preamble.

51. It is also consistent with private commercial mediation standards such as JAMS Mediators Ethics Guidelines (2003). Section VII of the Guidelines lists the circumstances under which a mediator should withdraw from the mediation: "A mediator should withdraw from the process . . . for any of the reasons set forth above: lack of informed consent. . . . A mediator should be aware of the potential need to withdraw from the case if procedural or substantive unfairness have undermined the integrity of the mediation process."

52. See B. Honoroff & S. Opotow, *Mediation Ethics: A Grounded Approach,* 23 Negotiation J. 155 (2007).

53. Nolan-Haley, supra note 43, at 825, 826.

54. L. P. Love & J. W. Cooley, *The Intersection of Evaluation by Mediators and Informed Consent: Warning the Unwary,* 21 Ohio St. J. on Disp. Resol. 45 (2005).

55. Z. Dubey, *Do ADR Mediators Have an Ethical Duty to Ensure an Agreement's Substantive Fairness?* 11 NYSBA N.Y. Litigator 26 (2006).

56. Nolan-Haley, supra note 43, at 821.

Chapter Six

1. See A. France, The Red Lily 95 (W. Stephens trans. 1910).

2. American Bar Association, Model Rules of Professional Conduct, Rule 2.4 (2005).

3. ABA Section of Dispute Resolution, Resolution on Mediation and the Unauthorized Practice of Law (2002), www.abanet.org/dispute /resolution2002.pdf.

4. Center for Dispute Settlement & Institute for Judicial Administration, National Standards for Court-Connected Mediation Programs, Standard 1.4 (1999), http://courtadr.org/files/NationalStandardsADR.pdf.

5. See Fla. R. Certified & Ct. App'ted Med., Rule 10.420(b), Conduct of Mediation (2010) (stating that "a mediator shall . . . adjourn or terminate any mediation which, if continued, would result in unreasonable emotional or monetary costs to the parties; [and a mediator shall] terminate a mediation entailing . . . the absence of bargaining ability, or unconscionability"); Ga. Alternate Disp. Resol. R., Appx C, Standard IV(A) (2009) (stating that "a mediator may refuse to draft or sign an agreement which seems fundamentally unfair to one party); Standards of Conduct for New York State Community Dispute Resolution Center Mediators, Standard VI, Quality of the Process, comment 11 (2005) (stating that "a mediator has an ongoing obligation to be sensitive to power imbalances between parties and to

ensure that the mediation process is conducted in a manner consistent with these Standards. If the mediator cannot ensure a quality process, the mediator should take appropriate steps to postpone the session, withdraw from the mediation or terminate the mediation"). See Va. Standards of Ethics and Professional Responsibility for Certified Mediators sec. L(2) (2002) (stating that "if, in the mediator's judgment, the integrity of the process has been compromised by, for example, ... gross inequality of bargaining power or ability, ... the mediator shall inform the parties. The mediator shall discontinue the mediation in such circumstances, but shall not violate the obligation of confidentiality").

6. See Ky. Mediation Guidelines for Court of Justice Mediators sec. 12, Comment (b) (2005) (stating that "a mediator should not convene the mediation if the mediator has reason to believe that a pro se party fails to understand that the mediator is not providing legal representation for the pro se party").

7. See Mass. Supreme Judicial Court Rule 1:18, The Uniform Rules on Dispute Resolution, Rule 9(c)(iii) (2005) (stating that "where a party is unrepresented by counsel and where the neutral believes that independent legal counsel and/or independent expert information or advice is needed to reach an informed agreement or to protect the rights of one or more of the parties, the neutral shall so inform the party or parties").

8. See N.C. Standards of Professional Conduct for Mediators, Standard V(D) (2010).

9. See State Bar of Texas, Alternative Dispute Resolution Section, Ethical Guidelines for Mediators, Guideline 11, Comment (b) (2005) ("A mediator should explain generally to pro se parties that there may be risks in proceeding without independent counsel or other professional advisors").

10. See, e.g., Ga. Alternative Dispute Resolution Rules, app. C, Ethical Standards for Neutrals, Standard IV(A) (1995); Fla. Rules for Certified and Court-Appointed Mediators, Rule 10.420(b)(4) (2006). See also Ind. R. Alternative Disp. Resol., Rule 7.5(B) (2010) (stating that "a neutral shall withdraw whenever a proposed resolution is unconscionable").

11. See Model Standards of Conduct for Mediators, Standard VI(A)(10) (2005) (stating that "if a party appears to have difficulty comprehending the process, issues, or settlement options, or difficulty participating in a mediation, the mediator should explore the circumstances and potential accommodations, modifications or adjustments that would make possible the party's capacity to comprehend, participate and exercise self-determination").

12. Id. at Standard VI(C).

Chapter Seven

1. Model Standards of Conduct for Mediators, Standard VI(A)(9) (2005).
2. See, e.g., Kans. Sup. Ct. Rule, Ethical Standards for Mediators, Rule 903(f), comment (2010); Washington Mediation Association, Standards of Practice for Mediators, Standard VI, comment (1997); Mo. Model Standards of Conduct for Mediators, Standard VI(A)(9) (2005).
3. Ala. Code of Ethics for Mediators, Standard 3(b) (2010).
4. Uniform Mediation Act sec. 5(c) (2001).
5. Id. at sec. 6(4).
6. See Fla. Stat. 44.405 4(a)(2) (2005).
7. See In re Petition of the ADR Rules and Policy Committee on Amendments to Florida Rules for Certified Court Appointed Mediators, 931 So. 2d. 877 (Fla. 2006).
8. See European Code of Conduct for Mediators, sec. 3.2, Fairness of the Process (2004): "The mediator if appropriate shall inform the parties, and may terminate the mediation, if:—a settlement is being reached that for the mediator appears unenforceable or illegal, having regard to the circumstances of the case and the competence of the mediator for making such an assessment."
9. See JAMS Mediators Ethics Guidelines sec. VII (2010). A Mediator Should Withdraw Under Certain Circumstances: "A mediator should withdraw from the process if the mediation is being used to further illegal conduct, or for any of the reasons set forth above."
10. Model Standards, supra note 1.
11. J. Macfarlane, *Mediating Ethically: The Limits of Codes of Conduct and the Potential of a Reflective Practice Model,* 40 Osgoode Hall L.J. 49 (2002).
12. See Standard VI(A)(9) of the Model Standards, supra note 1, which advises mediators who find themselves involved in negotiations that are "being used to further criminal conduct" to take "appropriate" action, which may include withdrawal or termination. The same language is found in the commentary to Principle VI of the SPIDR (now ACR) Code of Conduct for Mediators.
13. This also may be relevant to ascertaining the potential criminal liability of the mediator herself, for example, whether she is susceptible to a charge of criminal conspiracy under the criminal code.
14. See the further discussion in Macfarlane, supra note 11.
15. The cab-rank rule was developed at the English bar and requires English barristers to take any client who presents herself, in a similar fashion to a cab driver taking the next person in the taxi line. It is the subject of constant

controversy and may be more lip-service than common practice. See, e.g., A. Kramer, Bewigged and Bewildered? A Guide to Becoming a Barrister in England and Wales (2007).

16. For example, the Florida Rules for Certified and Court-Appointed Mediators speak of the responsibility of mediators "to preserve the integrity and quality of the profession." Fla. Rules for Certified and Court-Appointed Mediators, Rule 10.060 (1998).

17. See C. Argyris & D. Schön, Theory in Practice: Increasing Professional Effectiveness (1974); D. Schön, The Reflective Practitioner (1983); D. Schön, Educating the Reflective Practitioner (1987).

18. The same assumption runs through victim-offender programs. See, e.g., M. Umbreit, *Mediation of Victim Offender Conflict,* J. Disp. Resol. 85 (1988).

19. Although even where the outcome is perfectly lawful, as it was in this case, there is the additional question of whether a court would enforce such an agreement as contrary to public policy. This did not seem likely to be a practical concern for either Don or Clive.

Chapter Eight

1. See D. Peters, *When Lawyers Move Their Lips: Attorney Truthfulness in Mediation and a Modest Proposal,* 2007 J. Disp. Resol. 119 (2007). The twenty-three attorneys surveyed were asked to estimate the prevalence of various types of deceit advanced in mediation. These included material misrepresentations, lies regarding bargaining authority, lies about settlement alternatives, and lies about underlying client interests and priorities. The average estimate of prevalence of material misrepresentation in joint session was 25 percent (id. at 124); average estimate of prevalence of lies concerning the value of disputed items and claims was 35 percent (id. at 130); average estimate of prevalence of lies concerning reservation price or bottom line was 43 percent (id. at 130); and average estimate of prevalence of lies regarding bargaining authority was 36 percent (id. at 133).

2. A. Hinshaw & J. K. Alberts, *Doing the Right Thing: An Empirical Study of Attorney Negotiation Ethics,* CELS 2009 4th Annual Conf. on Empirical Legal Studies. Paper forthcoming at 16 Harv. Negotiation L. Rev. (2011).

3. Id. at 30.

4. See id. See also P. Reilly, *Was Machiavelli Right? Lying in Negotiation and the Art of Defensive Self-Help,* 24 Ohio St. J. Disp. Resol. 481 (2009) (reporting that of thirty attorneys surveyed, a significant minority would lie about settlement authority as well as the extent and severity of client injuries during negotiations).

5. Typically definitions of what constitutes a material fact hinge on the fact's influence on party deliberations. In the context of a house sale, one court defined a material fact as one for which "a reasonable purchaser would attach importance to its existence or nonexistence in determining the choice of action in the transaction in question." Ollerman v. O'Rourke, 94 Wis. 2d 17, 288 N.W.2d 95 (1980). In addition, facts are material if the speaker knows that this particular negotiator would attach importance to the fact, regardless of whether a reasonable person in similar circumstances would. See Restatement (Second) of Torts sec. 538 (1977) (stating that a "matter is material . . . if the maker of the representation knows or has reason to know that its recipient regards or is likely to regard the matter as important in determining his choice of action, although a reasonable man would not so regard it").

6. See Restatement (Second) of Torts, supra note 5, at sec. 551 (imposing a duty to disclose material facts if a fiduciary or confidential relationship exists or the customs of the trade or other objective circumstances would lead to a reasonable expectation of disclosure). See also N. W. Palmieri, *Good Faith Disclosures Required During Precontractual Negotiations,* 24 Seton Hall L. Rev. 70, 120, 125–141 (1993); See also K. D. Krawiec & K. Zeiler, *Common-Law Disclosure Duties and the Sin of Omission: Testing the Meta-Theories,* 91 Va. L. Rev. 1795, 1880, 1881 (2005) (finding that courts are likely to impose duties to disclose when disclosure would update or correct previously disclosed information, when a confidential relationship exists between informed and uninformed parties, and where undisclosed defects are latent as opposed to patent. In addition, disclosure is frequently required when the informed party acquired the information casually, without much cost, and the uninformed party lacks equal access to the information).

7. Model Standards of Conduct for Mediators, Standard VI(A)(4) (2005).

8. Va. Standards of Ethics and Professional Responsibility for Certified Mediators sec. L(2) (2002).

9. N.C. Standards of Professional Conduct for Mediators, Standard VIII(B) (2001).

10. Ala. Code of Ethics for Mediators, Standard 3(b) (2010).

11. Ore. Mediation Association: Standards of Practice, Standard VI (2000).

12. See Va. Standards, supra note 8 (mandating that "if, in the mediator's judgment, the integrity of the process has been compromised by . . . gross unfairness resulting from nondisclosure or fraud by a participant, the mediator shall inform the parties. The mediator shall discontinue the

mediation in such circumstances, but shall not violate the obligation of
confidentiality").

13. Beatrice guided Dante from Purgatory to Heaven in his epic poem,
    The Divine Comedy.

14. Restatement (Second) of Torts, supra note 5, at sec. 538.

15. Id. at sec. 551(2); see also Krawiec & Zeiler, supra note 6, at 1795.

16. In the language of the restatement, the question is whether "the
    relationships between them, the customs of the trade or other objective
    circumstances" would create a reasonable expectation of disclosure. See
    Restatement (Second) of Torts, supra note 5, at sec. 551(2).

17. See Mitchell v. Slocum, 7 Ohio Misc. 2d 33, 455 N.E.2d 20 (Ohio Mun.,
    1981); Miles v. McSwegin, 58 Ohio St. 2d 97, 388 N.E.2d 1367, 1369 12 O.O.
    3d 108 (1979).

18. Spaulding v. Zimmerman, 116 N.W.2d 704 (Minn. 1962); Virzi v. Grand
    Trunk Warehouse and Cold Storage Co., 571 F. Supp. 507 (D.C. Mich.
    1983) (overturning a settlement due to attorney's failure to disclose death of
    plaintiff in personal injury action). See also Kentucky Bar Ass'n v. Geisler,
    938 S.W.2d 578 (Ky. 1997) (reprimanding an attorney for negotiating set-
    tlement while failing to disclose death of client).

19. Hamilton v. Harper, 404 S.E.2d 540 (W. Va. 1991).

20. See Nash v. Trustees of Boston Univ., 776 F. Supp. 73 (D.R.I. 1990).

21. See Mohr v. Commonwealth, 421 Mass. 147, 653 N.E.2d 1104 (Mass. 1995).

22. See Fire Insurance Exchange v. Bell, 643 N.E.2d 310 (Ind. 1994). See also In
    re McGrath, 468 N.Y.S.2d 349 (N.Y. App. Div. 1983) (suspending an attor-
    ney from practice for failure to disclose the existence of additional insurance
    source).

23. Two formal ethics opinions authored by the ABA Standing Committee on
    Ethics and Professional Responsibility suggest the acceptable boundaries
    of attorney obfuscation. In Formal Opinion 93–370 (1993), devoted to an
    attorney's obligations in communicating with a judge in settlement nego-
    tiations, the committee noted that "while a certain amount of posturing or
    puffery in settlement negotiations may be an acceptable convention between
    opposing counsel, a party's actual bottom line or the settlement author-
    ity given to a lawyer is a material fact." That committee went on to suggest
    that an attorney should simply decline to answer pointed judicial inquiries
    rather than lie or misrepresent. In another opinion devoted to truthfulness
    in negotiations between attorneys, the committee reiterated this language,
    but clarified that "statements regarding negotiating goals or willingness to
    compromise ... ordinarily are not considered statements of material fact

within the meaning of the Rules." See Formal Opinion 06–439 (2006). It is notable that the former opinion does not directly address or elaborate on an attorney's treatment of settlement authority or bottom line in the context of mediation, or direct lawyer-to-lawyer negotiations, and that Formal Opinion 93–370's characterization of settlement authority and a client's bottom line as material fact took place in the context of judicially facilitated negotiations, where obligations of candor to the tribunal are in play.

24. See, e.g., G. Wetlaufer, *The Ethics of Lying in Negotiation,* 75 Iowa L. Rev. 1219 (1990); C. Menkel-Meadow, *Ethics, Morality and Professional Responsibility in Negotiation*, in Dispute Resolution Ethics: A Comprehensive Guide 119, 137–138 (P. Bernard & B. Garth eds. 2002); Peters, supra note 1, at 119; Hinshaw & Alberts, supra note 2.

25. This fact pattern is loosely based on the role-play *Saving the Last Dance,* produced in both textual and videotape form by the Center for Understanding in Conflict/Center for Mediation in Law and the President and Fellows of Harvard College, and reprinted in Folberg, Golann, et al. at B-277. Excerpts for viewing are available at www.understandinginconflict.org.

Chapter Nine

1. See Model Standards of Conduct for Mediators, Standard V(B) (2005) (stating that "a mediator who meets with any persons in private session during a mediation shall not convey directly or indirectly to any other person, any information that was obtained during that private session without the consent of the disclosing person").

2. See Standards of Conduct for New York State Community Dispute Resolution Center Mediators, Standard V (2005); State Bar of Texas, Alternative Dispute Resolution Section, Ethical Guidelines for Mediators sec. 8, Comment (c) (2005); Florida Rules for Certified and Court-Appointed Mediators, Rule 10.360(b) (1998); Rules Adopted by the Supreme Court of Kansas, Court Rules Relating to Mediation, Rule 903(e) (Comment) (2010) (stating that "if the mediator holds private sessions with a party, the nature of these sessions with regard to confidentiality should be discussed prior to undertaking such sessions").

3. Those states are Washington, D.C., Idaho, Illinois, Iowa, Nebraska, New Jersey, Ohio, South Dakota, Utah, Vermont, and Washington (introduced in Hawaii, Massachusetts, New York). See www.nccusl.org /update/uniformact_factsheets/uniformacts-fs-uma2001.asp.

4. See Uniform Mediation Act sec. 4 (2001).

5. See id. at sec. 6.

6. See S. R. Cole et al., Mediation: Law, Policy and Practice, sec. 9:12, chart in app. A (2nd ed. 2001) (describing a variety of state legislation conferring confidentiality protection on public and, in some instances, privately administered programs).

7. Alabama Civ. Ct. Mediation Rules, Rule 11 (1998); Cal. Rules of Court, Rule 3.854 (2010); Cal. Evid. Code sec. 1120, 1126. (2010); see also Mass. Gen. L. CH. 233 sec. 23C (2010).

8. Compare, for example, Fla. Stat. Ann. sec. 44 1011, 44 102 (2010) (privileging communications made during court-connected mediation, except for communications made in furtherance of a crime or fraud, information necessary for prosecution for criminal conduct, or in subsequent disciplinary procedure brought against a mediator), with Conn. Gen. Stat. sec. 52–235d (2010) (allowing disclosure in the following four circumstances: parties agree in writing; disclosure is necessary to enforce written agreement; disclosure is required by statute, regulation, or court; disclosure is required as a result of circumstances in which a court finds that the interest of justice outweighs the need for confidentiality).

9. See E. Deason, *The Need for Trust as a Justification for Confidentiality in Mediation: A Cross-Disciplinary Approach*, 54 U. Kan. L. Rev. 1387 (2006) (discussing the importance of trust in facilitating information sharing in the face of risk).

10. In re Marriage of Kieturakis, 138 Cal. App. 4th 56, at 68 (1st App. Dist. 2006).

11. See Cole et al., supra note 6, at sec. 8, app. A (listing state statutes conferring confidentiality protections on mediation proceedings in various contexts to varying degrees). See also Administrative Alternative Dispute Resolution Act of 1996, 5 U.S.C.A. 574(a) (4)(c) (stating that a dispute resolution neutral will not be compelled to disclose dispute resolution communication unless a court determines such disclosure is necessary to "prevent harm to the public health or safety").

12. See, e.g., Ore. Rev. Stat. sec. 36220(6) (2010) and Va. Code Ann. sec. 8.01–581.22 (2010) (providing confidentiality exceptions but removing confidentiality protections when "communications are intentionally used to plan, attempt to commit, or commit a crime or conceal an ongoing crime"); Kan. Stat. Ann. sec. 5–512(b)(3) (2010) (stating that confidentiality and privilege protections do not apply to "any information that is reasonably necessary to stop the commission of an ongoing crime or fraud or to prevent the commission of a crime or fraud in the future"). See Idaho

Evidence Rule 507(4)(D) (2010) (stating that there is no confidentiality privilege for mediation communication that is "intentionally used to plan a crime, attempt to commit or commit a crime").

13. See N.D. S. Ct. Rules of Court, app. A to Rule 8.7, Standards of Prof. Conduct, Rule IV, Confidentiality (2010) ("The mediator shall disclose a participant's threat of suicide or violence against any person to the threatened person and the appropriate authorities"). See also Ida. Evid. Rule 507(4)(D) (2010) (stating that there is no protection for communication that is "a threat or statement of a plan to inflict bodily injury or commit a crime of violence"); Va. Code Ann., supra note 12, at sec. 8.01–576.10 (stating that there is no confidentiality protection "where a threat to inflict bodily injury is made"); Me. R. Civ. P. 16B(k) (2010) (stating that "a neutral does not breach confidentiality by making such a disclosure if the disclosure is . . . necessary . . . to avoid subjecting others to the risk of imminent physical harm"); Arizona 12–2238(4)(D) (2010) ("threatened or actual violence that occurs during a mediation is not a privileged communication"); Kan. Stat. Ann. 5–512(b)(5) (2010) (exempting from confidentiality protection "any report to the court that a party has issued a threat of physical violence against a party, a party's dependent or family member, . . . [or] the mediator"); N.C. Rules of Court, Standards of Professional Conduct for Mediators, Standard III(C)(2) (2010) (removing confidentiality protection where "a party to the mediation has communicated to the mediator a threat of serious bodily harm or death to be inflicted on any person, and the mediator has reason to believe the party has the intent and ability to act on the threat").

14. See Ore. Rev. Stat. sec. 36.220(6) (2010); N.C. Rules of Court, Standards of Professional Conduct for Mediators, Standard III(C)(2)(ii) (2010) (stating that there is no confidentiality protection where "a party to the mediation has communicated to the mediator a threat of significant damage to real or personal property and the mediator has reason to believe the party has the intent and ability to act on the threat").

15. Uniform Mediation supra note 4, at sec. 6(a)(3),(4).

16. See D.C. Code sec. 16–4206 (2010) (stating that "a mediator may disclose . . . [a] mediation communication evidencing abuse, neglect, abandonment, or exploitation of an individual to a public agency responsible for protecting individuals against such mistreatment"). See also Me. R. Ev. 514 (e)(2)-(6) (2010). See also Fla. Stat. 44.405 4(a)(3) (2010); Indiana Rules of Court, Alternative Dispute Resolution 2.7(E), Rule 2.11 (2009) (requiring the mediator to preserve mediation confidentiality except when reporting

previously unreported child abuse); Texas Civ. Prac. and Rem. Code Ann. 154.073(f) (2010).

17. Uniform Mediation Act, supra note 15, at sec. 6(a)(7).

18. Even in the sacred space of attorney-client relations, the Model Rule of Professional Conduct for attorneys states that attorneys may disclose client confidences in order to prevent serious physical or financial harm to others. See American Bar Association, Model Rules of Professional Conduct, Rule 1.6 (2005).

19. See Idaho R. Evid. Rule 507(4)(D) (2010); New Jersey Rules of Court R. 1:40–4(d) (2010) (mandating mediators disclose to proper authority information obtained at mediation session if . . . "mediator has reasonable belief disclosure will prevent commission of illegal act likely to result in death or serious bodily harm"); North Carolina Standards of Professional Conduct for Mediators Standard 3(C)(2)(i) (2010) (excepting from nondisclosure requirement threat of serious bodily harm).

20. See Me. R. Civ. P. 16B(k)(3) (2010). See Illinois Fifteenth Judicial Circuit Court Rule 9A.7, Mediation of Child Custody or Visitation (2010) (prohibiting disclosure of information gained from parties in mediation, except "where there is a clear danger of imminent harm to a child or to a party").

21. See, e.g., Maryland Rule 17–109 (2010); Oklahoma Stat. Ann. Tit. 12, sec. 1805(F) (2003); Minn. State 595.02 (2010) (no privilege for complaints against mediators); Ga. Mediation Rule VII(b) (2010); Ark. Rev. Stat. sec. 12–2238(b)(2) (2010); Va. Code Ann., supra note 12, at sec. 8.01–576.10 (2010).

22. See Va. Code Ann., supra note 2, at 8.01–581.22 (2010) (no privilege where mediation communication is sought in action between mediator or mediation program and a party to the mediation for damages arising out of mediation).

23. Uniform Mediation Act, supra note 15, at sec. 6(a)(5),(6).

24. La. Rev. Stat. sec. 9:4112(A),(B)(1)(c) (2010). Conn. Gen. Stat. Ann., supra note 8, at 52–235d (allowing disclosure of mediation information where "disclosure is required as a result of circumstances in which a court finds that the interest of justice outweighs the need for confidentiality").

25. Maryland allows testimony regarding statements in mediation if claims are being made that a mediation contract should be rescinded due to fraud, duress, or misrepresentation. New Hampshire's rules allow testimony in divorce mediation when "a party is alleged to have made . . . a material misstatement of fact, which would have constituted perjury if made under oath." N.H. Rev. State Ann. 328-C-9 (2010). North Dakota excludes from

protection evidence that relates to either a crime or a civil fraud or where the validity of the mediated agreement is in issue. North Dakota Century Code 31–04–11 (2010).

26. Uniform Mediation Act, supra note 15, at sec. 6(b).

27. Id. at sec. 6(c) (2001).

28. See Model Standards, supra note 1, at Standard V(A)(1) ("If the parties to a mediation agree that the mediator may disclose information obtained during the mediation, the mediator may do so"). See also id., Standard V(D) ("Depending on the circumstance of a mediation, the parties may have varying expectations regarding confidentiality that a mediator should address. The parties may make their own rules with respect to confidentiality, or the accepted practice of an individual mediator or institution may dictate a particular set of expectations").

29. See Va. Code Ann., supra note 12, at sec. 8.01–576.10; Ariz. Rev. Stat. sec. 12–2238(b)(2) (2010).

30. Uniform Mediation Act, supra note 4, at sec. 6(a)(5).

31. See D. Ak. LR sec. 16.2(f)(5)(B) (2010); La. R.S. sec. 9:4112(B)(1)(c) (2010).

32. Md. Rule sec. 17–109(d).

33. See D. Ak. LR sec. 16.2(f)(5)(B) (2010); La. R.S. sec. 9:4112(B)(1)(c) (2010); Md. Rule sec. 17–109(d) (2010); Kan. Stat. Ann. sec. 5–512(b)(e) (2010).

34. See Valchine v. Valchine, 923 So. 2d 511, Fla. App. 4 Dist. (2006); Durham v. Durham 2004 WL 579224 (Tex. App. 2004); Chitkara v. N.Y. Tel. Co., 2002 WL 31005729 (2nd Cir., 2002); Zimmerman v. Zimmerman, 04–04–00347-CV, 2005 WL 1812613 (Tex. App. 2005).

35. See Guthrie v. Guthrie, 594 S.E. 2d 356 (Ga. 2004).

36. Model Standards, supra note 1, at Standard I(A): "A mediator shall conduct a mediation based on the principle of party self-determination. Self-determination is the act of coming to a voluntary, uncoerced decision in which each party makes free and informed choices as to process and outcome. Parties may exercise self-determination at any stage of a mediation, including mediator selection, process design, participation in or withdrawal from the process, and outcomes." Similarly, the ADR Institute of Canada Model Code of Conduct for Mediators states in section III(1) (2005): "Self-determination is the right of parties in a Mediation to make their own voluntary and non-coerced decisions regarding the possible resolution of any issue in dispute. It is a fundamental principle of Mediation which every Mediator shall respect and encourage."

37. From Model Standards, supra note 1, at Preamble: "Mediation is a process in which an impartial third party facilitates communication and negotiation and promotes voluntary decision making by the parties to the dispute."

38. Id. at Standard VI(A)(5): "The role of a mediator differs substantially from other professional roles. Mixing the role of a mediator and the role of another profession is problematic and thus, a mediator should distinguish between the roles. A mediator may provide information that the mediator is qualified by training or experience to provide, only if the mediator can do so consistent with these Standards."

39. From Uniform Mediation Act, supra note 4, at Comments on sec. 2(1). "Mediation": "The emphasis on negotiation in this definition is intended to exclude adjudicative processes, such as arbitration and fact-finding."

40. See also the ADR Institute of Canada Model Code, supra note 36, at sec. VI(3): "If the Mediator holds private sessions (breakout meetings, caucuses) with a party, he or she shall discuss the nature of such sessions with all parties prior to commencing such sessions. In particular, the Mediator shall inform parties of any limits to confidentiality applicable to information disclosed during private sessions."

41. Id. at sec. V(3) states: "The Mediator's commitment is to the parties and the process and he or she shall not allow pressure or influence from third parties (including, without limitation, persons, service providers, Mediation facilities, organizations, or agencies) to compromise the independence of the Mediator."

42. For example, Model Standards, supra note 1, at Standards VI(B) and VI(A)(9), state that if a mediator is made aware of domestic abuse or violence among the parties or a mediation is being used to further criminal conduct, the "mediator shall take appropriate steps including, if necessary, postponing, withdrawing from or terminating the mediation."

43. Requiring neutrals to make such decisions on their own may subject them to undue pressure, grievances, or potential liability and makes impossible the principled weighing process contemplated by laws like the UMA and Administrative Dispute Resolution Act for tough calls. Mediators, especially those who are not lawyers, may be less qualified than judges to decide, under applicable legal mandates, how to weigh arguably conflicting duties that may affect confidential treatment of communications.

44. These recently revised Standards, first adopted in 1994 by the American Arbitration Association, the Section of Dispute Resolution of the American Bar Association, and the Society of Professionals in Dispute Resolution (now the Association for Conflict Resolution), address the mediator's duties regarding issues like party self-determination, neutrality, bias, and confidentiality. See http://moritzlaw.osu.edu/dr/msoc/pdf/sep_draft.pdf. Other ethical standards include CPR-Georgetown Commission on

Ethics and Standards in ADR, Model Rule for the Lawyer as Third-Party Neutral (2002), and JAMS Mediators Ethics Guidelines (2003) (www.jamsadr.com/mediation/ethics.asp).

45. Expectations as to what disclosure may be reasonable may also be influenced by other specific factors: the practices and procedures of a mediator or mediation program; specific ethical, disclosure, or record-keeping duties imposed specifically on a mediator (for example, a government employee); what participants agree to in advance (for example, in an agreement to mediate); and even the ability of a mediator to communicate effectively to the parties his confidentiality duties and practice.

46. The CPR-Georgetown Commission on Ethics and Standards in ADR contains this language, as do the Model Rules of Professional Conduct for attorneys, which provide guidance to attorneys generally. The National Standards for Court-Connected Mediation Programs also authorize mediator disclosure of information that "reveals a danger of serious physical harm either to a party or to a third party."

47. Model Standards, supra note 1, at Standard VI addresses the "Quality of the Process" and counsels that the mediator should conduct a mediation in a manner that promotes "diligence, timeliness, [and] and safety." It also states that the mediator should promote honesty and candor between and among all participants. Some—though probably I [C.P.]—might interpret this vague language as a general injunction to keep both the safety of the parties and the general public in mind and as justification for ensuring that the threat of toxic contamination associated with the land deal is addressed.

48. The Administrative Dispute Resolution Act contains other protections. If the disclosure involves information that is required by statute to be made public, the act requires anyone seeking confidential information to try initially to obtain it from parties or other sources before looking to the neutral. Neutrals who are requested to disclose protected documents must make an effort to notify the parties of a demand for disclosure, and a party that does not offer to defend a neutral's refusal to disclose is considered to have waived any objection.

Chapter Ten

1. American Bar Association, Model Rules of Professional Conduct, Rule 8.3(c).

2. See Attorney U v. Mississippi Bar 678 So. 2d 963, 972 (Miss. 1996) (the "supporting evidence must be such that a reasonable lawyer under the circumstances would have formed a firm opinion that the conduct in question had more likely than not occurred"); Skolnick v. Altheimer and Gray 760

N.E.2d 4, 15 (Ill. 2000) (reporting required where "lawyer could reason-ably infer from the circumstances . . . that the reportable misconduct had occurred." See Douglas R. Richmond, *Professional Responsibilities of Law Firm Associates,* 45 Brandeis L J 199 (2007).

3. See Pennisi v. Grievance Comm. for the Second and Eleventh Judicial Dis-tricts, 559 N.Y.S.2d 365 (1990); In re Patrick Leiz, 728 So. 2d 835 (1999). See L. Gatland, *The Himmel Effect: "Snitch Rule" Remains Controversial but Effective, Especially in Illinois,* 83 A.B.A.J. 24 (1997). Rule 8.3 and its state corollaries also stipulate that reporting should take place only if it does not violate client confidentiality. If reporting would violate the attorney-client privilege, the requirement is waived.

4. See In re James H. Himmel, 125 Ill. 2d 531, 533 N.E.2d 790 (Ill. 1988).

5. Not every state professional responsibility code has a reporting require-ment. California's version does not. Georgia's version of rule 8.3 substitutes "should" for "shall," and Michigan's rule includes no-disclosure exceptions for attorneys working in a broad range of attorney assistance programs.

6. Of course, in this situation, other exceptions to mediator confidentiality would be called into play, including exceptions where mediation communi-cations reveal a past or future crime and disclosure is necessary to prevent future harm. See Chapter Nine, this volume.

7. See Kan. Stat. Ann. sec.38–2223(a)(2); La. Child Code Ann. art. 609(B) (2004); Va. Code Ann. sec. 63.2–1509(A)(10) (2002); Wis. Stat. 48.981(2)(c)(d) (2005). See generally Art Hinshaw, *Mediators as Mandatory Reporters of Child Abuse: Preserving Mediation's Core Values,* 34 Fla. St. U.L. Rev. 211 (2007).

8. See Hinshaw, supra note 7, at n. 120–122.

9. See id. See also Michael Moffitt, *Ten Ways to Get Sued: A Guide for Media-tors,* 8 Harv. Negotiation L. Rev. 81 (2003).

10. American Bar Association, Model Standards of Practice for Family and Divorce Mediation, Standard VIII (hereinafter "Divorce Mediation Stan-dards") (2000), www.afccnet.org/pdfs/modelstandards.pdf. Divorce Medi-ation Standards give suggestions for how mediators should help parents best use mediation to promote the best interests of children, from suggest-ing that the mediator refer parents to a specialist in child development to help children cope with the consequences of family reorganization to dis-cussing the level of detail that should be in parenting plans. Id. at Standard VIII(A)(1)-(5).

11. Model Standards of Conduct for Mediators, Standard VI(A)(4) (2005) ("A mediator should promote honesty and candor between and among all par-ticipants, and a mediator shall not knowingly misrepresent any material fact or circumstance in the course of a mediation").

12. Compelling circumstances are those situations where the personal safety of the child, or the accusing party, or the mediator is at risk. R. J. Racusin & J. K. Felsman, *Reporting Child Abuse: The Ethical Obligation to Inform Parents,* 25 J. Am. Acad. Child Psychiatry 485, 486 (1986); A. Taylor, The Handbook of Family Dispute Resolution 203 (2002). In this hypothetical, I (A.H.) am presuming there are no compelling circumstances, and the following suggestions for terminating the mediation are geared to keeping the situation under control.

13. See M. Moffit, *Ten Ways to Get Sued: A Guide for Mediators,* 8 Harv. Negot. L. Rev. 81, 113–116 (2003) (discussing mediator liability for maintaining confidentiality improperly).

14. I (A.H.) specifically used the term *suggestion* as it is not a technical term. For a layperson, it acts as a reasonable synonym for the reporting standard embodied in the reporting statute.

15. Divorce Mediation Standards, supra note 10.

16. Id. at Standard VII(B).

17. Model Standards of Conduct for Mediators (2005), see Appendix of this book.

18. Id. at Standard V(C).

19. See, e.g., Model Standards, Standard V(A): "A mediator shall maintain the confidentiality of all information obtained by the mediator in mediation, unless otherwise agreed to by the parties or required by applicable law." See also Divorce Mediation Standards, supra note 10, at Standard VII: "A family mediator shall maintain the confidentiality of all information acquired in the mediation process, unless the mediator is permitted or required to reveal the information by law or agreement of the participants."

20. National Conference of Commissioners on Uniform State Laws, Uniform Mediation Act, Prefatory Note (2001).

21. See Divorce Mediation Standards, supra note 10, at Standard IV(I): "A family mediator should withdraw … if the mediator believes the mediator's impartiality has been compromised or a conflict of interest has been identified and has not been waived by the participants."

22. G. Firestone, *Empowering Parents in Child Protection Mediation: Challenges and Opportunities,* 47 Family Court Rev. 98–115 (2009).

23. G. Firestone & J. Weinstein, *In the Best Interest of Children: A Proposal to Transform the Adversary System,* 42 Family Court Rev. 203–215 (2004).

24. See Uniform Mediation Act, supra note 20, at sec. 6.

25. Although parties may be required to give testimony in a "proceeding to prove a claim to rescind or reform or a defense to avoid liability on a contract arising out of the mediation" or to prove or disprove professional misconduct or malpractice that occurred during mediation, the mediator is

protected under the UMA from such compulsory disclosures. See Uniform Mediation Act, supra note 20, at sec. 6.

26. Florida F.S. 44.401–406.
27. Id. at 44.405(4)(a).

Chapter Eleven

1. See Model Standards of Conduct for Mediators, Standard III(E) (2005) (stating that if a mediator's conflict of interest might reasonably be viewed as undermining the integrity of the mediation, a mediator shall withdraw from or decline to proceed with the mediation regardless of the expressed desire or agreement of the parties to the contrary). See Fla. Rules for Certified and Court Mediators 10.340 ("After appropriate disclosure, the mediator may serve if all parties agree. However, if a conflict of interest clearly impairs a mediator's impartiality, the mediator shall withdraw regardless of the express agreement of the parties"). See Ala. Rules of Court, Standard Code of Ethics for Mediators, Standard 5(b)(6) (2010) (requiring that, regardless of disclosure and party consent, the mediator must withdraw if an existing conflict of interest compromises the mediator's ability to remain impartial); Ga. Ethical Standards for Neutrals app. C., ch. 1, III(e) (2010).

2. See Uniform Mediation Act sec. 9 (2001) ("Before accepting a mediation, an individual who is requested to serve as a mediator shall:

    1. "make an inquiry that is reasonable under the circumstances to determine whether there are any known facts that a reasonable individual would consider likely to affect the impartiality of the mediator, including a financial or personal interest in the outcome of the mediation and an existing or past relationship with a mediation party or foreseeable participant in the mediation; and"

    2. "disclose any such known fact to the mediation parties as soon as is practical before accepting a mediation").

3. See generally M. D. Gaines, Notes & Comment, *A Proposed Conflict of Interest Rule for Attorney-Mediators*, 73 Wash. L. Rev. 699 (1998).
4. See Model Standards, Standards V and II.
5. Model Standards, Standard III(A).
6. Poly Software Int'l, Inc. v. Su, 880 F. Supp. 1487 (D. Utah 1995).
7. See the analogues for Model Rule 1.12 in the following states: California, Georgia, Hawaii, Michigan, Tennessee, Texas, Virginia, and West Virginia. See also American Legal Ethics Library, *Topical Overview—Index of Narratives,* www.law.cornell.edu/ethics/comparative/index.htm#1.12. Similarly,

while certain jurisdictions and provider forums have adopted the Model Standards or variations of them, others have not.

8. See, e.g., McKenzie Construction v. St. Croix Storage Corp., 961 F. Supp. 857 (D.V.I. 1997) (disqualifying an attorney who joined the firm after she was the mediator in the identical action, and attorney's disqualification was imputed to the firm); Poly Software International, Inc. v. Su, 880 F. Supp. 1487 (D. Utah 1995) (disqualifying an attorney who was a mediator in a previous substantially related action because he failed to obtain consent of the original parties to the mediation); Cho v. Superior Court, 39 Cal. App. 4th 113, 45 Cal. Rptr. 2d 863 (1995) (disqualifying a former judge who participated personally and substantially from representing anyone afterward in the same matter because the judge was like a mediator and retained confidential information).

9. Model Standards, supra note 1, at Standard III(B).

10. Id. at Standard II(C).

11. Id. at Standard VI(A)(10).

12. I (S.N.E.) have researched general civil mediator standards of conduct that are available within all fifty states. Some states have court-connected standards. Some have standards promulgated by professional mediation organizations, and some states have both. In all, I have examined almost fifty different sets of standards, and all have some requirement of mediator impartiality.

13. Model Standards, supra note 1, at Standard II(A)(B); see Appendix of this book. See Va. Standards of Ethics and Professional Responsibility for Certified Mediators (G)(1) (2010).

14. Model Standards, supra note 1, at Standard II(B)(1); see Appendix of this book.

15. K. K. Kovach, Mediation Principles and Practice 151 (3rd ed. 2001) (noting that "mediation is about the disputants—not the mediator").

16. See id. at 65.

17. S. N. Exon, *How Can a Mediator Be Both Impartial and Fair? Why Ethical Standards of Conduct Create Chaos for Mediators,* 2006 J. Disp. Resol. 387 (2006). Appendix A of the article charts mediation standards of conduct in all fifty states. Standards within the following states require or encourage the mediator to ensure some type of fair result: Georgia, Illinois, Indiana, Massachusetts, Pennsylvania, and West Virginia.

Chapter Twelve

1. M. Arnold, "Culture and Anarchy" and Other Writings (S. Collin ed. 1993).

2. Id. at 79.

3. C. Levi-Strauss, Structural Anthropology (C. Jacobson & B. G. Schoepf trans. 1967).

4. See G. Hofstede, Cultures and Organizations: Software of the Mind: Intercultural Cooperation and Its Importance for Survival 4 (1991).

5. UNESCO, Mexico City, Declaration on Cultural Policies, World Conference on Cultural Policies 1 (July 26, 1982–Aug. 6, 1982), available at http:/portal.unesco/culture/en/files/12762/11295421661mexico-en.pdf.

6. See generally Hofstede, supra note 4.

7. See W. L. Adair & J. M. Brett, *Culture and Negotiation Processes,* in The Handbook of Negotiation and Culture 158, 159 (M. J. Gelfand & J. M. Brett eds. 2004).

8. See F. Trompenaars and C. Hampden-Turner, Riding the Waves of Culture: Understanding Diversity in Global Business 35–39 (2nd ed. 1998).

9. Hofstede, supra note 4, at 23–28.

10. See E. T. Hall, Beyond Culture, 105–128 (1976).

11. Hofstede, supra note 4, at 121–122.

12. Id. at 109, 110, 120–122.

13. See H. Abramson, *Crossing Borders into New Ethical Territory: Ethical Challenges When Mediating Cross-Culturally*, 49 S. Texas L. Rev. 921 (2008).

14. D. B. Syme, The Jewish Home: A Guide for Jewish Living 95–97 (1988); A. L. Goldman, Being Jewish: The Spiritual and Cultural Practice of Judaism Today 84–85 (2000).

15. See A. M. Shulman & T. Yoseloff, Gateway to Judaism: Encyclopedia Home Reference 449–452 (1971).

16. In a number of jurisdictions, civil law has sought to alleviate this power imbalance. In New York, for example, domestic relations law precludes the granting of a civil divorce unless the recalcitrant spouse agrees to remove all religious barriers to the remarriage of the other spouse. See N.Y. Dom. Rel. Law, sec. 253 (2010).

17. See generally J. J. Nasir, The Islamic Law of Personal Status (2nd ed. 1990).

18. I (C.M.-M.) have taken a course in Islamic law, given by an expert in Shari'a family law, so I know what I do not know.

19. Let me (H.A.) orient this discussion by placing it into the broader context of bridging cultural differences in mediations. Mediators more typically face cultural conflicts between the disputing parties or their representatives, and they employ various approaches to help participants bridge any cultural gaps. See, e.g., H. I. Abramson, *Mediation Representation: Advocating in a Problem-Solving Process* 173–181 (2004) (Five Steps: Develop Cultural Framework, Understand Own Culture, Learn Other Culture, Be Open Minded, and Bridge Gap). In this commentary, the five steps are reduced

to three (know your own culture, learn the other culture, and bridge the gap), with a fourth new step added on assessing whether to withdraw. In contrast with a mediation that fails due to an impasse between the parties and the parties terminating the mediation, the conflict here is between the mediator and the parties, and the mediator is weighing whether to withdraw.

20. For example, see New York cases that held agreements void when the husband withheld permission for a Jewish divorce (withheld giving a *get*) in order to extort unduly favorable terms. L. Zornberg, *Beyond the Constitution: Is the New York* Get *Legislation Good Law,* 15 Pace L. Rev. 703, 726–727 (1995); and see generally N. A. Welsh, *The Thinning Vision of Self-Determination in Court-Connected Mediation: The Inevitable Price of Institutionalization?* 6 Harv. Negot. L. Rev. 1, 59–78 (2001) (summarizes legal approaches for overturning settlement agreements).

21. It is worth noting that the Standards adopted by the Association of Family and Conciliation Courts for divorce cases back away from the "pure process" model, exhorting mediators instead to assess the fairness of the mediated agreement. Standard XI of the Model Standards of Practice for Family and Divorce Mediation (2001) requires mediators to "consider suspending or terminating the mediation when the mediator "reasonably believes" the agreement to be "unconscionable" or when parties are using the mediation to "further illegal conduct" or to "gain an unfair advantage."

22. These two examples are described in B. A. Venkatraman, *Islamic States and the United Nations Convention on the Elimination of All Forms of Discrimination Against Women: Are the Shari'a and the Convention Compatible?* 44 Am. U. L. Rev. 1949, 2000–2007 (1995).

23. This report was prepared to guide interpretations of the Convention on the Elimination of All Forms of Discrimination Against Women.

24. Also see, e.g., J. R. Wegner, *The Status of Women in Jewish and Islamic Marriage and Divorce Law,* 5 Harv. Women's L.J. 1, 20–23 (1982) (because the husband pays a marriage gift called the *mahr* to the bride as well as maintenance including food, clothing, and shelter for the duration of the marriage and for a period of time after any divorce, the wife cannot divorce the husband without the husband's permission).

25. K. Sorrell, *Cultural Pluralism and International Rights,* 10 Tulsa J. Comp. & Intl L. 369, 410 (2003).

26. Although the law was designed to address the exploitive withholding of the *get* by husbands in Jewish divorces, the legislation was drafted neutrally so that it would apply in a similar situation to other religions. N.Y. Dom. Rel. Law sec. 236(5)(h) (Consol. 2007). Even though this law is constitutionally suspect and controversial, it seems to have been effective in reducing the

unequal bargaining positions of the parties. Zornberg, supra note 20, at 756–763.

27. I (H.A.) realized that I needed more information before I could research the parties' BATNAs. It would have been helpful to know the name of the parties' local community and the mosque of the mullah because I learned that Islamic religious dispute resolution is not yet well developed in the United States. It seems that the current processes rely heavily on private conciliation and decision making by local mullahs and imams of each mosque, although a more formal private arbitration process, shaped by diverse religious and secular views, is emerging, especially in Canada. See C. L. Wolfe, *Note: Faith-Based Arbitration: Friend or Foe? An Evaluation of Religious Arbitration Systems and Their Interaction with Secular Courts,* 75 Fordham L. Rev. 427, 440, 459–465 (2006); N. Pengelley, *Faith-Based Arbitration in Ontario,* 9 Vindobona J. Int'l. Com. Law & Arb. 111 (2005); A. W. Sheikh Osman, *Islamic Arbitration Courts in America and Canada* (2005), www.hiiraan.com/op/eng/2005/dec/Prof_Abdulwahid 211205.htm.

28. One non-ADR colleague, Fabio Arcila, with a deep commitment to human rights, asked: "Is there ever an occasion when the culture is so foreign to you that you will not be able to achieve sufficient cultural competence and therefore should decline the appointment?" Clearly, the standard practice of mediators is to decline appointments for which they lack competence. This inquiry raised the prospect that some cultures may be so foreign that even diligent research will be insufficient. That is an interesting possibility for further study.

Chapter Thirteen

1. The report, Mandated Participation and Settlement Coercion: Dispute Resolution as It Relates to the Courts (1991), considered the effect that burgeoning mediation programs were having on individuals' experience with and access to the courts.
2. See CPR-Georgetown Principles, Preamble (2002).
3. See National Standards for Court-Connected Mediation Programs, Introduction (1999), http://courtadr.org/files/NationalStandardsADR.pdf.
4. See Principles, supra note 2, at Preamble (explaining the Principles' goal of "establishing a benchmark for responsible practice" and contributing to the ADR field's commitment to "self-regulation and high standards of practice").
5. See id. at Definition, Comment (stating that the definition intends to cover all private and public entities, including roster creation, referral to neutrals, administration and management of processes, and similar activities).

6. See id. at Principle V, Comment ("At issue is the potential for actual or perceived conflicts of interest involving ADR participants [such as businesses, public institutions, and law firms] that have continuing professional, business or other relationships with the ADR Provider Organization. For example, an ADR Provider Organization may be under contract to an institutional party to provide a volume of ADR services; or a law firm may regularly choose a particular ADR Provider Organization by contract or de facto business relationship. Under this Principle, disclosure of such relationships between the Organization and repeat player parties or other repeat players to the other parties to the dispute would be required").

7. The National Standards, supra note 3, at Standard 8.1(b), discuss individual mediators' duty to disclose "circumstances that may create or give the appearance of a conflict of interest" but do not address the possibility that the ADR provider organization as a whole may be embroiled in relationships that call the neutrality of its operating procedures or those of its individual mediators into doubt.

8. See id., at Standard 3.2.

9. See CPR-Georgetown Principles, supra note 2, at Principle IV, Accessibility of Services.

10. See id. at Principle IV, Comment.

11. See National Standards, supra note 3, at Standard 1.0, Commentary ("Specifically, courts should not make mediation available based on whether the parties are able to pay, whether they are represented, whether they have a particular physical disability or might have difficulty speaking or understanding English").

12. Interestingly, the Principles allow providers to absolve themselves of responsibility for the quality of the service offered if a "clear and prominent disclaimer" is offered. See CPR-Georgetown Principles, supra note 2, at Principle I, Quality and Competence of Services.

13. National Standards, supra note 3, at Standard 2.1.

14. See CPR-Georgetown Principles, supra note 2, at Principle 1, Comment, Quality and Competence of Service, fn. 15 (citing Ensuring Competence and Quality in Dispute Resolution Practice, Report No. 2 of the SPIDR Commission on Qualifications [April 1995]).

15. See id. at Principle 1, Quality and Competence, Comment.

16. See id.

17. See National Standards, supra note 3, at Standard 6.1, Qualifications of Mediators, Comment (other skills include: "Ability to earn trust and maintain acceptability; . . . Ability to screen out non-mediable issues; . . . Ability

to help parties to invent creative options; . . . Ability to help the parties identify principles and criteria that will guide their decision making; . . . Ability to help parties make their own informed choices; and . . . Ability to help parties assess whether their agreement can be implemented").

18. See id. at Standard 6.1, Commentary.
19. See CPR-Georgetown Principles, supra note 2, at Principle III, Fairness and Impartiality, Comment.
20. See id.
21. See National Standards, supra note 3, at Standard 1.4, Comment.
22. See id. at Standard 4.0, Selection of Cases and Timing of Referral, Comment.
23. See id. at Standard 4.2.
24. See id. at Standard 5.1, Mandatory Attendance.
25. See id. at Standard 11.1 (suggesting courts adopt special procedures, including liberal opt-out provisions, for particular parties, including those who have suffered physical or psychological victimization).
26. See id. at Standard 11.0–11.2, Inappropriate Pressure to Settle.
27. See id. at Standard 6.5 ("Courts should continue to monitor the performance of mediators to whom they refer cases and ensure that their performance is of consistently high quality") and Standard 6.6 (prescribing removal of mediators from the roster for failure to meet performance expectations).
28. See id. at Standard 2.6 ("Complaint Mechanism[:] Parties referred by the court to a mediation program whether or not it is operated by the court, should have access to a complaint mechanism to address any grievances about the process").
29. See P. M. Young, *Take It or Leave It. Lump It or Grieve It: Designing Mediator Complaint Systems That Protect Mediators, Unhappy Parties, Attorneys, Courts, the Process, and the Field,* 21 Ohio St. J. Disp. Resol. 721 (2006).
30. Id. at 741–775.
31. Id. at 775.
32. Id.
33. Id.
34. See National Standards, supra note 3, at Standard 16.1, Commentary.
35. See CPR-Georgetown Principles, supra note 2, at Principle IV, Complaint and Grievance Mechanisms.
36. See id. at Principle VI, Comment ("The organizational oversight provided through these mechanisms is concerned primarily with complaints

about the conduct of the neutral, or deficiencies in process and procedures used. The complaint and grievance mechanisms are not intended to provide an appeals process about the results or outcome of the ADR proceeding").

37. See id. at Principle IX, Confidentiality ("An ADR Provider should take all reasonable steps to protect the level of confidentiality agreed to by the parties, established by the organization or neutral, or set by applicable law or contract").

38. See id. at Principles IX(a)-(c), Confidentiality.

39. See National Standards, supra note 3, at Standard 9.1.

40. See id.

41. See id. at Standard 9.1(d), Comments.

42. See S. Raines et al., *Best Practices for Mediation Training and Regulation: Preliminary Findings,* 48 Fam. Ct. Rev. 541, 545 (2010).

43. See CPR-Georgetown Principles, supra note 2, at Principle I(b). ("The ADR Provider Organization's responsibilities . . . decrease as the ADR parties' knowing involvement in screening and selecting the particular neutral increases"). See id. at Comment (4). Principle I(b) reflects, and is consistent with, ADR standards honoring party autonomy and knowing choice. It provides that when knowledgeable parties have meaningful choice in the identification and selection of individual neutrals, the duty for ensuring the quality of the competence of the neutral chosen transfers in part from the administering organization to the parties themselves. Where party choice is limited by contract, statute, or court rules, the ADR provider organization retains responsibility for maximizing the likelihood of individual neutral competence and quality.

44. See T. Relis, Perceptions in Litigation and Mediation: Lawyers, Defendants, Plaintiffs and Gendered Parties (2009).

45. See CPR-Georgetown Principles, supra note 2, at Principle I, Quality and Competence of Services ("The ADR Provider Organization should take all reasonable steps to maximize the quality and competence of its services, absent a clear and prominent disclaimer to the contrary").

46. Model Standards, Standard VI.

47. J. P. McCrory, *Mandated Mediation of Civil Cases in State Courts: A Litigant's Perspective on Program Model Choices*, 14 Ohio St. J. Disp. Resol. 813, 832 (1999).

48. R. Delgado et al., *Fairness and Formality: Minimizing the Risk of Prejudice in Alternative Dispute Resolution,* 1985 Wis. L. Rev. 1359 (1985).

49. McCrory, supra note 47, at 835.

50. Model Standards, supra note 46, at Standard I(A)(2).

51. Some analysts of court-connected landlord-tenant mediations suggest that when unrepresented tenants leave a mediation satisfied, that satisfaction may reflect the false bliss of ignorance, not informed consent. J. Kurtzberg & J. Henikoff, *Freeing the Parties from the Law: Designing an Interest and Rights Focused Model of Landlord/Tenant Mediation,* 1997 J. Disp. Resol. 53, 54 (1997). The issue of mediating cases where the law rests almost wholly on the landlord's side remains problematic.

52. See S. N. Exon, *How Can a Mediator Be Both Impartial and Fair? Why Ethical Standards of Conduct Create Chaos for Mediators,* 2006 J. Disp. Resol. 387, 398 (2006).

53. This may present the most challenging option, for it requires attorneys to relinquish traditional roadblocks to nonattorney assistance in legal matters. On the other hand, the dearth of legal representation for the working poor and lower class may require a serious revisit of the prohibitions against unauthorized practice of law, since the landlord's ability to access legal counsel in evictions against pro se tenants is so pervasive. See R. Engler, *And Justice for All—Including the Unrepresented Poor: Revisiting the Roles of the Judges, Mediators and Clerks,* 67 Fordham L. Rev. 1987, 1988, 2033 (1999).

54. This option presents a mechanism to ensure that private justice and public policy remain in reasonable alignment, responding to a longtime critique of mediation. See O. M. Fiss, *Against Settlement,* 93 Yale L.J. 1073 (1984).

55. See Model Standards, supra note 46, at Standard I(A), Self-Determination: "A mediator shall conduct a mediation based on the principle of party self-determination. Self-determination is the act of coming to a voluntary, uncoerced decision in which each party makes free and informed choices as to process and outcome." See also id. at Standard VI(A), Quality of the Process: "A mediator shall conduct a mediation in accordance with these Standards and in a manner that promotes diligence, timeliness, safety, presence of the appropriate participants, party participation, procedural fairness, party competency and mutual respect among all participants."

56. National Standards, supra note 3, at Standard 5.1: "Mandatory attendance at an initial mediation session may be appropriate, but only when a mandate is more likely to serve the interests of parties (including those not represented by counsel), the justice system and the public than would voluntary attendance. Courts should impose mandatory attendance only when: (a) the cost of mediation is publicly funded, consistent with Standard 13.0 on Funding; (b) there is no inappropriate pressure to settle, in the form of reports to the trier of fact or financial disincentives to trial; and (c) mediators or mediation programs of high quality (i) are easily accessible; (ii) permit party participation; (iii) permit lawyer participation when the parties

wish it; and (iv) provide clear and complete information about the precise process and procedures that are being required."

57. See Model Standards, supra note 46, at Standard I(A): "Self-determination is the act of coming to a voluntary, uncoerced decision in which each party makes free and informed choices as to process and outcome."

58. See id. at Standard III(A).

The Editor

Ellen Waldman, J.D., L.L.M., is professor of law and founder and director of the Mediation Clinic at Thomas Jefferson School of Law in San Diego. She teaches a variety of courses that traverse the general areas of dispute resolution and ethics, including advanced mediation, therapeutic jurisprudence, and bioethics. She has served as a mediator in a variety of disputes, sits on the ethics committees of local health care institutions, and speaks and conducts trainings nationally and internationally on the intersection of mediation and health care ethics. She has authored over twenty-five articles on related topics.

The Contributors

Harold Abramson is a full-time faculty member at Touro Law Center, New York, where he teaches, trains, and writes on how attorneys can effectively represent clients in domestic and international mediations. He serves as cochair of the International Mediation Institute committee in The Hague that is designing an intercultural mediator certification program. Abramson is the author of *Mediation Representation: Advocating as a Problem-Solver in Any Country or Culture*, which received the 2004 Book Award from the CPR Institute, and coauthor of *International Conflict Resolution-ADR Consensual Processes*.

Phyllis Bernard is a professor of law at Oklahoma City University (OCU) School of Law and the founding director of its Center on Alternative Dispute Resolution. For a decade, OCU School of Law hosted the Oklahoma Supreme Court's mediation program, Early Settlement Central (ESC). As director of ESC, Bernard selected, trained, and supervised an average annual roster of sixty volunteer mediators. She has served on the governing councils of the American Bar Association Section of Dispute Resolution, Section of Administrative Law and Regulatory Practice, and ABA Africa. She is a former chair of the Alternative Dispute Resolution Section of the Association of American Law Schools.

John Bickerman is an internationally recognized mediator and arbitrator, specializing in complex environmental, public policy, commercial, and tribal disputes. In the past twenty years, he has logged over twenty-five thousand hours and resolved more than $3 billion dollars in claims in over thirty-five states. Prior to starting his practice as a neutral, he practiced environmental and insurance coverage law at Kaye Scholer. He is past chair of the American Bar Association Section of Dispute Resolution. He has also taught classes in dispute resolution, mediation, and negotiation to undergraduates and law students at Cornell University and Georgetown University Law Center. He has been selected as one of the Best Lawyers in America for the past five years.

———

Melissa Brodrick is the ombudsperson for Harvard University's Medical School, School of Dental Medicine, and School of Public Health and their affiliate institutions. In this role, she is a designated impartial and independent dispute resolution practitioner whose major function is to provide confidential and informal assistance to faculty, staff, students, and trainees. Since 1985 she has also served as a mediator, trainer, and facilitator, helping clients engage in effective communications and problem solving while navigating high-impact workplace and family issues. Her clients have included academic institutions, health care organizations, Fortune 500 companies and other corporations, state and federal agencies, and nonprofit groups.

———

Dorothy J. Della Noce has been active in the dispute resolution field for more than two decades as a researcher, practitioner, trainer, educator, and policymaker. Her publications have appeared in *Ohio State Journal on Dispute Resolution, Pepperdine Dispute Resolution Law Journal, Hofstra Labor and Employment Law Journal, Negotiation Journal, Mediation Quarterly, Conflict Resolution Quarterly,* and *Communication Teacher.* She coauthored the book *Mediator Communication Competencies: Problem Solving and Transformative Practices* (5th ed., 2005) and has contributed chapters to other books. An award-winning teacher, she has taught undergraduate, graduate, and professional students for a variety of institutions since 1994.

———

Dan Dozier is a partner in Press, Potter & Dozier, LLC, where his practice focuses on providing the full range of alternative dispute resolution services. He has mediated hundreds of complex multiparty environmental, public policy, civil litigation, and land use cases. Dozier was an adjunct professor at the Vermont Law School, where he taught environmental dispute resolution from 1989 to 2000. He has been admitted to the practice of law in Michigan, the District of Columbia, and Maryland.

———◊◊◊———

Bill Eddy is the senior family mediator at the National Conflict Resolution Center in San Diego. Previously he provided psychotherapy for twelve years to children and families at psychiatric hospitals and clinics. He is president of High Conflict Institute and has provided training to legal professionals in over twenty-five states, several provinces in Canada, Australia, and France on personality disorders in legal disputes. He is the author of several books, including *High Conflict People in Legal Disputes* and *It's All Your Fault!*

———◊◊◊———

Susan Nauss Exon is a professor of law at the University of La Verne College of Law in Ontario, Canada, where she teaches mediation, negotiation, alternative dispute resolution, civil procedure, and related seminars. She received an L.L.M. in dispute resolution from Pepperdine University and has over twenty years of combined experience as a business litigator, practicing mediator, and law professor. She speaks frequently on ethical and alternative dispute resolution topics and has been a featured speaker for the PBS television show *Contemporary Legal Issues.* She is cochair of the Ethics Committee for the American Bar Association Section of Dispute Resolution and serves on the section's Ethical Guidance Committee. She has published extensively on mediation ethics and civil procedure topics.

———◊◊◊———

Gregory Firestone is director of the University of South Florida Conflict Resolution Collaborative and has been a practicing mediator, mediation trainer, and clinical psychologist for more than twenty-five years. He has been influential in shaping alternative dispute resolution public policy through service as Florida Supreme Court Alternative Dispute Resolution Rules and Policy Committee member (including seven years as vice chair); member of the boards of directors of the Academy of Family Mediators (AFM) and the Association of Family and Conciliation Courts; editorial board member of *Family Court Review;* legislative chair of the Association for Conflict Resolution

(ACR); official observer on behalf of ACR and the AFM to the National Conference of Commissioners on Uniform State Laws Uniform Mediation Act Drafting Committee; and Florida Supreme Court Mediation and Arbitration Training Committee member. In 2002, he was awarded the Association for Conflict Resolution Presidential Award.

—*◊◊◊*—

Dwight Golann is professor of law at Suffolk University in Boston and an active mediator of legal disputes. He has led seminars for courts, the American Bar Association, the European Union, the People's Republic of China, and law firms in the United States and Europe. He is the author of *Mediating Legal Disputes* and a DVD, *The Skills of a Legal Mediator,* and coauthor of *Resolving Disputes, Mediation: The Roles of Lawyer and Advocate,* and *Lawyer Negotiation.* He is an honorary member of the American College of Civil Mediators.

—*◊◊◊*—

Art Hinshaw is clinical professor of law and director of the Lodestar Dispute Resolution Program at the Sandra Day O'Connor College of Law, Arizona State University. His research and teaching interests lie in the field of alternative dispute resolution (ADR), primarily mediation and negotiation. Hinshaw is active in the ADR community, having served on several academic and professional committees at the state and national levels. He is a senior fellow at the Center for the Study of Dispute Resolution at the University of Missouri School of Law and a contributor to Indisputably, the ADR Prof Blog.

—*◊◊◊*—

Jeremy Lack is a partner with Etude Altenburger in Geneva, Switzerland. He is also a door tenant with Quadrant Chambers in London, counsel to Pearl Cohen Zedek Latzer LLP in New York City, and an adjunct professor with the University of Neuchâtel in Switzerland. He serves on several alternative dispute resolution committees, including the Independent Standards Committee of the International Mediation Institute; the American Bar Association Section of Dispute Resolution's International Committee, for which he is cochair; the

CPR Institute's European Advisory Board; the Chartered Institute of Arbitrators' Mediation Practices and Standards Subcommittee; the Swiss Chamber of Commercial Mediation's Regional Committee for Western Switzerland; the Geneva Chamber of Commerce's Advisory Council; and the board of directors of the Global Negotiation Insight Institute.

—*ᴧᴧᴧ*—

Carol B. Liebman is a clinical professor at Columbia Law School, where she is the director of the Columbia Law School Mediation Clinic and the Negotiation Workshop. She has designed and presented mediation training for a variety of groups, including the certification program in bioethics of the College of Montefiore Medical Center; the New York City Bar Association; and high school students, parents, and teachers, and she has taught about negotiation and mediation in Vietnam, Israel, Brazil, and China. She is the coauthor with Nancy Dubler of the forthcoming *Bioethics Mediation: A Guide to Shaping Shared Solutions* (2nd ed.).

—*ᴧᴧᴧ*—

Lela P. Love is a professor of law at Benjamin N. Cardozo School of Law, Yeshiva University, in New York City, and directs the law school's Kukin Program for Conflict Resolution. In addition to more than two decades of teaching, training, consulting, and writing in the dispute resolution field, she serves as a mediator, arbitrator, and dispute resolution consultant in a wide range of cases. A former chair of the American Bar Association Section of Dispute Resolution, she serves on a variety of committees to promote dispute resolution initiatives. Love is the author of *The Middle Voice*, as well as numerous articles and textbooks.

—*ᴧᴧᴧ*—

Julie Macfarlane is professor at the faculty of law of the University of Windsor. She has researched and written extensively on dispute resolution and, in particular, the role of lawyers, including *The New Lawyer: How Settlement Is Transforming the Practice of Law* (2008). She is also the author of a forthcoming book, *Sustaining the Islamic Imagination: Marriage and Divorce Among North American Muslims*. She is an active mediator and consults on conflict resolution interventions, training, program evaluation, and systems design for a range of public and private sector clients.

———

Carrie Menkel-Meadow is Chancellor's Professor of Law at the University of California, Irvine, and A. B. Chettle, Jr., Professor of Law, Dispute Resolution and Civil Procedure at Georgetown Law Center, where she teaches civil procedure, legal ethics and the legal profession, negotiation, mediation, advanced multiparty dispute resolution, international dispute resolution, and international legal analysis. She is the author or editor of over ten books, including, most recently, *Dispute Resolution: Beyond the Adversarial Model* (2nd ed., 2010), *Negotiation: Processes for Problem Solving* (2006), *Mediation: Theory, Practice and Ethics* (2006), and *What's Fair: Ethics for Negotiators* (2004), and over 150 articles in leading law reviews.

———

Bruce E. Meyerson is a mediator, arbitrator, and trainer in Phoenix, Arizona. He is also an adjunct professor at the Arizona State University College of Law, where he teaches courses in all aspects of dispute resolution. He has served as the chair of the State Bar of Arizona Committee on Alternative Dispute Resolution and chair of the Arizona Supreme Court Alternative Dispute Resolution Advisory Committee for seven years. He is a member of the Commercial and Employment Panels of the American Arbitration Association and arbitration panels of the National Arbitration Forum. He is a past chair of the American Bar Association Section of Dispute Resolution.

———

Michael Moffitt is the associate dean for academic affairs and Orlando J. and Marian H. Hollis Professor of Law at the University of Oregon School of Law, where he teaches negotiation, dispute resolution, and civil procedure. He is also the associate director of the Appropriate Dispute Resolution Center at the University of Oregon. He was formerly a lecturer on law at Harvard Law School and served as the clinical supervisor of the Harvard Mediation Program. A graduate of Marietta College and Harvard Law School, he has authored or coauthored two books and more than twenty articles on dispute resolution.

―◦◦◦―

Forrest S. Mosten is a mediator and collaborative family lawyer in Los Angeles and adjunct professor of law at UCLA School of Law. He trains professionals in conflict resolution from basic to advanced courses and is in demand worldwide as a conference keynote speaker. Mosten is the author of the *Complete Guide to Mediation* (1997), *Unbundling Legal Services* (2000), *Mediation Career Guide* (2001), and *Collaborative Divorce Handbook: Helping Families Without Going to Court* (2009). Mosten has received numerous awards including the ABA Lawyer as Problem Solver Award and the ABA Lifetime Legal Access Award.

―◦◦◦―

Jacqueline Nolan-Haley is a professor at Fordham University Law School, where she directs the conflict resolution program and teaches courses in alternative dispute resolution, international and interethnic conflict resolution, Catholic perspectives on conflict resolution, and mediation. She has also conducted conflict resolution workshops in Northern Ireland and the United States. Nolan-Haley's scholarship focuses on ethical issues related to mediation and international conflict resolution. She is a member of the Mediation Ethics Advisory Committee of the New York State Unified Court System and chairs the Education Committee of the Dispute Resolution Section of the New York Bar Association.

―◦◦◦―

Bruce Pardy is a professor in the faculty of law at Queen's University in Kingston, Ontario, Canada, and sits on the Ontario Environmental Review Tribunal as an adjudicator and mediator. He has written extensively on environmental governance, ecosystem management, climate change, water policy, and environmental liability, and he has taught environmental law in Canada, the United States, and New Zealand. Previously he was a litigation lawyer at Borden Ladner Gervais LLP in Toronto.

―◦◦◦―

Charles Pou has twenty-five years of experience in conflict management. For ten years, he directed the dispute resolution program at the Administrative Conference of the United States, the agency designated in the Administrative Dispute Resolution Act of 1990 with lead responsibility for promoting federal alternative dispute resolution (ADR) use. Pou coauthored that statute and spearheaded the government's implementation of consensus-based processes. Since 1995, he has served in a variety of regulatory and other conflicts; consulted with agencies setting up conflict resolution programs; and written on quality, ethics, and related issues involving governmental bureaucracies employing ADR. His Outstanding Contribution to Improved Dispute Resolution was honored by the Washington, D.C., chapter of ACR. Pou graduated from Rice University and Harvard Law School.

Mary Radford is the Catherine C. Henson Professor of Law at the Georgia State University College of Law, where she has taught since 1984. Her teaching areas include wills, trusts and estates, and elder law. She is the president-elect of the American College of Trust and Estate Counsel. She served as the reporter for the Probate Code Revision Committee of the State Bar of Georgia, which drafted the 1998 Georgia Probate Code; the Georgia Guardianship Code Revision Committee, which drafted the 2005 Georgia Guardianship Code; and the Georgia Trust Code Revision Committee, which drafted the 2010 Georgia Trust Code. Radford graduated from Emory Law School.

R. Wayne Thorpe has been an Atlanta lawyer and mediator for over thirty years. Mr. Thorpe has mediated more than one thousand cases and arbitrated more than four hundred. Mr. Thorpe is chair of the ABA Section of Dispute Resolution. He has been recognized in both *Georgia Super Lawyers* and *The Best Lawyers in America* for alternative dispute resolution (ADR). Previously he was a litigation partner at Alston & Bird and a law clerk to a federal judge. He was an editor on the *Georgia Law Review*.

John Winslade is a professor and associate dean of the College of Education at California State University San Bernardino and part-time associate professor at the University of Waikato in New Zealand. He is coauthor of *Narrative Mediation: A New Approach to Conflict Resolution* (2000) and *Practicing Narrative Mediation: Loosening the Grip of Conflict* (2008). He edits *Explorations: An E-Journal of Narrative Practice* and has taught workshops on narrative mediation in North America, Australasia, Europe, and the Middle East.

—◁/\/\▷—

Roger Wolf is an emeritus professor of law at the University of Maryland School of Law, where he created and directed the school's Center for Dispute Resolution, directed the mediation clinic, and was a former director of the clinical law program. He is a trainer and mediator, a member and past cochair of the American Bar Association's Section of Dispute Resolution's Ethics Committee, and a member of the Section's Ethical Guidance Committee.

—◁/\/\▷—

Susan M. Yates is executive director of Resolution Systems Institute, a nonprofit that strengthens justice by enhancing court alternative dispute resolution (ADR) systems through program development, monitoring, and assessment, and a national court ADR resource center. She has chaired and served on many court, nonprofit, and bar committees, including serving as one of two American Bar Association representatives to the 2005 revision of the Model Standards of Conduct for Mediators. She is coeditor of the *ADR Handbook for Judges* and author of *Accessing Justice: Pathways for Poor and Low-Income Disputants*. She is a mediation trainer and has been an adjunct instructor at several law schools. She has been a mediator since 1983.

⟶ Index

Page references followed by *fig* indicate an illustrated figure.

A

Abramson, Harold, 311, 327–337
Absolute duties notion, 8
Accommodations for diminished capacity, 31
Accountability: debate over mediator, 117–118; of mediator for impartiality, 295, 334
Administrative Dispute Resolution Act, 248, 250
ADR (alternative dispute resolution) provider organizations: ADA mediation Guidelines of, 45; biased roster issue for, 351–352; capacity as defined in, 45; case: Physician Mediators, 348–353; case: A Recurring Landlord-Tenant Pattern, 353–367; CPR-Georgetown Principles of, 340, 341–348, 352; ensuring fairness of mediation models of, 250–251; ethical issues faced by private and public, 339–340; National Standards of, 340–341, 342–347; quality and mediator work conditions under, 352–353. *See also* Mediation
Advertising (Standard VII), 377
Alabama state code: codes of ethics, 12–13; on nondisclosure of material facts, 207; on promoting party truth telling, 203
Alberts, Jess, 200
All-or-nothing thinking, 58
American Arbitration Association, 10

American Association on Intellectual and Developmental Disabilities (AAIDD), 46
American Bar Association (ABA), 10, 178. *See also* Model Rules of Professional Conduct for Attorneys (ABA)
American Psychiatric Association, 46
Americans with Disabilities Act, 35, 40, 51
Anger: biases related to, 58; description and impact of, 57–58; disputant autonomy and, 58–59; Harry's Will case on, 64–66; Laurie and Paul's Divorce case on, 67–85. *See also* Conflict
Anxiety: description and impact of, 59–60; disputant autonomy and, 60–61
Appreciation capacity component, 30
Arkansas state code, 118
Arnold, Matthew, 306
Association for Conflict Resolution, 10
Attorney misconduct: case: An Attorney's Wrongful Termination Claim, 256–259; Model Rules mandate to disclose, 255–256
Attorneys: case: An Attorney's Wrongful Termination Claim, 256–259; conflicting interests of, 216–217; power imbalance and role of, 108; question on competency of, 216. *See also* Malpractice; Model Rules of Professional Conduct for Attorneys (ABA)

An Attorney's Wrongful Termination
Claim case, 256–259
Autonomy. *See* Disputant autonomy

B

BATNA (best alternative to a negotiated
agreement): anger and resistance to,
59; case: Tunemaker "Attorney"
consideration of, 164–165,
168*fig*–169, 175; case: Who Owns
the Dance?, 210; case: Ziba and
Ahmed's Iranian-American Divorce
possible use of, 334–335, 337;
ill-informed disputant and
perceived, 144. *See also* Negotiations
Bernard, Phyllis, 354–358, 366–367
Beyond Reason (Fisher and Shapiro), 56
Bickerman, John, 182, 183–187,
196–197
A Boutique Relationship case:
background information on, 284;
Bruce E. Meyerson's comments on,
284–287, 291–292; editor's thoughts
and comments on, 291–293; Model
Rules on conflict of interest in, 286,
287, 289–292; Model Standards on
conflict of interest in, 285–286,
288–289; Wayne Thorpe's
comments on, 287–291, 292
Bridging cultural gaps, 312–313,
331–333
Brodrick, Melissa, 220–222, 225
Brown v. Board of Education, 129
Bully tactics problem, 107
Bush, Robert A. Baruch, 22, 123

C

CAL (guardian ad litem), 269
California state code, 120–121
Can Mary Mediate Her Residency? case:
background information on, 31–32;
capacity to bind oneself question of,
33–35; capacity to participate
question of, 32–33
Capacity: accommodations for, 31;
ADA mediation Guidelines'
definition of, 45; cases on, 31–53;
components for mediation, 30;

medical versus legal, 28; state
criteria for legal, 29
CASA (court-appointed special
advocate), 269
Cases: An Attorney's Wrongful
Termination Claim, 256–259; A
Boutique Relationship, 284–293;
Can Mary Mediate Her Residency?,
31–35; A Costly Snap, 159–163;
Divorce, Custody, and Domestic
Violence, 88–89, 92–93; Divorce
and Possible Child Abuse, 260–275;
Duties of Care—Mediating with a
Crooked Doctor, 236–240; An
Employment Termination,
212–226; Hannah and Yoav's
Brooklyn Divorce, 313–318; Harry's
Will, 64–66; Hey, Neighbor—Don't
Touch My Clothesline or Compost!,
133–135; Kevin's Disability—
Dreams and Duress, 35–53; Laurie
and Paul's Divorce, 67–85;
Outrageous Offshore, 180–182;
Physician Mediators, 348–353; A
Recurring Landlord-Tenant Pattern,
353–367; Shady Leaves, 182–198;
Super Tom, 102–111; Sympathy for
the Tenant?, 293–303; Tennis
Center Negligence?, 281–284;
Tongan Slip and Fall, 135–153; The
Toxic Playground, 240–253;
Tunemaker "Attorney," 163–176;
Vulnerable Workers and an
Oppressive Employer, 130–133;
Who Owns the Dance?, 208–212;
Wrongful Death, 136–153; Ziba and
Ahmed's Iranian-American
Divorce, 318–337
Catastrophizing bias, 58
Center for Dispute Settlement, 340
Center for Public Resources
(CPR)-Georgetown Commission on
Ethics and Standards of Practice. *See*
CPR-Georgetown Principles
Chartered Institute of Arbitrators
(CIArb), 189
Charybdis versus Scylla problem, 2

Child abuse: appropriate disclosures related to, 264–265; case: Divorce and Possible Child Abuse, 260–275; confidentiality expectations when reporting, 267–272; ending the mediation session and making report on, 263–265; evaluating the likelihood of, 262–263; GAL or CASA mediation participation in cases of, 269; inquiring into allegation of, 266–267; mediators' reporting duties related to, 259–260. *See also* Domestic violence

Child Protective Services: appropriate disclosures to, 264–265; child abuse criteria by, 274; loss of self-determination to, 261; mediation participation by, 269

Civil disobedience, 186–187

Collectivist cultures, 307–308, 309

Comments to Rule 4.1: case: Who Owns the Dance? on, 210–211; description of, 207–208

Communication: as capacity component, 30; influence of listeners, 81

Competency: diminished capacity and, 28, 30–53; mediator Shari'a law, 321; of misinformed and ill-informed disputants, 113–153; National Standards and CPR-Georgetown Principles on mediator, 343–346; question on lawyer's, 216; Standard IV on, 374; unrepresented disputants' informed consent and, 155–176, 215–216

Confidentiality: case: An Attorney's Wrongful Termination Claim, 256–259; case: Divorce and Possible Child Abuse, 260–275; case: Duties of Care—Mediating with a Crooked Doctor, 236–240; case: A Recurring Landlord-Tenant Pattern issue of, 363; case: The Toxic Playground, 240–253; child abuse reports and expectations of, 267–272; criminal conduct as annulling, 178, 185–186; as critical value in mediation, 247; defendants' misrepresentation of assets and issue of, 217–218; duty to keep disputant disclosures secret, 228–231; as evidentiary privilege, 229; explaining scope and limits of, 265–266; factors affecting expectations of, 247–249; Florida Mediation Confidentiality and Privilege Act on, 271; Model Rules of Professional Responsibility on, 200–201, 217; Model Standards on, 200–201, 217–218, 228, 234–235, 243, 248, 266, 270, 285, 363, 374–375; National Standards and CPR-Georgetown Principles on, 347; nondisclosure of material facts and mediator, 207; tailoring parties' expectations of, 234–236; Uniform Mediation Act (UMA) on privilege of, 178, 185–186, 229, 231–232, 250. *See also* Disclosures; Mediation ethical values

Conflict: CPR-Georgetown Principles on disclosing, 341–342; intervention as act of temerity, 26; narrative mediation approach to, 23–24; research on how power generates and sustains, 103; transformative mediation perspective on, 22, 68. *See also* Anger

"Conflict-saturated story," 23

Conflicts of interest: case: A Boutique Relationship, 284–293; case: A Recurring Landlord-Tenant Pattern issue of, 362–363; case: Sympathy for the Tenant?, 293–303; case: Tennis Center Negligence?, 281–284; case: Ziba and Ahmed's Iranian-American Divorce and mediator, 322; dealing with personal or professional ties, 278–280; Standard III on, 278–279, 294, 322, 373–374; ties based on subject matter alliances, 280–281; when party's attorney has, 216–217.

Conflicts of interest *(continued)*
See also Impartiality; Interests;
Mediators
Convention on the Elimination of All
Forms of Discrimination Against
Women (UN), 331, 333–334
Copyright dispute mediation: case: A
Costly Snap, 159–163; case:
Tunemaker "Attorney," 163–176;
case: Who Owns the Dance?,
208–212. See also Property rights
mediation
A Costly Snap case, 159–163
CPR-Georgetown Principles: on
confidentiality, 347; description of,
340–341; on disclosing conflicts and
curbing the profit motive, 341–342;
on ensuring quality and disputant
choice, 343–346; on ethics for
mediators, 347; on mediator work
conditions ensuring quality, 352
Criminal conduct: case: Duties of
Care—Mediating with a Crooked
Doctor, 236–240; case: Outrageous
Offshore, 180–182; case: Shady
Leaves, 182–198; civil disobedience
as, 186–187; confidentiality
annulled in case of, 178, 185–186;
considering nature of the, 186–187,
192–193; mediating with parities
engaged in past, 188–189; mediator
attitudes and values regarding rule
of law and, 179–180, 193–196;
Model Standards and state codes on
"furthering," 177–179, 181,
185–186, 189; working with parties
to avert future, 189–191
Cultural differences: bridging gap
between, 312–313, 331–333;
buyer-seller example of
complications of, 310–311; case:
Hannah and Yoav's Brooklyn
Divorce, 313–318; case: Ziba and
Ahmed's Iranian-American
Divorce, 318–337; four steps in
dealing with, 311–313, 329–335;
individualistic versus collectivist,

307–308, 309; in legal age for
self-determination, 321–323;
low-context versus high-context,
308; low-power-distance versus
high-power-distance, 308, 309–310;
low-uncertainty-avoidant versus
high-uncertainty-avoidant, 309;
monochronic versus polychronic,
308–309; self-determination and
issues of, 321–323; universalist
versus particularist, 308; when to
consider withdrawal due to, 313,
333–335. See also Disputants
Culture: bridging gaps between
different, 312–313, 331–333;
current definition of, 306–307;
disputing style related to, 307–310;
doing research on other, 312,
330–331; Jewish Orthodoxy versus
secular, 315–316; mediator
understanding one's own, 311–312,
329–330; Model Standards as
providing the primary lens for,
329–330; parties and shared
understanding of, 324
Culture and Anarchy (Arnold), 306

D

Decision making: disputant's
diminished capacity for, 28–53;
facilitating disputants in their, 27;
Model Standards on voluntary, 106.
See also Ethical decision making
Depression: description of, 62;
disputant autonomy and, 62–63
*Diagnostic and Statistical Manual of
Mental Disorders* (DSM-IV), 46
Diminished capacity: accommodations
for, 31; case: Can Mary Mediate Her
Residency?, 31–35; case: Kevin's
Disability—Dreams and Duress,
35–53; cautions when declaring
disputant, 28; components of, 30; in
legal settings, 29
Disclosures: case: An Attorney's
Wrongful Termination Claim,
256–259; child abuse report and
appropriate, 264–265; interests

advanced by protecting mediation from, 229–231; legal rules requiring, 235; mandate for attorney misconduct, 255–256; mediator duty to keep secret disputant, 228–231; permitted in case of malpractice, 237–240; preventing future harm by, 231–232; righting past wrongs through, 232–234; UMA procedures for judicial direction on, 250. *See also* Confidentiality

Disputant autonomy: conditions which may put at risk, 27; determining capacity for, 25, 28–53; evaluative versus facilitative mediation support of, 20–21; of misinformed and ill-informed disputants, 113–153; relationship between emotions and, 55–85; tensions between substantive fairness and, 113–153; as underlying mediation value, 3–4; unrepresented disputants and, 155–176, 215–216, 353–3567. *See also* Power imbalance; Self-determination

Disputant autonomy capacity: accommodations for, 31; case: Can Mary Mediate Her Residency?, 31–35; case: Kevin's Disability—Dreams and Duress, 35–53; cautions when declaring disputant unfit, 28; components of, 30; in legal settings, 29; medical versus legal, 28; of misinformed and ill-informed disputants, 133–153; penetrating inquiry required to determine, 25, 28; of unrepresented disputants, 155–176, 215–216

Disputant autonomy and emotions: Harry's Will, 64–66; Laurie and Paul's Divorce, 67–85

Disputants: dealing with lies told by, 199–226; declared unfit, 28; determining need for support person, 48–49; facilitating decision making by, 27; "favored nation"

status of, 279; grievance procedures for dissatisfied, 345–346; handling bully tactics by, 107; the misinformed and ill-informed, 113–153; "reasonable person" inquiry on relationships with, 279; unrepresented, 155–176, 215–216, 353–367. *See also* Cultural differences

Ditech "People Are Smart" logo, 145

Divorce mediation: case: Divorce, Custody, and Domestic Violence, 88–89, 92–93; case: Divorce and Possible Child Abuse, 260–275; case: Hannah and Yoav's Brooklyn Divorce, 313–318; case: Laurie and Paul's Divorce, 67–85; case: Super Tom, 102–111; case: Ziba and Ahmed's Iranian-American Divorce, 318–337; ethical intuitionism applied to, 15–16; going beyond the ethical pale in, 17–18; range of acceptable action in, 16–17

Divorce Mediation Standards. *See* Model Standards of Practice for Family and Divorce Mediation

Divorce and Possible Child Abuse case: Art Hinshaw comments on, 260–265, 273, 274, 275; background information on, 260; editor's thoughts and comments on, 273–275; evaluating likelihood of abuse in, 262–263; explaining scope/limits of confidentiality and privilege, 265–266; Gregory Firestone comments on, 265–275; preliminary concerns regarding, 261; promoting children's best interests in, 261–262; sending the session and making the report, 263–265

Domestic violence: assessing red flags and resilience in cases of, 91; assessing whether mediation is an option, 92–93; autonomy and power imbalance due to, 88–89,

Domestic violence *(continued)* 92–93; substance abuse, mental illness, and, 90; types of imbalance in cases of, 89–91. *See also* Child abuse

Dozier, Dan, 171–174, 175–176

Dred Scott v. Sandford, 6

Duties of Care—Mediating with a Crooked Doctor case: background information on, 236–237; ethical side of disclosures in, 238–240; legal realities of disclosures in, 237–238

Duty-based ethics, 7–8

Duty-to-warn rule, 252

E

Eddy, Bill, 106–109, 110–111

Educable mentally retarded, 46, 51

Einstein, Albert, 145

Emotions: anger, 57–59, 64–66, 67–85; anxiety, 59–61; case: An Employment Termination case (version 1), 215; case: Harry's Will, 64–66; case: Laurie and Paul's Divorce, 67–85; defined as "felt experience," 56; depression and, 62–63; positive and negative, 57; relationship between autonomy and, 55–56; sadness and grief, 61–62; shame and guilt, 63

Employment mediation: case: An Attorney's Wrongful Termination Claim, 256–259; case: An Employment Termination, 212–226; case: Vulnerable Workers and an Oppressive Employer, 130–133

An Employment Termination case (version 1): avoiding assumptions and looking for facts, 220; defendants' misrepresentation of assets issue, 217–218; description of, 212–213; Dwight Golann's comments on, 214–218, 225; editor's thoughts and comments on, 225; lawyer appears incompetent issue, 216; lawyer has conflicting interests, 216–217; mediator role in, 221–222; mediator suspects dishonesty, 212–213, 214–218; Melissa Brodrick's comments on, 220–222, 225; plaintiff seems distraught issue, 215; unrepresented disputant issue, 215–216

An Employment Termination case (version 2): defendants' misrepresentation of assets issue, 218–219; description of, 213; Dwight Golann's comments on, 218–219, 225; editor's thoughts and comments on, 225–226; mediator on perceptions and assumptions in, 222–224; on mediators staying humble, 224; mediator's suspicions of dishonesty are verified, 213, 218–219; Melissa Brodrick's comments on, 222–224, 225

Empowerment, 22

Equal Employment Opportunity Commission (EEOC), 126, 127

Equal mediation discussions, 100

Equal Pay Act (1965), 126–127

Ethical decision making: beyond the ethical pale in, 17–18; case: Duties of Care—Mediating with a Crooked Doctor, 238–240; using codes as basis of, 10–14; limitations of ethical codes for, 14; range of acceptable action, 16–17; rejecting rigidity in mediation and, 15–18; tough choices required for, 1–2. *See also* Decision making; Mediation ethics

Ethical intuitionism: applied to divorce mediation, 15–16; mediation and, 9; theory of, 7

Ethical theories: Kantian deontology, 7–8; Ross's theory of ethical intuitionism, 7, 8–9; utilitarianism, 7, 8

Evaluative mediation model: autonomy supported by, 20–21; comparing substantive fairness perspective of facilitative and, 21; description of, 20; Super Tom case application of, 107–108

Evaluative mediators: comparing substantive fairness perspective of facilitative and, 21; facilitating informed decision making with justice, 132; informed consent and substantive fairness approach by, 123, 144–145

Exon, Susan Nauss, 297–303

F

Facilitative mediation model: autonomy as defined and supported by, 20–21; comparing substantive fairness perspective of evaluative and, 21; description of, 19–20

Facilitative mediators: comparing substantive fairness perspective of evaluative and, 21; facilitating informed decision making with justice, 132; informed consent and substantive fairness approach by, 122–123

"Fairness interventions," 146–147. *See also* Substantive fairness

"Favored nation" status, 279

Fear and power imbalances, 96

Fees/other charges (Standard VIII), 378

Financial resources, 94

Firestone, Gregory, 265–275

Fisher, Roger, 56, 75

Fiss, Owen, 118

Florida Mediation Confidentiality and Privilege Act, 271

Florida state code: concern for substantive fairness in, 118–119; on confidentiality of criminal activity, 186; Rules for Court-Appointed Mediators on informed consent, 119

Folger, Joseph P., 22, 123

Foucault, Michel, 79

"The four legals" (Virginia), 70–71

Friedman, Gary, 325

Fuller, Lon, 124

G

Gadlin, Howard, 324

Geertz, Clifford, 75

Get (Jewish certificate ending the marriage), 314

Golann, Dwight, 214–218, 225

Goldilocks intervention approach, 170, 175

Grief and sadness, 61–62

Grievance procedures, 345–346

Guidelines on Termination of Mediation (CIArb), 189

Guilt and shame: description and impact of, 63; Harry's Will case on, 64–66; Laurie and Paul's Divorce case on, 67–85

Gunning, Isabelle, 322–323

H

Hannah and Yoav's Brooklyn Divorce case: background information on, 313–315; finding balance during, 317–318; Jewish Orthodoxy versus secular culture, 315–316; self-identification issue of, 316; validating Hannah's choice during, 316–317

Harry's Will case: assessing the emotions of disputants, 64–65; background information on, 64; two possible tracks by mediator, 65–66

Hey, Neighbor—Don't Touch My Clothesline or Compost! case: background information on, 133–134; facilitating parties to formulate their own norms, 134–135

High-context culture: low-power-distance compared to, 308; Ultra-Orthodox Jewish, 316

High-power-distance culture, 308, 309, 310

High-uncertainty-avoidant cultures, 309

Himmelstein, Jack, 325

Hinshaw, Art, 200, 260–265, 273

I

Ill-informed claimants: case: Tongan Slip and Fall, 135–153; case: Wrongful Death, 136–153;

Ill-informed claimants *(continued)* mediator impartiality and, 141, 144; power imbalance issue for, 141–142

Impartiality: case: A Boutique Relationship, 284–293; case: A Recurring Landlord-Tenant Pattern issue of, 362; case: Sympathy for the Tenant?, 293–303; case: Tennis Center Negligence?, 281–284; case: Ziba and Ahmed's Iranian-American Divorce issue of, 321; ill-informed claimants and, 141, 144; mediator subject matter expertise issue of, 300; Standard II on mediator's responsibility for, 295, 334, 372; Standard VI Quality of the Process on, 116, 148, 172, 295, 334. *See also* Conflicts of interest; Mediators

Indiviudalistic cultures, 307–308

Informal mediation environment, 97

Information: leveling the informational field, 100–101; mediator "knowledge" of legal outcomes, 142–143, 145; power imbalance due to limited, 97; substantive fairness/informed consent of ill-informed claimants, 135–153

Informed consent: case: A Costly Snap, 159–163; case: Hey, Neighbor—Don't Touch My Clothesline or Compost!, 133–135; case: Tongan Slip and Fall, 135–153; case: TuneMaker "Attorney," 163–176; case: Vulnerable Workers and an Oppressive Employer, 130–133; case: Wrongful Death, 136–153; evaluative mediator approach to, 123, 132, 144–145; facilitative mediator approach to, 122–123, 132, 144–145; factors influencing attitudes toward, 121–124; factual context of case influencing, 122; mediator impartiality required for, 141, 144; of misinformed and ill-informed claimants, 135–153; Model Standards on, 106, 114–115;

norm-advocating model on, 126–127, 129–130; norm-educating model on, 125–126, 128–129; norm-generating model on, 124–125, 128; process of selecting model for, 127–130; state codes on, 119–121; unrepresented disputants' competency and, 155–176, 215–216. *See also* Self-determination

Institute of Judicial Administration, 340

Interests: advanced by protecting mediation from disclosures, 229–231; attorneys with conflicting, 216–217; promoting children's best, 261–262; of unrepresented third party, 243–244, 246, 249. *See also* Conflicts of interest

Internal threats, 4

J

Jewish Orthodoxy culture, 315–316

Jurisdiction issue, 68–69

K

Kant, Immanuel, 7–8

Kantian deontology, 7–8

Kentucky state code, 158

Kevin's Disability—Dreams and Duress case: background information on, 35–36; Carol B. Liebman's comments on, 36–44, 51, 52; determining Kevin's capacity for, 42–44, 45–49; editor's thoughts and comments on, 51–53; Mary Radford's comments on, 44–51, 52–53; maximizing Kevin's ability to participate, 49–51; structuring the mediation for, 37–42; What should the mediator do in advance? question of, 37–38

Knowledge resources, 94

L

Lack, Jeremy, 182, 187–191, 197

Landlord-tenant mediation: case: A Recurring Landlord-Tenant Pattern, 353–367; case: Sympathy for the

Tenant?, 293–303. *See also* Property dispute mediation
Laurie and Paul's Divorce case: background information on, 67; creating agenda of respect, 81–82; Dorothy Della Noce's transformative perspective on, 67–73, 82, 83, 84–85; editor's thoughts and comments on, 82–85; influence of the listener in, 81; inquiring into relations of power, 79–80; John Winslade's narrative perspective on, 73–82, 83, 84–85; policy of the jurisdiction impact on, 68–69; reflexivity used in, 78–79
Law and Public Policy Committee of the Society for Professionals in Dispute Resolution report (1991), 340
Lawyers. *See* Attorneys
Lazarus, Richard, 56–57
Legal capacity: medical versus, 28; of misinformed and ill-informed disputants, 113–153; state criteria for, 29; of unrepresented disputants, 155–176, 215–216
Lerner, Harriet, 60
Liebman, Carol B., 36–44, 51, 52
Lies. *See* Misrepresentation
Listeners' mediation influence, 81
Love, Lela P., 136–146, 151, 152, 153
Low-context culture: high-power-distance compared to, 308; secular liberal democratic, 316
Low-power-distance culture, 308
Low-uncertainty-avoidant cultures, 309
Lyotard, Jean-François, 74

M

Macfarlane, Julie, 182, 191–196, 197–198
Malpractice: permitted disclosures related to, 237–240; repudiating mediated settlement due to, 233–234; UMA (Uniform Mediation Act) approach to, 233–234. *See also* Attorneys
Marijuana trafficking case, 182–198
Massachusetts state code, 158

Material facts: avoiding assumptions and looking for, 220; nondisclosure of, 207; Rule 4.1 on representation of, 207–208, 210–211
Mediation: CIArb's Guidelines on Termination of Mediation, 189; cultural issues related to, 305–337; ethical intuitionism and, 9; "furthering" criminal conduct issues of, 177–198; mediator conflicts of interest, 278–303; as option in case of domestic violence, 92–93; power imbalance as general issue in, 93–102; power sources in, 94–95; rejecting rigidity in, 15–18; repudiating settlement due to malpractice, 233–234; Standard IX on advancement of practice of, 378–379; state codes on pro se court-connected, 158–159; time allocations for, 359–361; unrepresented third parties to, 243–244, 246, 249, 252. *See also* ADR (alternative dispute resolution) provider organizations
Mediation ethical codes: Americans with Disabilities Act Mediation Guidelines, 11; conclusions regarding limitations of, 14; CPR-Georgetown Principles, 340, 341–348, 352; inconsistencies among, 11–13; inconsistencies within, 13–14; Model Rules of Professional Responsibility, 200–201, 217; Model Standards of Practice for Family and Divorce Mediation, 11, 12–13, 266, 268, 270; National Standards of ADR, 340–341, 342–347; Victim-Offender Mediation Association Recommended Guidelines, 11. *See also* Model Rules of Professional Conduct for Attorneys (ABA); Model Standards of Conduct for Mediators; State codes
Mediation ethical values: balancing, 6–9; balancing competing as, 18;

Mediation ethical values *(continued)* disputant autonomy as, 3–4; procedural fairness as, 3, 4–5; substantive fairness as, 3, 5–6, 21. *See also* Confidentiality; *specific value*

Mediation ethics: balancing competing values of, 6–9; case: Physician Mediators, 348–353; case: A Recurring Landlord-Tenant Pattern, 353–367; effect of mediation model or philosophy on, 24; loss entailed by, 1; National Standards and CPR-Georgetown Principles on, 341–348; policy of the jurisdiction issue of, 68–69; questions and lessons posed by, 2; underlying values of, 3–6. *See also* Ethical decision making

Mediation models: effect on ethical deliberation, 24; evaluative, 20–21, 107–108, 123, 132, 144–145; facilitative, 19–21, 122–123, 132; narrative, 23–24, 74–82, 123–124; personal growth, 22–24; problem-solving, 19–21; relationship-building and personal growth, 22–24. *See also* Mediator philosophy

Mediation quality: ADR provider organization provisions ensuring, 252–253; autonomy versus mediator responsibility for, 67, 106, 110; balancing disputant autonomy and information for, 73; case: Divorce, Custody, and Domestic Violence on problem of, 88–89, 92–93; case: Physician Mediators on ADR provider responsibility for, 348–353; case: A Recurring Landlord-Tenant Pattern issue of, 359–361, 364; case: Sympathy for the Tenant? promotion of, 295–296; case: Ziba and Ahmed's Iranian-American Divorce case issue of, 322; codes are not enough to ensure, 14; conditions required for preceding over, 106–107; conflict as providing opportunity to improve, 22, 68; determining diminished capacity impacting, 51; legal or social norms used to measure, 83; mediator skills in facilitating, 36; misinformed/ill-informed disputants issues for, 113–153; National Standards and CPR-Georgetown Principles on ensuring, 343–346; Standard VI on impartiality and, 116, 148, 172, 295, 334, 364, 375–377; state codes on requirements for, 118–119; time allocations to ensure, 359–361; unrepresented disputants and challenges for, 155–176, 215–216. *See also* Power imbalance

Mediator interventions: "fairness," 146–147; Goldilocks option to, 170, 175; handling disputant bully tactics, 107; "helping" the unrepresented party, 159, 215–216; implications of, 167–170; measures to help cope with power imbalance, 100–102, 356–358; prohibition from advocating for weaker participant, 97–98; unrepresented parties and three basic options for, 165–167

Mediator philosophy: balancing competing value commitments and, 18; effect on mediation ethics by, 24; fees and other charges by, 378; informed consent and substantive fairness attitudes, 122–124. *See also* Mediation models

Mediators: advancement of mediation practice by, 378–379; advertising and solicitation by, 377; assessing a depressed disputant, 62–63; balancing competing value commitments, 18; CIArb's Guidelines on Termination of Mediation by, 189; criminal conduct issues and attitudes/values of, 179–180; dealing with an angry disputant, 59; debate over accountability of, 117–118; determining disputant capacity for autonomy, 25, 28–53; duties to promote truth telling and to be truthful, 201–203; duty to avoid harm by, 26; An Employment Termination case on role of, 221–222; facilitative, 19–21; "the four legals" of, 70–71; "knowledge" of outcome by the, 142–143, 145; mediating multiculturally, 305–337; Model Standard on postmediation relationships by, 285, 288; National Standards and CPR-Georgetown Principles on competence/ethics of, 343–347; personal values/attitudes about rule of law, 179–180, 193–196; protecting reputation of, 109; self-examination of impartiality by, 300–301; on staying humble, 224; subject matter expertise of, 300; understanding of their own culture by, 311–312, 329–330; when to consider withdrawal due to cultural differences, 313, 333–335; work conditions under ADR provider organizations, 352–353. *See also* Conflicts of interest; Impartiality; Model Standards of Conduct for Mediators; State codes

Mencken, H. L., 365

Menkel-Meadow, Carrie, 320–327, 335–337

Mental illness/domestic violence relationship, 90

Mental retardation: AAIDD definition of, 46; educable, 46, 51; factors impacting functioning of persons with, 46–47; Kevin's Disability—Dreams and Duress on, 35–53; maximizing ability to participate in case of, 49–51

Merit as power, 94

Meyerson, Bruce E., 284–287, 291–292

Misinformed disputants: case: Hey, Neighbor—Don't Touch My Clothesline or Compost!, 133–135; case: Tongan Slip and Fall, 135–153; case: Vulnerable Workers and an Oppressive Employer, 130–133; case: Wrongful Death, 136–153; classification systems on norms and informed consent of, 124–130; mediator's attitudes toward, 122–124; Model Standards on informed consent and, 114–115; Model Standards on substantive fairness and, 115–118; state codes on informed consent and, 119–121; state codes on substantive fairness and, 118–119

Misrepresentation: case: Duties of Care—Mediating with a Crooked Doctor, 236–240; case: An Employment Termination, 212–226; case: Who Owns the Dance?, 208–212; of defendants' assets, 217–219; fraudulent misstatements of material fact, 204–205; Model Rules of Professional Conduct on, 200–201; Model Standards on mediator duties related to, 201–203; nondisclosure of material facts, 205–207; opinions as to value, authority, and the bottom line, 207–208; pervasiveness of mediation-told, 199–201; reasons for pervasiveness during negotiations, 200–201; Rule 4.1 on, 207–208, 210–211; rules regulating attorney conduct during negotiation, 203–208

Model Rules of Professional Conduct (ABA): on clarifying roles for unrepresented parties, 156–158; mandate to disclose other attorneys' misconduct, 255–256; on mediator conflict of interest and impartiality, 286, 287, 289–292; on nondisclosure of material facts, 205; pervasive confusion over obligations under, 200–201; Rule 4.1 of, 207–208, 210–211. *See also*

Model Rules of Professional Conduct (ABA) *(continued)* American Bar Association (ABA); Attorneys; Mediation ethical codes

Model Standards of Conduct for Mediators: allowing disclosures, 257; balancing autonomy with fairness using the, 114–121; on confidentiality (Standard V), 200–201, 217–218, 228, 234–235, 243, 248, 266, 270, 285, 363, 374–375; on conflicts of interest (Standard III), 278–279, 294, 322; on conflicts of interest (Standard V), 285–286, 288–289; description of, 10–11, 370; on duties related to truth/lies (Standard VI), 201–203; inconsistencies between other codes and, 12–13; inconsistencies within, 13; on informed consent, 106, 114–115; placing burden of impartiality on mediator (Standard II), 295, 334; on postmediation relationships (Standard III), 285, 288; on providing enough time for quality process, 359–360; as providing the primary cultural lens for disputes, 329–330; on Quality of the Process and impartiality (Standard VI), 116, 148, 172, 295, 334, 364, 375–377; regarding "further criminal conduct," 177–179, 181, 185–186, 189; self-determination as defined by, 139, 147, 148, 171–172; on substantive fairness, 115–118; on voluntary decisions and absence of undue influence, 106. *See also* Mediation ethical codes; Mediators; State codes

Model Standards of Conduct for Mediators (August 2005): note on construction, 371; preamble of, 370; Standard I. Self-Determination, 371–372; Standard II. Impartiality, 372; Standard III. Conflicts of Interest, 373–374; Standard IV.

Competence, 374; Standard IX. Advancement of Mediation Practice, 378–379; Standard V. Confidentiality, 374–375; Standard VI. Quality of the Process, 375–377; Standard VII. Advertising and Solicitation, 377; Standard VIII. Fees and Other Charges, 378

Model Standards of Practice for Family and Divorce Mediation: description of, 11, 12–13; on explaining scope/limits of confidentiality and privilege, 266; on honoring party expectations of confidentiality, 268, 270

Moffitt, Michael, 164–170, 175, 176

Monk, G., 23

Monk, Gerald, 123

Monochronic culture, 308–309

Moral conviction, 94–95

Mosten, Forrest S., 103–106, 110

Multicultural mediation: case: Hannah and Yoav's Brooklyn Divorce, 313–318; case: Ziba and Ahmed's Iranian-American Divorce, 318–337; disputing style related to culture, 307–310; self-identification issue of, 307–310, 316

N

Nader, Laura, 118

Narrative mediation model: on informed consent and substantive fairness, 123–124; Laurie and Paul's Divorce case application of, 74–82; overview of, 23–24

National Conference of Commissioners on Uniform State Laws, 178

National Standards for Court-Connected Mediation Programs: on confidentiality, 347; description of, 340–341; on educating litigants about mediation process, 342; on ensuring access to mediation services, 342–343; on ensuring quality and disputant choice, 343–346; on ethics for mediators, 347–348; on mandatory referrals, 359; on unrepresented parties, 158

Nazi soldiers ethical problem, 8–9

Negative imputation of motive bias, 58

Negotiations: reasons for misrepresentation during, 200–201; rules regulating attorney conduct during, 203–208. *See also* BATNA (best alternative to a negotiated agreement)

Noce, Dorothy Della, 67–73, 82, 83–85

Nolan-Haley, Jacqueline, 146–150, 151–153

Norm-advocating model: importance of autonomy in, 126; informed consent perceived through, 126–127; issues to consider when selecting, 129–130

Norm-educating model: autonomy commitment by, 125; informed consent perceived through, 125–126; issues to consider when selecting, 128–129

Norm-generating model: informed consent perceived through, 124–125; issues to consider when selecting, 128

North Carolina state code: concern for informed consent in, 120; concern for substantive fairness in, 119; on nondisclosure of material facts, 207; on pro se court-connected mediation, 158–159; on promoting party truth telling, 203

O

Odyssey (Homer), 2

Oregon state code: on nondisclosure of material facts, 207; on promoting party truth telling, 203

Outrageous Offshore case, 180–182

Overgeneralization bias, 58

P

Pain infliction, 95

Pardy, Bruce, 241–245, 251–253

Particularist cultures, 308

Perception resource, 95

Personal conflict of interest, 278–280

Personal growth mediation models, 22–24

Personal traits: argumentative skills as, 96–97; power through, 95

Peters, Don, 199

Physician Mediators case: ADR provider responsibility for mediation quality, 349–350; background information on, 348–349

Policing intimidating behavior, 100

Polychronic cultures, 309

Pou, Charles, 246–253

Power imbalance: assessing domestic violence red flags, resilience, and, 91; benefits of mediating versus the alternative in face of, 98–100; case: Divorce, Custody, and Domestic Violence, 88–89, 92–93; case: A Recurring Landlord-Tenant Pattern case, 353–367; case: Super Tom, 102–111; deciding on mediation option in domestic violence, 92–93; domestic violence and types of, 89–91; enlisting nonattorney party assistants in case of, 357; as general mediation issue, 93–102; ill-informed claimants and issue of, 141–142; mediator measures to help cope with, 100–102, 356–358; risks of mediating in face of extreme, 96–98; role of attorneys in, 108; weighing risks and benefits of, 95–96. *See also* Disputant autonomy; Mediation quality; Substantive fairness

Power/power relations: conflict generated and sustained by, 103; informal mediation environment and perceived, 97; low-power-distance versus high-power-distance culture, 308; sources in mediation, 94–95; three techniques to balance, 100–101

Preexisting duties, 7–8

Preventing future criminal conduct, 113

Preventing future harm, 231–232

Problem-solving mediation models: evaluative, 20–21; facilitative, 19–21

Procedural fairness, 3, 4–5. *See also* Substantive fairness

Professional conflict of interest: case: A Boutique Relationship, 284–293; Model Standards' guidance on, 278–280

The Promise of Mediation (Bush and Folger), 22

Property dispute mediation: case: The Toxic Playground, 240–253; fraudulent misstatements of material fact on, 204–205; nondisclosure of material facts in, 205–207; opinions on value, authority, and bottom line, 207–208. *See also* Landlord-tenant mediation

Property rights mediation: case: A Costly Snap, 159–163; case: Hey, Neighbor—Don't Touch My Clothesline or Compost! on, 133–135; case: Tunemaker "Attorney," 163–176. *See also* Copyright dispute mediation

Q

Quality of the Process. *See* Mediation quality

R

Radford, Mary, 44–51, 52–53

Real estate. *See* Property disputes

"Reasonable person" inquiry, 279

A Recurring Landlord-Tenant Pattern case: attempted to redress the power imbalance during, 355–356; background information on, 353–354; debunking the default argument, 355; editor's thoughts and comments on, 366–367; fairness issues during, 361–363; mediator planning to resolve issues of, 364–365; modifying city ordinance to address, 358; Phyllis Bernard's comments on, 354–358,

366–367; Susan M. Yates's comments on, 358–365, 366–367

Reflective sadness, 61–62

Relationship-build mediation models, 22–24

Reporting duties: case: An Attorney's Wrongful Termination Claim, 256–259; case: Divorce and Possible Child Abuse, 260–275; for child abuse, 259–260; mandate on attorney misconduct, 255–256

Reputation (mediator), 109

Respect, ethical agenda of, 81–82

Riskin, Len, 19

Ross, W. D., 7, 8–9, 15

Rule 4.1 (Comments): case: Who Owns the Dance? on, 210–211; description of, 207–208

Rule of law: case: Ziba and Ahmed's Iranian-American Divorce and relevance of, 324–326; description of, 6; fairness issue and, 5–6; mediator attitudes and values regarding the, 179–180, 193–196; requiring specific disclosures, 235; social norms embodied in, 25–26. *See also* Shari'a law

S

Sadness and grief, 61–62

Sanford, Dred Scott v., 6

Scylla versus Charybdis problem, 2

Section 551(2) [Restatement of Torts], 205

Section of Dispute Resolution (ABA), 10, 178

Self-determination: as autonomy, 3–4; case: A Recurring Landlord-Tenant Pattern on essence of, 362; as critical to mediation, 45; cultural differences issues and determining, 321–323; loss to Child Protective Services in case of child abuse, 261; Model Standards on, 139, 147, 148, 171–172, 371–372; protecting integrity of, 107; Virginia Standards favoring, 71. *See also* Disputant autonomy; Informed consent

Self-identification: case: Hannah and Yoav's Brooklyn Divorce issue of, 316; cultural differences of, 307–310

Sexual harassment: case: Vulnerable Workers and an Oppressive Employer, 130–133; Title VII regulations on, 132

Shady Leaves case: avoiding complicity in future misconduct, 185–186; background information on, 182–183; codes and future criminal conduct in, 189; editor's thoughts and comments on, 196–198; Jeremy Lack's comments on, 182, 187–191, 197; John Bickerman's comments on, 182, 183–187, 196–197; Julie Macfarlane's comments on, 182, 191–196, 197–198; mediating with parties engaged in past criminal conduct, 188–189; mediation should not be used to shield criminal activity in, 183–185; mediator's moral judgment considered in, 193–196; nature of the crime as issue in, 186–187, 192–193; working with parties to avert future criminal act, 189–191

Shame and guilt: description and impact of, 63; Harry's Will case on, 64–66; Laurie and Paul's Divorce case on, 67–85

Shapiro, Dan, 56

Shari'a law: American divorce and relevance of the, 325; issue of shared cultural acceptance of, 324; mediator competency in, 321; religion-based mediation using, 320; UN Universal Declaration found to violate norms of, 334. *See also* Rule of law; Ziba and Ahmed's Iranian-American Divorce case

Situational threats, 4

Slip and Fall. *See* Tongan Slip and Fall case

"Snitch rule," 256

Solicitation (Standard VII), 377

State codes: allowing disclosures, 257; concern for informed consent in, 119–121; concern for substantive fairness in, 118–119; on confidentiality expectations in child abuse cases, 270–271; evidentiary protections conferred by, 229; on future criminal conduct, 189; on pro se court-connected mediation, 158–159; regarding "further criminal conduct," 177–179, 186. *See also* Ethical codes; Mediators; Model Standards of Conduct for Mediators; *specific state codes*

Stulberg, Josh, 117–118

Subject matter alliances: assessing mediator's, 280–281; case: Tennis Center Negligence?, 281–284

Subject matter expertise, 300

Substance abuse/domestic violence relationship, 90

Substantive fairness: case: Hey, Neighbor—Don't Touch My Clothesline or Compost!, 133–135; case: Physician Mediators on ADR provider model's, 350–353; case: A Recurring Landlord-Tenant Pattern and issues of, 361–363; case: Tongan Slip and Fall, 135–153; case: Vulnerable Workers and an Oppressive Employer, 130–133; case: Wrongful Death, 136–153; definition of, 3; evaluative mediator approach to, 21, 123, 132, 144–145; facilitative mediator approach to, 21, 122–123, 132; factors influencing attitudes toward, 121–124; factual context of case influencing, 122; ill-informed claimants and, 135–153; Model Standards on, 115–118; narrative mediation, 24; state codes on, 118–119; tensions between disputant autonomy and, 113–153; as underlying mediation value, 5–6. *See also* "Fairness interventions";

Substantive fairness (continued)
Power imbalance; Procedural
fairness
Super Tom case: background
information on, 102; Bill Eddy's
comments on, 106–109, 110–111;
editor's thoughts and comments on,
110–111; ethical questions raised
by, 106–109; Forrest S. Mosten's
comments on, 103–106, 110
Support person: determining need for,
48–49; nonattorney party assistants
as, 357
Suspicious bias, 58
Susskind, Lawrence, 117–118
Sympathy for the Tenant? case:
background information on, 293;
deciding to take the case, 294–295;
dilemma for tenant-oriented
mediator, 298; editor's thoughts and
comments on, 302–303; ongoing
tension and dilemma during,
301–303; possible actions by
mediator during, 298–301;
promoting mediation quality
during, 295–296; remaining
impartial during, 296–297; Roger
Wolf comments on, 294–297,
302–303; Susan Nauss Exon's
comments on, 297–303

T
Tax evasion case, 180–182
Tennessee state code, 120
Tennis Center Negligence? case:
background information on,
281–282; keeping subject matter
bias in mind, 283–284;
postmediation activity, 283; taking
and continuing the, 282–283
Texas state codes, 159
Third party: determining need for
support person, 48–49;
duty-to-warn, 252; interests of
unrepresented, 243–244, 246, 249;
Model standards on rebalancing
power strategies by, 355–358;

nonattorney party assistants for
support, 357
Thorpe, Wayne, 287–291, 292
Threats: autonomous decisions and
internal, 4; autonomous decisions
and situational, 4
Time allocations: ensuring quality of
process through adequate, 359–360;
working to expand the mediation
session, 360–361
Title VII, 132
Tongan Slip and Fall case: background
information on, 135–136; editor's
thoughts and comments on,
151–153; informed consent issue of,
138; Jacqueline Nolan-Haley
comments on, 146–150, 151–153;
Lela P. Love comments on,
136–146, 151, 152, 153; substantive
fairness issue of, 136–138
The Toxic Playground case:
background information on,
240–241; Bruce Pardy's comments
on, 241–245, 251–253; Charles
Pou's comments on, 246–253;
confidentiality duty in, 243; editor's
thoughts and comments on,
251–253; factors affecting
confidentiality expectations,
247–249; interests of unrepresented
third party in, 243–244, 246, 249;
limited role of the mediator in,
241–242; mediation ethics during,
244–245; mediator not as fact finder
in, 242–243; possible mediator
strategies for, 249–251; what the
mediator is permitted to do during,
245
Transformative mediation model: on
informed consent and substantive
fairness, 123; Laurie and Paul's
Divorce case application to, 68,
69–70; overview of, 22–23
Truth-telling: case: An Employment
Termination, 212–226; case: Who
Owns the Dance?, 208–212;
fraudulent misstatements of

material fact, 204–205; Model Rules of Professional Conduct on, 200–201; Model Standards on, 201–203; nondisclosure of material facts, 205–207; Rule 4.1 on requirements for, 207–208, 210–211; rules regulating attorney conduct in negotiations, 203–208

Tunemaker "Attorney" case: allowing disputants to have control, 174; background information on, 163–164; BATNA arguments and response in, 164–165, 168*fig*–169, 175; Dan Dozier's comments on, 171–174, 175–176; determining competence issue of, 171–172; editor's thoughts and comments on, 175–176; good mediation practice recommended for, 172–173; Michael Moffitt's comments on, 164–170, 175, 176; paying attention to intangibles in, 173–174

U

Ultra-Orthodox Jewish culture, 315–316

Ulysses, 1–2

UN Convention on the Elimination of All Forms of Discrimination Against Women, 331, 333–334

UN Universal Declaration of Human Rights, 333–334

Understanding capacity component, 30

Undue influence, 106

Uniform Mediation Act (UMA): on confidentiality as evidentiary privilege, 229; on confidentiality waived in case of criminal activity, 178, 185–186; on disclosure related to malpractice, 237–238; expansive approach to malpractice by, 233–234; on party expectations of confidentiality, 267–268, 270–271; on preventing future harm through disclosure, 231–232; on procedures for judicial direction on disclosures, 250

United Nations Educational Scientific and Cultural Organization, 306

United Nations Report of the Committee on the Elimination of Discrimination Against Women, 330

Universalist cultures, 308

Unknowability principle, 142–143, 145

Unrealistic demanding bias, 58

Unrepresented parties: case: A Costly Snap, 159–163; case: An Employment Termination case (version 1), 215–216; case: A Recurring Landlord-Tenant Pattern, 353–367; case: Super Tom on, 102–109; case: Tunemaker "Attorney," 163–176; complexities with, 155–156; guidance from the codes on, 158–159; mediator "help" to, 159; mediator's explanation on procedures to, 156–157; third party neutral's strategies for rebalancing power of, 355–358; three basic options for mediators with, 165–167

Ury, William L., 76

Utilitarian, 7, 8

V

Vermont Law Review, 117

Victim-Offender Mediation Association Recommended Guidelines, 11

Virginia state code: concern for informed consent in, 120; favoring self-determination, 71; "the four legals" of, 70–71; Laurie and Paul's Divorce case application of, 69–73; on nondisclosure of material facts, 207; on promoting party truth telling, 202–203; relevance of, 68–69

Vulnerable Workers and an Oppressive Employer case: background information on, 130–131;

Vulnerable Workers and an Oppressive
Employer case *(continued)*
facilitating informed decision
making with justice, 131–133

W

Who Owns the Dance? case, 208–212
Winslade, John, 23, 73–82, 83, 84–85,
123
Wolf, Roger, 294–297, 302–303
Wrongful Death case: background
information on, 136; editor's
thoughts and comments on,
151–153; informed consent issue of,
138; Jacqueline Nolan-Haley
comments on, 146–150, 151–153;
Lela P. Love comments on,
136–146, 151, 152, 153; substantive
fairness issue of, 136–138

Y

Yates, Susan M., 358–365, 366–367

Z

Ziba and Ahmed's Iranian-American
Divorce case: background
information on, 318–319; BATNA
possibility in, 334–335, 337; Carrie
Menkel-Meadow's comments on,
320–327, 335–337; clash between
religious, communitarian and legal
systems, 320–321, 328;
cross-cultural four-step approach
to, 328–335; editor's thoughts and
comments on, 335–337; Harold
Abramson's comments on,
327–335; mediator conflict of
interest in, 322; quality of process
issue of, 322; relevance of the law in,
324–326; self-determination issues
of, 321–323; shared cultural
understanding by parties in, 324. *See
also* Shari'a law

Printed in Poland
by Amazon Fulfillment
Poland Sp. z o.o., Wrocław
28 October 2020

df49bf1a-67b4-451f-9324-cb9d46064becR01